Blows Against the Empire
Trotskyism in Ceylon
The Lanka Sama Samaja Party, 1935-1964

Revolutionary History, Volume 6, no 4
Porcupine Press
Socialist Platform Ltd

Revolutionary History

Editor: Al Richardson

Deputy Editor: Ted Crawford

Continental Contributing Editor: Fritz Keller

Reviews Editor: José Villa

Business Manager: Barry Buitekant

Production and Design Manager: Paul Flewers

Editorial Board: Ian Birchall, Tony Borton, Paul Hampton, Baruch Hirson, Mike Jones, Stuart King, Bahir Laattoe, George Leslie, Sheila Leslie, John Plant, Jim Ring, Ernest Rogers, Bruno Simon, Phil Walden

ISBN 1 89943 826 2

ISSN 0953 2382

Copyright © 1997 Socialist Platform Ltd

Web site: http://www.compulink.co.uk/~jplant/revhist

E-mail: tcrawford@revhist.datanet.co.uk
jplant@cix.compulink.co.uk
revhist@uk.pi.net

Socialist Platform Ltd, BCM 7646, London WC1N 3XX

Porcupine Press, 10 Woburn Walk, London WC1H 0JL

Typeset by voluntary labour

Printed in Britain by BPC Wheatons Ltd, Exeter

A list of available back issues of *Revolutionary History* appears on page 218

Contents

Editorial	2
The Origins of the Lanka Sama Samaja Party	4
The Politics of the LSSP	36
The Defence of Mark Bracegirdle	47
The LSSP Turns to Trotskyism, 1939-41	57
The LSSP, 1939-60	71
The LSSP Against Imperialist War, 1939-45	84
The 1945 Split in the LSSP	99
The Dispute over Independence, 1948	126
The Unification of the LSSP in 1950	136
The Great Hartal of 1953	145
Tamil Rights: The LSSP Against Sinhala Only, 1955-56	153
The LSSP Against the People's Front, 1956-60	170
The Years of Crisis, 1960-64	177
Charles Wesley Ervin, Trotskyism in India, 1942-48	218
Obituaries	242
Work in Progress	257
Reviews	259
Letters	302
Reader's Notes	308
Back Issues of *Revolutionary History*	318

Editorial

THIS ISSUE of our magazine fulfils the promise we made some time ago to assemble material charting the development of the Trotskyist movement in Ceylon, now Sri Lanka, from its foundation up to the time when the party joined a bourgeois coalition government in 1964. Having already produced issues devoted to Greece, Vietnam and Bolivia, we have therefore been able to cover four fifths of the countries where Trotskyism gained for itself a significant following amongst the working class. And it was probably in Sri Lanka where the Trotskyists were most prominent of all, for over many years their parties led the greater part of the organised working class. As we have said more than once, the lessons to be gained from a mass movement with a Marxist leadership are far more significant than the doings and sayings of marginal groups. We hope to be able to publish in the future material on the history of Trotskyism in Belgium in the 1930s.

The picture we assemble inside these covers does not, of course, amount to a history: rather it provides a few of the materials on the basis of which such a history could be written. The selection has been deliberately slanted towards documents and accounts coming from the movement in Ceylon itself, for although our bibliographies show that an extraordinary amount has been published on this movement, practically all of it is a by-product of conflicts between the different Trotskyist organisations in the USA and Western Europe. The development of Ceylonese Trotskyism has therefore been seen only through the distorting prism of outside concerns, and surprisingly little has been done to uncover the motor forces of its development within the conditions actually existing in the country. Our determination to use Ceylonese sources to the exclusion of others as our guiding principle has unfortunately had the effect of making our materials bitty and episodic, and we can only apologise to our readers for this. But we are sure that they will realise that they have gained from seeing the movement from the inside, in its own terms, as opposed to being fitted into historical straitjackets imposed by the polemics of revolutionaries elsewhere.

The assembling of so many varied materials has been a difficult and exhausting task, and it is only just that we should put on record that nearly all the work of editing and collecting them has been done by Bob Pitt. His resignation from our board does not alter the extent of our debt and gratitude to him.

We draw readers' attention to our Internet site, details of which are given below. We extend our thanks to John Plant for setting it up.

Editorial Board
Revolutionary History

Revolutionary History On-line!

The Web page of *Revolutionary History* can be found at < http://www.compulink.co.uk/ ~ jplant/revhist >. It provides full details of previous issues, subscription rates and links to Socialist Platform Ltd and Porcupine Press.

We have three e-mail addresses, but all orders for journals and correspondence about arrangements for payment are to go to Ted Crawford at < tcrawford@revhist.datanet.co.uk >.

John Plant at < jplant@cix.compulink.co.uk > and José Villa at < revhist@uk.pi.net > are happy to correspond with readers. John can handle Russian, José is fluent in Spanish, Portuguese and Italian, while Ted can deal with French.

I: The Origins of the Lanka Sama Samaja Party

Our first two items were selected to explain the formation and prewar growth of the LSSP, which was to develop towards the politics of Trotskyism and become the leading party of the working class in Ceylon. They are reprinted here from the Ceylonese *Young Socialist* (new series), no 1, March 1980, pp11-29. The *Manifesto of the Lanka Sama Samaja Party* was first issued on 18 December 1935, but we owe the introductory narrative to the generosity of Kumari Jayawardene, the author of *The Rise of the Labour Movement in Ceylon* and *The Origins of the Left Movement in Sri Lanka* (Sanjiva Books, Colombo, nd). We have expanded the footnotes in the original article to include information that has become available since. Some more general background to the history of the Ceylonese workers' movement can be gleaned from NSG Kuruppu, 'A History of the Working Class Movement in Ceylon' (parts 1-3, Ceylonese *Young Socialist*, 1962), and Robert M Kearney, *Trade Unions and Politics in Ceylon*, Berkeley, California, 1971.

A similar full-length study is Yodage Ranjith Amarasinghe's *Trotskyism in Ceylon: A Study of the Development, Ideology and Political Rôle of the Lanka Sama Samaja Party, 1935-1964*, a PhD dissertation submitted to the University of London in 1974. As the author was a member of the LSSP, he is able to speak from personal experience and a position of some insight. The only other detailed treatments of this early period of the party's history are George Jan Lerski's *The Origins of Trotskyism in Ceylon* (Stanford University Press, 1968), which ends in 1942, and Pierre Broué's 'Notes sur l'histoire des oppositions et du mouvement trotskyste en Inde dans la première moitié du XXè siècle' (*Cahiers Léon Trotsky*, no 21, March 1985, pp24-8 and 30-2), which takes the story up to the end of the Second World War. Other surveys covering a longer time-span are those of James Jupp, *Sri Lanka: Third World Democracy*, 1978, pp72-8, 102-5 and 261-5, and Robert J Alexander, *International Trotskyism, 1929-1985: A Documentary Analysis of the Movement*, 1991, pp159-78. The pamphlet *Ceylon: The JVP Uprising of April 1971* (Solidarity London, no 42) deals with the period of the party's history up to 1964 on pp17-29, as do Michael Ross, *The Struggle for Trotskyism in Ceylon* (Bulletin Pamphlet Series, no 9, February 1972), and Chrisantha Madapatha, 'Popular Frontism in Sri Lanka' (*Militant International Review*, no 9, June 1974, pp24-40).

The contacts of the future leaders of the LSSP with the Trotskyists in Britain are barely mentioned in accounts published so far. But we know that Philip Gunawardena and Colvin R de Silva were supporters of Aggrawala, the leader of the Congress students' organisation in London, and a member of the Marxian League of FA Ridley and Hugo Dewar, and the Ceylonese were afterwards associated with the Communist League of Reg Groves, Henry Sara and Harry Wicks (S Bornstein and A Richardson, *Against the Stream*, London, 1986, pp52 and 121). At the same time, in line with the Communist League's orientation towards the Communist Party, Philip managed to get published 'The Indian Masses Move Forward' in Palme Dutt's *Labour Monthly* (Volume 14, no 2, February 1932, pp87-92).

A number of surveys of this early period of a more general character help to fill up some of the gaps in our knowledge. Leslie Goonewardene wrote two outline sketches, *A Short History of the Lanka Sama Samaja Party* (Colombo, December 1960) and *The History of the LSSP in Perspective* (Colombo, December 1978), the second of which was reviewed by Colvin R de Silva in 'A New Look at the Past', *Socialist Nation*, Volume 4, no 2, February 1979. The special anniversary issue of *The Nation* (Volume 12, no 46, 19 December 1975), entitled '40 Years After', also carried Colvin's general summary, 'The Issue Today is no Longer Socialism, But the Road to It', along with a statement by NM Perera, 'Forty Years of Struggle'. EP de Silva's *NM: A Short Biography of Dr NM Perera* (Colombo, 1975), whilst not being particularly well organised, helps to round out the picture. Edmund Samarakkody also published a preliminary historical sketch, 'The Root and the Flower (A Short History of the LSSP)' for the *Samasamajist* (Volume 24, no 16, 1 March 1960), which was reprinted as an appendix in Paolo Casciola's tribute, *Edmund Samarakkody (1912-1992)* (Centro Studi Pietro Tresso, June 1992). Edmund expanded considerably upon this in 'The Struggle for Trotskyism in Ceylon', which occupied an entire issue of the *Spartacist* (no 22, Winter 1973-74). Prins Rajasooriya's analysis is to be found in an interview he granted to Bob Pitt, 'Sri Lanka: The Fight for Trotskyism' (*Workers News*, October-November 1990). Bob Pitt's own conclusions appear in 'The Road to Coalition: How the LSSP Betrayed Trotskyism' (*Workers News*, June-July and August 1989).

Calvin A Woodward, 'The Trotskyite Movement in Ceylon' (*World Politics*, Volume 14, 1962, pp308-21), and Robert N Kearney, 'The Marxist Parties of Ceylon' (in Paul Brass and Marcus P Franda [eds], *Radical Politics in South Asia*, Cambridge, Massachusetts, 1973, pp401-39) provide the odd additional detail, as does Alfred J Wilson, 'Socialism in Sri Lanka', in Helen Defosses and Jacques Levesque (eds), *Socialism in the Third World* (New York, pp255-90).

Kumari Jayawardene

The Background to the Formation of the Lanka Sama Samaja Party[1]

THE IMPLANTATION of capitalism in a colonial economy led to important changes both in the class composition and the political superstructure of Ceylon. The new classes that emerged with the development of the plantation sector and the consequent urbanisation were the British and Ceylonese capitalists, the urban petit-bourgeoisie, and the working class composed of plantation and urban labour. The rise of a Ceylonese bourgeoisie and the growth of wage labour relationships marked the beginning of the demands for democratic rights in Ceylon, including trade union rights for the working class. However, there was a gap of a hundred years between the introduction into the country of plantation capitalism[2] in the 1830s and the rise of the labour movement on the plantations in the 1930s. The reason was that plantation labour recruited from South India was not wage labour in a competitive market, but was semi-feudal in character. Payment of wages was partly in kind, and the workers, who had to buy their provisions from shops run by the estate, were further tied to the planter and the *kangany* by bonds such as indebtedness. Independent activity and organisation amongst this group of semi-wage labour was thereby retarded.

However, the growth of transport and urban workshops ancillary to the plantation economy, and the emergence of a nucleus of skilled and unskilled wage labour, resulted in an urban labour movement led by a section of the Ceylonese bourgeoisie. Urban wage labour, divorced from the traditional means of production in the village, found itself in a new form of employer-worker relationship in the towns. Being 'free' agents, selling their labour power on the market, a section of the urban working class sought to improve its position

1. I am very grateful to Mr Hector Abeyawardena, Mr Philip Gunawardena, Mr James Rutnam, Mrs Doreen Wickremasinghe and Dr SA Wickremasinghe for their helpful comments on this article.
2. The term 'plantation capitalism' has been expressly used because there is a view that plantations were not a completely capitalist mode of production.

through organisation and joint action. In addition, the emergence of a Ceylonese bourgeoisie — whose wealth was derived from coconut, rubber, timber, cinnamon, graphite, arrack renting, cart contracting and urban property — led to the growth in the demands for basic political rights in keeping with the economic power of the new class. During the 50 year period between 1880 and 1930, the workers' agitation for trade union rights was linked with the movement for constitutional reforms. This struggle of the bourgeoisie and the urban workers for democratic rights can be divided into three phases.

The first phase, between 1880 and 1920, was a period of religious revival and nationalism. The challenge to British rule came in an indirect form with the Buddhist and Hindu revival movements of the 1880s led by the Sinhalese and Tamil intelligentsia. This cultural self-assertion of the 'national' religions against the religion of the foreign rulers and their agents, the Christian missionaries, was a form of incipient nationalism. Significantly, it was a Buddhist Theosophist teacher (AE Buultjens), and other middle class reformers associated with various protest movements, who started the first trade union in Ceylon in 1893 (the Ceylon Printers Union, formed after a strike at Cave and Co). In the period up to 1920 there were numerous strikes, the most important being the strikes of laundrymen in 1896, carters in 1906, railway workers in 1912, and port and railway workers in 1920. These strikes were led by the unorthodox radical fringe of the Ceylonese bourgeoisie which included Buddhist revivalists, Theosophists, social reformers, temperance workers and the more politically conscious nationalists. These middle class leaders were mainly paternalistic, advocating conciliation and moderation to the working class, but nevertheless championing the workers' basic right to organise into trade unions. They were people who were themselves involved in claiming their rights, which included the right of middle class suffrage, political representation, racial equality and equal opportunity vis-à-vis British officialdom in Ceylon.

The 1920s form the second phase of the movement for democratic rights. This was a period of militant trade union struggle which began in 1923, when the Ceylon Labour Union under the leadership of AE Goonesinha[3] organised a general strike in Colombo of 20 000 workers. It was followed by a wave of successful strikes, in the harbour in 1927, and amongst taxi drivers and industrial workers in 1928, culminating in the violent tramway strike of 1929, during which police

3. Alexander Ekanayake Goonesinha (1871-1967) can be regarded as the founder of the labour movement in Ceylon, having become Secretary of the Ceylon Labour Union in 1922. [He subsequently became a champion of Sinhala chauvinism, and refused to defend the rights of Tamil workers in Ceylon when they came under attack in the late 1940s. Editor's note]

firing led to five deaths. The leadership of urban wage labour of the 1920s came from the radical section of the Ceylon bourgeoisie, most notably the staunch nationalist AE Goonesinha, who took the fight for democratic rights a stage further than the moderate reformers of the Ceylon National Congress. In a society where wage labour relationships existed alongside vestiges of feudalism, where there were class, caste, communal and religious divisions, and where the exploiting class was both foreign and local, the important political slogans of the period were freedom, equality and social reform. Goonesinha's Ceylon Labour Union and Ceylon Labour Party called for political independence, universal suffrage, political rights irrespective of race, religion or sex, the recognition of trade unions and the right to strike, and minimum wages, pensions and other social legislation for the working class.

The ideology of the 'advanced' elements of the bourgeoisie of the pre-1920 phase had been Gladstonian Liberalism tinged with Buddhism, Theosophy and humanitarianism. The demands were essentially upper middle class demands for moderate political reform, limited suffrage and equal rights. But during the 1920s — a period of economic boom, when the Ceylonese bourgeoisie increased in economic power, and urban wage labour expanded in size and acquired greater class consciousness — certain radical sections of the bourgeoisie and a section of the petit-bourgeoisie came into prominence, and were shrill in their agitation for political reforms and social changes. This was the 'Goonesinha era' with its ideology of Social Democracy. However, during the severe economic depression of the early 1930s, the trade union and political movement led by AE Goonesinha collapsed, and an era of radical agitation with a new leadership began. The aim of this article is to discuss the events leading to this phase in the struggle for democratic rights which commenced in the early 1930s, and led to the formation in 1935 of the Lanka Sama Samaja Party, the first Socialist political party in Ceylon.

The International Situation

The Socialism of the 1930s in Ceylon resulted from the fusion of two political strands of the radical bourgeoisie and petit-bourgeoisie. First was the group of locally educated Ceylonese nationalists who formed Youth Leagues in various parts of Ceylon, and led an anti-British political campaign; these young radicals were strongly influenced by militant Indian nationalism, but were not Socialists. The second group provided the ideology. These were the Ceylonese students who had absorbed Socialist ideas abroad, and who, on returning to Ceylon, assumed the leadership of the Youth Leagues, which they regarded as the most radical indigenous political group. In discussing the events leading to the formation of the LSSP in 1935, some comment on the contemporary international situation in relation to revolutionary movements is therefore necessary.

In the late 1920s and early 1930s, left forces in the world had suffered several setbacks, including the defeat of the General Strike in Britain in 1926, the consolidation of Mussolini's Fascist rule in Italy, the defeat of the Communists in China in 1927, and the rise to power of Hitler in 1933. The emergence of a Left Opposition in the Soviet Union, which resulted in the expulsion from the country of Leon Trotsky in 1929, reflected the internal problems of the Communist movement. This was also a period when the Communist International had to face several important tactical issues concerning the threat of Fascism, the attitude to Social Democracy, and the policy to be adopted towards the national bourgeoisie in colonial countries.

Between 1927 and 1935 there were important changes in the policy of the Communist International. In 1927 the Communists had formed the League Against Imperialism to include 'all political organisations, parties, trade unions and persons, fighting against capitalist imperialist domination'. The League declared that its task was to mobilise 'in a world-wide resistance to the imperialist offensive, all the revolutionary forces fighting *for freedom and democracy* in the oppressed colonial countries'.[4] The Executive Council of the League included many non-Communist nationalists like Nehru,[5] Mohammed Hatta (from Indonesia)[6] and Lamine Senghor (from French West Africa).[7] But by 1931 the attitude of the League towards these nationalists had changed, and warnings were issued against 'illusions spread by these nationalist reformists concerning the possibility of winning national independence without a revolutionary struggle'. During this period Nehru, Gandhi[8] and Subhas Chandra Bose[9] were denounced as traitors and agents of imperialism.[10] But in 1935, in view of the 'towering menace of Fascism to the working class', the Seventh Congress of the Communist International changed its line to that of a 'People's Front Against Fascism'. Communists were urged to act

4. League Against Imperialism, General Council Resolution, December 1927.
5. Jawaharlal 'Pandit' Nehru (1889-1964) was an Indian nationalist leader, and the first Prime Minister of the independent state (1947-64). [Editor's note]
6. Mohammed Hatta (1902-1986), an Indonesian nationalist, was Prime Minister of Indonesia (1948-1950), and later Vice-President. [Editor's note]
7. Leopold Senghor (1906-), a Senegalese leader and a proponent of moderate African Socialism, was later President of Senegal (1960-1980). [Editor's note]
8. Mohandas Karamchand 'Mahatma' Ghandi (1869-1948) was the leader of Indian nationalism. [Editor's note]
9. Subhas Chandra Bose (1897-1945) led a national struggle against British rule in India during the Second World War in alliance with the Japanese. [Editor's note]
10. League Against Imperialism, Executive Council Resolution (1931).

jointly with Social Democrats in the political field, and with existing trade unions in industrial matters.[11]

Amongst the Ceylonese students who were in London, there emerged for the first time, in the late 1920s, a group which was influenced by Marxism, which became active in left wing politics, and which was influenced by the critical issues which faced the Communist movement at the time.

The Socialist Student Group

Before the First World War, Ceylonese students who went to universities in Britain were drawn from the families of large landowners and those in the liberal professions. With the boom in all agricultural products and plantation crops in the 1920s (especially coconut and rubber), a section of the newly-prosperous rural middle class was able to afford a foreign university education for its children. Whereas the earlier progression of rich students had been from a few select Christian schools in Colombo to Oxford and Cambridge, the new type of student often went from provincial or Buddhist Theosophist schools to the University of London.

In London in the 1920s, the Ceylon Students Association became an important centre of political discussion amongst young Ceylonese. The Association was dominated by a group of Socialist students, who whilst active in the broad student organisation, would also meet separately to discuss questions of Socialism and the possibility of forming a Socialist party in Ceylon. The group included Philip Gunawardena,[12] Leslie Goonewardene,[13] Colvin R de Silva,[14] NM Perera[15] and

11. In 1935 the Comintern declared that Communist parties had to 'reach agreements with the organisations of the toilers of various political trends for joint action on a factory, local district, national and international scale' (*Resolutions of the Seventh World Congress of the Comintern*, 1935). At this time the importance of joint trade union activity was stressed by Georgi Dimitrov when he said: 'We must base our tactics not on the behaviour of individual leaders of the Amsterdam unions no matter what difficulties their behaviour may cause in the class struggle, but on the question of *where the masses are to be found and make the question of struggle for trade union unity the central issue.*' (G Dimitrov, *The Working Classes Against Fascism*, my emphasis) [The central feature of the Popular Front strategy, however, as distinct from the earlier united front policy, was that it advocated anti-Fascist unity between working class and bourgeois political parties. Editor's note]

12. Don Philip Rupasinghe Gunawardena (1901-1972) was a son of Boralugoda Ralahamy, who had been sentenced to death and reprieved by the British during the 1915 Riots. After this episode, Gunawardena was taken from a Christian school (Prince of Wales College, Moratuwa) and sent to Ananda College. The Principal at the time was a Theosophist, Fritz Kunz, of Wisconsin University where there were several Marxists including Scott Nearing and John Commons. Kunz was a liberal, and was sympathetic to Indian nationalism. Gunawardena

Dr SA Wickremasinghe[16]. Except for Leslie Goonewardene, none of them belonged to the Christianised elite, but came from the Sinhala-speaking, rural landowning class. They were educated in Buddhist Theosophist or government schools, and were from Buddhist families whose nationalism had been influenced by Anagarika Dharmapala's

> also attended Wisconsin University. [He was probably the main inspiration behind the evolution of the LSSP in the direction of Trotskyism. After the Second World War, he came into conflict with the organisation, now part of the Bolshevik-Leninist Party of India, and, along with NM Perera, split from the BLPI to set up a rival group under the name of the LSSP. He refused to take part in the unification of the two parties in 1950, forming first of all the Viplavakeri (Revolutionary) Samasamaja Party, and then the Mahajana Eksath Peramuna. He was MP for Avisawella. The MEP entered an alliance led by the UNP, and Philip joined the government, being Minister of Food and Agriculture (1956-58), and of Industry (1965-70), and died as a right winger. Editor's note]
>
> 13. Leslie Simon Goonewardene (1909-1983), whose father was a doctor in Panadura, came from a landowning Westernised family. He went to St Thomas' College and to a public school in Wales. He did a BSc (Economics) degree at the London School of Economics, and qualified as a barrister. Whilst in London, Goonewardene was very active in left wing political groups. [He was Secretary of the LSSP from 1935 to 1977, and was its main authority on Stalinism and on the history of the LSSP. He was MP for Colombo North and then Panadura. He was Minister of Transport in the second SLFP coalition government (1970-75). Editor's note]
>
> 14. Colvin Reginald de Silva (1907-1989) was from a rural middle class family. He was educated first at St John's, Panadura and later at Royal College. He did a degree and PhD at London University, and was called to the Bar. His thesis was on British rule in Ceylon in the period before 1833. In 1926 de Silva was Secretary of the Ceylon Students Association. He visited the Soviet Union in 1931. [Apart from being a brilliant and powerful orator and perhaps the island's leading criminal lawyer, he wrote a major two-volume work, *Ceylon Under British Occupation, 1795-1833* (Colombo, 1953), based upon his university PhD thesis. He was Minister of Plantation Industries in the coalition government led by the SLFP. Editor's note]
>
> 15. NM Perera (1905-1979) was from a middle class family, and was educated at Ananda College. He did a PhD on the Weimar Republic at the London School of Economics, and later obtained a DSc for a thesis on parliamentary procedure. He was influenced by Professor Laski. [He was elected to Colombo Municipal Council in 1950, and was Mayor of Colombo during 1954-56. He was elected 'Man of the Year' in 1956 by the *Ceylon Observer*, and served as Minister of Finance and Governor of the Bank of Sri Lanka in both of the SLFP's coalition governments. Editor's note]
>
> 16. SA Wickremasinghe (1901-) was from a landowning family in South Ceylon. He was educated at Mahinda College (Galle) where the Principal was FL Woodward, a liberal and a Theosophist, and the Vice-Principal, F Gordon Pearce, was a member of the Independent Labour Party. During the 1915 Riots, Wickremasinghe, who was a schoolboy at the time, witnessed acts of repression by British troops. Wickremasinghe qualified as a doctor in Ceylon, and went to Britain in 1926. In London he was President of the Ceylon Students Association in 1927. [He later became a leader of the Communist Party of Ceylon. Editor's note]

Buddhist nationalist crusade, and by the repression that followed the riots of 1915.

The two important political influences on this group of Socialist students were the Indian nationalist movement and Marxism. The late 1920s was a period when Indian nationalism was going through a militant phase; the Simon Commission on constitutional reforms had been boycotted by the Indian National Congress, and within Congress the Communists and left wing factions were becoming influential. In London, the Indian students were active in nationalist agitation conducted principally through their student organisation, the London Majlis. Some members of the Ceylon Students Association (notably SA Wickremasinghe) worked closely with both the Majlis and the Indian League in London, whose leading members were Krishna Menon,[17] Fenner Brockway[18] and the Reverend Sorenson. However, Philip Gunawardena opposed Krishna Menon's policies, and he joined the Indian Communist students' group in London. Philip was later joined by Leslie Goonewardene. Whilst in America, Berlin and Paris, he worked with groups of Indian revolutionaries including MN Roy, the best-known Indian Communist at that time.[19]

Amongst both Indian and Ceylonese students at the time there was great disillusionment with the British Labour Party, which was regarded as imperialist in colonial policy and reformist in home affairs. Hence the revolutionary slogans of the Communist Party and the left wing of the Labour Party seemed to have greater relevance and appeal to many of the students from colonial countries. In addition, the fact that two of the leading members of the British Communist Party were Indian (Rajani Palme Dutt[20] and Shapurji Saklatvala[21]) led to close contact between the Communist Party and the Indian and Ceylonese students.

17. Vengali Krishnan-Krishna Menon (1897-1974) was a prominent Indian nationalist, and was High Commissioner for India in London from 1947, and later Indian Minister of Defence. [Editor's note]
18 . Archibald Fenner Brockway (1888-1988), Secretary of the Independent Labour Party, was active in the League Against Imperialism. [Editor's note]
19. Manabendra Nath Roy (Battacharia) (-1954) was won to Communism whilst in Mexico in 1919. Active in the Communist International, especially in India and China, he sided with the Brandler-Thalheimer Opposition, and was expelled from the Comintern in 1929. He later formed a movement based upon radical humanism. [Editor's note]
20. Rajani Palme Dutt (1896-1974) was actually half-Indian, his mother being Swedish. He was the British Communist Party's main theoretician and expert on India, and used his considerable intellectual powers to provide a sophisticated gloss for every Stalinist twist and turn. [Editor's note]
21. Shapurji Dorabji Saklatvala (1874-1936) was a member of the Communist Party of Great Britain, and was for a while an MP in Battersea on a joint Labour/Communist ticket. [Editor's note]

In 1928 the conference of the Communist-sponsored League Against Imperialism, which was held in London, attracted the attention of the colonial students. (Philip Gunawardena was on the Executive Council of the League during 1929-31.) The policy of the League was one of condemnation of the Socialist Second International and the British Labour Party, which was accused of having 'made common cause with the British imperialists' by participating in the Simon Commission.[22]

Several of the Ceylonese students acquired a knowledge of Marxism through contact with Marxist intellectuals and with Socialist teachers at British and American universities, and practical experience was obtained through membership of various Communist organisations, especially the British Communist Party. The Left Opposition's views within the Communist movement influenced Philip Gunawardena, who, on his way back to Ceylon, contacted Trotskyist groups in France and Spain.

It is important to note to what extent the views of this group of Socialist Ceylonese students differed from the opinions of other political associations in Ceylon. This can be gauged from the stand they took on two vital issues: the question of political reforms, and the rôle of the trade union movement. At a time when the Donoughmore reforms and AE Goonesinha's Labour Party were supported by the British Labour Party, the Socialist student group in London made known their opposition to the reforms and to Goonesinha's trade union policy.

Attitude to Reforms

One important area of disagreement concerned the rôle of the national bourgeoisie in Ceylon. After the publication of the recommendations of the Donoughmore Commission in 1928,[23] the Ceylonese students in London held a series of weekly discussions at which Krishna Menon, S Saklatvala and DB Jayatileka were the main speakers. A critical examination of the proposed reforms was made, and reports of these discussions were published as a pamphlet in 1928 by SA Wickremasinghe and Krishna Menon. The students disagreed with the attitude of the British Labour Party and AE Goonesinha towards the national bourgeoisie. The British Labour Party regarded

22. League Against Imperialism, General Council Resolution (1927).
23. A Commission was set up by the British government in 1927, led by the Earl of Donoughmore, to investigate the constitution and government of Ceylon. It recommended that certain powers and responsibilities be given to Ceylonese politicians, whilst strengthening the powers of the Governor. It also called for universal suffrage and for the ending of communal representation.

the Ceylon National Congress as a set of oligarchs, and Goonesinha's objections to the Ceylonese leaders were so strong that he said he was against more responsible government, unless the franchise was broadened. But the Ceylonese students in London adopted the prevalent Marxist line that the national bourgeoisie should be supported in the fight against foreign rule. They held that the indigenous oligarchy was preferable to a foreign one because the former 'had the knowledge of the land and people, [were] of the same stock and tradition, and formed a wider oligarchy with the inherent possibility of ceasing to be one'.

On the question of universal suffrage, the students' group argued that, although it was desirable, its immediate significance was not to be overestimated because of the danger of a 'large number of votes being at the mercy of those who have the economic power to manipulate them'. The Donoughmore Commissioners were accused of 'treating the problem in the old way, of looking at political and evading economic issues', and of neglecting to report on labour conditions in Ceylon, which 'would have at least served to draw the attention of the British parliament, and greater attention from the government of Ceylon and the ILO'. They alleged that this was deliberately omitted as the findings would have discredited the British administration and planter interests; in this connection, the Labour MP Dr Drummond Shiels,[24] who was a member of the Donoughmore Commission, was accused of shirking a duty which 'he owed to the labour world as a whole'.[25]

Attitude to AE Goonesinha

The Ceylon student group in London opposed the policy and leadership of AE Goonesinha in the Ceylon Labour Union and the Ceylon Labour Party. It was essential for the students to take a stand on Goonesinha's position, because from 1922 until the years of the depression the Labour Union had led the trade union struggles of Colombo workers, and the Ceylon Labour Party (formed in 1923) had been the most radical force on the political scene. The younger generation of nationalist Ceylonese supported Goonesinha in the fight for *swaraj*,[26] universal suffrage, trade union rights and better pay. But dissatisfaction with Goonesinha grew especially after the Labour Un-

24. Sir Thomas Drummond Shiels (1881-1953) was a well-known Labour politician, and was Under-Secretary at the Colonial Office during 1929-31. [Editor's note]
25. Ceylon Students Association, *Study of the Report on the Constitution*, London, 1928.
26. Independence, a term taken from the struggle led by the Indian National Congress. [Editor's note]

ion signed a collective agreement with the employers in 1929 under which lightning strikes were renounced in return for recognition of the union.

The first theoretical Marxist analysis of the rôle of Goonesinha and the labour movement of the 1920s was given by Philip Gunawardena in an article entitled 'Whither Ceylon?', written in 1931. Goonesinha was given credit for the militant battles he had fought on behalf of the workers, and was called 'a man of tremendous initiative and daring'. According to Philip Gunawardena, the crucial strike in Ceylon, which marked the culmination of a period of offensive action by the workers, was the tramway strike and riot of 1929, during which the workers set fire to the Maradana police station:

'The workers rose to an extraordinary pitch of revolutionary energy, enthusiasm and self-sacrifice to defend their class interests and smash the symbol of capitalist authority... [They] displayed rare initiative and an ability to cope with a critical situation when parliamentarians were wasting their time in hair-splitting arguments over constitutional authority. The weakened nationalists shivered in their shoes and knelt at the altar of imperialism, begging it to save them from their class enemies. Their class fear was far more potent than their fear of foreign conquerors.'

Gunawardena claimed that the strike weapon was 'the manifestation of the class struggle at a fairly acute stage', and that during the tram strike, the workers 'who were not interested in the law and order of a capitalist society', were able to 'put out of commission the authority of the decadent capitalist society'. Though the workers had neither preparation nor correct leadership, they were able to challenge 'the armed forces of the mightiest empire the world has ever seen'. In contrast to the militancy of the workers, Goonesinha was accused of failing to give the required revolutionary leadership during the strike, and of displaying 'a lamentable confusion'. Goonesinha's praise of the British police officials, and the cheers that he asked the workers to give the chairman of the Chamber of Commerce after the settlement of the strike, were referred to as 'tactical blunders' of the first magnitude.[27]

Attack on the British Labour Party

In the late 1920s the Communists and the left wing of the Labour Party in Britain were highly critical not only of the political leader-

27. P Gunawardena, 'Whither Ceylon?', *The Searchlight*, 9 November 1931.

ship of the Labour Party, but also of the policy of the British trade union movement, and especially of the Mond-Turner negotiations. These talks between Sir Alfred Mond, the chairman of the large combine of ICI (Imperial Chemical Industries)[28] and Ben Turner, the chairman of the British Trade Union Congress,[29] were an attempt to obtain industrial peace through collaboration between employers and labour.

Influenced by the Communist line on these two questions, the Ceylonese student group criticised the close association between the British Labour Party and AE Goonesinha in both political and trade union matters. Labour personalities such as Ramsay MacDonald,[30] Drummond Shiels and George Lansbury[31] were said to have introduced Goonesinha 'to the wonders of Fabian mysticism', and in the trade union sphere British union officials were said to have explained the nature of 'Mondism' to Goonesinha, who after his visit to England in 1928 returned to Ceylon 'a devout apostle of industrial peace and a class collaborator'. The signing of the collective agreement in Ceylon in 1929 was also attributed to this influence. Philip Gunawardena alleged that soon after Goonesinha returned from England, the Chairman of the Ceylon Chamber of Commerce, SP Hayley, 'a high priest of industrial peace, hurriedly formed the Employers Federation to collaborate with the trade unions... Hayley addressed the business community in the tones of a Hebrew prophet, and an agreement was signed to prevent lightning strikes'. Gunawardena also claimed that Goonesinha's conciliatory attitude towards the Employers Federation was proof that very few leaders of the working class could escape the temptations of capitalist society. Goonesinha, he said, having risen to power 'on the shoulders of the workers, [was] looking round for an official position in the framework of imperialism, and the Labour government of England makes the temptations doubly attractive'.

In order to counteract the influence of the British Labour Party, the young Socialists urged the Ceylon unions to maintain contacts abroad only with 'genuine working class organisations', and with the 'revolutionary trade union movement' in India; warnings were made

28. Sir Alfred Moritz, later Baron Melchett (1868-1930), approached the union leaders for discussions about cooperation between labour and capital. [Editor's note]
29. Ben Turner, later Sir Benjamin (1863-1937), headed the National Union of Textile Workers, and was a leading right winger. [Editor's note]
30. James Ramsay MacDonald (1866-1937) was a leader of the Labour Party, Prime Minister in the Labour governments elected in 1924 and 1929, and defected to head the National Government in 1931. [Editor's note]
31. George Lansbury (1859-1940), a pacifist, was for a brief period leader of the Labour Party. [Editor's note]

against attempts to ally the Ceylon labour movement to the ILO and the Socialist Second International, and trade union bureaucrats 'of the English and American type' were denounced.[32]

The views of the Ceylonese Socialist students in London presented a new departure in ideology for the Ceylonese political and labour movement. Whilst these students remained abroad, their agitational activities were confined to student organisations and foreign nationalist or Communist groups. The impact of these ideas was felt in Ceylon between 1930 and 1933 when all the active members of the Ceylon students' group returned home. On their return they emphasised the need for a new political party with a Socialist basis; this was formed in 1935, but until then the young Socialists joined the radical Youth League movement which had already taken root in the country.

The Youth League Movement in Ceylon

Amongst the radical youth who had studied in Ceylon during the 1920s, there was great dissatisfaction with the existing political organisations, and the need for a new approach to political, social and economic issues was keenly felt. The Ceylon National Congress was regarded as a conservative organisation, dominated by the 'old guard' leaders, who were against mass political action or any extension of the franchise. Some of the radicals — K Natesa Aiyar, George and Susan Caldera and Valentine Perera — had joined Goonesinha's Labour Party, hoping that his party would provide a vigorous and progressive alternative to the Congress, but many of them dropped out after conflicts with Goonesinha.

Attempts were made in the 1920s to form a radical political party when SWRD Bandaranaike[33] returned from Oxford. His views on economics and politics and his defiance of the older politicians made him for a time the hope of the young Ceylonese. In 1926 the Progressive Nationalist Party, formed with Bandaranaike as its President, attracted many young nationalists and students. The aim of the party was full self-government for Ceylon, and by 'fostering the spirit of nationalism' to widen the scope of political agitation, which had 'hitherto been the monopoly of a few'.[34] This attempt to unite the existing radical forces failed, and Bandaranaike continued his political

32. P Gunawardena, 'Whither Ceylon?', *The Searchlight*, 9 November 1931.
33. Solomon West Ridgeway Dias Bandaranaike (1899-1959) was subsequently a leader of the Sri Lanka Freedom Party, which was formed in the early 1950s and took office in 1956, with Bandaranaike as Prime Minister. He was assassinated by a Buddhist monk in 1959. [Editor's note]
34. *Ceylon Independent*, 6 September 1926.

career in the Ceylon National Congress. The existing dissatisfaction with Goonesinha's one-man leadership of the trade union movement resulted in efforts to break his control over labour. In 1927 Bandaranaike contested and defeated Goonesinha at a municipal council election.

There was a heightened interest in politics in Ceylon with the arrival of the Donoughmore Commissioners in 1927, when issues such as the degree of self-government for Ceylon and the extension of the franchise were hotly debated. The politically conscious youth, who had no faith in the Ceylon National Congress or the Ceylon Labour Party, began to group themselves into Youth Leagues in order to protest against the new constitution. The first Youth League was formed in Jaffna (led by Handy Perimpanayagam and C Balasingham) and active Youth Leagues sprang up in Colombo and elsewhere. In 1931, the Youth Leagues came together to form the Youth Congress, which had Aelian Pereira (a lawyer) as its President, and Valentine Perera and George Caldera (also lawyers and former members of the Labour Party) as Secretaries.

Anti-Imperialism

An important source of inspiration for the Youth League movement came from the militant section of the Indian national movement. In India by the late 1920s, the Socialists had formed a group within the Indian National Congress, and in 1931 left wing members of the Congress, Jawaharlal Nehru and Kamaladevi Chattopadyaya, who were visiting Ceylon, addressed a meeting of the Youth Congress. Links with India were also maintained through personal contacts by some Youth League members who travelled to India frequently.

The political outlook of the Youth Leagues can be divided into two phases: the purely nationalist, anti-imperialist phase when the Leagues concentrated on agitating for political independence for Ceylon, and the second phase when the Socialist students who returned to Ceylon during the depression years gave the Youth Leagues a Socialist orientation, and directed them to an interest in economic issues.

In the earlier phase, the activities of the Youth Leagues were dominated by political questions connected with the Donoughmore Constitution. In May 1931 a resolution was moved by Stanley de Zoysa declaring that the youth of Ceylon had completely lost faith in British rule, which was 'fraught with incalculable detriment to the social, economic, political and cultural life of the people', and that an intensive campaign be launched for the immediate attainment of *swaraj*. At the Youth Congress in December 1931, Valentine Perera called for 'downright unadulterated independence', and stated that no halfway measures would be acceptable. The Donoughmore Constitution was also described as 'a setback in the political history of Ceylon', and 'a flagrant invasion of our cherished rights calculated to wound our national self-respect'.[35]

The Youth Leagues also launched several boycott campaigns. Influenced by the methods of the Indian national movement, the Youth Leagues called for a boycott of the general elections (held in June 1931) as a protest against the new constitution. On election day, Youth League members demonstrated with placards near polling stations, urging people not to vote. The boycott was only successful in Jaffna, mainly because the Tamil population had their own special grievances against the constitution. There was also a campaign by the Youth Leagues to boycott foreign goods — especially rice, liquor, cloth and tobacco — and Ceylonese were urged to join the *swadeshi* movement launched by the Youth Leagues to encourage local products. The Colombo South Youth League opened a *swadeshi* cooperative store which only sold local products. Terence de Zylva, one of the most active members of the youth movement, declared that as Ceylon was 'held in bondage by military force and repression', the only weapon the Ceylonese could use was the boycott of foreign goods and the fostering of national industries. Another boycott sponsored by the Youth Leagues was the King's birthday celebrations, on the ground that such occasions fostered a 'lamentable form of slave mentality', and were bound to be regarded as a 'willing acquiescence to be governed and controlled by Great Britain'.[36]

The Youth Leagues were also critical of the country's education system, which, according to Terence de Zylva (the founder of Kolonnawa Vidyalaya), was 'in the hands of Empire builders who had used it as a political weapon'. At the Youth Congress sessions in 1931, CC Sabaratnam proposed and Terence de Zylva seconded a resolution declaring that the existing system of education was injurious to Ceylon's 'political, cultural and economic well-being', and

35. *Morning Leader*, 18 May and 29 December 1931. The Youth League and (after 1935) the LSSP leaders retained their contacts with India. SA Wickremasinghe spent two months in India on his way back from Britain in 1928, where he attended the sessions of the Indian Trade Union Congress. He revisited India frequently. He was in Benares when the news arrived of Gandhi's arrest during the Salt March in 1931, and he rendered medical aid to the injured after the police fired on the demonstrators. He also visited Gandhi in jail, and spent some time at Santiniketan, where he met Tagore in 1933. In 1936 Philip Gunawardena attended the Indian Trade Union Congress sessions in Bombay, and in 1937 Colvin R de Silva, NM Perera and Philip Gunawardena attended the sessions of the Indian National Congress.

36. *The Searchlight*, 13 February 1932; *Morning Leader*, 26 May 1931.

urged that a national system of education in *swabasha* be implemented.[37]

In the absence of a broad nationalist movement led by the national bourgeoisie, a small group of radicals in the Youth Leagues became the vanguard of the nationalist movement during this period.

Economic Issues and Socialism

In 1931 Nehru, addressing the Youth Congress, had emphasised the inadequacy of nationalism alone without an understanding of the working of capitalism. At that time the left wing in the Indian National Congress believed that political independence would be of little value without revolutionary social changes; Nehru advised the Youth League members to consider how national freedom would affect the masses in the country, and to try to understand the nature of imperialism and capitalism: 'How will you free the men, women and children of Ceylon? Freedom is worth striving for, but you must see how it affects the bottom dog in your country.' At the same meeting, Kamaladevi Chattopadyaya spoke of Gandhi's campaign of civil disobedience in 1930, and said that it was 'not only imperialist violence that Gandhi was up against, but also the violence of the capitalists who exploited the poor'.[38]

As a result of the trade depression and the prevailing high rates of unemployment, economic problems were frequently highlighted by the Youth League movement. For example, in January 1932 Terence de Zylva declared that the aim of Ceylon youth should include 'freedom from the vulgar pride of wealth and the monopoly of the necessities of life by self-seeking capitalists', and he called on the youth to liberate the country 'from alien domination and economic exploitation'.[39] In May 1932 the monthly journal *Young Ceylon*, published by Youth League members, declared that its aims were complete independence, economic stability and national solvency. In 1932 the Colombo South Youth League issued a pamphlet entitled *The Present Economic Crisis* which aimed at showing that political and economic freedom were 'inextricably bound up with each other'. This pamphlet referred to British economic interests in the country as 'a constant drain of the country's wealth', and it condemned the system of Imperial Preference as 'disastrous to the economic stability of the island'. The Youth Leagues called for a more equitable distribution of wealth, to be obtained through 'the reorganisation of tariffs, taxation

37. *Morning Leader*, 24 December 1931.
38. *Morning Leader*, 18 May 1931.
39. T de Zylva, 'Our Duty', *The Searchlight*, 27 January 1932. [*Swabasha* is the implementation of education in Sinhalese and Tamil. Editor's note]

and finance'. It is significant that in 1932 Socialism was not one of the slogans that was openly used, and the equal distribution of wealth was advocated through financial reform rather than by means of a revolutionary change in the social order. But it must be noted that a few of the Youth League members in Ceylon (notably Terence de Zylva and Susan Caldera) had already shown interest in Socialist ideas.

However, by the latter half of 1932 and in 1933 there were significant changes in the politics of the Youth Leagues, when the Socialist students who had studied abroad returned to Ceylon and became leaders of the Youth League movement. For the first time in Ceylon, Communism and the experiences of the USSR received favourable comment. In September 1932 Dr Colvin R de Silva, who had joined the Colombo South Youth League, wrote an article in *Young Ceylon* proclaiming Communism as the new ideology to be followed. In the same journal Robin Rutnam, another member of the Youth League (who had studied in Canada), argued that the need for economic planning was 'the most significant lesson the outside world was learning from the great social experiment in Russia', and he forecast that the youth of Ceylon had a great opportunity to create 'a new social order'. The pages of *Young Ceylon* from the latter half of 1932 onwards contained references to Lenin.[40]

In the years preceding the formation of the Lanka Sama Samaja Party, the Youth League movement made its influence felt in several ways. The Youth Leagues, under new Socialist leadership, turned the anti-Poppy Day campaign into a platform for anti-imperialist propaganda against the British; during the malaria epidemic of 1934, the Socialists played an active part in the relief of distress; in 1933 they led a strike and gained valuable experience in trade union agitation; and from 1931 to 1935, through their first representative in the State Council, the young Socialists entered the field of parliamentary politics.

The Suriya Mal Movement, 1931-1933

One of the issues that brought the Youth Leagues to the forefront of nationalist political activity was the anti-Poppy Day campaign. This campaign had its beginnings amongst a group of radical students in 1926, was carried on by the Ceylon Ex-Servicemen's Association and

40. R Rutnam, 'The Need For a Planned National Life', *Young Ceylon*, September 1932. In the same issue there was a review of *The Speeches of Lenin* in which Lenin was referred to as 'the greatest moral force in the proletarian revolution'. In *Young Ceylon*, October 1932, there was a review of Lenin's *Socialism and War* which wrote of the 'alert, resourceful and clear mind of Lenin'.

the Youth Leagues in 1931, and was given a distinct militantly anti-British appeal when the Colombo Central Youth League took over the movement in 1933.

Remembrance Day on 11 November used to be observed in the 1920s with a great deal of fervour by government officials and the British residents. On that day, poppies were sold by enthusiastic organisers, and there was a reaffirming of faith in the Empire by means of military parades, church services and banquets held with great pomp and ceremony. The jingoistic annual Poppy Day displays caused resentment amongst some of the young Ceylonese nationalists, who criticised Ceylon's contribution to the Poppy Fund, which was one of the largest in the Empire.

In 1926 AWH Abeysundera, a law student, complained in a letter to the press that although Ceylon was a poor country, vast sums of money, disproportionate to its revenue, were being sent out of the country in the form of Poppy Day collections, and that only an insignificant portion of that money went towards helping Ceylonese ex-servicemen. This letter aroused the interest of a group of young Ceylonese who called themselves the Cosmopolitan Crew (Harry Gunawardena, James Rutnam, DNW de Silva, C Ponnabalam, Valentine Perera), and who in 1926 organised a public meeting and demonstration to protest against Poppy Day. These young men were nationalists, some of whom had been associated with AE Goonesinha's labour activities, and were to become active members of the Youth Leagues.

In 1931 a more positive step against the Poppy Day collection was taken when the Ceylon Ex-Servicemen's Association, whose President, Aelian Pereira, was also the President of the Youth Congress and an ex-serviceman himself, launched a rival fund called after a local flower, the suriya mal, in order to collect money for Ceylonese ex-soldiers and for local charities. Pereira said that there were many Ceylonese servicemen who were disabled, destitute and in urgent need of help. 'There is an idea', he wrote, 'that it is dirty and mean to sell the suriya flower on Armistice Day', but he explained that this particular day was chosen as it had special significance to all servicemen.[41] The Youth Leagues took up the Suriya Mal campaign with great enthusiasm, and made the occasion into an anti-British demonstration.

The sale of the rival flower on Poppy Day in 1931 created a great interest in Colombo and other towns. There were brisk sales, especially in the working class areas of Colombo, where there were more suriya flowers than poppies, and it was reported that pedestrians in

41. *Times of Ceylon*, 10 November 1931.

Colombo 'showed preference for the Suriya Mal, but most cars had poppies'. The leading Christian schools of Colombo refused to let the Suriya Mal sellers enter their premises, and some British business firms warned their employees against wearing a suriya flower to work.[42]

The Ceylon Ex-Servicemen's Association which had sponsored the Suriya Mal was alarmed by the political character of the campaign and by the opposition that it aroused, and in 1932 the Association decided to discontinue the movement. This was the opportunity for the Socialists, and in 1933 the Colombo Central Youth League took over the Suriya Mal campaign and elected a committee for this purpose whose President was Mrs SA Wickremasinghe (née Doreen Young), the principal of Ananda Balika Vidyalaya. This committee included many of the Socialists who had come back to Ceylon from abroad, and also the most radical members of the Youth Leagues. The movement also attracted many other nationalists, including SWRD Bandaranaike, who was in charge of the Suriya Mal funds, and Wilmot Perera, at whose school (Sri Palee in Horana) the Suriya Mal annual meetings were held. It should also be mentioned that several young persons were drawn into political activity through participation in the Suriya Mal movement. The money collected was used for the education of a child of a 'depressed' community, and for the publication of literature. The Ananda Balika principal's house became the headquarters of the movement, and each year hundreds of yellow suriya flowers were made by the enthusiastic staff, who included Helen de Alwis, Eva de Mel, Violet Gamage, Lilian Bandaranaike and Winifred Silva.

The Suriya Mal, which had originated as a campaign for ex-servicemen, dropped any reference to Ceylon's disabled soldiers, and took on an open political and anti-British character. This led to a great deal of anger and resentment on the part of the authorities, the British residents in Ceylon, and certain newspapers. The new organisers of the Suriya Mal were accused of a 'lack of decent sensibility', and the campaign was called a 'crude political move utterly in bad taste'.[43]

Several new political slogans were introduced into the Suriya Mal campaign by the Youth Leagues. In 1933 Leslie Goonewardene wrote: 'We have yet to be shown that Britain fought for us during the war or that she has disinterestedly done anything for us in peace. The purchase of the Poppy in Ceylon is only too often an extension of blind admiration for the mighty British Empire.' Terence de Zylva

42. *Morning Leader*, 10 November 1931; *Ceylon Independent*, 11 November 1931.
43. Editorial in *Ceylon Independent*, 11 November 1933.

declared that the movement was 'definitely anti-war', and that they should prevent money going out of the country 'to help the British Empire to wage wars for the purpose of partitioning the world'. For the first time a Socialist slogan was used in the campaign when de Zylva in 1933 ended an article entitled 'Suriya or Poppy' with an appeal: 'Unite in this battle to establish a Socialist, Democratic Ceylon.'[44]

Trade Union Activity

In the years before the founding of the LSSP, the Youth Leagues also gained experience of trade union agitation when they took over the leadership of a strike at the Wellawatte Spinning and Weaving Mills in 1933. This was a turning point in the working class history of Ceylon because the Labour Union led by AE Goonesinha, which had abandoned its radical policy after the onset of the depression, was effectively challenged in the trade union field by the militant elements of the Youth Leagues.

The Indian-owned Wellawatte Spinning and Weaving Mills (established in 1890) was the largest textile mill in Ceylon, employing 1400 skilled and semi-skilled workers. In 1923, 1926 and 1929 under Goonesinha's leadership there had been strikes at the mills. In February 1933, as a result of the economic depression and the increased competition of Japanese textiles on the market, the management announced a reduction in wages. This led to a strike of the entire labour force, instigated, according to the management, by 'veteran ringleaders' amongst the workers. The strikers sent a petition to the Minister of Labour, and appealed to Goonesinha to intervene on their behalf. To the surprise of the workers, Goonesinha advised them to return to work on the grounds that striking without giving the required notice was a breach of the collective agreement between the union and the Employers Federation, and also because the Labour Union membership of the majority of the strikers had lapsed.

The strikers then appealed for support to a lawyer (H Sri Nissanke, a Youth League member) who lived opposite the mills; he advised them to put their case to Dr Colvin R de Silva, who had recently returned from Britain. De Silva and other members of the Colombo South Youth League took up the question, and the Wellawatte Mill Workers Union was formed on 23 February at a mass meeting of the workers, with de Silva as President, and two active Youth League members (Vernon Gunasekera[45] and JW Senanayake) as Secretaries.

44. See *Young Ceylon*, October 1933 for Leslie Goonewardene's article, and *The Searchlight*, 18 October 1933 for Terence de Zylva's.
45. Vernon Gunasekera (1908-1996) was the first General Secretary of the LSSP, and

Philip Gunawardena, NM Perera, SA Wickremasinghe, Robert Gunawardena, Susan Caldera and several militant workers including Appuhamy, Kattan and Ramiah helped in organising the strikers, spoke at mass meetings, collected funds, and distributed relief.

During the strike, which lasted two months, Goonesinha's aim was to prevent recognition being given by either employers or government to the new union. The manager of the mills refused to open negotiations with the newly-formed Wellawatte Mill Workers Union, and said that he was only prepared to accept Goonesinha as the accredited representative of the workers. Goonesinha denounced the Youth League as a political organisation which was misleading the workers for the 'sinister purpose' of disrupting organised labour. In tolerating the 'scandalous interference' of the Youth League in the strike, Goonesinha said the Controller of Labour was 'encouraging Anarchism'. The new union leaders were accused by Goonesinha of having 'imbibed fantastic ideas from Russia and America', and of seeking to introduce 'aggressive methods into the life of the labourers in Ceylon'.[46]

The strike at the mills was aggravated by the introduction of communal issues into the dispute. Because of the composition of the mill workers, of whom two-thirds were Malayalis and one third Sinhalese, Goonesinha was able to stir up anti-Malayali feeling at a time when communal racial tensions were strong in Colombo due to the extensive unemployment during the depression. The Secretary of the new union condemned 'the mischievous, irresponsible activities of Mr Goonesinha who through a campaign of vilification, insults and abuse of a highly inflammatory character is trying to raise inter-racial animosity in this dispute'.[47] Because the majority of the strikers were Malayalis, the attempt by Goonesinha to introduce Sinhalese black-legs into the mills increased the tension. Harbour workers were sent in lorries to the mills by Goonesinha, who claimed that the purpose was to afford protection to the strikers who were willing to go back to work. The police stated that Goonesinha 'by deliberately importing rowdies' had provoked clashes between Malayalis and Sinhalese, and had brought about a 'most serious state of affairs'.[48]

In view of the increase of communal tension, the Minister of La-

---

was a brilliant criminal lawyer. He was largely instrumental in arranging the escape of the LSSP leaders from Bogambara jail during the Second World War, and helped to mastermind the Bracegirdle affair. See ZM Razik, 'Kandy Bar Pays Tribute to Vernon Gunasekera', *Daily News* (Sri Lanka), 14 November 1996.

46. Ceylon Labour Department, File T15, letter of 15 March 1935; *Ceylon Daily News*, 2 May 1933.

47. Letter to the editor, *Ceylon Daily News*, 22 March 1933.

48. Ceylon Labour Department, File T6, police report, 21 March 1933.

bour informed the Governor that 'the disturbances which... [had] already arisen and the risks of racial clashes... [were] too substantial to be set aside'.[49] The government therefore decided to intervene, and appointed a commission for the settlement of the dispute under the Industrial Disputes Ordinance of 1931.

This was the first occasion when the provisions of the ordinance were used in the conciliation of a trade dispute. The commission in its report reprimanded the workers for striking without first trying to negotiate with the management, and Goonesinha's efforts to persuade the men to return to work were described as reasonable. The commission agreed that the mills needed financial relief, and that 'wages should make a contribution of some substance towards this relief', but they recommended a maximum reduction of wages by 12 per cent, which would be covered by the fall in the cost of living during the depression. The demands for a reduction in the hours of work from 60 to 54 a week was turned down as impracticable, as mills in India were also working a 60-hour week. The commission stated also that the financial difficulties of the time made it impossible for them to recommend the other improved amenities that the workers demanded.[50]

The report was welcomed by Goonesinha, and a meeting of the Ceylon Labour Union was organised to celebrate the occasion, at which Goonesinha gave an account of all the concessions he had obtained for the workers in past years. In contrast, Colvin R de Silva, the President of the Wellawatte Mill Workers Union, said that unlike Goonesinha, the workers did not greet the report with a 'hallelujah chorus' as it was neither 'fair, just nor reasonable'. On the question of wages he said: 'We cannot accept that principle that wages should invariably vary with the cost of living. This is based on the utterly unwarrantable assumption that the prevailing wage rates are just.'[51]

The government was concerned at the appearance of a new militant trade union to challenge Goonesinha's Labour Union, which at this date had become acceptable to both the government and the employers. The Controller of Labour reported that the manager of the mills was 'in a very embarrassing position... for we do not seem to be dealing with a trade union, but a political body'.[52]

The Malaria Epidemic, 1934

In common with the labour leaders of previous decades, the leaders of the labour movement of the 1930s were also involved in relief activ-

49. Ceylon Labour Department, File T15, letter of 23 March 1933.
50. Ceylon Labour Department, File T15, report of April 1933.
51. *Ceylon Daily News*, 25 May 1933.
52. Ceylon Labour Department, File T15, letter of 14 March 1933.

ity amongst the masses which brought them into direct contact with the problems of poverty and disease. The malaria epidemic came after two seasons of severe drought and failure of crops, and according to an official report, 'found ready victims among a population already debilitated by lack of food owing to the economic depression'. The official estimate was that in the area of Ceylon affected by the epidemic, where the population was three million (out of the island's total of 5.5 million), there were 1.5 million cases of malaria by April 1935, and over 100 000 deaths between September 1934 and December 1935.[53]

The severity of the epidemic caused conditions of famine in some districts of Ceylon, and government and private organisations were active in organising relief of distress in the worst stricken areas. The government appointed a Commissioner for Relief, voted half a million rupees to deal with the epidemic, and opened a Malaria Relief Fund to which a lakh[54] was subscribed. The money was used for distributing food, clothing and medicine, and organising relief work. Volunteers from various organisations helped in collecting supplies, and making house-to-house visits distributing medicine and food.

The Suriya Mal movement was very active in providing relief in the Kegalle district. A dispensary was opened, and Dr SA Wickremasinghe, Dr Colvin R de Silva, Harry, Philip and Robert Gunawardena, Dr NM Perera, Robin Rutnam, Dr Mary Rutnam, Selina Peiris and some teachers of Ananda Balika worked in the area for many months. The house of Boralugoda Ralahamy (Philip Gunawardena's father) was the centre for the Suriya Mal workers in that area. The Commissioner of Relief in his report stated that 'intelligent and systematic voluntary workers were the most efficient', and made mention of the 'admirable service' rendered by the Suriya Mal workers.[55]

The devastation caused by the malaria epidemic was blamed by the Youth League and the Suriya Mal workers on the apathy of the administration. The epidemic, which was referred to as one of 'the great national disasters', was held to be 'the direct result of the callousness and indifference of the state'. The legislature was accused of a total neglect of the peasantry during the critical years of depression,

53. Sessional paper 5 of 1936, p17.
54. A lakh is 100 000. [Editor's note]
55. Report of FC Gimson, Sessional paper 5 of 1936. The report of the Assistant Government Agent, Kegalle, also referred to 'the most useful work of the Suriya Mal Society' in Kegalle, and especially to one of its members, Robin Rutnam, who made 'excellent arrangements for the distribution of relief and performed very useful service in a locality which was particularly badly stricken'.

drought and epidemic, and the Ceylon National Congress was criticised for failing to put forward a policy 'for the regeneration of the villages and the improvement of the peasantry'. The leader of the State Council, DB Jayatilaka, who was reported to have said that the malaria epidemic was due to the past sins of the people, came under fierce attack from the Young Socialists. He was accused of avoiding 'the political implications of the malaria epidemic' by 'playing on the credulity of the ignorant and the superstitious', and of using the taxpayers' money to celebrate the Royal Jubilee in 1935 'while the country was being reduced to a graveyard'.[56]

Colvin R de Silva alleged that while thousands were dying of hunger and malaria, 'the so-called national leaders had been entertaining Royal Dukes, celebrating Royal Jubilees, hunting for knighthoods, relieving the rich of their responsibility by repealing estate duty, and lightening the taxes paid by foreign exploiters'.[57] The Ceylon Labour Party was also blamed by the Youth Leagues for failing in its 'special responsibility' of rousing public opinion 'to a consciousness of the needs of the poor and working classes'. The enthusiasm of the party, it was stated, had been exhausted by 'the craze for political heroics', and it was 'more concerned with exploiting the labourer than improving his condition'.[58]

Young Ceylon described the work of the Suriya movement during the epidemic as a remarkable effort by educated young men and women who had given a new meaning to the idea of relief. In a report made by the Suriya Mal Malaria Relief Committee, the political importance of the work was emphasised. The report stated that 'the medical and material aid we rendered was nothing compared to the moral value of the contact' between peasants and the Suriya Mal workers:

'Not until now did we really begin to understand and appreciate the full implications of a crude feudalism, and the nature and extent of the oppression, misery, want and moral degradation that could prevail within such a system... our sympathetic treatment of the villager as our equal was a revelation to him, accustomed as he was to be bossed, abused, and treated like a dog by his so-called social superiors.'[59]

The Young Socialists, who launched the attack on the Ceylon Na-

56. 'The Epidemic', *Young Ceylon*, December 1934; Vernon Gunasekera, 'Malaria and Politics', *Young Ceylon*, June 1934.
57. *Young Ceylon*, December 1934.
58. *Young Ceylon*, December 1934.
59. *Young Ceylon*, September 1935.

tional Congress and the Ceylon Labour Party for their failure to tackle the urgent problem of economic and social reform, became more than ever aware of the need in the country for a Socialist political party.

Agitation Through the State Council

In the years preceding the formation of the LSSP, the Socialists also had their first experience of parliamentary politics. Although a section of the Youth League movement had been against contesting the elections, another group believed that the State Council would be a valuable forum for agitation and propaganda, with the added advantage of parliamentary immunity. From 1931 until 1936, Dr SA Wickremasinghe, who had been active in the Suriya Mal campaign, malaria relief work and the Wellawatte strike, was the member of the State Council for Morawaka. In the State Council, Wickremasinghe kept up a vigorous attack on the British colonial government and on the political and economic policy of the Ceylonese Board of Ministers, and used every occasion to highlight the problems facing the masses during these years of economic depression. He criticised the medical and social service facilities, and made an important dissenting report on the Commission on child servants. He opposed wasteful expenditure on royal visits, and on the occasion of the King's Jubilee in 1935 he moved an amendment to the message of loyalty which stated: 'The condition of the masses has not improved one bit within the 25 years of your Majesty's reign... they are subjected to disabilities, harsh legislation and exploitation... and the fruits of this negligence and criminal indifference of Your Majesty's advisers has been garnered in the shape of poverty, disease and starvation.'[60] During the malaria epidemic, Wickremasinghe constantly exposed the inadequacy of the relief services, and claimed that the lesson of the epidemic was 'the need for political emancipation'.[61]

In the State Council, Wickremasinghe also led the campaign of opposition to the Trade Union Act of 1935. The Ceylon government had tried to pass repressive legislation to control trade unions in 1929, but this had been rejected by Lord Passfield (Sidney Webb), the Secretary of State in the 1929 Labour government,[62] and only the non-controversial ordinance to govern trade disputes was passed in 1931.

60. *Ceylon Daily News*, 8 May 1935.
61. State Council of Ceylon, *Hansard*, Debate of 15 January 1935, p34.
62. Sidney Webb (1859-1947) was a leading theoretician of Fabianism, headed the Colonial Office in the second Labour government, and with his wife Beatrice was responsible for a mammoth apology for Stalinism, *Soviet Communism: A New Civilisation?*. [Editor's note]

By 1935, however, when Ceylon was beginning to recover from the after-effects of the depression and renewed labour activity was therefore a possibility, the first ordinance to regulate trade unions was adopted by the legislature.

The main provisions of the Trade Union Ordinance of 1935 were the compulsory registration of all trade unions, regulations concerning 'contracting in' by members with respect to the political fund of a trade union, and provision that not more than half the officials of a trade union could be 'outsiders'. The Youth Leagues claimed that the government was trying to crush the trade union movement, and in the State Council SA Wickremasinghe, as a member of the Standing Committee to discuss the ordinance, made a dissenting rider in which he stated:

'The Bill is designed to restrict the legitimate activities of workers to form trade unions, but does not provide any protection against victimisation by the employers. In a country where there is no legislation for insurance against unemployment, sickness, old age, maternity, accidents and any other form of social insurance, it is very unwise to introduce legislation to restrict the formation and activities of voluntary associations.'[63]

The Formation of the LSSP

The activities of the Youth League movement in the years before 1935 had consisted of Socialist-inspired, anti-British, anti-feudal campaigns for obtaining democratic rights. The nationalist agitation of the Youth Leagues and the Suriya Mal movement expressed the radical middle class' hostility to British rule. Through the relief work done during the malaria campaign, the social requirements of the rural masses and the feudal oppression that existed in the villages were highlighted. During the severe economic depression when AE Goonesinha had abandoned militant trade unionism, the Youth Leagues led the struggle for trade union rights and workers' demands. In addition, they used the State Council as a platform from which all these political and economic problems could be aired.

The need for a separate political party to carry on broad political and trade union agitation was felt, and on 18 December 1935 the most active members of the Youth Leagues founded the Lanka Sama Samaja Party.[64] The new party issued a manifesto which was intended

63. Labour Department File T1, part II.
64. The founder members of the LSSP included C Balasingham, George Caldera, Susan Caldera, BJ Fernando, Philip Gunawardena, Robert Gunawardena, Leslie Goonewardene, Vernon Gunasekera, Corbett Jayawardena, Jack Kotelawala,

to be a broad programme of 22 'immediate demands for day-to-day agitation and struggle'. The manifesto claimed that the aims of the party were the abolition of social and economic inequality and oppression arising from differences of class, caste, race, creed or sex, and the socialisation of the means of production, distribution and exchange. However, measures involving socialisation were not included in any of the 22 demands, which enumerated the legislative measures needed to ameliorate economic and social conditions in Ceylon.

On behalf of urban workers the manifesto called for minimum wages, unemployment insurance and relief, an eight-hour day, factory legislation, slum clearance, cheaper housing, and the abolition of compulsory registration for trade unions. Relief for the peasantry was urged in the form of free pasture lands, seed paddy free of interest, and the abolition of irrigation rates and forest laws relating to the removal of brushwood. In the interests of children, demands were made for free school books, free milk, and the abolition of child labour. On economic questions, the manifesto advocated higher income tax, estate duty, the abolition of Imperial Preference and the Japanese Quota, and the abolition of indirect taxation which affected goods consumed by the poor. The manifesto also recommended the use of *swabasha* in the lower courts, police stations and government departments.[65]

This was a programme of minimum demands intended to popularise the new party amongst a wide section of the population. None of the demands called for revolutionary change, and the party at its formation did not intend to establish itself as a Marxist party. Even organisationally the party was not a tightly-knit revolutionary party with a restricted membership. Membership was open to anyone who affirmed that he was a Socialist, and agreed with the aims of the party.

The decision — 18 years after the October Revolution — to form the LSSP as a broad-based radical party instead of a strictly Marxist party was influenced by the absence in Ceylon of a militant nationalist movement led by the national bourgeoisie. The need of the day was felt to be the establishment of a party which could include radical nationalists and Socialists, and which could

MG Mendis, Roy de Mel, NM Perera, Selina Perera, Robin Rutnam, JW Senanayake, Colvin R de Silva, SA Wickremasinghe, Terence de Zylva and Stanley de Zoysa.

65. *Young Ceylon*, February 1936. [Imperial Preference was a means of forcing British colonies to purchase British-made goods. The Japanese Quota restricted the importation of Japanese goods into Ceylon. Editor's note]

give a Socialist direction to the struggle for political freedom and democratic rights.[66]

Manifesto of the Lanka Sama Samaja Party

AFTER 140 years of British rule, the people of Ceylon are faced with poverty amidst all the material prerequisites of prosperity, and with disease and recurring epidemics despite the researches of modern medical science. We are still attempting to maintain life with primitive and unproductive methods of agriculture, and in an age characterised by the fruitful application of science to agriculture. Illiteracy and ignorance are widespread with us, though ever fresh fields of knowledge are being conquered by modern thought. Indeed, the majority of our people are condemned to work and die in poverty, squalor, ignorance and disease while a small majority enjoy the comforts, privileges, leisure and opportunities which their disparate wealth affords them.

There were those that believed that some radical improvement in the condition of the people would result from the acquisition of some semblance of political power by the Ceylonese. Particularly was it hoped that the pressure of popular opinion functioning through a full adult franchise would operate to that end. The result has belied the hope.

Four and a half years have now lapsed since a State Council was elected on a universal franchise. Limited as are the powers of the State Council under the Donoughmore Constitution, our accepted national leaders have not lacked the opportunity of influencing policy in the interests of our people. Instead, the apathy of these leaders in the face of political crises, their cooperation in imposing hardship and injustice on the people, together with their pronounced antipathy to measures of social amelioration and even to political struggle, prove

66. It appears that the decision to form the LSSP as a broad party had no connection with the Communist International United Front policy of the time. However, after the party was formed, the inner group of Marxists (Philip Gunawardena, Robert Gunawardena, Leslie Goonewardene, NM Perera and Colvin R de Silva), who were influenced by the ideas of the Left Opposition, began to take control of the party. Under their influence the LSSP had by the late 1930s made a revolutionary impact in the plantation sector, and by 1940 the party emerged as a Trotskyist party. Philip Gunawardena states that the Communist International made several attempts to influence the LSSP, and sent British and German emissaries to Ceylon in the 1930s for this purpose.

conclusively their readiness to subordinate the national interest to personal ascendancy.

The representatives of popular emancipation have become the agents of class domination. While blow after blow has been struck at the standard of living of the poor by taxation of necessary foodstuffs, etc, by Imperial Preferences, Japanese Quotas, etc; while the army of unemployed has mounted to stupendous proportions uncalculated and unprovided for; while over 90 000 have in a few months died of hunger and preventable malaria, reducing the countryside to a grave-yard, our national leaders have been entertaining Royal Dukes and celebrating Royal Jubilees at public expense, hunting for knighthoods and other 'honours', indulging in the most open forms of family bandyism and impudent jobberies, relieving the rich of their responsibilities by repealing the estate duty and lightening the taxes paid by foreign exploiters.

It is no wonder therefore that 70 per cent of our people are existing on the verge of starvation. There is scarcely a wage earner who has not to support many unemployed relatives — yet the government has neither provided real relief, nor even ascertained the number requiring such relief. Half the children of school-going age have neither the opportunity nor the means to go to school. Our figures of infant and maternal mortality are better only than those of India. Preventable disease annually takes a shocking toll of lives. The average span of life in Ceylon, when not disturbed by epidemics, has not been officially estimated, but is in the neighbourhood of 27 years, as compared with 53 years of average life per person born in England.

In short, the history of the last few years demonstrates that there is no real advantage to the toiling masses in merely choosing every four years which members of the oppressing classes should repress them in Council.

Never were the national leaders of our country more satisfied with themselves and with the administration than now; and never were the conditions of poverty, unemployment and disease among our people more desperate than today!

This self-satisfaction derives from the absence of a genuine opposition basing itself on a coherent body of economic and political principles. Nothing more clearly demonstrates the urgent need for an organised political party formulating openly and boldly the needs of our people.

It is not enough, however, merely to voice the felt demands of our people; it is the rôle of a party to base the struggle for them on a body of coherent principles, and it is the function of true leadership to take the road to their attainment.

All the world over there is today a fundamental conflict between two sets of principles, which may form the basis of government policy — they are the principles of disintegrating capitalism and those of advancing socialism. Recent history has amply demonstrated the inability of capitalism to ensure a decent existence to the large majority of humankind. In every country there is an increasing body of informed opinion which has become inalienably convinced that Socialism provides the only practicable alternative to capitalism. What is more, it is now being increasingly realised that Socialism alone can give the universal opportunity of a full life.

That there is a growing volume of Socialist opinion in Ceylon has been apparent for some time. It will therefore be no cause for surprise that those elements have now coalesced into the Lanka Sama Samaja Party.

The primary aim of the LSSP is the establishment of the Socialist society in Ceylon. The essential economic basis of such a society is socialised production, distribution and exchange of commodities. Through socialisation alone can the popular needs be fulfilled.

The struggle for socialisation will inevitably bring to the surface the reality of foreign domination. The fight for popular rights involves a fight against the dominant power. The dominant power in our social system is held by the capitalist class, the predominant section of which are the British exploiters.

Behind the British capitalists stand the forces of British imperialism. The greatest barrier to the establishment of Socialism in Ceylon is therefore the existence of imperialist rule. Accordingly, for us the assault on capitalism necessitates the assault on imperialism by the struggle for full national independence.

The only elements in our society which can wholeheartedly and effectively carry out the struggle against imperialism are the toiling masses. They cannot emancipate themselves without emancipating all society from the tyrannies, superstitions and prejudices of class, race, caste, creed and sex which keep society divided and enslaved.

Thus the need of the hour in our country is for a common front, of all the elements striving for emancipation, with the battle-front of Socialism which alone can lead society to victory. The victory of Socialism means the political supremacy of the toiling masses, and therewith the abolition of every form of exploitation by the constitutional use of the new state power.

It will be the rôle of the LSSP to prepare the toiling masses for the exercise of this power and for a consciousness of their historic mission for which already they are being provided, both with the opportunity and with the power, by the economic condition for their very existence.

The *fundamental objective* of the LSSP is the establishment of a Socialist society. This necessarily means:

★ The socialisation of the means of production, distribution and exchange of commodities.
★ The attainment of national independence.
★ The abolition of economic and political inequality and oppression arising from differences of class, race, caste, creed and sex.

The LSSP formulates the following immediate demands on behalf of the toiling masses:

★ Abolition of domestic or industrial exploitation of child labour.
★ Free supply of school books to children in primary schools.
★ Free meals and milk to all children in primary schools.
★ Free pasture lands in every rural district.
★ Supply of seed paddy free of interest to cultivators.
★ Permanent abolition of irrigation rates.
★ Abolition of the assignability of Tea and Rubber Coupons.
★ Abolition of Forest Laws relating to removal of brushwood and the transport of timber.
★ Establishment of unemployment insurance for all workers.
★ Provision of work or maintenance for all in need.
★ Establishment of a minimum wage so that all workers may maintain a decent level of life.
★ Establishment of an eight-hour day for all workers.
★ Abolition of the compulsory registration of trade unions.
★ Factory legislation to ensure decent working conditions.
★ Introduction of a Rent Restriction Act.
★ Clearance of slums and provision of better and cheaper housing for workers.
★ Use of vernaculars in the lower courts of law, and in entries and recorded statements at police stations; and the extension of this use to all government departments.
★ Introduction of a scheme of national health insurance paying: i. sick benefits; ii. old age benefits; iii. maternity benefits.
★ Steeper graduation of income tax on the higher incomes.
★ Reimposition of estate duty on estates of Rs25 000 and over.
★ Abolition of Imperial Preference and the Japanese Quota.
★ Progressive abolition of all indirect taxation.

II: The Politics of the LSSP

In March 1936 Philip Gunawardena and NM Perera of the newly-founded party were elected to the Ceylon State Council. The following piece, which consists of some extracts from a speech made on the occasion of the budget on 28 August 1936, shows that Philip seized the opportunity to make known the policies of the LSSP to a wider public. A similar short exposition by Colvin R de Silva, 'What is Communism?', had already been published in the *Ceylon Daily News* on 11 November 1935 (reprinted in the Ceylonese *Young Socialist*, no 19, Volume 4, no 4, pp139-41).

Philip Gunawardena
Speech to the State Council, 28 August 1936 (excerpts)

DURING THE last few years, world forces, progressive movements, the advance of scientific thought, have touched even the shores of this island, and during the last two or three years we have witnessed the spectacle of a really scientific Socialist movement growing out of the soil of this country. But during the general elections and the few months preceding the general elections, the Honourable Leader of this House principally, and the leaders of the National Congress, went throughout the country speaking of Socialism and what they call 'Communism' with the most infantile superficiality.

I hope you will permit me, Sir, to read a very short passage from the *Communist Manifesto* of 1847 written by the two great founders of scientific Socialism, Karl Marx and Frederick Engels:

'A spectre is haunting Europe — the spectre of Communism. All the powers of old Europe have entered into a holy alliance to exorcise this spectre: Pope and Tsar, Metternich and Guizot, French Radicals and German police spies. Where is the party in opposition that has not been decried as Communistic by its opponents in power? Where is the opposition that has not hurled back the branding reproach of

Communism, against the more advanced opposition parties, as well as against its reactionary adversaries? Two things result from this fact: firstly, Communism is already acknowledged by all European powers to be itself a power; secondly, it is high time that Communists should openly, in face of the whole world, publish their views, their aims, their tendencies, and meet the nursery tale of the spectre of Communism with a manifesto of the party itself.'

Sir, that was written, as I said before, in 1847. Now, nearly 90 years later, I believe it is true, and its application to this country is evident even to those who are most ignorant of the ideas of Socialism. In December last year, because of the violent and false propaganda indulged in by the leaders of the Ceylon National Congress, we were compelled to meet together and form ourselves into a party. Our party is not a Communist Party of Ceylon. Our party is the Lanka Sama Samaja Party, and as its programme and platform of action indicate, it is a party which is very much less militant and demanding less than the Communist Party of India or any other Communist Party or section of the Communist or Third International.

Sir, the fundamental objective of the Lanka Sama Samaja Party is the establishment of a Socialist society. This necessarily means the following: firstly, the socialisation of the means of production, distribution and exchange of commodities; secondly, the attainment of national independence; thirdly, the abolition of economic and political inequality and oppression arising from differences of class, race, caste, creed and sex.

The Lanka Sama Samaja Party formulates the following immediate demands on behalf of the toiling masses: [he lists the 22 demands contained in the LSSP manifesto — Ed]. Sir, I was compelled to read the demands of my party when I realised that there was such abysmal ignorance even among the Honourable Ministers of this House.

The Honourable Minister of Agriculture and Lands when introducing the Budget for 1935-36 spoke of our coffers being 'brimful of revenue', and he was hoping 'to bask in the noonday sunshine of a dazzling prosperity'. But he is faced with a deficit. Sir, if he is basking in the noonday sunshine of a dazzling prosperity, surely the year for which he was responsible for introducing the Budget should have shown a surplus. But that is by no means the case. That shows that our Board of Ministers can see only as far as their noses, and no further. When they have received a blow on the nose, they realise that they have received it, that it hurts, and that all is not well with the world — but that is the measure of their wisdom. The more daring surmise that it came from a fist.

Again, Sir, as to the accumulated surplus that they put into the different tills about the middle of last year, at what cost was this surplus obtained? I wish to remind, particularly, the Honourable Minister of Agriculture and Lands, who was the Acting Leader of this House for some time last year, that in order to accumulate that surplus of 27 millions this country had to kill — thanks to the efforts of the Ministers — this country, I repeat, had to kill 180 000 people. I say so because it was their cutting down of essential services, especially in matters pertaining to health, that made the malaria epidemic so acute. When the malaria epidemic came, the country was poorer from the point of view of health considerations, namely, the hospitals were understaffed, the dispensaries were undermanned, and some hospitals had actually been closed. If the Honourable Minister of Agriculture and Lands says that he is responsible for accumulating this surplus of 27 millions, he must also shoulder responsibility for the death of 180 000 of my countrymen. He said that he was proud of his achievement: does he point with pride to 180 000 graves?

I do not want to go through the amounts they spent from 1931 up to last year, but it will be seen that on every side there was an attempt to cut down expenditure. In other countries, a time of depression is considered the opportune time to incur additional expenditure on social services. That is a time when the people are undernourished, are even starving, when there is no employment, and when all the means of livelihood of thousands of workers of the country have disappeared. That is the very time when social services must be extended, when adequate unemployment relief should be given, when maternity benefits as well as other services of that type must be provided. It is during a depression that the producing workers of the country and the peasants have to go through really trying times. That is not the time to accumulate surpluses. But what did the Ministers do? They handed over 2.5 millions of rupees to the rich parasites of this country and of England. That is what the abolition of death duties means.

Sir, when you examine very closely the question of death duties, you will find that it is only the rich that pay. And by relieving his beloved capitalists, the Acting Leader of this House did not hand back money only to the rich people of this country, but also to the capitalists of England — the greedy sharks of Park Lane. I think that the reimposition of death duties is an absolute necessity. It is not a burden on the country. It is a burden only on those who are able to bear taxation. Our taxation in this country is regressive, that is, its incidence is heavier on the poorer classes. And if you are to have a progressive form of taxation, it is necessary to shift more and more of the burden onto the shoulders of those that are able to bear, and must bear, the incidence of taxation.

If you consider the matter you will find that the wealth in this country is accumulating in the hands of a fewer and fewer number of individuals, that the peasants in our country are compelled by the operation of the Land Partition Ordinance, and by the activities of the usurious money-lenders, to sell their land; and their land is being forcibly sold. Today those who own land are either Chetties or foreign companies or a few land-grabbing new-grown capitalists of this country masquerading as national saviours. The depression helped this process, because I believe the depression reduced considerably the number of landowners in this country. And this process in continuing. It is impossible to stop it, as we are a part of the capitalist system, and the actual wealth of this country will pass more and more into the hands of a fewer number of the people of this country; and 80 to 90 per cent of our people must of necessity be landless, being either workers, lower middle class elements, or professional elements of one kind or another: this is the inexorable social law of capitalist accumulation.

This process is continuing, and we must rely more and more on the rich to get our revenue. That is absolutely necessary because those who own property, those who own the means of production, those who receive the dividends, those who receive the profits must of necessity pay for the services that they receive from the state. It is only because the state provides them with these services such as roads, canals, railways, police forces and all the other necessary services that they are able to accumulate these profits. And for accumulating these profits they must be made to pay, because the workers and the peasants get hardly enough to eke out a miserable standard of living. They are unable to pay taxes, and in the future will be increasingly unable to pay. Indirect taxes must go. Direct taxes alone must come to the rescue of the state.

That is the situation that must be faced by all of us in this country. Of course, there are the wildcat schemes of the Honourable Minister of Agriculture and Lands. He believes that some day Minneriya will come to the help of this country. But if Minneriya is ever developed, it will not be developed by the present methods of peasant colonisation. It is impossible to apply advanced modern technique in agriculture to petty five, two and three acre farms characteristic of primitive agriculture. It is impossible. It cannot be done. You must have large units. Why cannot an experiment be tried on a commercial scale? Why cannot the Minister of Agriculture and Lands mark out an extensive tract of land of 4000 or 5000 acres in Minneriya and introduce modern advanced agricultural machinery, and think less of Parakama and more of Henry Ford? Use tractors more and buffaloes less. If you apply these methods, if you have large farms of this nature, I believe it is possible to develop Minneriya and other parts of the dry zone, and to give the people who develop and live in those areas — the peasant workers who happen to develop these areas — a decent living, decent housing, up-to-date medical services and all the amenities of, I might even say, town life. If these methods are applied, I say it is possible to develop these tracts in Minneriya.

Sir, I should like to say a few words on the headmen system.[1] I think enough has been said about the corruption that is to be found in the headmen system: it is corrupt from top to toe. Bribery, favouritism, nepotism, all these evils are found in the headmen system. It is my belief — and this is the attitude of my party — that the headmen system must go. We cannot make a few modifications here and there; hole and corner reforms here and there will not do. The headmen system must go lock, stock and barrel. And it is only by extending the powers of local self-governing institutions, by extending the powers of Village Committees, Urban District Councils and other local bodies that this country must be governed. If they can do it in other countries — in Denmark and in most countries of Europe and America — there is no reason why we cannot do it in this country. The headmen system must go.

I was very much struck by what I saw during the Perahera season, when I happened to be one night at Kandy. I thought I was living in the middle ages. I saw the pomp and splendour of a faded past being paraded in the streets of Kandy, and I felt I was in the middle ages. I am for the complete abolition of the headmen system, not only in the Kandyan districts, but also in the low country. The *mudaliyars*, the *muhandirams*, the *vidane arachchies* and *vidanes* are just as bad and just as corrupt as the Kandyan *Ratemahatmayas*, *koralas* and *arachchies*, and they must all go if we are to make any progress. They oppress the villager at every point. When it is a question of counting the number of rubber trees in a certain area, in the case of smallholdings, it is the village headman who is required to go round and count the trees, and unless the villager pays a few rupees to these minor cogs in the state machine they can never get the work done: it is delayed. It is because of these exactions that I say that the whole system must go if we are to make any progress. Otherwise there is no meaning in hav-

---

1. The headmen system, the exercise of power by the head of a village, was already in operation prior to the establishment of British colonial rule. Headmen became to be appointed by government agents, and acted as stooges of the colonial authorities.

ing full adult franchise: there is no meaning in our coming to this House.

Of course, the honourable member for Balangoda, representative of that decadent headmen system, said that he was elected by the people of Balangoda electorate. Sir, I have with me the figures of that election, and Mr Goonesekera, the honourable member for Balangoda, was returned by a minority vote. The other two candidates received 18 333 votes, whereas he received only 14 000-odd votes. And I believe that even this 14 000-odd was largely due to the influence of European planters. They simply marched the estate population to the polling stations. Unfortunately, the honourable member for Hatton was not present in that area, and I believe that that is the reason why the planters were able to march these estate voters to the polling stations in the manner they did.

In this connection I wish to refer to another matter, that is the position of the depressed classes in the island. Sir, at a time when we were ready to give equal rights to every man and woman in this country — equal political rights — it was very unfortunate, Sir, that certain leaders of the National Congress practised methods of brutality and terrorism in certain electorates by driving back members of the depressed classes who had come to vote; defenceless men and women were beaten by hired gangsters and thugs. Very prominent, very influential and very powerful leaders of the National Congress were responsible for enacting this most disgusting scene in certain areas of the Kandyan districts. The depressed classes who were just waking up from their age-long torpor, who were throwing off the influence of the headmen, the depressed classes who were trying to throw off this oppressive yoke and rise to the full stature of manhood, were beaten back by the influence of feudal lords of the Kandyan districts as well as by the powerful leaders of the National Congress, and still we are asked by Congress leaders to sink our differences, to unite together, to form a united front and ask for certain things that the leaders of the National Congress want.

Sir, it is necessary to bring practice nearer your professions, if you are to get the support of the defenceless and downtrodden members of the depressed classes. And I wish to ask particularly the Honourable Minister for Agriculture and Lands to go round the country and see that these things are done. Sir, I do not wish to speak at length on the activities of certain leaders during the elections. I think the country knows the truth. And truth must out.

Coming back to the work of the Honourable Minister of Agriculture and Lands, when I was in the United States I had the good fortune to visit and see some of the advanced technique applied to paddy cultivation in particular places in Southern California and Louisiana. In the United States 1090 pounds of rice are produced per acre. I believe the average yield in this country is in the neighbourhood of 650 pounds per acre. Generally, it is very much lower in the smaller holdings in this country. Rice is predominantly a peasant cultivation. Productive technique is very primitive. The activities of the Department of Agriculture have not affected the peasants' method of cultivation. What is the reason, Sir? From generation to generation, due to the operation of the inheritance laws of our country, plots of paddy land that our peasants cultivate are getting smaller and smaller. Fragmentation of these holdings has reduced the size of the holding to an uneconomic unit. You cannot apply machine technique to these small plots.

Then again there is the tremendous problem of agricultural indebtedness. The cooperative movement in this country has barely scratched the surface. It has to some extent succeeded in centralising credit, but it has not replaced the money-lender or limited the money-lending operations of the village boutique-keeper. Unless the cooperative movement extends and replaces the money-lender — who does not live in the village, but is an absentee money-lender — unless the cooperative movement restricts the activities of, or eliminates entirely, the money-lender and the money-lending operations of the village boutique-keeper, I do not believe that the problem of rural indebtedness will be satisfactorily solved. The cooperative movement has succeeded, as I said, in centralising to some extent the credit of the village, and the credit of the rural areas by the different Cooperative Societies and the Central Cooperative Banks — it has by these means succeeded to some extent in centralising credit facilities. But those who receive benefits from the cooperative movement today are the upper strata of the village, the fairly well-to-do of the countryside. The poor peasantry, particularly the peasantry responsible for the cultivation of paddy, are yet untouched by the operations of the cooperative system.

Till you eliminate the rural indebtedness of the peasantry, till you provide the means of modern technique to the peasant, till you introduce advanced modern technique in agriculture, that is till you introduce a plough which instead of scratching the surface of the field will plough at least six or seven inches, till you introduce buffaloes if it is impossible to get tractors — I believe the Honourable Minister's kraal at Nikaweratiya or some place nearby has captured enough buffaloes for this purpose — till you bring these facilities within the reach of the peasant, our production of paddy per acre will never be increased.

It is criminal to think of encouraging food production by raising the tariff against rice and the other necessities of the poor. It is only by improving technique, it is only by extending easier credit to the peasantry, by better marketing facilities, that you can resolve the problem of food production. My party is ready to support a scheme for subsidising food production in this country, but, Sir, my party and myself will always fight against any demand on the part of the Honourable Minister for Agriculture to raise the tariff against rice and other necessities of the poor.

I do not propose, Sir, to take very many more minutes, because I do not think there is much use going over item by item, Ministry by Ministry, the different financial proposals. I think in the Committee stage myself and my party could examine more closely the expenditure side of the budget. But I wish to make a few remarks on the work of the Ministry of Health.

Sir, I am not opposed to the half a million vote asked for anti-malaria work. I say it is not enough and that is should be supplemented by work in the other Ministries, particularly the Ministry of Agriculture and the Ministry of Labour, Industry and Commerce. Unless we raise the physical vitality of our people, malaria will always remain a problem. Malaria is essentially a problem of poverty, and unless the problem of poverty is solved malaria will be a curse to Ceylon either in epidemic or in endemic form, and that is the stark fact that we must face. With the accumulation of wealth in the hands of a few people in the Cinnamon Gardens and in London with consequent growing poverty on the other hand, with increasing numbers of our young men and young women being driven from rural areas to the cities because they cannot earn a living in agriculture and other rural occupations, and with increasing numbers of unemployed from the cities roaming all over the country in search of work, work which they can never find — when we are faced with these problems I say that by a mere technical medical attack the problem of malaria can never be tackled. It can only be tackled or eradicated if the Ministry of Agriculture succeeds in producing more coconuts per acre, and in raising the income of the rural peasantry. And it is only by that method, I repeat, that malaria can be eradicated from this country.

Sir, I wish to congratulate the Minister of Education on the vote of 800 000 Rupees for the feeding of school children. As I mentioned before, that was one of the planks, one of the fighting demands of our party during the elections, and I am sorry to have to say that during the elections the Honourable Leader of the House went to several meetings in my constituency and opposed this particular measure. We are not satisfied with 800 000 Rupees. We want every poor child, in the vernacular schools at least, of our country to be provided with a midday meal. We would go a step further: we want not merely rice and a little curry, but we want the younger children to be given a glass or two of milk in the rural schools of our country, because unless we raise the physical fitness of the coming generation the country may in a few years be faced with the problem of a population physically unable to resist any sort of disease, with reduced physical vitality and reduced economic efficiency, and even intellectually and culturally a third-rate people. That is a problem which must be faced, and I hope that in the coming years this vote will be increased, indeed we propose to ask for more in this item during the Committee stage.

Coming to the question of quotas and imperial preference, the only satisfactory solution, from our point of view, is the total abolition of quotas. Our people cannot go naked. Our poor brothers and sisters in the rural areas, the workers in the cities, want the cheapest kind of clothing possible. We are not particularly enamoured of the imperial products of Lancashire. The Empire can sell its produce to the rich bloodsuckers of Mayfair, if they have an excess of cloth. Our poor people cannot foot the bill to fill the pockets of the capitalists of England. If they find that it is impossible for them to compete with the cheap but efficiently produced Japanese article or the efficiently produced Indian article, then they must look for other markets. Ceylon should not be a dumping ground for their produce, and the time will come — the time must come — when the peasantry of this country will refuse to bear these imperial burdens. And if this State Council does not tackle this problem seriously and intelligently, the time will come, the time must come, when the rural masses in this country, when the working classes and peasants in this country, having lost all confidence in their elected representatives, will rise as they have risen in other countries, and throw off this brutal and oppressive yoke of British imperialism.

We can only cause developments to take place constitutionally if we act intelligently and in the interests of the workers and peasants and the other lower middle class elements of this country. But if we do not give serious attention to these problems and find a satisfactory solution to them, the workers and peasants will rise in desperation and will overthrow this iniquitous, this oppressive, this exploitative system of imperialism, and work out a system that will give them food, clothing and the shelter which they require. That will come if we do not act intelligently. I appeal to members of this House to consider this matter seriously, because, after all, they are our masters, they sent us here — the vast majority of the peasants and workers. Because of the adult franchise they are our masters, and we must serve our masters. No one can serve two masters! The British imperialist representatives who exist in this country are not our masters. They have the bombing plane, the battleship and the guns. They rule over us by reason of their armed might. But they are not our masters. We must serve the people.

I will not occupy the floor of this House for more than a few more minutes. I wish to appeal particularly to the members of the Labour Party to join with the members of the Lanka Sama Samaja Party to put forward a united front on behalf of the working classes. Unless we do so, we cannot compel the capitalist classes to grant to the poor even the minimum of relief. I make this appeal to the members of the Labour Party as well as other representatives of the peasants. The voice of the peasants was heard through the mouth of the honourable member for Hambantota the other day, and I do appeal to all the democratic elements of this House to form a united front as has been done so successfully in other countries, such as France and Spain, to oppose the imperialists and their lackeys, the capitalists of this country represented by the Honourable Leader of this House.

Sir, our party was attacked by several members because of our attitude in regard to the Defence vote. The honourable member for Gampola accused the Lanka Sama Samaja Party of irresponsibility. He spoke of them as a body of people who were afraid to shoulder their responsibilities. These are his words: 'They want privileges without responsibilities and corresponding duties. My friends of the Lanka Sama Samaja Party want the millennium without sacrifice.' I find it difficult, Sir, to express the attitude of mind of the honourable member for Gampola. If there is a group of people who are ready to go through any sacrifice for ridding humanity of the curse of militarism, of the curse of ignorance, superstition and poverty, I believe that group must of necessity be a Socialist group. Throughout the world in the face of the most ruthless brutality, barbarism and terrorism, the Communists and Socialists have fought and fought for what they believe to be the correct attitude in life. And, Sir, the members of the Lanka Sama Samaja Party are ready to fight even with guns if necessary for the cause that they believe in — the cause of Socialism — humanity's leap from the realm of necessity to the realm of freedom.

Sir, we are not ready to fight the battles of the imperialists. We refuse to be cannon fodder for coining money for the dividend hunters of England. When my honourable friend the member for Gampola and the Minister of Local Administration organise a really national revolutionary army, then the members of the Lanka Sama Samaja Party will join them. But we are now not ready to join the units of the Ceylon Defence Force because we believe that the imperialists will use these units for fighting the battles of England, and not for fighting the battles of the people of this country. We refuse to be a party to any imperialist war. We will fight only in wars of national and social liberation. We are not 'conscientious objectors'. We oppose imperialist war. But we are ready to take our place in the battles of national wars, such as wars for the liberation of the working classes and the peasantry of the country. We are determined to oppose this vote on Defence. As long as we remain in this House we will try our best to prevent even one red cent being spent for the Ceylon Defence Force, or any other imperialist army.

Sir, as I said before, I wish to reserve my remarks for the Committee stage on the important questions of flood control, unemployment, and things of that type. I hope that I have not taxed the patience of the House too much.

III: The Defence of Mark Bracegirdle

A dramatic incident that brought the LSSP into public notice attended the appearance of Mark Bracegirdle in Ceylon in 1936. This section includes an account by Kumari Jayawardene, for which we tender our thanks, and an interview conducted with Mark Bracegirdle himself in Wandsworth by Bob Pitt on 4 October 1995.

Kumari Jayawardene

The Bracegirdle Affair

THE MOST spectacular incident in which the LSSP was involved in the 1930s was the 'Bracegirdle affair', which raised important political and economic issues, and caused the biggest political storm and constitutional crisis of the time, resulting in a short wave of popularity and publicity for the LSSP.

Mark Bracegirdle was born in England in 1913, and had emigrated to Australia. He came to Ceylon in 1936 as a trainee planter on the Regulas Tea Estate. In Australia, he had been an active member of the Sydney Communist League, and soon after his arrival in Ceylon he began to take an interest in conditions of labour on the estates, and he joined the LSSP, writing in their journal under an assumed name. The superintendent of the estate dismissed him, and informed the acting Inspector General of Police that as a result of Bracegirdle's activities, the labour force had 'started to give trouble... there was a general slackness... and the pruners were impertinent and would not work'. After the superintendent had dismissed five labourers, between 50 and 60 others left the estate, and this was attributed to the 'disaffection which Bracegirdle had stirred up'.[1]

Bracegirdle began to appear at public meetings of the LSSP, and being an ex-planter, his violent speeches against planters and British

1. Deportation of Bracegirdle, CGA File CF/131/37.

rule attracted large crowds. When Mrs Chattopadyaya toured Ceylon in 1937, Bracegirdle was a prominent speaker at the mass meetings that were held. The police reported him as saying:

'You see those white hills there, those white bungalows, where the whites live in luxury... they suck your blood, they are parasites. I know the secrets of the planters... I came here as I heard it was a rich country... but all the riches have gone into the pockets of the white men. Do you know what amount he pays to the club as his drink bill? It is enough to keep a hundred families out of starvation.'[2]

For a non-Ceylonese to be linked with the LSSP and to be actively engaged in such propaganda led to alarm among official circles. In a confidential report, the acting IGP said that it was 'dangerous to allow a European youth of this type to remain in Ceylon stirring up feelings of disaffection against employers of labour and against the British government', and recommended that he be deported from Ceylon.[3] The Governor reported to the Secretary of State that Bracegirdle 'went about the country making violent speeches abusing Europeans and inciting labour to rise against the planters. As ignorant coolies tend still to attach importance to speeches of white men, the police and I have considered him a public danger.'[4] The policy of the government had always been that foreign Communists and 'agitators' were a greater menace than their local counterparts, and deportation and restrictions on landing in Ceylon had often been carried out on these grounds.[5] The Governor confirmed this attitude when he wrote to the Secretary of State that 'even if we can afford to disregard the activities of local Communists, it is obviously dangerous to allow them to be reinforced by external agitators'.[6] One of the Governor's

2. Bracegirdle Commission Report, Session Paper 18 of 1938.
3. Report of Acting IGP, CGA File CF/137/37.
4. Confidential Telegram 95 of 12 May 1937, CGA File CF/137/37.
5. Dr Manilal Shah, an Indian Communist, was deported in 1922. Egon Kisch, a Czech Communist, was prevented from coming ashore when his ship touched Colombo in 1935, but Dr Wickremasinghe intervened with the authorities, and Kisch was allowed briefly to visit Ceylon.
6. Confidential Dispatch of Governor, 15 May 1937, CGA File CF/137/37. AE Goonesinha claimed that the Governor, speaking of Bracegirdle, said: 'I do not mind the whole of Ceylon turning Communist, but I do not want Europeans to come and meddle here.' Goonesinha added that the British administration believed that Bracegirdle was seriously compromising 'the prestige of the white man' (*Hansard*, 1938, p4053). The LSSP took the same view of the matter, NM Perera compared the episode with the Meerut Trial in India (where three British Communists were tried for conspiracy along with local Communists), and said that it was an 'outstanding example that so long as the natives, the black people, take part in an agitation there is no great objection, but the moment Europeans

advisers in the Civil Service held that though the activities of the LSSP did not constitute 'an immediate threat to public security', the activities of a European, who had been a planter, 'inciting estate labourers and others to down tools does constitute a real danger of unrest leading to breaches of the peace, and might well endanger the economic stability of the island'.[7]

Under an old Order in Council of 1896 which had fallen into disuse, the Governor issued a deportation order on Bracegirdle. Helped by the LSSP, he went into hiding, and the party launched a campaign against the action of the government. In a letter to the Chief Justice, Bracegirdle protested against the 'high-handed action of the Governor' and 'the gross interference with the rights of a British subject', and added that he had as much right to be in Ceylon 'as the Governor or any one of his lesser paid officials'.[8] In a statement to the press, Bracegirdle declared: 'I am not leaving Ceylon until I am thrown out... perhaps the Governor will have to carry me out on his shoulders under the proclamation of 1896... that will be better than a state drive.'[9]

The LSSP was able to raise the issue of constitutional liberties, and on this point to gain the support of all the ministers, the great majority of the state councillors, and arouse popular sympathy all over the country. The President of the LSSP stated that 'the real issue is the undermining and the denial of the liberty of the subject in Ceylon... for the sole bulwark of liberty is recourse to the ordinary courts of the land'.[10] The *Daily News* was able to agree on this issue, and stated that 'the existence of this kind of legislation... is a continuing menace to the ordinary rights of British citizenship'.[11]

At a mass meeting on 5 May 1937, Bracegirdle, whom the police were trying to arrest, made a dramatic appearance and spoke to a vast crowd of 50 000, who according to the LSSP were 'delirious with enthusiasm'.[12] Bracegirdle was later arrested, and his lawyer applied for a writ of habeas corpus. The judges who heard the case decided that the Governor had acted ultra vires, and that the Executive did not have the right to use emergency laws where there was no emer-

come on the scene, the position is changed' (*Hansard*, 1938, p4673). Writing several years later, Colvin R de Silva observed that 'Bracegirdle had broken no law except the unwritten law of colonialism, that the whites do not join the coloureds but stand together against them' (*Samasamajist*, 8 January 1953).

7. Minute of 1 May 1937, File CF/131.
8. *Times of Ceylon*, 5 May 1937.
9. Op cit.
10. Letter to the Editor, *Ceylon Daily News*, 24 April 1937.
11. Editorial, *Ceylon Daily News*, 24 April 1937.
12. *Samasamajist*, December 1937.

gency.[13] Bracegirdle was freed and left for England of his own accord later in the year, and after making a few appearances on left wing platforms in England, lapsed into obscurity. The incident had several repercussions in the political field. The deportation order had been issued by the Governor on the advice of the Chief Secretary, without the knowledge of the elected Minister of Home Affairs. The Board of Ministers unanimously condemned this action of the Governor, for they held that the matter was one on which the Minister for Home Affairs should have been consulted.[14] A resolution condemning the Governor for acting unconstitutionally and asking that the deportation order be rescinded and the Order in Council repealed, was carried in the State Council by 34 votes to seven, all the Ministers voting in favour.[15]

Attacks were made on the use of an outdated Order in Council by the Governor where no emergency existed, and on the special powers of the Governor. A commission was appointed to go into the whole episode; the findings of the Commission, which exonerated the police and government officials, were also condemned by the State Council by 34 votes to 14.

The Bracegirdle incident was important from the LSSP's point of view for several reasons. It gave a great deal of publicity to the party, and the opportunity to show leadership on two fronts: against British rule and against the strongest group of capitalists in Ceylon, the British planters. It also brought into the open the growing alarm of the government towards the activities of the LSSP.

In his annual report for 1937, Colvin de Silva stated that there was not a great amount of feeling against capitalism in Ceylon 'as that is really concentrated on the plantations', and said that labour on estates was not yet 'sufficiently conscious to become the main centre of the attack on capitalism'.[16] When the agitation over Bracegirdle commenced, the LSSP accused the planters of having put pressure on the government to secure deportation. In the State Council, Philip

13. The case became a cause célèbre; Ceylon's leading lawyer, HV Perera, appeared free of charge for Bracegirdle, and the case was heard by three Supreme Court Judges, including Sir Sydney Abrahams, the Chief Justice.
14. The Governor in a letter to the Minister said 'it never occurred to me that the expulsion of an Australian undesirable could be of a matter of sufficient importance to justify me in troubling the Board', to which the Minister replied that they regretted that '... Your Excellency should have regarded the deportation of Mr Bracegirdle as a matter of such trivial importance not to justify consultation with the Board of Ministers before issuing an order. The Board should be consulted whoever the person concerned may be.' (Letters of 18 May and 21 May 1937, File CF 131/37)
15. *Hansard*, 5 May 1937.
16. *Samasamajist*, December 1937.

Gunawardena said 'the step has been taken at the request of the planters'.[17]

As a method of protesting against the Governor, on the occasion of his address to the State Council, the LSSP organised a filibuster in order to keep him waiting, and on this occasion Gunawardena gave notice of motion that 'as it is evident that a state of imminent emergency has arisen by virtue of the conspiratorial meetings of certain sections of the planting community, and by virtue of the fact that in their less sober moments a sort of Klu Klux Klan has been formed... the House is of the opinion that no planter should be allowed to possess firearms...'[18]

The same year the LSSP President said that the Bracegirdle affair showed that European planterdom would be the source from which Fascism in Ceylon would 'find its main strength'.[19]

The LSSP's Secretary admitted that the deportation order gave Bracegirdle and the party 'marvellous popularity, and advertised the party in the remotest corners of the land.'[20] The Bracegirdle affair was referred to as the party's 'first clear engagement with imperialism', in which the honours went entirely to the LSSP.[21]

The question of Communism in Ceylon was first treated by the government and the press as a matter of importance during the Bracegirdle incident. In a confidential dispatch to the Secretary of State, the Governor described the LSSP as a 'small local party run by young men with more money than brains';[22] the Governor indicated that the influence of the LSSP was growing, and stated:

'Hitherto no notice has been taken of the antics of the local Communist Party, who are generally regarded as half-wits or degenerates. I am inclined to think that we have been far too lenient in this respect, and I am now considering what steps it is desirable to take in view of information I have received from many sources as to the spread of Communist opinions among the lower classes. The organ of the Communist Party, the *Samasamaja*, is becoming more and more scurrilous. For example, in a recent number Her Late Majesty Queen Victoria was referred to by a Sinhalese phrase meaning "the woman Victoria".'[23]

17. *Hansard*, 5 May 1937.
18. *Hansard*, 12 May 1937.
19. Speech of Colvin R de Silva, *Samasamajist*, December 1937.
20. Op cit.
21. Op cit.
22. Confidential despatch from Governor of Ceylon to the Secretary of State, 15 May 1937, File CF 131/37.
23. Op cit.

A violent campaign against the LSSP was also carried on by the *Times of Ceylon*, which contrasted the severe measures taken in India against Communists with the Ceylon government's alleged weakness in dealing with the LSSP:

'In Ceylon, not only are the Samasamajists allowed to proclaim their views openly in the State Council, but we allow them to import "comrades from India"... the government cannot claim to be doing its duty in protecting the ignorant masses from their pernicious teachings.'[24]

The Times kept up its onslaught for several weeks, complaining that 'blatant preaching of the most subversive doctrines... [had] gone on for some time in Ceylon',[25] and claiming that 'red agents are overrunning the island preaching class hatred and sedition among the ignorant masses'.[26]

The need for a control of LSSP activities was urged by both *The Times* and the Governor. *The Times* remarked 'the deportation of a single Communist does not by any means make Ceylon safe... Unless his comrades profit by this lesson... strict measures must be taken to curb their activities';[27] it also warned that 'a watch must be kept on the more dangerous indigenous agitators, [and] to deal with seditionists such as these, the law must be amended promptly'.[28] The Governor informed the Secretary of State that if the powers under the Order in Council of 1896 were held to be ultra vires, it would be essential 'to pass immediately — with or without the consent of the State Council — legislation giving the Governor, or possibly the Minister of Home Affairs, adequate powers to deal with such cases.'[29]

The Secretary of State did not agree with the Governor, and the disapproval of the Colonial Office with the Governor's mishandling of the situation was reflected in the replacement in June 1937 of Governor Stubbs by a new Governor who was considered to be more in touch with the times.

The LSSP had on all points scored a remarkable political victory in the Bracegirdle affair. On the issue of constitutional rights, a virtual united front of all Ceylonese was achieved; in the political field, a decisive rebuff was given to the Governor on the use of outdated leg-

24. *Times of Ceylon*, 24 April 1937. The 'comrades from India' is a reference to Mrs Chattopadyaya
25. *Times of Ceylon*, 30 April 1937.
26. *Times of Ceylon*, 3 May 1937.
27. *Times of Ceylon*, 30 April 1937.
28. *Times of Ceylon*, 5 May 1937.
29. Confidential Despatch from Governor to Secretary of State, 15 May 1937, File CF/131/37.

islation, and on the question of consulting the elected Ministers. In the context of the labour movement, the issue aroused mass excitement, both in the towns and on the estates; Bracegirdle was represented as a 'white man' who in his championing of the rights of the workers, had incurred the wrath of the planters' police and the Governor, and the LSSP became identified with a militant policy of challenge to authority.

Interview with Mark Bracegirdle

Could you tell us something about your family background and your early life?

I was born in Chelsea, and I was brought up in the country in Oxshott. My mother was a Socialist and also a very active suffragette. She eventually thought there was no future in this country for a young man, so we emigrated to Australia. I was in Australia for 10 years, and during that time I was a jackaroo, which is the same sort of thing as a creeper. You know what a creeper is? Somebody learning how to be a planter. A jackaroo is someone learning a particular type of farming in Australia. I used to run a station, on both the agricultural and livestock side.

Were you at all politically involved at that time?

I joined the Young Communist League, round about 1935 I suppose. I then applied to become an apprentice in Ceylon.

What was it decided you to go to Ceylon?

Well, mainly the fact that I was going to learn a new type of agriculture, but nothing really political at that time. I had no knowledge of the politics of Ceylon. Then, when I went to Ceylon and I was on the estate, we heard of the left wing movement, and I had a young planter with me, a chap named Simpson Hayward. We contacted Vernon Gunasekera, who arranged a meeting with us, and everything started from there.

The thing that really made me befriend the movement was the bad treatment of the workers on the estates. Because in order to work you had to get a note from the planter, and he would go down the lines, which was where the people lived in little houses, and he would be quite brutal in forcing them to go to work. Despite many people having malaria or suffering badly from the results of malaria, he would insist on them picking. He used to do another thing that used to annoy me, and that was to go to the school and say: 'It is far better that they should learn to pick than that they should learn the rubbish they learn at school.' Learning to read and write was only copying white men, he used to say, and it does them no good at all, and will give them ideas in later life above their station. So he used to take them off and make them pick tea.

Gradually I became more involved. The LSSP had a Central Committee, and I was eventually invited to become a member of the committee. I used to work on the paper, which was made on a flat-bed, by hand, and we had to get something like 3000 copies out in the night. It was really hard work. We had little boys there who folded the paper up, and then it was put on the buses to be sent all over Ceylon. I persuaded BJ Fernando to start a fighting fund, so we could mechanise the paper, which would save us a tremendous amount of work. We did this, and I remember BJ sitting there opening letter after letter, taking out rupees in paper money, hundreds of letters.

Then it came to the point when having spoken publicly for the LSSP a couple of times they decided to arrest me, but they didn't arrest me immediately. I told them I was going to leave Ceylon and go back to Australia, but I didn't do this. As I'm pretty good in the bush, I decided to 'go bush'. The party wanted me to go to a safe house, but I'd had some experience of this safe house business, and it didn't work out very well. So I went bush, just taking enough food to last me for eight to 10 days. This was just before May Day, and I was going to come out and we would have a big meeting and I would speak. And that is what happened.

I found it very difficult, this Robinson Crusoe living. For instance, I couldn't light a fire because somebody would see it, and the police would be coming up after me. One of the most difficult things I found was keeping an accurate calendar. I decided to cut the days in a stick. But you think to yourself: 'Did I cut it today or not?' Anyway, I got it right.

Came the day when I should return, and I got up to go down to where the meeting place was. And there was a man stealing wood, and he made this big heap of wood to put on his back to carry off. But it was still daylight, and he didn't want to go until it got dark. I wanted to get down to the meeting place, and he wouldn't move off. So it delayed me. And when I came to walk down I found between me and the road there was a cliff some 30 feet high, and I couldn't climb that. The only way I could get down was to grab these plants that hung down — called lanias — and I found one of these and pulled on it to make sure that it wouldn't let me down, and then eventually I climbed down that.

By now it was dark, because it gets dark so quickly. Then I began to see the lights of the cars in the sky coming up towards me up the hill. I'd said: 'When you come to collect me, you must get out of the cars and stand around at the front in the headlights so that I know it's comrades and not police.' And then I knew that we were on our way back, and I was going to be alright.

On May Day we were going to have this big workers' meeting, and when we had the meeting the problem was that the whole place was surrounded by policemen. How was I going to get to the platform? Vernon said: 'No problem, just go straight through the crowd.' And we did, pushing people aside and saying 'make way, make way'. And we walked through the crowd, and I climbed up on the platform to a terrific cheer. The police came rushing in with the ejection notice, and my lawyers got hold of it and they said: 'It's out of date.'

My lawyer was made a King's Counsel on the day I appeared in court. One judge was Lord Justice Abrahams, a Jewish judge, and there were two Burgher judges. The court was somewhat in my favour from the very early stages, and this came out when the two Burgher judges said that the court must be responsible here, because Mr Bracegirdle might be thrown out of Ceylon and might not be accepted by Australia, and then he'd 'go wandering around the world like a Wandering Jew'. And quick as a flash Abrahams said: 'Or a Flying Dutchman!'

On the LSSP Central Committee who impressed you most?

Well of course we held Philip Gunawardena in the greatest regard. Philip had been through a revolution, in Brazil. He had more experience than any of us in those days. I think the man who had the greatest understanding of theory was Vernon. He could write articles, and he also read the works of other great Socialists. Colvin R de Silva and NM Perera didn't get on terribly well. It was political differences really. In those days there was always the trouble we had about Trotsky, which has been largely dissolved now. I'll tell you another man who was interesting — Terence de Zylva. I don't know if he was a member at that time, he certainly wasn't on the Central Committee, but he had a school, and many of his ex-students were in the LSSP and were all very strong Trotskyists.

The differences between NM and Colvin were around that, you think, because Colvin was a supporter of Trotskyist views and NM was not?

That's right.

It's uncertain to us, looking back, when that trend emerged in the LSSP, because when it was founded it was a broad-based Socialist party.

It appeared quite early, especially as they turned more left, and this discussion came up. I personally, in a way I feel unfortunately, was very anti-Trotsky due to the fact that the youth in Australia were badly let down by the Trotskyists who got into our movement. Philip Gunawardena and I got on very well. When I first got to Ceylon the Trotskyist thing hadn't raised its head to any great degree. I fact I think that I was possibly somebody who triggered it because I was openly Marxist, you see.

When you came back to England, after you left Ceylon, you joined the Communist Party here?

I did after a while, yes, and I was attacked for it by Krishna Menon, physically. You see Krishna was promoting me in parliament — he got me to talk to Dingle Foot.[30] He also got me appointments to speak at the Oxford Union and the Cambridge Union about Ceylon, which I did. But at the same time he didn't want to be seen promoting a Communist. And so he was furious with me when he heard I'd joined the party. He attacked me with his umbrella in New Oxford Street, just outside the India Office!

What further contacts did you have after leaving Ceylon?

A very curious thing happened to me, just before I retired. I went and did a year's service in Zambia in the flying doctor service. And while I was there — I'm very interested in birds — and our birdwatching group said: 'Oh you must come and have tea with us tomorrow, we're going to Mr Stubbs.' And you know who Mr Stubbs was? The ex-Governor of Ceylon! He shook my hand and said: 'Where have I heard that name before?' I just smiled.

---

30. Sir Dingle Mackintosh Foot (1905-1978) was a well-known Labour politician. [Editor's note]

IV: The LSSP Turns to Trotskyism (1939-1941)

The items in this section were collected to illustrate the process by which the LSSP broke its links with Stalinism and moved over to a Trotskyist position.

Our first piece, 'An Interview with a Comrade: Ceylonese Masses Want No Part Of Bosses' War', is reprinted from *Socialist Appeal*, the paper of the American Trotskyists (10 November 1939). The comrade in question was Selina Perera, whose attempt to visit Trotsky in Coyoacan from the United Sates had just been prevented. She was the wife of NM Perera, and was Treasurer of the LSSP. The circumstances surrounding this interview are explained in Lerski's *Origins of Trotskyism in Ceylon* (pp177-9), where the correspondence of James Cannon, Joseph Hansen and Selina Perera is quoted in full, along with Trotsky's 'India Faced with Imperialist War' (25 July 1939) and 'Letter on India' of 24 November 1939 (*Writings of Leon Trotsky, 1939-40*, New York, 1973, pp28-34 and 108-9), which were first published in *New International*, Volume 5, no 9, September 1939, pp263-6, and *Permanent Revolution*, the organ of the Bolshevik-Leninist Party of India (Volume 1, no 3, July-September 1943).

We next reproduce the text of Leslie Goonewardene's anti-Stalinist pamphlet published by the LSSP in March 1940 entitled *The Third International Condemned!*, along with the obituary of Trotsky that appeared in *Samasamajaya* on 30 August 1940, which, though already printed in Wesley Muthiah and Sydney Wanasinghe's *Britain, World War Two and the Sama Samajists* (pp67-74 and 166-7), are so central to our story as to require a place here. Leslie Goonewardene expanded his exposure of Stalinism into a full-length book, the *Rise and Fall of the Comintern*, published by the Spark Syndicate in Bombay in December 1947 over the pseudonym of 'K Tilak', which draws heavily upon CLR James' *World Revolution* (new edition by Humanities Press, 1993).

A clash with the Stalinists in 1954 produced two further polemics, Leslie Goonewardene's *The Differences between Trotskyism and Stalinism* (seven articles from the *Samasamajist*, LSSP publication, March 1954; reprinted by the Centro Studi Pietro Tresso, April 1995), and Colvin R de Silva's *Their Politics and Ours* (13 articles from the *Samasamajist*, LSSP publication, September 1954). Colvin went on to publish an *Outline of the*

Permanent Revolution as a study guide for the training of party cadres (LSSP publication, January 1955).

The short piece that completes the section is an excerpt from the programme adopted by the LSSP in 1941 which first appeared abroad in 'The Road to Freedom for Ceylon', *Fourth International*, Volume 3, no 4, April 1942, pp117-8, and was later reproduced by the British *Militant*.

An Interview with a Comrade

Ceylonese Masses Want No Part Of Bosses' War

A COMRADE from the island of Ceylon representing the Ceylonese Socialist Party which is conducting a struggle for the independence of their country from the British imperialists had the following to say when interviewed by the *Socialist Appeal*.

Ceylon's six million workers and peasants are absolutely opposed to giving any sort of support to England in the present imperialist war. The reason for this is simple. This war is not being fought for democracy. This war is fought for who shall have the privilege of standing on our necks and exploiting our people. Ceylon, one of the colonies of the British and French Empires, is a bone over which the imperialist dogs are fighting. The people of the colonies will have nothing to do with either gang.

Whatever democratic liberties we had won during the course of the last three and a half years were being smashed by the British 'democrats' who feared the tremendous growth of our liberation movement. The English have organised an illegal terrorist militia which they are beginning to employ against the workers' and peasants' unions throughout Ceylon. The British-appointed Governor General has suspended the constitution, and now governs by military decree, in the fashion of Hitler.

If the Ceylonese people were able to express themselves by means of a democratic vote 80 to 90 per cent would vote to break away from the British Empire, which they feel is strangling them. But since this right is not given to them, they must employ other means to obtain their freedom.

And this is where the work of our party, the Ceylonese Socialist Party, comes in. We are definitely opposed to the Second International, which endorses the war aims of the Allied imperialists. Likewise we denounce the Third International, which is for the defence of one imperialist bloc as against another. Our policy is the policy of internationalism — that is, the workers of every country must act independently of their rulers and oppressors. They must fight for their own freedom and for Socialism.

It is our belief that the colonial peoples will be the first to raise the banner of revolt against this imperialist war. When that time comes we know that class conscious American workers will be of real aid to us in assuring our victory. From what I have observed in America, the Socialist Workers Party is the only anti-war, revolutionary party that is preparing to lead the workers to Socialism. We Socialists and revolutionists of Ceylon wish to extend our fraternal greetings.

Leslie Goonewardene

The Third International Condemned!

' IN VIEW of the failure of the Third International to guide itself by the needs of the international revolutionary working class, the Lanka Sama Samaja Party, while reaffirming its support for and solidarity with the Soviet Union, the first workers' state, declares that it no longer has confidence in the Third International.' This resolution was recently passed by the Executive Committee of the Lanka Sama Samaja Party by 29 votes to five. Since the reasons for the passage of the resolution are of vital interest to all conscious revolutionaries, they are deserving of recapitulation.

Communist Parties Support the War

The present imperialist war started on 3 September 1939. The Lanka Sama Samaja Party recognised from the start that it was an imperialist war, and explained its true significance openly in its papers. What happened in England? As was to be expected, the reformist British Labour Party, playing its customary rôle as loyal servant to imperialism, supported the war. But one had the right to expect that at least the Communist Party which claims to be following the international revolutionary path of Leninism would oppose the war and give a bold revolutionary lead to the working class of Britain. But alas! The Communist Party of that country shamelessly supported the war, declaring that it was not an imperialist war, but a war against Fascism. The leader of the party, Harry Pollitt, even published a booklet entitled *How to Win the War*. For a month and four days the Communist Party of Britain followed this disgraceful policy. It is true that the Communist Party then changed its policy and opposed the war. But the question remains to be answered — *how did they come to support the war for a month?*

The French Communist Party in like manner also supported the war for almost as long. Again, what is the explanation for this?

The French and British Communist Parties are sections of the Third International. The Third International was founded under the leadership of Lenin because the older Second International had betrayed the working class in 1914-18. Besides, after the Russian Revolution, it was for the same reason that on the advice of Lenin the Bolshevik Party changed its name from Socialist to Communist. Since all the European parties outside Russia appearing under the name 'Socialist' had supported the war, Lenin held that the word Socialist itself had been besmirched as a result. This was how the Communist Parties of today came to acquire the name Communist. But two prominent parties bearing the name Communist have supported the war, and disgraced the name they bear.

How can we explain this? Everybody makes mistakes. But for a mistake as serious as this, there must surely be a deep cause. A colossal blunder of this nature cannot be the result of a single temporary deviation. The Communist Parties of these countries must of necessity have been for some time past following a wrong policy for them to have committed so flagrant a violation of international revolutionary principles.

If we are to explain this apparently inexplicable riddle of Communist Parties supporting an imperialist war, we must go back for a few years into international events.

Hitler Threatens the Soviet Union

In 1933 Hitler came to power in Germany. In keeping with his previous declarations, he threatened attack on the Soviet Union. The Soviet government replied with the Franco-Soviet Pact of 1935. According to this pact, the two parties promised to come to the aid of one another in the event of German aggression. It needs hardly be said that the rightist government in France at the time made this pact not through love of the Soviet Union, but as a safeguard against the German invasion which they feared.

As a result of this pact any anti-Soviet action that Hitler may have contemplated was checked for the moment. But there was no abatement of Hitler's open threats of invasion of the Soviet Union. He started conspiring with Italy and Japan to draw them against the Soviet Union. In 1936 the Rome-Berlin Axis was formed, and soon after the Anti-Comintern Pact of Germany, Japan and Italy came into existence.

On the other hand, the Soviet Union began to feel that the Franco-Soviet Pact was not a sufficient guarantee of her own security. It is true that France, in panic after Hitler's advent to power, entered into a pact with the Soviet Union in 1935. But as time went on, it became clear that France was unwilling to be embroiled in a war without the assured military support of Great Britain. The Conservative British bourgeoisie, in turn, intended diverting Hitler eastwards against Russia, and consistently followed a policy of weaning France away from her Soviet allies. Russia was in danger of being isolated. Therefore the Russian government devoted its efforts to securing a pact with England, France and the Soviet Union against Germany. The Munich Pact of September 1938, marking the culmination of the British attempt to isolate Russia, served to redouble the efforts of the Soviet Union to secure the Anglo-Franco-Russian Pact.

There are some who might say that the Soviet Union, being a workers' state, should not compromise its position by entering into an alliance with capitalist states. But this view is not correct. The Soviet Union, which is surrounded by capitalist enemies, has a right for its own self-protection to form such alliances, and so to take advantage of the divisions and conflicts in the capitalist world. Therefore no blame attaches to the Soviet Union for attempting to enter into an alliance with England and France.

But what is wrong is that the policy of the Third International should be subordinated to the foreign policy of the Soviet Union.

Change of Policy of the Communist International

After the advent of Hitler to power, the Seventh Congress of the Third International met in August 1935, after a gap of seven years. It was at this Congress that the tactic of the Popular Front was put forward. The purpose of this idea was to defeat Fascism, not by a united front of the working class, but by a multi-class or Popular Front including sections of the capitalists opposed to Fascism. The result of this policy was the side-tracking and weakening of the class struggle of the proletariat. However, this was but one evil effect of the disastrous Popular Front policy followed by the Communist Parties.

In 1937 the Popular Front idea was extended to the international plane. The workers of England and France were told by their Communist Parties that not only the Fascists in their own countries, but also Hitler was their enemy. They raised the cry that their governments should form a pact with the Soviet Union against Hitler. In 1938 and 1939 the main agitation of the Communist Parties of England and France was centred around the demand for the Anglo-Franco-Soviet Alliance against Hitler.

In March 1939, not as a result of this agitation, but for its own imperialist purposes, Britain entered into negotiations with the Soviet Union for an alliance. The enthusiasm of the Popular Fronters knew no bounds. Expecting the Anglo-French-Soviet 'peace' alliance, the British Communist Party began openly to prepare to help Britain in the war. It was the same with the French Communist Party.

If the Anglo-French-Soviet Pact had Materialised

Was this in keeping with the principles of international Socialism? Let us suppose for a moment that the present war was a war with France, England and the Soviet Union on one side and Germany on the other. What would be the duty of British workers, or of colonial people like ourselves? To support the war because Russia is on the side of Britain, *or to oppose the war and make the revolution*?

It is true, opposing such a war and making a revolution in Britain would appear to be to the military disadvantage of the Soviet Union. But such a disadvantage, if any, would be temporary. But a workers' government in Britain would be the best ally the Soviet Union could have. Therefore the best way that the British working class could contribute to the ultimate defence of the Soviet Union would be to make their own revolution and establish a workers' government.

On the other hand, British imperialists would be in such a war, not to help the Soviet Union, but for their own imperialist purposes. To support the war would therefore be an act of treachery to the British working class. But on the instructions of the Third International, it was precisely this act of treachery that the Communist Parties of England and France were preparing for. Expecting to be on the same side as England and France in the coming war, the Soviet government through the Third International instructed the Communist Parties of England and France to support the war. The Communist Party of France even supported conscription. Its leader, Thorez, enlisted in the French imperialist army, with the full approbation of the French Communist Party press.

There may be some who say that neither the Third International nor the Communist Parties of Britain and France planned such treachery. But that there was such preparation for betrayal is proved by the French Communist Party voting for conscription and supporting the war for several weeks, and by the British Communist Party supporting the war for over a month.

How the Third International Misled the Communist Parties

These Communist Parties, placing their trust in the Third International and its leader Stalin, prepared for a war against Hitler, by England, France and the Soviet Union. But without the least warning to his supporters, Stalin turned a volte-face on 20 August. He entered into a non-aggression pact with Germany.[1]

On 3 September the war began against Hitler, but without the Soviet Union. The Communist Parties of England and France, stunned by the Russo-German Pact which had come like a bolt from the blue, continued loyally to follow their old orders. The Communist International had evidently not had time to change its instructions. This is the reason why the Communist Parties of England and France continued to support the war for some time!

But in due course they apparently received new instructions from the Communist International. Since Stalin was no longer on the side of England and France, the Communist International, which saw no point in the Communist Parties of England and France supporting the war, sent fresh instructions to them to oppose the war. This is how the Communist Parties that were supporting the war suddenly came to oppose it. The Communist Party of England, which had been propounding for a month that this was a war against Fascism, suddenly discovered that it was an imperialist war! Apart from orders from the Third International, the Communist Parties of England and France had no reasons to change their views on the war. Thus we see that the Communist Parties of England and France both supported and opposed the same war for one and the same reason — they slavishly followed the Third International.

The Disastrous Effects of this Policy

A policy of this nature must surely be suicidal to the international working class movement. The confusion and distrust that must follow when a Communist Party asks the workers one day to support the war and the next day to oppose it can well be imagined. But a much more disastrous effect than the discrediting of the Communist Parties has resulted from this policy. For the last two years the British Communist Party has been attacking Chamberlain. Why? Because he refused to enter a pact with the Soviet Union and against Germany. They accused Chamberlain of secretly helping Hitler to seize Austria and Czechoslovakia. They demanded that Chamberlain unite with the governments of France and Russia to put an end to Hitler's rapacious conquests.

1.   The German-Soviet Pact of Non-Aggression was actually signed by the respective Foreign Ministers on 23 August 1939. [Editor's note]

And what do the British workers see today? Chamberlain has gone to war with Hitler, but without the help of the Soviet Union! British imperialism must indeed be really thankful to the British Communist Party for having done their war propaganda much more effectively than they could ever have done it themselves. Both the British and the French Communist Parties have by their disastrous policies helped the imperialists to deceive the workers, and drag them into the war.

Subordination of the Revolutionary Movement to Soviet Union Foreign Policy

The reason for the identically wrong policies of the Communist Parties of Britain and France flows from the fact that they are members of the Third International. The Third International is the central organisation of the Communist Parties of the world. Conversely, the Communist Parties of the world are sections of the Comintern, whose headquarters is Moscow. The Comintern helps financially its different sections, and since the Russian Communist Party is larger and more influential than all the other Communist Parties of the world put together, it is easy to see how the Russian party has a preponderating power in the International. The policy of the Third International is determined by the Communist Party of the Soviet Union. It should now be clear how the policy of the Communist International comes to be subordinated to the foreign policy of the Soviet Union.

That is why, when the Soviet Union was hoping to come to an alliance with England and France, the Communist Parties of the various countries were instructed to carry on propaganda in favour of it.

Expecting England and France to be on the side of the Soviet Union in the coming war, the Communist Parties of these countries were further instructed to prepare to support the war. Accordingly, when Russian foreign policy changed and the German-Soviet Pact came into existence, these very same parties were instructed to oppose the war. It is thus seen that the policy of the Communist International and Communist Parties affiliated to it is determined and changed not by the needs of the revolutionary movements in these countries, but according to the immediate demands of the foreign policy of the Soviet Union.

This is a very dangerous state of affairs. If the workers are to be victorious anywhere, the proletarian revolutionary movement of a particular country should be directed towards the victory of the revolution in that country. We are therefore forced to the conclusion that the leadership of the international proletarian movement by the Communist International is a danger to the cause of World Revolution and World Socialism.

World Revolution, far from being a disadvantage to the Soviet Union, is the path to the ultimate victory of Socialism in the Soviet Union itself. This goal will be reached when the Soviet Union is surrounded, not by hostile capitalist countries, but by friendly workers' governments. The greatest service the workers of any country can perform in the interests not only of World Revolution but of the defence of the Soviet Union itself is to make their own revolution, and establish a proletarian dictatorship. Therefore, workers' revolutions taking place in the capitalist states of the world must necessarily be a great aid to the cause of Socialism in the Soviet Union.

If that is so, should not the leaders of the Soviet Union and the Communist International, if only because of self-interest, be guided by the principles of international revolution? Why should Stalin and his supporters be guided by the short-sighted policy of the temporary success of the Soviet Union's foreign policy, and so betray the international revolutionary movement? There is a reason for this too.

Why was Faith in World Revolution Lost?

In 1917 the workers of Russia made their Socialist revolution, after having undergone untold suffering during the war. At that time Lenin and all the Bolshevik leaders awaited revolution in other countries (especially Germany). They did not expect the Russian Revolution to be successful without proletarian revolution in other countries. Lenin at that time held that the duty of the Russian working class was somehow to maintain power till the proletariat of the Western countries came to their aid.

This policy was followed. Till 1921 the Red Army had to fight the interventionist armies of the capitalist world. Pinning their faith to the cause of international revolution, the Russian working class fought on, despite untold difficulties and widespread famine in 1921. Indeed if not for the solidarity of the international working class, the young workers' state must surely have perished. The British working class threatened a general strike, a mutiny occurred in the French fleet, and the capitalist governments gradually desisted from their interventionist war against the Soviet Union.

But the long awaited revolutionary successes did not take place in these countries. Now the enormous task of building Socialism in Russia fell to the lot of the Russian workers, numbering less than one-tenth of the total adult population of Russia. Despite the tremendous odds, the Russian working class has worked valiantly to accomplish this enormous task. But their belief in international revolution has temporarily declined. When one considers the above-mentioned facts, this is not surprising.

The Russian working class has today got leaders who reflect in exaggerated form the attitude of the masses. The weariness of the Russian masses after years of struggle made it possible for a section of the leadership of the Bolshevik Party under Stalin to attain leadership. This new leadership had lost faith in international revolution, and putting forward the un-Marxist slogan of 'Socialism in One Country' thereby made the military defence of the Soviet Union their last resource, to which they were prepared to subordinate and sacrifice all else. This is how leaders like Stalin, who had no faith in international revolution, have come to the position of leadership in the Soviet Union. But the danger of the situation lies in the fact that the leadership of the international Communist movement should be in the hands of a group that has no faith in world revolution.

Why it is Necessary to Raise this Question Without Delay

It only remains to explain why it is of such importance that this issue be clarified without delay. There may be some who are of the opinion that in the interests of unity this issue should not be raised at the present moment. In this connection, it is interesting to note what Engels wrote to Bebel in a letter dated 20 June 1873, on this subject:

'One must not allow oneself to be misled by the cry for "unity". Those who have this word most often on their lips are the ones who cause most of the discord, just as at present the Jura Bakuninists in Switzerland, who have provoked all the splits, clamour for nothing so much as for unity. These unity fanatics are either narrow-minded people who want to stir everything into one nondescript brew, which, the moment it is left to settle, throws up the differences again but in much sharper contrast, because they will all be in one pot (in Germany you have a fine example of this in the people who preach reconciliation of the workers and the petit-bourgeoisie) or else they are people who unconsciously (like Mülberger, for instance) or consciously want to adulterate the movement. It is for this reason that the biggest sectarians and biggest brawlers and rogues shout loudest for unity at certain times. Nobody in our lifetime has given us more trouble and has caused more quarrels than the shouters for unity.'[2]

2. K Marx and F Engels, *Selected Correspondence*, Moscow, 1975, p266. Mikhail Bakunin (1814-1876) had support for the ideas of Anarchism from the Jura watchmakers. Arthur Mülberger (1847-1907) was a follower of Proudhon. [Editor's note]

Lenin never hesitated to discuss and clarify exhaustively theoretical questions, however unimportant they appeared to be. All deviations from the revolutionary path he criticised mercilessly. For he never underestimated the importance of revolutionary theory to a revolutionary party. He never hesitated to risk even splits in the party on such occasions, for he realised that in the end the party would only be the stronger for its internal conflict.

For some time before the outbreak of the last war, Karl Liebknecht and his revolutionary followers were faced with the problem of splitting the reformist Social Democratic Party of Germany and of forming a revolutionary party independent of it. Guided by considerations of unity, Liebknecht rejected this course. This was one of the main reasons why the German revolution when it occurred at the end of the war had no party to lead it, and was thus destroyed.

The Second International betrayed the working class in the war of 1914-18. Today the Third International, by subordinating the international revolutionary movement to Soviet Union foreign policy, is committing another betrayal. It is our duty to point out this fact. And this is a task that must be accomplished today.

For it is now that we must discuss all the important questions that will arise in the critical years to come. We in Ceylon still enjoy the legal freedom to meet and clarify all these issues. Tomorrow it may not be so. It is therefore of the utmost importance that all these questions be clarified today. And the rôle of the Third International is one of the most important of these questions.

Murder of Trotsky the Leader of the World Revolution Stalin's Evil Deed

LEON TROTSKY, the greatest revolutionary leader in the world, has been killed by a Stalinist assassin. For 13 years the thugs of Stalin's secret police have harassed Trotsky and threatened his life. The death of this great man demonstrates the treacherous activities of Stalin against the working class of all countries.

'I am sure of the victory of the Fourth International. Go forward!' were Trotsky's last words. His death will give a fresh impetus to the great movement he headed.

Trotsky is now no longer among the living. But the results of his work will remain forever. Trotsky was not only the greatest revolutionary leader, but also a silver-tongued orator.

Trotsky shared with Lenin the leadership of the Russian Revolution. He fought shoulder to shoulder with the workers in the revolutions of 1905 and 1917. It was Trotsky who commanded a battle front of 7000 miles against 21 armies sent by England, America, Germany, France and Japan with the aim of destroying the young government established through the workers' seizure of power. The Russian Revolution would without doubt have fallen victim to the capitalist armies had it not been for Trotsky and the Red Army.

The guiding principle of Trotsky was to go forward, despite all obstacles in his way. When Stalin adopted a reactionary course of action, Trotsky defended the ideas of Leninism, and said that the basic objective of Russia was to bring about a world revolution. Stalin banished him, and now he has murdered him. The Chinese and Spanish revolutions were defeated as a result of Stalin's betrayals.

But Trotsky continued the fight despite all obstacles. Adhering to the principles of Marx, Engels and Lenin, he took the lead in establishing the Fourth International in 1938. The killing of Trotsky shows the mean level to which Stalin's Third International has descended. We announce with shock and sorrow that Trotsky, who sacrificed his life for the benefit of the workers and peasants, has breathed his last in a hospital in Mexico.

Down with the Third International!

Long live the Fourth International!

The Struggle Against Imperialism

THE FIRST and foremost task facing the toiling masses in Ceylon is the overthrow of British imperialism. With the entry of the anti-imperialist struggle to the openly revolutionary stage, the native bourgeoisie will completely side with the imperialists. Neither the urban petit-bourgeoisie nor the petit-bourgeois intelligentsia, because of their position of dependence on the capitalist class, can play an independent rôle in the revolution. Yet because there is no prospect whatsoever of improving their conditions under imperialism, but on the contrary they are faced with actual decline and pauperisation, they are forced on the revolutionary road.

Although the Ceylon economy is mainly agricultural, the Ceylon peasantry is not subject to the usual form of tenure prevailing under landlordism. The bulk of the peasantry are still proprietors, although of uneconomic holdings. The fragmentation of holdings, and the joint ownership of fragmented holdings, the heavy load of peasant indebtedness, the absence of credit and marketing facilities, and the heavy indirect taxation of necessities, all continue to drive the peasant into a chronic state of degradation and misery. At the same time, the number of landless peasants has increased, and is increasing even more rapidly. By reason of the fact that these landless peasants and even sections of the small peasant proprietors do part-time work in the plantations, they constitute a link between the working class and the peasantry. For these reasons and because of the comparatively high literacy and the already noticeable growth of political consciousness among them, the peasantry will play an important rôle. Nevertheless because of their isolation, lack of cohesion, political backwardness and because of the veiled nature of their exploitation by imperialism, the peasantry cannot play an independent revolutionary rôle.

The only class capable of leading the struggle against imperialism to a successful conclusion is the working class. The concentration and discipline induced by its very place in the capitalist economy, its numerical strength, the sharpness of the class antagonisms which daily bring it into direct conflict with the imperialists who are the biggest capitalists in Ceylon, its organisation and experience of struggle, and the vital position it occupies in the economy of the country, as well as its steadily worsening conditions under imperialism, combine to make the working class the natural and inevitable organiser and leader of the toiling masses for the overthrow of imperialism.

In India today the bourgeoisie is either openly with the imperialists, or is engaged in utilising the growing anti-imperialist mass tide for striking a bargain with British imperialism, while simultaneously diverting the mass movement into innocuous channels. The revolutionary foreground is already occupied by the proletariat, which is the only class capable of leading the peasant majority against imperialism, landlordism and the native princes. This opens to the Indian workers the prospect of capturing power before this takes place in the advanced countries of the world. The Indian revolution to be victorious must result in the establishment of the dictatorship of the proletariat.

In Ceylon, the social tasks of the bourgeois democratic revolution, namely the liquidation of landlordism and of other feudal forms, have already been accomplished in the low country through the impact of repeated foreign invasions, and in the up-country by the British to meet the needs of the plantation development on capitalist lines. Consequently, the development of the struggle against imperialism leads directly to the proletarian revolution. But this does not mean that the seizure of power by the workers of Ceylon can take place only after the proletarian revolution has occurred in the advanced countries of the world. Since the revolution in Ceylon is dependent on and is indeed an integral part of the Indian revolution, the prospect of proletarian revolution, before that can take place in the more advanced countries, arises for Ceylon as much as for India.

For this purpose the working class must win the support particularly of the peasantry, with whom links exist already in the landless peasants and the small peasant proprietors working on capitalist estates. The proletariat can win for itself the support of the peasants by the slogan of 'land to the landless', and establish with this support the dictatorship of the proletariat.

The dictatorship of the proletariat neither in India nor in Ceylon, however, can maintain itself permanently against imperialist reaction, without the support of the international proletariat. Nor can the proletariat of either country, isolated from the world proletariat, solve the economic problems of the country. Only with the support of the international proletariat, through world revolution, can the dictatorship of the proletariat be finally established, and the victory of the Socialist revolution be completed.

V: The Lanka Sama Samaja Party, 1939-1960

These notes on the history of the LSSP were written in 1994-96 by the veteran Sri Lankan Trotskyist Meryl Fernando (born 1923), to whom we tender our thanks. He joined the LSSP during the Second World War whilst still a university student. In the immediate postwar period he was active organising match factory workers in his home town, Moratuwa. He was a member of the Moratuwa Urban Council, and later its Chairman. This was the first local council in which the LSSP was able to wrest power from the ruling UNP in 1951. Meryl was arrested and jailed during the Great Hartal of August 1953.

Meryl broke with the LSSP in 1964 along with Edmund Samarakkody, Bala Tampoe, Prins Rajasooriya, V Karalasingham and others when the party joined the coalition government of Mrs Sirimavo Bandaranaike, and he helped to found the LSSP(R). He represented the LSSP and the LSSP(R) as MP for Moratuwa from 1956 to 1964.

Meryl Fernando
An Account of the LSSP, 1939-1960

THE LSSP from the start characterised the Second World War as an imperialist war. NM Perera and Philip Gunawardena, the two members of the party in the State Council, refused to vote for war supplies. Commencing in November 1939, there was a wave of strikes on the plantations in the Central and Uva provinces. When the wave reached its zenith in the Central Province in the Mooloya Estate strike, and when it spread to the Uva Province, the Samasamajists were in the leadership.[1] Because of the LSSP's opposition to the war and the militant leadership provided to the plantation workers in the strike wave of 1939-40, the colonial government moved against the LSSP. In June 1940 four leaders were arrested, and the govern-

---

1. See Leslie Goonewardene, *A Short History of the LSSP*, pp11-13.

ment issued a warrant for the arrest of Leslie Goonewardene, who evaded arrest. Furthermore, the government adopted repressive measures against party activity.

In June 1941 Hitler attacked the Soviet Union. The LSSP stuck firmly to the view that the war between Britain (and later the USA) and Germany, Italy and Japan was an imperialist war. In relation to the war between Germany and the Soviet Union, the LSSP called for the unconditional defence of the Soviet Union. The Communist Party, like their fraternal parties in other countries taking their cue from the Kremlin, now supported the war effort of the colonial rulers in Ceylon, and while calling upon the workers to produce more and more towards the war effort, organised certain sections of the workers like the tea and rubber packing workers in the Ceylon Trade Union Federation (CTUF). The LSSP was proscribed, and those who escaped imprisonment had to function underground, whereas the Communist Party and CTUF operated in the open with the blessings of the British War Commander in Ceylon. Despite the class-collaborationist rôle of the Communist Party and the CTUF, certain sections of government workers on the railway and in the hospitals under the influence of the Samasamajists struck work during the war.

In May 1942 the Bolshevik Leninist Party of India (BLPI), with the LSSP as the Ceylon unit, was founded with the active participation of Philip Gunawardena and NM Perera. In an article in the LSSP's illegal Sinhalese newspaper, *Sama Samajaya*, dated 17 August 1942, entitled 'The Coming Indian Revolution', Philip Gunawardena said that from the decision of the All-India Congress Executive Committee to launch a civil disobedience movement, it was manifest that a revolutionary situation was maturing rapidly in India. With the escalation of the Second World Imperialist War to its zenith, British imperialism had to face a political crisis in India. He stated:

'The Indian National Congress threatens to launch a civil disobedience movement to be in the vanguard of the worker-peasant mass struggle that is undoubtedly gradually unfolding as a result of the attacks on the people due to the war. The mass movement in India is gathering strength against the war and imperialism... Strikes of workers have been transformed into struggles where shooting by government forces is the result. Thus with every passing day the working class demonstrates its militancy and its determination to give leadership to the mass movement... The Indian bourgeoisie will start a civil disobedience movement. When this movement develops and is transformed into a mass movement, the working class will wrest its leadership from the bourgeoisie. Under the unstained red banner of the

Fourth International, the Bolshevik Leninist Party of India will show the way to the working class. It is only under the leadership of the working class that the Indian revolution can be guided to victory.'

Considering the fact that the Bolshevik Leninist Party of India was founded a mere three months before, and was unknown to the working class, not to speak of the teeming millions of peasants, the optimism displayed was not at all justified by the objective situation.

Having spoken of the rôle the BLPI would play in 'the coming Indian revolution' in such terms, after the war ended in August 1945 Philip Gunawardena, along with NM Perera, dissociated himself from the BLPI, and set up another political party, calling it the Lanka Sama Samaja Party, and describing it as Fourth Internationalist. The Central Committee of the BLPI expelled Philip Gunawardena and NM Perera, and adopted a resolution explaining the expulsion and stating that the other political organisation, also known as the Lanka Sama Samaja Party, was the real unit of the BLPI. Towards the end of 1943 Philip Gunawardena and NM Perera had written a document from prison entitled *The Indian Struggle: The Next Phase*. The Central Committee of the BLPI criticised this document, and pointed out that the result of accepting the ideas contained in the document would be the creation of a petit-bourgeois organisation in place of a disciplined closely-knit working class party. However, the LSSP led by Philip Gunawardena and NM Perera was a cadre-type party. This was seen at the two later unifications between the BLPI (Ceylon Unit) and the LSSP.

When the war ended and repressive legislation against the LSSP and the working class was revoked, the Samasamajists had the overwhelming support of the Colombo working class, who had correctly drawn the distinction between the anti-imperialist LSSP and the class-collaborationist Communist Party. There were now two Samasamaja parties: the Lanka Sama Samaja Party, Ceylon Unit of the Bolshevik Leninist Party of India (BLPI), section of the Fourth International, and the Lanka Sama Samaja Party, which claimed to be Fourth Internationalist, and of which the leaders were Philip Gunawardena and NM Perera. The latter had more working class support than the former, and also more support among the urban and rural poor. In two major strikes of the Colombo proletariat in 1946 and 1947 both parties played a rôle, but the LSSP played a dominant rôle with NM Perera being the spokesman for the workers on strike. It was also in these two years that the white-collar employees in government service became radicalised and organised in the Government Clerical Service Union. They, too, struck work in 1947. The leadership was under the influence of the two Samasamaja parties, as well as the Communist Party.

The Ceylon National Congress (CNC), which was named after the Indian National Congress, was a feeble replica of the party of the Indian bourgeoisie. It was content to go to Whitehall, the seat of the British government, begging for constitutional reforms with the aim of obtaining Dominion Status within the British Empire. On the other hand, the LSSP was the only organisation to call for complete independence from British rule from its inception in 1935. During the war, the younger leaders of the CNC, Dudley Senanayake and JR Jayawardene, had a disagreement with the leader, DS Senanayake.[2] They wanted independence from British rule to be the objective of the CNC, whereas DS Senanayake stood for Dominion status. There was another matter which separated the younger leaders from DS Senanayake. They joined the Friends of the Soviet Union in Ceylon, and the Communists joined the CNC. DS Senanayake was opposed to this alliance. Disagreeing on both counts, he left the CNC.

Thus when the war ended in 1945, the Ceylon bourgeoisie did not have a real political organisation of their own. By contrast, the Samasamajists, though split into two organisations, enjoyed extensive support amongst the workers, particularly in Colombo and its environs, the urban and rural poor in certain areas, and also limited support among the plantation workers. They had the potential of being the unifying force to rally the anti-imperialist forces around the slogan of 'Independence from British Rule', and by calling upon the British to quit Ceylon. In such a situation there was the possibility of drawing the minorities behind the working class banner by guaranteeing democratic rights, and in particular the Tamil minority the right of self-determination. Although this was on the agenda of the day, both the LSSP and the Ceylon Unit of the BLPI failed to launch a struggle to compel the British to leave Ceylon. In the meantime, in 1946 DS Senanayake brought together the various bourgeois organisations and groups into one political organisation — the United National Party. The Samasamajists lost the opportunity of giving leadership to the anti-imperialist and toiling masses.

2.   Don Stephen Senanayake (1884-1952) was Minister of Agriculture and Lands during 1931-36, and Leader of the House of Representatives and Vice-President in 1942. His son, Dudley Shelton (1911-1973), was Minister of Agriculture and Lands (1947-52), and Prime Minister (1952-53), resigning as a result of the Great Hartal, and during 1960-73. Junius Richard Jayawardene (1906-1996) was a lawyer and a leading bourgeois nationalist politician. Secretary of the Ceylon National Congress during 1940-47, he became a leader of the United National Party in 1947, and held responsible positions in UNP governments. He became Prime Minister in 1977, and President from 1978 to 1989. An early proponent of Sinhala chauvinist policies, he also adopted a pro-Western diplomatic and economic orientation. [Editor's note]

During a short-lived merger of the two parties in 1946, an agreed list of candidates was drawn up for the parliamentary elections due to take place on a new constitution drawn up by Britain to take effect in 1947. After the two parties split again, this list was honoured at the elections held in September 1947. The popular support the two Samasamaja parties enjoyed was in reality demonstrated at these 1947 parliamentary elections, when the two parties and sympathisers won between them 15 seats in a parliament of 101 members.

The 1946 unification happened all of a sudden without the differences between the two organisations being discussed. The only issue was the accusation Philip Gunawardena had made that Doric de Souza[3] was a police spy. Kamalesh Bannerjee was appointed as a one-man commission to inquire into the accusation. Philip Gunawardena appeared before him. At the end of the inquiry Bannerjee came to the conclusion that the accusation was baseless, and wanted Philip Gunawardena to withdraw it unconditionally. The latter refused, and the unification broke down. At this unification it was manifest that although the LSSP was the more popular party, and had a wider mass base than the BLPI, its membership was not disproportionate when compared with that of the latter. At the 1950 unification, too, the position with regard to the membership was the same.

The divergent politics of the two parties are demonstrated by the following. In 1975, when the Prime Minister, Mrs Sirima Bandaranaike, sacked the three LSSP ministers from her cabinet, NM Perera availed himself of the parliamentary practice afforded to a dismissed minister to state his case. In his speech in Sinhala in parliament on 3 September 1975, he recalled the attempt in 1947 after the first parliamentary elections in Ceylon to form a coalition to make SWRD Bandaranaike Prime Minister, and to keep DS Senanayake out. He said:

3. Anthony Theoderic Armand Doric de Souza (1914-1987) was a founding member of the LSSP. He was MP for Wellawatte North (1946-52), and then a member of the Senate (1957-69), where he was leader of the opposition. He became Minister of Plantation Industries in Mrs Bandaranaike's government. In the mid-1940s he submitted evidence to the Soulbury Commission on behalf of the trade unions, where he argued for separate representation for the workers on the grounds that they were a 'minority' as defined by the commission. He wrote the main critique of the resulting constitution on behalf of the Bolshevik Samasamaja Party, 'On Conspiracy Against the People'. He also made a special study of the peasantry and agrarian economics, as reflected in his unpublished manuscript, *The Agrarian Economy of India*. In fact, Philip Gunawardena's famous Paddy Lands Act was drafted by his secretary, GVDS de Silva. He was also the author of the duplicated summary of Harold Isaac's *Tragedy of the Chinese Revolution* that circulated around India and Ceylon after the first edition of that invaluable work had become unavailable (*Revolutionary History*, Volume 2, no 4, Spring 1990, p4, n11). [Editor's note]

'After the 1947 parliamentary elections, all sections opposed to Mr
DS Senanayake met at "Yamuna", the residence of Mr Sri Nissanka,[4]
and took a decision after a discussion. What was our decision? We
saw that Mr SWRD Bandaranaike commanded a majority of votes in
parliament. With our joining, Mr Bandaranaike would be in a position to defeat Mr DS Senanayake, become Prime Minister, and form
a government of his own... As far as I remember, it was Mr Nissanka
whom we sent to meet Mr Bandaranaike and inform him of our decision that we were prepared to make him Prime Minister and to support him. Although this request was made of Mr Bandaranaike, he
rejected it. He did so because in his mind it was evident there were
two things which every person in Ceylon accepted. Firstly, there was
a strong view that after Mr DS Senanayake, Mr Bandaranaike would
be Prime Minister. Everyone in Sri Lanka knows that. There was
such an expectation. Secondly, leftist ideas had not matured politically in him very much. He did not start on such ideas. He did not
start as a Socialist. Perhaps you know his history. He started as a
Ghandian on the ideas of Gandhi. It was after starting like that that
his political ideas matured gradually, and he leaned completely towards Socialism. This is the true position. We cannot blame him. We
need not be surprised that at the level of his political development
then, in view of his political ideas, he was unwilling to form a government by joining hands with the Marxists.'[5]

This episode is politically important, since it distinguishes the LSSP
from the BLPI, which refused to enter into a coalition to make Bandaranaike Prime Minister in 1947. The fact that the BLPI opposed
this move by the LSSP and others was well known at the time.

A further conflict between the two parties emerged over the granting of independence to Ceylon in 1948. Whereas the LSSP saw this as
a step forward, the BLPI denounced it as 'fake independence'. Independence had in fact been granted on the basis of certain agreements
entered into between the governments of the UK and Ceylon on defence, external affairs and certain matters affecting public officers.
What was conferred on 4 February 1948 was not fully responsible
status within the British Commonwealth of Nations. The UK government was provided with bases and facilities at Katunayake and
Trincomalee, which were taken back by Bandaranaike in 1956. But
more important, as JR Jayawardene stated many years later, under
the terms of the Defence Agreement, the UK government could intervene in Ceylon if an occasion arose. The Queen of the UK ceased

4.   Sri Nissanka was elected to the 1947 parliament as an Independent.
5.   *Hansard*, 3 September 1975, author's translation.

to be the head of Ceylon only in 1972, with the adoption of the republican constitution.

The Bolshevik Samasamaja Party, as the Ceylon Section of the Fourth International was now called, and the Lanka Sama Samaja Party merged in May 1950 to form the LSSP, Ceylon Section of the Fourth International. Again, however, the merger was not the outcome of a discussion of the differences between the two parties by the leaderships of the parties, the realisation that there was no justification for the two parties to exist separately, and that whatever differences that existed could be contained within a democratic centralist organisation. There was absolutely no discussion of the differences. On the contrary, the merger was the expedient consequence of a series of political incidents.

The immediate political incident that precipitated the merger was a physical assault organised by Philip Gunawardena of the LSSP on several leading members of the BSP when they were returned to Colombo by motor-car after participating in a parliamentary by-election in 1949 in the Gampaha constituency close to Colombo, which was contested by the two parties and the ruling UNP. During the election campaign there had been a number of clashes between supporters of the two parties. The constituency had been contested by the LSSP at the general election in September 1947. The LSSP was furious that the BSP should have dared to contest the by-election. After the polling was over, Leslie Goonewardene, Doric de Souza, Edmund Samarakkody and Bala Tampoe were travelling by motor-car to Colombo when they were set upon by a mob organised by Philip Gunawardena a few miles from Colombo. In the assault Leslie Goonewardene suffered an injury in one knee. It was this assault that caused members of both parties to criticise the absurdity of having two parties fighting against each other. The cry for unity became rampant.

There were other happenings as well. A few months before the above by-election, Edmund Samarakkody as the BSP candidate defeated Robert Gunawardena of the LSSP in a triangular contest in a by-election for a vacant seat in an urban council just south of Colombo. Several working class members of the LSSP who held leading positions in the LSSP one by one joined the BSP, claiming that the latter was the correct party. Two MPs of the LSSP, W Dahanayake and Lakshman Rajapakse,[6] crossed over from the LSSP to the BSP. The BSP was in the ascendant, and the LSSP's fortunes were declining. It was in this atmosphere that the merger took place.

6. Lakshman Rajapakse (1924-1976) was MP for Hanbantota (1947-52). He joined the MEP and was Deputy Minister of Commerce and Trade. He later joined the SLFP. [Editor's note]

Philip Gunawardena refused to join in the 1950 unification. Here I think there were two factors. Firstly, as events in his post-1950 political career were to indicate, it is possible that towards the end of the 1940s he was considering pursuing another road to what he considered to be 'a Socialist goal' — a national road in collaboration with bourgeois and Stalinist forces. This possibility becomes more real in view of the fact that he, along with NM Perera, had been prepared to extend his support to making SWRD Bandaranaike Prime Minister in 1947. Further, speaking in parliament on 28 November 1947, in the debate on the Governor's address to parliament, he characterised the Communist Party of Ceylon as a revolutionary party:

'Mr DPR Gunawardena: He [the Prime Minister] is under the impression that he can frighten the members of the Lanka Sama Samaja Party and the other two revolutionary political parties whose representatives sit in this House. I say that in the opposition there are three revolutionary parties. I do not claim that ours is the only revolutionary party.

'The Hon Mr Bandaranaike: Do not libel the Communists; they are not revolutionaries.

'Mr DPR Gunawardena: I say three — the Communist Party of Ceylon, the Bolshevik Leninist Party and the Lanka Sama Samaja Party — for the edification of my friend the Minister of Transport and Works.'[7]

Thus Philip Gunawardena equated the Communist Party of Ceylon with his Lanka Sama Samaja Party, both of which a couple of months back had been prepared to make Bandaranaike Prime Minister. He labelled the Communist Party revolutionary in spite of the well-known Trotskyist position at the time that Stalinism was counter-revolutionary.

In 1945 he had broken with the Fourth International organisationally, and thereafter did not have any perspective of building an international revolutionary organisation. He could have raised the matter of his and NM Perera's expulsion from the Bolshevik Leninist Party with the International Executive Committee of the Fourth International, which he did not. In fact, he and NM Perera were thwarted from doing so by their very act of attempting to pose as the Ceylon Unit of the Bolshevik Leninist Party. In the alternative, if he really was interested in building a Trotskyist International, however difficult the task would have been, he should have made an attempt towards such a goal. But he did not do this. Thus, although his or-

7. *Hansard*, 28 November 1947.

ganisation claimed to be Fourth Internationalist, it was confined to Ceylon.

Secondly, there was the subjective factor. Philip Gunawardena had been from 1945 the principal leader of the new Samasamaja Party. In a situation where leading worker-members and others known to the masses in the LSSP had joined the Bolshevik Samasamaja Party, he would not have been able to play a dominant rôle in a unified party.

In a pamphlet entitled *Left Disunity*, a response to a unity-wallah who advocated unity among the left parties 'at all costs' which was written about the time of the 1950 unification of the LSSP and BSP, Colvin R de Silva said that after the Gampaha by-election in 1949, in which the two parties clashed with each other:

'Once again the BSP renewed its offer for united action leading to the unification of the two parties. The majority of the LSSP also called for unity, and struggled for it against the sectarians who opposed it. At the LSSP conference of January 1950 the policy of unity was carried in the LSSP, and a new process of unification was set going on the basis of equality of status, comradeship in arms, and the identity of the programmes of the LSSP and BSP. The sectarian elements were isolated and finally defeated. Many who had earlier supported them through misunderstanding turned after Gampaha into strong adherents of unity, and their will was strengthened by the actual experience of the two parties working together after January.[8] And today at the time of writing, the first joint conference of the two parties, which will also be the founding conference of the new united party, is due in a week. Everybody is coming in except a small group round Philip Gunawardena which has withdrawn itself by deliberate choice and decision to cling to their sectarianism in isolation.'

When the LSSP and BSP merged in May 1950, the unified party — called the LSSP — presented a stronger organisation to the country. It was not only numerically larger, it contained worker-leaders on the workshop floor, in workplaces and offices and in important sectors of the economy. Thus the trade union base became stronger, and the broad masses which supported the party had increased confidence in the party. This was reflected in the local government elections which followed. In December 1950 the LSSP was able to capture power in an urban council 10 miles south of Colombo, inhabited by hundreds of workers employed in government and private sector workplaces in Colombo and the neighbouring suburban areas, and dotted with

8.   Joint councils of the two parties were set up at the leadership level and at the local level.

hundreds of small carpentry workshops. This was the first occasion that the LSSP was able to wrest power from the ruling UNP in a local council. In the 1950s the LSSP was able to capture power in the Colombo Municipal Council (in 1954), in several important towns and several village committees. This development was, of course, strengthened by the Hartal of August 1953.

In 1951 SWRD Bandaranaike, a minister of the ruling UNP, broke away from the UNP to found the Sri Lanka Freedom Party (SLFP), a liberal bourgeois party focusing attention on nationalism, the Sinhala language and national culture. The leader of the UNP, Prime Minister DS Senanayake, died in March 1952, and his son, Dudley Senanayake, was made Prime Minister. In the parliamentary elections that followed in the same year, the LSSP and SLFP both fared badly, each party winning only nine seats. The main factor which influenced the election result was the boom in the economy due to the steep rise in the price of rubber because of the Korean War. The UNP won the elections comfortably, and secured the support of 74 MPs in a parliament of 100 members.

In this election, the LSSP asked the electorate for a parliamentary majority. Consequent to the defeat of the LSSP and the SLFP, a section of the party put forward in 1952 the thesis that in the elections the LSSP should have formed an alliance with the SLFP to defeat the UNP. At the highest level, there was the possibility of an LSSP-led government, and at the lowest level there was the possibility of a Bandaranaike-led government. This thesis was defeated at the party congress in 1952.

The euphoria of the 1952 UNP election victory was short-lived. In July 1953 the UNP government raised the price of rice, the staple food of the people, by nearly 200 per cent, and cut back social welfare. The opposition protested. But when 12 August 1953 was fixed as a day of protest against the government's anti-people measures, the SLFP kept out, and the protest was organised by the LSSP, the Communist Party and Philip Gunawardena's organisation, known as the Revolutionary LSSP (Viplavakeri Lanka Sama Samaja Party). It was the LSSP that played the dominant rôle in the Hartal. However, the LSSP leadership did not have the perspective of assessing the strength of the struggle and continuing it. In certain areas militants went into action on 13 August as well, but the LSSP leaders discouraged them, and asked them to stop their activities on the plea that the protest was meant only for one day, and that it had been successful. In certain areas the Hartal assumed the proportions of an uprising. The Hartal broke the backbone of the UNP government, and was the high water mark of class action against capitalist rule.

The minority of the party that put forward the thesis of an alliance with the bourgeois SLFP against the UNP raised the issue again after the Hartal, that same year. They were defeated again, and a section of the party broke away, at first to form a united front with the Communist Party and Philip Gunawardena's organisation, but later to fritter away in different directions.

In the following period the state language question became the most important political issue of the day. From 1944 the leading Sinhalese politicians — DS Senanayake, SWRD Bandaranaike and others — had accepted that both Sinhala and Tamil should be the official languages of the government. This was the position up to 1955. In 1954 the UNP Prime Minister, John Kotelawela,[9] while on a visit to the north of the country inhabited predominantly by Tamil people, promised parity of status to the Sinhalese and Tamil languages. Bandaranaike's SLFP reacted quickly, and took up a position that Sinhala alone should be the state language, with Tamil as a regional language in Tamil-speaking areas and also as a language permissible in parliament. The VLSSP of Philip Gunawardena took up a similar position, but did not express its view on the use of Tamil in parliament. The LSSP stood for the adoption of Sinhala and Tamil as the state languages of Ceylon with parity of status throughout the country. The Communist Party also called for the Tamil language to be given official status.

The state language question became a communal issue, and the political atmosphere was dangerously explosive. The Communist Party held a public meeting on 13 October 1955 at the Town Hall in Colombo in support of the demand for official status for Tamil. It was wrecked by mobs of supporters of 'Sinhala Only' led by Buddhist monks. The LSSP held a public meeting at the same venue a few days later in support of the demand for parity of status for Sinhala and Tamil. This meeting was also attacked by mobs of 'Sinhala Only' supporters led by monks. LSSP militants thronged the entrance to the hall to prevent the attackers from gaining entry. A bomb that was lobbed at the entrance by a man in monk's robes hit Reginald Mendis, a leading militant in the Colombo Pettah local, and his hand had to be amputated at the wrist.

In the 1956 parliamentary elections, Bandaranaike won and formed a government. The Sinhala Only Act was passed by parliament in June that year with the LSSP, Communist Party and Tamil MPs voting against. On the day that the Sinhala Only Bill was presented in parliament, the Federal Party, the largest Tamil party with

9. Sir John Lionel Kotelawela (1897-1980) was Minister of Agriculture and Lands (1933-36), and became Prime Minister in the 1950s. [Editor's note]

nine MPs, organised a *Satyagraha* — non-violent protest — against the bill on Galle Face Green close to the parliament building. Thousands of Sinhalese held a counter-demonstration. The Federal Party leaders and supporters who were passively seated on the Green were physically attacked. Tamil people in other parts of Colombo were assaulted, and shops and houses were looted. Violence against Tamil people for being Tamil started on that day. A few days later, while the debate on the bill was proceeding in parliament, anti-Tamil riots took place in the Tamil-populated areas in the East, Amparai and Batticaloa. At the Colombo Municipal Council elections held at the end of the year, NM Perera was defeated because of the LSSP's stand on the language question. The LSSP suffered a temporary setback. Nevertheless, the party firmly maintained the stand it had taken.

After 1956, under the SLFP government, the LSSP unions led hundreds of strikes, but the worker leaders by and large remained trade union activists without any orientation towards revolutionary working class politics. This became clear that when NM Perera, after the defeat of the SLFP in the parliamentary elections of March 1960, called for a coalition government with the SLFP with LSSP members accepting portfolios, and the working class members of the party had on their own come to the same conclusion.

The main reason why the party rank and file voted in large numbers for NM Perera's resolution calling for a coalition government with the SLFP was the abysmally low political level of the members — at the special conference of the party in May 1960, NM Perera's resolution received 269 votes with only 128 against. The party had characterised the SLFP as the alternative bourgeois party up to 1959. But the party had not educated the members that the various reformist measures adopted by the Bandaranaike government of 1956-59 — such as the nationalisations, the take-over of imperialist bases at Trincomalee and Katunayake from the British government, the setting up of the Employees' Provident Fund, the Paddy Lands Act (an agrarian reform to increase the share of the tenant cultivator), the establishment of diplomatic relations with the Soviet Union and the other workers' states — did not constitute Socialism. There was confusion in the minds of the workers that the Bandaranaike government was a 'progressive' government quite different from the earlier UNP government. If the party had seriously attempted to educate the members through internal discussions and debates, there is no doubt that the party would have succeeded, particularly because the party had given leadership to hundreds of strikes both in the private and public sectors during the Bandaranaike regime.

In the absence of attempts to raise the political level of the members, certain socio-economic reforms after the end of the Second World War which had a cumulative effect would also have influenced working class members. There was free education from the kindergarten to the university, the medium of education was the mother-tongue, government skilled and unskilled labour became pensionable as a result of the 1946 general strike, employees in the private sector could contribute to the Employees' Provident Fund, and in the late 1950s it was possible for skilled government workers to build their own homes by obtaining housing loans. In calling for a coalition government after March 1960, NM Perera argued that social revolution is not possible in a country where there is universal franchise and free education!

In the March 1960 election, the party's manifesto included the following statement on the language question:

'Sinhala has by law been made the official language. Provision should also be made by law to make Tamil also an official language. Thus, on the one hand the right of the Tamils to have relations with the state in their own language, and to be educated and examined in their own language, will be safeguarded, while on the other hand the rightful place of the Sinhalese language, which is the language of the majority of the people, is safeguarded without any injustice being done to the Tamil people.'

When the party adopted NM Perera's resolution calling for a coalition government with the SLFP at the May 1960 Special Conference, it was only a matter of time before the party would change its position of parity of status for Sinhala and Tamil as state languages. This it did in 1963 when it formed a United Left Front with Philip Gunawardena's organisation and the Communist Party.

VI: The LSSP Against Imperialist War (1939-1945)

The present chapter was compiled to illustrate the politics of the party during the Second World War, and so should be studied alongside the richer documentation of Muthiah and Wanasinghe's *Britain, World War Two and the Samasamajists*, which has already been reviewed by Bertram Bastiampillai, 'The Secret Files — *Britain, World War Two and the Samasamajists'*, *The Island*, 17 March 1996; by *Workers News* in 'The LSSP at War' (May-June 1996); and by Ray Athow, 'Sri Lanka: The LSSP: From Revolution to Counter-Revolution', *Marxist Review*, August 1996.

The first piece is an extract from Reggie Perera's article 'Jail Break!: The Escape of the Political Prisoners', from the *Ceylon Observer*, 9 September 1962, in which he describes the escape of LSSP leaders Philip Gunawardena, NM Perera, Edmund Samarakkody and Colvin R de Silva from jail in April 1942. Ranawakarachchige Arthur Reginald Perera (1915-) had already been arrested in June 1940, along with Selina Perera, Boyd Wickremasinghe and eight others at a mass meeting in Colombo to protest at the arrest of the LSSP leaders. He subsequently was MP for Dehiowita during 1947-52, and at the time of the writing of this article, he represented the LSSP in the Ceylon Senate. The second piece was first published in the *Samasamajist* on 10 June 1942, and then reproduced under the title of 'The Real Situation in Ceylon' in *Fourth International*, Volume 3, no 10, October 1942, pp301-3. The final document is an article published by Philip Gunawardena using the pseudonym of 'Rup Singh' in *Permanent Revolution*, the theoretical organ of the Bolshevik-Leninist Party of India, Volume 1, no 2, April 1943, pp39-44.

Most of the general accounts listed in our first introduction cover this period, and so need not be repeated here. To them should certainly be added Charles Wesley Ervin's 'Trotskyism in India' (*Revolutionary History*, Volume 1, no 4, Winter 1988-89, pp22-34; see *Cahiers Léon Trotsky*, no 39, September 1989, pp77-111), and the summary compiled at the time by 'DG' (Douglas Garbutt) for the *Internal Bulletin* of the Revolutionary Communist Party, 'Report on the Fourth International Movement in India'. A more rounded report of the illegal activity of the party was published in the American *Fourth International* and again in *Workers International News* ('News from Indian Fourth Internationalists', Volume 5, no 4, October-November 1943, pp1-3).

Garbutt and Fred Bunby were with the British forces in India, and so were able to make contact with the LSSP leaders in the underground on behalf of the British Trotskyists. Bunby even acted as a courier between Colvin R de Silva and his wife back in Ceylon (S Bornstein and A Richardson, *War and the International*, pp85-6). Towards the end of 1941 the Formation Committee of the BLPI adopted a policy document, part of which was printed under the title of 'Thesis of Indian Fourth Internationalists' in *Workers International News* (Volume 5, nos 3-4, Summer 1942). The full text of the *Draft Programme of the Bolshevik Leninist Party of India* of 1942 was republished by the LSSP(R) in December 1970.

Most of the leaders of the LSSP were not to remain at liberty in India for very long. In July 1943 NM Perera was apprehended in Ahmedabad, and Philip in Bombay, and the other LSSP leaders were arrested there and in Madras. On 8 February 1944 Philip and NM were brought before a magistrates' court in Kandy, where they made a spirited revolutionary defence, which was published in the American *Militant* (14 October 1944), and in *Workers International News* ('Statement of Indian Trotskyists on Trial', Volume 5, no 7, December 1944, p15). It can be conveniently consulted in D North, *The Heritage We Defend* (Detroit, 1988, pp92-7), and so need not be repeated here.

On 4 August 1944 the BLPI's Political Committee formulated a number of theses, 'On the Present Political Situation in India', which were adopted at the party's second conference on 20-25 September ('Trotskyism in India', *Fourth International*, Volume 5, no 10, pp299-307; 'Le Mouvement Trotskyste aux Indes: La situation politique actuelle aux Indes', *Quatrième Internationale*, new series nos 20-21, July-August 1945, pp25-38). A further 'Appendix to the Program of the BLPI on the Tasks of Ceylon' ('The Program for Ceylon', *Fourth International*, Volume 7, no 10, October 1946, pp316-9) was issued later, but by that time the party had split, as will be recounted in our next section.

Reggie Perera

Jail Break!

The Escape of the Political Prisoners

THE FAR Eastern theatre of war was becoming extremely critical for the Allies. The Japanese war machine was pushing relentlessly into regions which had hitherto been the exclusive hunting grounds of Western imperialist powers. The pride of the British navy was being blown to smithereens by intrepid Japanese airmen. On the memorable Easter Monday of 5 April 1942, Colombo was bombed by a squadron of Japanese planes. That same time the four detainees broke jail and sought the fresh air of freedom which had been denied them for over two years. To the chagrin of the authorities, they discovered that the escaping prisoners had not only left four empty beds behind, but had taken their warder with them — jail guard Solomons.

It is no secret that the four detainees had in the course of their incarceration won the sympathy and affection of their warders. Almost to a man, they were ready to help the detainees in every way possible. Study classes on Socialism had been conducted by the detainees for the benefit of the warders; thus some of them were also tied to the LSSP leaders by the bonds of a common cause.

The jailer in charge was Mr Neville de la Motte, a genial man who had been extremely generous and kind to his prisoners — a personal aspect which made the getaway a little difficult. Political decisions have to be made irrespective of personal relations. Mr de la Motte, who was dismissed from the service, is now a reputed journalist. Several years later, when NM and Philip were charged for their jail break, Mr de la Motte had to testify formally for the prosecution; he did not reveal even a trace of bitterness against his former prisoners and friends. In the course of his examination, Mr de la Motte was asked whether he was dismissed from the service. 'No', he said blandly, 'I was sacked!'

It was zero hour on that memorable night. Powerful cars were outside with their friends; some of them were armed. Jail guard Solomons unlocked the door for the last time, and the detainees stepped out one by one. Everything seemed to be moving with clockwork precision. But wait! NM is walking back to his cell. Something wrong? Something important? No, he was going to retrieve a pair of old bathroom slippers he had left behind.

The fugitives from justice tarried awhile in Ceylon, and then left for India, where political events were rising in a feverish crescendo. In August 1942 Mahatma Gandhi, after the breakdown of negotiations with the imperial rulers, launched the 'Quit India' movement against foreign oppression and for India's freedom. How did these men, hunted and pursued by the police and military intelligence, cross over to India? This question is asked often. They crossed over the same way that thousands of wrist watches and fountain pens find their way from Ceylon to India today, the same way that hundreds of illegal immigrants find their way to our shores. Four men with a will to fight in a frail boat reached India, and were soon active in the revolutionary Socialist movement. The police of two countries now commenced to look for them.

The decision to be intensely active in the Indian political movement partially stemmed from a rather romantic concept that the Ceylon Trotskyist movement would give leadership to the revolutionary Socialist movement of India. It was the same perspective that gave abortive birth to the Bolshevik Leninist Party of India and Ceylon. This political romanticism crept into the party at a time when the leaders were in jail, and the party was cut off from work among the people. This infection was in time to develop into a gangrenous malady.

The lives of the leaders, whose wives subsequently joined them in wartime India, were certainly no bed of roses. On one occasion when Philip, NM and Colvin were travelling together, an astute pickpocket relieved both Philip and Colvin of their purses. Until such time they had received money from Ceylon, they had to depend on all the money that NM possessed. NM used to dwell at length on the desperate nature of their financial position and the necessity of being frugal when ordering meals in restaurants. However, Colvin could not resist a nice roast or a tasty joint, and would talk NM around to a hesitant consent.

The jail break provoked the government into taking immediate action against several active members of the party. Many were arrested and detained. For others there was a 'hue and cry'. The police came to arrest me at Ruanwella, and just as they drove in I had just enough time to get away and evade arrest, accompanied by a schoolboy friend — BHS [Boyd Wickremasinghe — ed] — who loyally elected to share my trials. We walked from sunset to dawn to reach the Kandy Road, intending to take temporary refuge with a friend in Hewaheta. When two constables stopped the bus at Hingula Bridge, I thought that our escapade was coming to a premature end. It turned out that all traffic was stopped because the Japanese raiders were bombing Trincomalee Harbour.

Our intended plan to stay at Hewaheta was abandoned when a few miles from our destination I heard a voice behind me on the bus saying: 'That is Reggie Perera; he is a Sama Samajist.' I turned around and recognised a young student from Panadura. After a few days we were given sanctuary by a generous family at Kiriella. However, a few days after the newspapers carried the offer of large rewards for information leading to the arrest of the four jail-breakers, a suspicious neighbour, mistaking me for one of the jail-breakers, carried information to the police with the hope of reward.

I was arrested, handcuffed and brought to the police headquarters in Colombo for questioning. I was grilled for nearly three days by a coarse-mouthed Superintendent, finger-printed, and photographed in convict style...

The Real Situation in Ceylon

THE FALL of Singapore, Rangoon and Port Blair, the air raids on Colombo and Trincomalee, and the imminent westward drive that Japan is organising in order to link up directly with her Axis partners, have thrust Ceylon into the international headlines. All the world is keen for information about this island. And British propaganda has hastened to assure the world that all is perfect in this imperialist garden.

If we are to believe their propagandists, this is a prosperous and democratically-ruled country with a contented population among whom disloyalty is rare and fifth columnists unknown. Here, if we are to believe them, no ripple of resistance disturbs the even tenor of British rule, and everybody loves to be oppressed by profane Britishers and even to kiss the iron heel that grinds them down — or rather, according to them, there is neither oppression nor iron heel, but only mutual cooperation arising from the people's faith in British benevolence and the people's belief in British justice. In a word, here imperialism has apparently changed its very nature, and transformed itself into democracy and justice.

What a charming picture! And how charmingly untrue!

Ceylon is certainly rich in natural resources, and grows products that are sold in the markets of the world. It has vast tea and rubber plantations which bring swollen profits and fat dividends to their owners. But who are the owners? Ninety per cent of the tea plantations and 60 per cent of the rubber plantations in Ceylon belong to the foreign imperialists who rule and exploit this island. And they certainly are prosperous.

But what of the masses? What of the army of workers who toil and sweat on these very plantations to produce these profits? They are among the most fiercely exploited workers in the world. Held in semi-slave conditions, they eke out a bare existence. The standard wage of a fully employed adult male on the plantations is about 70 cents a day. Women, of course, receive far less.

What of the Colombo workers, who are supposed to be in a somewhat better condition? Their average wage before the present crisis was about one rupee a day. And how many got even that? Ac-

Revolutionary History, Volume 6, no 4

cording to official statistics, there were in Colombo over 40 000 registered unemployed in 1939; the actual number was much greater. Since the population of Colombo at the time was about 350 000, this signifies that at least every third adult in Colombo was unemployed!

Turn to the peasantry. What is the condition of these folk, who constitute the major section of the toiling masses in Ceylon? The word 'prosperity' in relation to them is sheer blasphemy. The official government rural surveys have shown that fully 60 per cent of the people in our countryside do not earn enough to get a regular two full meals a day. And fully 20 per cent go through life without even knowing what it is to have a decent full meal.

So much for the vaunted prosperity of Ceylon. What of the democracy alleged to prevail in it? The propagandists delight to point to the State Council as proof of its existence.

Of all the institutions in Ceylon, the State Council is easily the biggest fraud. It is a painted screen behind which an autocratic Governor operates. Its Ministers are but puppets, while the Governor pulls the strings. For the Governor has the power — and frequently exercises it — to legislate independently and against the will of the State Council. In fact, today, this country is openly ruled by the Governor's legislation without even the pretence of consulting the State Council. And none dare protest, as is shown by the failure of even a single Councillor to protest against the utterly inhuman conditions that have been imposed on political detainees. More, the Governor has detained with impunity even two State Councillors, and threatened publicly even a Minister.

Finding the State Council to be useless as an instrument for bettering their conditions, the workers have increasingly resorted to independent and direct action. The last few years have witnessed wave after wave of strikes in Ceylon up in the plantations. The long-suffering workers rose at last, and, with incredible tenacity in the face of rank brutality, fought time after time during a whole year and more for increased wages, and for their right to form unions. The government and the planters met them with police brutality and Fascist thuggery. Workers were shot, maimed, beaten, dismissed in droves, imprisoned in crowds, and victimised by the thousand. But they fought on grimly, and won grudging recognition of their unions.

Meantime the war had begun. There followed a sharp upward swing of prices, and an increase in unemployment. Conditions became so intolerable, especially in the urban centres, that the workers were driven to use the strike weapon once more. In Colombo and its environs a wave of strikes spread from factory to factory and from workplace to workplace. The government promptly struck back with prosecutions under the Defence Regulations. But the wave rose higher and higher until it culminated in a widening series of strikes at that nerve centre of imperialism, the Colombo Harbour, just about the time that the Japanese came into the war.

Taking advantage of the war situation, the government struck fiercely at the workers. It banned strikes and illegalised even efforts at organised protest against working conditions. By sheer legal trickery and administrative bludgeoning, it emasculated the trade union movement in Ceylon.

Today the government has gone further. It has conscripted labour under the guise of creating military units on the railways and in the harbour. It has set up scab squads in the guise of the so-called Essential Services Labour Corps. It has illegalised strikes and even resistance to employers' oppression as hampering the war effort. It has made trade union work impossible not only by such legislation, etc, but also by promptly arresting trade union organisers and militants. Trade union offices have been raided by the police, their documents seized, and their occupants arrested, beaten up and tortured until trade unions had to close down from the sheer impossibility of carrying on with their work. There is no longer any freedom of speech, writing or organisation; no hope of successful defence in the courts where terror-stricken magistrates hasten to convict workers on the flimsiest of evidence, and no possibility of public protest with even the State Council bullied into hushed acquiescence. An utterly Fascist regime has come into being, with a military dictator at the head. Admiral Layton has become the dictator of Ceylon.

The battered and oppressed working class has met the ever-tightening repression with an ever-growing revolutionary movement directed against imperialism itself. As far back as 1935 this movement found organisational expression in the Lanka Sama Samaja Party, the only revolutionary party in Ceylon. This party is now a section of the revolutionary Fourth International, the only international organisation which upholds the banner of proletarian revolution since the degenerate Comintern turned traitor to the working class.

The LSSP has led the workers in their political and economic struggles since its formation. In June 1940, four of its principal leaders were detained under the Defence Regulations, thus becoming the first political prisoners in Ceylon. At the same time, the party press was confiscated, and many of its members jailed. The government hoped thus to smash the party. But the party resolutely continued its work, both legally and illegally, and with considerable success. Thereupon the government banned the party, and also struck at its ancillary organisations. The party promptly went underground, and retaliated with even more militant activity, including the dramatic escape of its four imprisoned leaders in April. It has not been deterred by police raids and police brutality, by prosecution and frame-ups, and by the imposition of intolerably inhuman conditions on political prisoners drawn from its ranks. There can be no doubt that on the not distant date when the mass upsurge against imperialism comes in Ceylon, the LSSP will be at the head.

In that task the workers of Ceylon look for help to the British workers in uniform who have come to Ceylon. There are no fifth columnists among the Ceylon workers. They are not pro-Japanese, but anti-imperialist. The only pro-Japanese fifth column elements in Ceylon are to be found among the native bourgeoisie, among the Kotelawalas and their ilk, who tomorrow will lick the boots of the Japanese imperialists as cheerfully as they today lick the boots of their British imperialist master.

Among the British soldiers here are large numbers of trade unionists and politicals. We ask them: Can you in the conditions of Ceylon believe you are fighting for democracy? Can you believe that claim when our working class organisations are banned and our trade unions are smashed, when our leaders are imprisoned and our rank and file are prosecuted and persecuted, when we are denied the right of free speech, publication and organisation, and when the very capitalist press is gagged and harnessed to the purposes of imperialist war and imperialist oppression? Can you not see that the British bosses have created in Ceylon only a bastion of Fascism? Can you not see that only the workers, through revolutionary action, can convert it into a veritable bastion of freedom?

Rup Singh (Philip Gunawardena)

Revolutionary Defeatism

'REVOLUTIONARY ACTION in wartime is impossible without incurring *the defeat of the home government, and every defeat of the home government in a reactionary war facilitates revolution*, which alone can bring about a lasting and democratic peace... Finally, it is necessary to tell the masses that without *their own illegal organisations created by themselves, and a press free from military censorship, that is, an illegal press*, it is impossible to render serious support to the nascent revolutionary struggle, its development, the criticism of its individual steps, the correction of its errors, and the systematic broadening and sharpening of the struggle.' (Lenin in Krupskaya's *Memories of Lenin*, p184. Italics by RS)

The virus of opportunism has begun to attack the top leadership of the Socialist Workers Party of America. The February 1942 issue of the chief theoretical organ of the Socialist Workers Party of America contains an article which attempts to revise, modify and castrate the principles of revolutionary defeatism of Marx, Lenin and Trotsky. The editors of that publication labour to draw a sharp distinction 'between the principled position on the war and the application of the principled position in mass agitation'. They go to the extent of dubbing those revolutionary Marxists who use the slogans of 'Revolutionary Defeatism' and 'Turn the Imperialist War into Civil War' ultra-left sectarians. This is an index to the depth of their opportunism. Lenin was called an ultra-left sectarian by a great many internationalists who even attended the Zimmerwald and Kienthal Conferences during the Imperialist World War of 1914-18. But that did not prevent him and the Bolsheviks from using the slogans of 'Revolutionary Defeatism' and 'Turn the Imperialist War into Civil War'. Lenin's strategy and tactics proved superior to the strategy and tactics of the Mensheviks of the day. Lenin always emphasised and repeated again and again the necessity for building illegal organisations and an illegal press for the effective prosecution of the revolutionary struggle, particularly in time of war.

Our comrades in the SWP fail to realise that you can go on broadening the struggle of the proletariat as to make it flat, anaemic and lifeless. That is why Lenin emphasised the urgency for sharpening the struggle. The necessity for putting up a legal defence in the courts of even 'democratic' America should not make our comrades dilute the principles of revolutionary defeatism. Civil liberty even in 'God's own country' is an ephemeral phenomenon that will disappear with the sharpening of the class struggle. Our American comrades should by all means utilise to the fullest possible extent legality as long as they are permitted to do so. But the problem of legality should not delay or prevent them from taking the necessary steps for illegal work. It has ceased to be a mere organisational question, and has assumed the proportions and character of a political problem, if we are to judge the question from the political line that the editorial in the February 1942 issue of the *Fourth International* seeks to formulate.

The American masses are fast shedding their democratic illusions. Our comrades in the SWP should not try to act as a brake on this process, by hitching their party to the chariot wheels of Roger Baldwin's Civil Liberties outfit. Popular Frontism in smart American clothes is attempting to flirt with the American proletariat. The Independent Labour Party advocated by the top leadership of the SWP of America is symptomatic of the opportunism that is rearing its ugly head inside the SWP of America.

Let us examine the editorial of February 1942 of the *Fourth International* more minutely. We have not been able to obtain a copy of the January 1942 issue of the *Fourth International* in which we are told an authoritative statement by Comrade James Cannon on the war appeared. We are assured that Comrade Cannon's statement gave 'the correct attitude on the war'. We are further informed that 'revolutionaries could not expect anything less from Comrade Cannon — a Trotskyist, that is, a revolutionary Marxist'. But we did and do expect a little more from the editors of the organ of the SWP of America. Yes, a little more clarity and light.

The editors state clearly and concretely that 'this war on the part of all nations, except the Soviet Union and China, is imperialist in character'. Then they go on to state that 'it is a reactionary imperialist war on the part of all nations involved except the Soviet Union, a degenerated workers' state, and China, a colonial nation fighting for its independence'. We endorse this characterisation of the war unreservedly. We stand for the fullest aid to the Soviet Union — a degenerated workers' state — in her war against the counter-revolutionary armies of Hitler and his Axis partners. We state emphatically that the principles of revolutionary defeatism do not apply to the Soviet Union in this war until all the gains of the October Revolution — particularly those of the state ownership of industry and the state monopoly of foreign trade — are liquidated. We stand for victory for the Red Army even under the Stalinist bureaucracy. This does not mean that the international proletariat has in any way given up its struggle for the elimination of the Stalinist bureaucracy even in the course of the war. It only means that vis-à-vis the Red Army and the counter-revolutionary armies of the Axis powers, we stand for the defeat of the Axis armies and military victory to the Red Army even under its present leaders. As a matter of fact, we are in favour of prosecuting the struggle for the elimination of the Stalinist bureaucracy more intensively. As the political alliance between Anglo-American finance capital and the Soviet Union becomes closer, we will begin to put greater emphasis on the urgency of overthrowing the Stalinist regime by means of a political revolution in the course of this war. If a temporary peace treaty is signed by Hitler and Stalin, this struggle for the elimination of the Stalinist bureaucracy will take the chief place in the activities of the international proletariat so far as the Soviet Union is concerned. That is our position so far as aid to the Soviet Union and the elimination of the Soviet bureaucracy are concerned.

We consider that so far as China is concerned the international proletariat must render aid to the national liberationist armies of China even under the Guomindang flag. It is true that Chiang Kai Shek and his military camarilla in Chungking are only the tools of Anglo-American finance capital — more particularly American finance capital. We stand for the organisation of independent workers' and peasants' armies under the revolutionary proletarian party in China for the overthrow of Chiang Kai Shek and the Guomindang camarilla — the hirelings of American finance capital. We stand for a more effective prosecution of the war against Japanese imperialism by these independent armies of the colonial masses of China, Melanesia and Indonesia. We support the resolution of the Fourth International on aid to China and the character of that aid. That the sending of American armed forces to China converts the war of national liberation of the Chinese armies into an inter-imperialist war between the United States and Japan for the domination of China and the Pacific is clear. This makes the organisation of independent worker and peasant armies under the proletarian party not merely a propagandist slogan, but a practical task. Our aid to the Chinese masses must be not merely political, but military. That is, military organisational problems must be tackled just as much as the political organisational problems. China seems to afford the most fertile field for this work in the entire colonial and semi-colonial world. We stand for the fullest material and organisational aid to the masses of China for their struggle against the Guomindang and world imperialism. That Japanese imperialism is their chief enemy today is not overlooked. But the menace of American imperialism in the Pacific is emphasised.

On the fundamental principled position on the war, we are in complete agreement with the editors of the *Fourth International*. Now, let us see how the leaders of the American SWP attempt to translate their principled position on the war into practice. That is to say, let us examine their strategy and tactics in this war.

The editors characterise the war as a reactionary imperialist war on the part of all nations taking part in it except the Soviet Union and China. 'There follows from this analysis', they write, 'the necessity on the part of revolutionary Marxists to oppose the war, to oppose the class in control of all the capitalist imperialist states involved in the war.' So far so good. But it is beautifully vague yet. 'Opposition to the war', they declare, 'is a political concept, synonymous with non-support of the war.' We are assured that this political concept is not one which Comrade Cannon and his disciples meditate and hold secret communion with. Oh no. 'It is, of course, an active opposition', they say, 'in the sense that revolutionary Marxists are obliged at all times to tell the working masses the true nature of the war and what they should do to assure peace for themselves and future generations.' This active opposition is yet of the Nirvanic variety. The learned editors attempt to elaborate further their strategy and tactics. They state: 'The revolutionary party has no alternative but to say: This is not our war, we refuse to take responsibility for it.' Now, how can a party ask the proletariat to work for 'the defeat of the home government' with negative, hesitant and wobbling propaganda of this nature? This is not all: 'So long as we are in a minority, we cannot help but go to war ourselves.' No revolutionary party will be in the majority of the nation except for a few days or weeks during the revolutionary crisis leading to the revolutionary situation. Till that day dawns, Comrade Cannon and his disciples will continue to tell the American proletariat 'to go' to fight. At first, opposition to war is a political concept synonymous with non-support of the war. Then this non-support of the war is transformed into telling workers that as the proletarian revolutionary party is as yet in a minority, they 'cannot help but go to war' themselves. This is how the leaders of the SWP of America fight for the defeat of their government in this war.

Their opportunism takes them a few steps further on the road to shamefaced social-patriotism when they say 'revolutionary defeatism does not mean that we prefer the defeat of our own imperialism at the hands of Japanese imperialism'. They shame-facedly attempt to cover their social-patriotism by adding that they 'favour the continuation of the class struggle for the purpose of defeating the imperialists by the revolutionary forces of the nation'. This is deliberate evasion. This is sowing confusion in the ranks of the militant proletariat of America. Lenin is very concrete and precise on this point. He writes that '*every defeat of the home government* in a reactionary war facilitates revolution'. So, defeat of the home government even at the hands of German or Japanese imperialism must facilitate revolution in America. Why do the leaders of the SWP of America say that they do not 'prefer the defeat of American imperialism at the hands of German or Japanese imperialism', if 'every defeat of the home government facilitates revolution', no matter at whose hands the defeat takes place? The leaders of the SWP of America are willing to wait till the 'majority decide to take their fate into their own hands' to attempt to transform the imperialist war into a civil war. That is why they take shelter under the statement that 'by and large the masses are not moved by propaganda'. That is why they refuse to rise above the political level of 'the more mundane working masses'.

The American proletariat demonstrated from 1930 onwards that it is not so 'mundane' as Comrade Cannon and his colleagues would make us believe. The writer of this article wrote in August 1941:

'Our best and strongest forces are in the Americas. Our American comrades are taking a prominent part in the mighty class battles of the proletariat which are shaking to its very roots the Dollar Republic. Our American comrades by their heroic example and ceaseless endeavour are exposing the social-patriotism of the Stalinist Browders and Minors, and preparing the militant proletariat of America for the gigantic revolutionary battle for the Socialist revolution that is looming on the immediate horizon beyond the mists of blood and carnage of this war.' (*Bolshevik-Leninist*, January 1942)

We still hold these views. We feel that the militant proletariat of America will compel the leadership of the SWP of America to travel the revolutionary road. We hope there is enough virility and political honesty left within the SWP of America to abandon opportunism and revert to the revolutionary Marxism of Lenin and Trotsky. The vanguard of the proletariat must show the way, must lead, instead of attempting to descend to the level of the most backward sections of the American proletariat.

The editorial states, 'revolutionary Marxists are opposed to sabotage. The capitalist government officials know they need not fear sabotage on the part of revolutionary Marxists.' This is evidently addressed to the American bourgeoisie, more particularly, the government officials. It cannot possibly be directed to the working class. Sabotage has its time and place in the class struggle of the proletariat. Revolutionary Marxism does not condemn sabotage as a general principle. It is the duty of the revolutionary party of the proletariat to explain to the working masses where and when to engage in acts of sabotage. Marxism is not Gandhian pacifism. Even the votaries of non-violence do not condemn acts of sabotage in such general terms as do the leaders of the SWP of America. We cannot help coming to the conclusion that since the entry of America into the war, the leadership of the SWP has got cold feet. This is made quite clear by their attitude on legality. 'The problem of legality', declares the editorial, 'is, of course, not to be disregarded. The criminal code exists, and revolutionaries do not disregard it when it comes to the question of tactical approach — *what to say and how to say it in order to be within the law*.' [Our emphasis — RS] Besides the criminal code there are special war emergency powers; even military powers are assumed by the President of the USA and American government officials in restricting, stifling and crushing the class struggle of the American pro-

letariat. So, the desire to remain within the law means not only cur-
tailing the activities of the party, but also sowing legalist illusions in
the ranks of the proletariat. The important thing is not to remain
within the law, but how to reach the proletariat and help it organise
itself despite the law. This can be done only by building illegal organisations of the party, and setting up an illegal press for conducting
undiluted, uncensored propaganda and agitation in the ranks of the
proletariat, including therein the armed forces. 'What to say and how
to say it, in order to be within the law' can never be even a substitute
for revolutionary propaganda in war time. This propaganda can be
conducted only by an underground organisation and an underground
press.

We propose to deal with the growth of opportunism in the SWP
of America in a more comprehensive way and at greater length as
soon as we succeed in obtaining all the relevant publications of our
brother party in America. For the present, we wish to conclude this
article by reiterating that the proletariat everywhere must work for
the defeat of one's own home government in a reactionary war. The
present war is a reactionary imperialist war on the part of all nations
participating in it, except the Soviet Union and China. Defeatism is
inapplicable to the Soviet Union and China. It must be applied by the
proletariat of all other nations participating in this war. The USA —
the most powerful imperialist nation in the world — cannot be an
exception. It is the duty of the proletariat of the USA to work for the
defeat of their government in this war, even at the hands of German
and Japanese imperialism. The menace of Fascism to the American
and the world proletariat is from the American bourgeoisie even
more than from the Axis powers today. The defeat of American imperialism, even at the hands of Japanese or German imperialism, will
produce such a gigantic revolutionary crisis in America and throughout the world that the proletariat of America will be faced with the
capture of power not in the distant future, but in the immediate future. No other section of the international proletariat is better
equipped for this historic task than the American proletariat, since
the German proletariat capitulated to Fascism in 1933 and made possible this world war and the victory of the counter-revolution in
Europe. A heavy responsibility rests on the ample shoulders of the
vanguard of the American proletariat. We have no doubt whatever
that the virile elements of the SWP of America will rise to this responsibility.

The Bolshevik-Leninists of India are applying the principles of
revolutionary defeatism. They work for the defeat of their home
government — British imperialism. They cooperate with all Fourth

Internationalists throughout the British Empire to make this work effective and fruitful to the proletariat. We have no doubt that Fourth Internationalists in Germany, Italy and Japan are working for the defeat of their own home governments, even 'at the hands' of the 'democratic' united nations, not because they favour a victory of the democratic powers, but because the defeat of their own home governments will facilitate revolution, and bring nearer the day of the victory of the world revolution of the international proletariat.

A correct characterisation of the war is not enough. Revolutionary defeatism demands that the party of the proletariat outlines concretely and sharply the line of march of the proletariat in this war. This is proletarian strategy in this war. Then it must tell in unmistakable and bold terms the proletariat the counter-moves that it must make to every move by the imperialist government. This is proletarian tactics in war. The fundamental principled position is translated into strategy over a long period; it is translated into tactics over a short period — day-to-day work. The sharp distinction between the principled position on the war and the application of this principled position in mass propaganda is unreal, and betrays a tendency to refuse to apply the principles of revolutionary defeatism in mass work.

VII: The 1945 Split in the LSSP

This section starts with a section of Yodage Ranjith Amarasinghe's *Trotskyism in Ceylon: The LSSP 1935-1964*, a PhD Thesis that was prepared for the University of London in 1974. The author was a member of the LSSP's Youth League in the 1960s, and we are most grateful for his permission to reproduce this extract, which comprises pages 107-128 of the thesis.

This is followed by a contribution by Philip Gunawardena to the *Internal Bulletin* of the LSSP (March 1947), and a statement on the split issued to the *Ceylon Daily News* on 18 October 1945 by Colvin R de Silva and Leslie Goonewardene. Next comes the text of the resolution expelling Perera and Gunawardena from the BLPI, and a counter-statement by them that appeared in the *Ceylon Daily News* on 22 October 1945, and following this is an editorial by RCL Attygale from *Fight* (13 November 1945), the new paper of the BLPI, explaining the reasons for the existence of two separate Trotskyist parties in the island. The section finishes with an article by Colvin R de Silva from *Fight* (11 and 18 January 1946) which considers the possible political orientations that the new LSSP would adopt.

Biographical details for NM Perera, Colvin R de Silva and Philip Gunawardena can be found above on pages 10-11 (nn10, 12 and 13). More biographical material relating to Colvin R de Silva can be found in GL Peiris, *Some Themes in the Life of Dr Colvin R de Silva* (Colvin R de Silva memorial Lecture, 1991); Ernest Mandel's 'Homage to Colvin de Silva' (*International Viewpoint*, no 163, 15 May 1989, p27); and in 'Colvin R de Silva, 1907-1989' (*Cahiers Léon Trotsky*, no 38, June 1989, p126).

The Fourth International continued to recognise the Ceylon Unit of the BLPI as its representative in the island ('La victoire électorale des Trotskystes et le projet d'independence de Ceylan', *Quatrième Internationale*, Volume 6, nos 1-2, January-February 1948, pp54-5), which later assumed the name of the Bolshevik Samasamaja Party, and Colvin R de Silva attended the Second World Congress on its behalf, presenting the report of the Colonial Commission, and presiding over the second session on 12 April 1948. The LSSP refused to conclude a united front with the Bolshevik Samasamajists, and demanded instead a fusion of the two Trotskyist organisations ('Our Reply to the United Front Propaganda of the Bolsheviks and Stalinists', *Samasamajist*, Volume 3, no 6, 25 June 1948). Unification discussions were held from time to time, and a premature report published in *Quatrième Internationale* ('Une grève dirigée par les trotskystes', December 1946, p56) describing the arrest of NM Perera suggested that this had already taken place. It was not to happen until 1950, as we shall later learn.

YR Amarasinghe
The Samasamajists Divided

IN SEPTEMBER 1945 Philip Gunawardena and NM Perera announced the launching of a political party under the old name of the Lanka Sama Samaja Party.[1] This announcement triggered the formalisation of the split amongst the Samasamajists. The BLPI, whose leaders were still in India, decided to 'expel' NM Perera and Philip Gunawardena.[2] With this, hopes of any reconciliation between the two antagonistic Samasamajist groups diminished, at least for the time being. From this point onwards, there were two separate Samasamajist political formations in Ceylon.

Two 'Samasamaja' Parties

Both these new Samasamaja parties claimed allegiance to Trotsky and the Fourth International, and each of them also claimed to have inherited the mantle of the old LSSP. The group led by Philip Gunawardena and NM Perera not only took the old name, the Lanka Sama Samaja Party, but also the name and premises of the traditional party organ, the *Samasamajist*. However, the important asset of official recognition from the Fourth International continued to be with the BLPI section, which in Ceylon came to be known as the Bolshevik Samasamaja Party (BSP), led by the group around Colvin R de Silva and Leslie Goonewardene.[3]

1. See Philip Gunawardena and NM Perera's letter to the editor, *Ceylon Daily News*, 22 October 1945.
2. The Central Committee resolution of the BLPI that approved the expulsions is reproduced in full in Susan de Silva, *Wrecking of the LSSP*, pp10-14. See also Colvin de Silva and Leslie Goonewardene's letter to the editor, *Ceylon Daily News*, 13 October 1945.
3. The LSSP called itself 'Followers of the Fourth International' when the Bolsheviks introduced themselves as 'The Ceylon Unit of the BLPI, Section of the

Being Trotskyist, the two parties naturally had no fundamental differences, yet they were not without mutual hostility and petty squabbles. The Bolshevik Samasamajists criticised the LSSP's line as 'organisational Menshevism'. The basis for their contention was the advancement by Philip Gunawardena and NM Perera of the need to broaden the base of their party by associating with other radical groups in the country. Philip Gunawardena and NM Perera had put forward such views whilst in exile in India. The militants who had then rejected these ideas and opted for a well-knit revolutionary organisation were the same men who later on came to lead the Bolshevik section. The new party of Philip Gunawardena and NM Perera, the LSSP, started its operations in Ceylon by collaborating with several different non-Marxist organisations.[4] The Bolsheviks alleged that this policy was leading to the adoption of a 'loose petit-bourgeois party in contradistinction to a well-knit disciplined party integrated with the proletariat'.[5] They also maintained that the LSSP became a separate section for 'no principled reason', and that there were many non-revolutionary elements within its ranks. In spite of these accusations, the Bolsheviks at this stage conceded that the LSSP did not clearly deviate from the programme of the Bolshevik Leninist Party of India.

Philip Gunawardena and NM Perera, on the other hand, justified their setting up of a separate organisation as a measure taken to correct the wrong policies of the men who led the Samasamajists whilst they were in prison. The two leaders of the LSSP accused the Bolsheviks who led the wartime organisation of 'abject neglect of party work', and condemned their 'lack of interest in trade union work'. Another complaint was concerned with the aloofness of the leadership from the party rank and file; the LSSP called these leaders 'a bureaucratic group'.[6] Another regular criticism by the LSSP revolved around the alleged 'academic intellectual arrogance' of the Bolshevik leadership. Their alleged 'petit-bourgeois conspiratorial methods' were also condemned.[7] Apart from these accusations and counter accusations, the parties were unable to present differences of any fundamental nature. The different leadership groups, however, represented two tendencies that existed within the main Samasamaja

Fourth International'.
4. At the outset the LSSP collaborated very closely with the communally-organised Ceylon Indian Congress, which controlled the mass of the Indian plantation workers, and with some independent Socialists and liberals.
5. *Fight*, 20 November 1945.
6. Statement issued on behalf of the LSSP by Philip Gunawardena and NM Perera, *Ceylon Daily News*, 22 October 1945.
7. *Samasamajist*, 4 January 1946.

movement; the LSSP reflecting the pragmatist side, and the BSP the revolutionary and rather dogmatic line. The LSSP wanted to broaden the organisational base of the party, and consequently was more conciliatory than the BSP towards other radical groups. The BSP, concerned about the maintenance of theoretical purity and the retention of a cadre character of the party, was against any form of collaboration at an organisational level. These differences were to remain as a dividing line between the two parties right up to the unification in June 1950. In fact, even after the unification these differences were manifested within the unified party; the members who once belonged to the Bolshevik group often tended to act in a group on the left wing of the party. It was these members who were most interested in the maintenance of the links with the Fourth International, and in carrying on the Trotskyist polemics with the other leftist groups. Fourteen years after the unification, at the Special Conference in June 1964, the leaders of the two groups that opposed the right wing majority's desire to join with the SLFP to form a coalition came almost exclusively from amongst the Bolsheviks of the earlier period.

Whatever the reasons, the Samasamajists entered the significant postwar period divided. This was a tremendous handicap for the whole Trotskyist movement in Ceylon. As the official historian of the LSSP admits,[8] this prevented the Samasamajists from reaping the full benefits of the prestige they had gained by their activities during the war. This was all the more disadvantageous because the period immediately following the war was one of great working class upsurges and political change.

The Divided Samasamajists, 1945-50

Within months of their release from prison, the Samasamajists of both parties commenced their agitation and propaganda activities in earnest. These activities were mainly centred upon the economic issues of unemployment, the rising cost of living, and rights of association for government workers, together with the political issues of the dissolution of the State Council (due as early as 1941), the need to hold fresh elections, and the release of the remaining political prisoners. One area in which the Samasamajists were particularly active was the field of trade unions. As their old trade unions were in complete disarray since the banishment of the party in April 1942, there was much work to be done in this field. The Communist Party of Ceylon, which arose during the war, had made full use of its privileged

8.   L Goonewardene, *A Short History of the LSSP*, p32.

position of legality, and had acquired a very strong position within the trade union movement. In their competition for influence in the trade unions and other fields, the Samasamajists had the edge over the Communists because of their stand of unwavering opposition to the 'imperialists' during the war. At a time when the Samasamajists were 'suffering in the service of the people', the Communists were playing a supportive rôle to the British and the local establishment. This record was continued by the Samasamajists in the labour disputes that occurred during the first few months of their freedom.[9]

In the political sphere the most important event that took place in the early postwar period was the announcement of the new constitutional reform proposals made by the commission headed by Viscount Soulbury.[10] The new proposals recommended a cabinet type of government. According to these proposals, a House of Representatives with full powers on domestic matters, including finance, would replace the existing State Council, and only a few specifically mentioned items, defence and external affairs, were to be kept under the power of Westminster through a Governor General. The reforms also proposed a redivision of electorates. Although the Ceylon National Congress officially rejected cooperation with the Commission, once the proposals were made they were considered adequate, and the national political leaders had them approved by the State Council by an overwhelming majority.

The Samasamajists, however, condemned the new constitutional proposals without reservation. The LSSP's May Day rally of 1946 called for the rejection of these reforms, which were dubbed the 'Senanayake-Soulbury proposals'.[11] The Samasamajists particularly disliked the cabinet format proposed by the commission, which was

9.   Within a few months of their release from prison, several Samasamajists were charged by the police with criminal offences arising out of their participation in labour disputes in defiance of government regulations restricting such participation. Leslie Goonewardene, Philip Gunawardena and NM Perera were taken to court on charges arising out of a strike at the South Western Bus Co; of the three NM Perera was given a jail sentence of three months, and was later released on bail. In relation to a strike speech made at the harbour, another Samasamajist, WJ Perera, was sentenced to three months imprisonment.

10.   Herwald Ramsbotham, Viscount Soulbury, headed a constitutional commission to Ceylon, which was set up in 1945. The commission was sent to Ceylon in response to Ceylonese complaints about the vague nature of British proposals for constitutional reform. It proposed that universal suffrage should continue, with territorial voting so that minorities would be represented in parliament. The Governor General would have full powers over external affairs and defence matters, otherwise Ceylon would have full self-government. Its recommendations were implemented in May 1946.

11.   DS Senanayake was the leader of the State Council, and was instrumental in getting the reform proposals approved by the Council.

considered as offering inferior opportunities to individual members comparable with the executive committee system that existed in the State Council. It was considered as a reactionary means designed to keep real power entrenched in a handful of loyalists. On one occasion, NM Perera referred to the proposed reforms as 'impending fascism' which the political leaders of Ceylon were planning 'through their slave Soulbury Constitution'.[12]

The Bolsheviks were even more forceful in their rejection of the reform proposals. When the contents of the new proposals came to be known, they claimed that the aim of the British as reflected in the reform proposals was to make Ceylon into an 'Asiatic Ulster, a bastion for the Empire against the long overdue Indian revolution', and claimed that the 'Ceylonese bourgeoisie was quite ready to be bribed and pampered into allowing the British to point a pistol at the heart of India from Ceylon'. The Bolshevik Samasamaja Party held a mass meeting to protest against the acceptance of the reforms; at the meeting a resolution was adopted calling upon 'the masses to defeat the attempts to impose a new slave constitution... and to go forward with the masses of India towards the overthrow of imperialism, and the establishment of a government of workers and peasants'.[13]

The Samasamajists saw the reform proposals as a deal made by the British colonial rulers with the established political leaders of Ceylon, a deal that would satisfy the local leaders whilst enabling the British to continue their domination. The new delimitations which had in effect given weight to rural areas, and the proposal to establish a Senate which would be composed wholly of nominated members, were seen as means devised to facilitate the retention of power in the hands of the 'loyal stooges' of British imperialism. The proposals were viewed with suspicion, as they were thought to evade the substantive issue of the complete withdrawal by the British. This they thought was not likely to happen in the near future. The Samasamajists stated that the British wanted to hold on to their possessions in India despite the changed political atmosphere after the war, and for this they wanted to keep Ceylon as a staging base. Moreover, they thought that the British would never withdraw voluntarily, and that they would have to be pushed by force; therefore there was no room for a negotiated settlement, as the national political leaders in Ceylon claimed. An additional reason for the refusal to accept the reform proposals would have been the fact that the Samasamajists were kept away from the actual negotiations, as well as from the deliberations in the State Council, on the acceptability of the proposals.

12. *Samasamajist*, 1 May 1946.
13. *Fight*, 20 November 1945.

Within months of the Soulbury proposals becoming effective, announcements were made about the British intention to withdraw completely from Ceylon. By then the political prospects of the Samasamajists had also changed quite considerably. The general elections held between August and September of 1947 under the Soulbury proposals brought major electoral successes to both the Samasamajist parties, particularly to the LSSP. The elections in fact came at a time when the objective political situation did not appear to be very favourable to the Samasamajists. They had failed to arouse any public opinion against the new reform proposals. Moreover, the elections were held within months of disastrous strike failures that resulted in thousands of instances of victimisation, and the decline of the influence of all the left wing political parties within the unions. The divided Samasamajists had to face the national political leaders, who were in a position to offer the attractive promise of immediate independence if they were returned to power. Nevertheless, the Samasamajists, contesting 39 of a total of 95 seats, won 15, and emerged as the second biggest political party in the new parliament.[14] The election results convinced at least a section of the Samasamajists that they were not completely outside the pale of electoral politics; this section thought that through having been so successful in a not particularly favourable situation, they would have stood an even better chance had the conditions been different. This feeling was perhaps instrumental in making a substantial section of the Samasamajists more cautious in expressing their opposition to the granting of further constitutional reforms.

The next stage of constitutional reforms was the granting of complete political independence, which was to be effective from February 1948. Both of the Samasamajist parties were sceptical about this latest development in the constitutional evolution of Ceylon, and questioned the motives of the British. Because of their inherent disbelief that the British would withdraw from Ceylon peacefully, the Samasamajists firmly held that the withdrawal was merely nominal, and that real political as well as economic power was still in the hands of the British.[15]

Even on this matter the difference in the degree of militancy between the two Samasamajist parties came to the surface. The LSSP agreed that independence, though incomplete, was an improvement

14. The LSSP won 10 out of the 28 seats it contested, and the BSP had five of their 11 candidates returned. The seats in which they were successful included urban as well as rural areas.

15. It was believed that there were secret agreements that gave power to Britain to take back effective control of Ceylon when it was deemed necessary by the Imperial government (Goonewardene, op cit, p37).

on the existing constitutional status. When the Prime Minister under the new constitution moved a proposal expressing 'jubilation' on the granting of independence by His Majesty's government, NM Perera proposed an amendment that reflected the LSSP's thinking on independence.[16] This amendment 'appreciated' the granting of independence, but regretted that it was an 'incomplete independence'. The LSSP considered it incomplete mainly on three grounds. Firstly, independence had been negotiated by a handful of established national political leaders with hardly any reference to the people or to the legislature of Ceylon. Secondly, the signing of three agreements seemed to have been made a prerequisite for the granting of 'independence'. Thirdly, there was the absence of provisions enabling the Ceylonese legislature to amend the whole constitution, and the retention of the right to legislate for Ceylon by the parliament in Westminster.[17]

Another substantial criticism by the LSSP was that the new status did not alter the economic domination of Ceylon by British capital. The LSSP alleged that the implementation of the new constitution meant the 'complete freedom for the Ceylonese bourgeoisie to exploit the workers and peasants', whilst 'at the same time British capital invested in Ceylon and the armed forces of British imperialism stationed in Ceylon at the request of the Ceylonese government will pull the strings behind the scenes and influence the government of Ceylon'.[18] Despite these shortcomings, the LSSP conceded, the new status was an 'advancement', and it therefore did not reject it out of hand.

The Bolsheviks, however, took a somewhat different stand. They rejected outright the new status as a big fraud, and called it a 'fake independence'. They used arguments similar to those presented by the LSSP, but went further in their condemnation of the status of independence. In a special article entitled 'Independence', the leader of the BSP, Colvin R de Silva, stated that the granting of independence was a measure 'consistent' with the British Labour government's policy of 'reconstructing imperialism'. He held that the only change resulting from the new status for Ceylon was a shift from direct to indirect methods of control. He considered the Defence Agreement to be the key in the transfer of power, and he thought that this agreement permitted the British to use Ceylon as its military base and 'imperial fortress' in the Indian Ocean. He went on: 'Ceylon is thus

16. See NM Perera's speech, House of Representatives of Ceylon, *Debates*, Volume 1, 1947, particularly columns 590-610; and his review article of Sir Ivor Jennings' Constitution of Ceylon in the *University of Ceylon Review*, no 8, 1950, pp65-8.
17. House of Representatives of Ceylon, *Debates*, Volume 1, 1947, column 587.
18. *Samasamajist*, 10 February 1948.

not free, but continues to be in chains. Only now our imprisoned nation has a new and locally recruited warder. Mr Senanayake is but the head jailer of the British imperialist prison house.'[19] The Bolsheviks repeatedly denounced the impending independence as a 'fraud', and as a condition that would give ample opportunities for the imperialist economic and military exploitation of Ceylon.[20] Accordingly, the BSP group in parliament voted against the proposal of DS Senanayake that called on the nation to 'rejoice' at the grant of independence.

The LSSP, however, reflecting its ambiguous position, chose to abstain from voting on that particular motion.[21] When, eventually, the status of independence was formally declared in February 1948, the BSP took the lead in organising a boycott of all celebrations related to the granting of independence. The LSSP stayed away from the ceremony that was organised to express jubilation over the declaration of independence, but attended the opening of the new parliament of independent Ceylon. The Bolsheviks not only boycotted all the ceremonies, but also organised a well-attended rally immediately following the massive state celebrations to protest against what they called 'fake independence'. These activities of the Bolsheviks were severely criticised by the more moderate LSSP. The BSP's demonstrations against the granting of independence were denounced as 'exhibitionist, ultra-leftist and adventurist' actions.[22] The LSSP considered the period was one when the 'masses were faced with reaction', and when 'the class issues have temporarily got blurred'. This situation was thought to have arisen because of the failure of the strikes, the rise of 'ultra-nationalist' sentiments with the transfer of power, and the 'jingoism' of the bourgeoisie. In view of these circumstances, the LSSP advised that revolutionary parties should lie low and watch the situation calmly, rather than indulge in 'cheap adventurist and snobbish exhibitionism'.[23] These criticisms were, of course, answered with counter-accusations and insinuations made with equal venom by the Bolsheviks.[24] The different positions taken on these

19. Colvin de Silva, 'Independence', *Fight*, 21 November 1947.
20. *Ceylon Daily News*, 18 November 1947.
21. For the vote on the 'Independence' motion, see House of Representatives of Ceylon, *Debates*, Volume 1, 1947, column 739. The Communist Party also voted against the motion. The LSSP condemned the BSP's negative vote as 'traitorous' (*Times of Ceylon*, 10 December 1947). The BSP denounced the LSSP's passive stand as a sign of its demoralisation and as reflecting its petit-bourgeois standards (see Doric de Sousa's statement, *Times of Ceylon*, 17 February 1948).
22. Letter from NM Perera, *Times of Ceylon*, 13 February 1948.
23. Op cit.
24. See Doric de Sousa's statement for the BSP in the *Times of Ceylon*, 17 February 1948.

crucial issues were to weaken any prospects of an early unification between the two Samasamajist parties. In fact, during this period the militant Bolsheviks were closer to the Communist Party, which had now assumed a very radical position, than to their sister party the LSSP, and the squabbles between the Samasamajists continued. The lack of unity amongst the Samasamajists prevented the leader of the LSSP group getting the post of the Leader of the Opposition in parliament, and the two groups were to clash very badly in the electoral arena on several occasions.[25]

Unification

It was unanimously agreed that these quarrels between the Samasamajist parties were retrogressive in their effect on the morale of the whole Trotskyist movement in the country. It also gave a golden opportunity to the Communist Party to consolidate its own organisation and influence, undermining those of the quarrelling comrades.[26] Furthermore, the period following the elections witnessed a rapid strengthening of what was an almost unchallenged government. It was able to pass several discriminatory pieces of legislation, such as the Indian and Pakistani Citizenship Act and the Public Security Act of 1947. In this situation the Samasamajists felt it essential to unite their two organisations, or at least to cooperate on major issues, if they were to make any impression on the policy of the government and thereby to enhance their position in the country. Consequently, almost continual attempts were made to establish some degree of unity between the Samasamajists.

The first major attempt at unification came in mid-1946 on the initiative of the Bolsheviks. After some preliminary talks, a unified conference of all the Samasamajists was held at Gangodawila, at which the superiority of the LSSP came to be accepted by the Bolsheviks. However, the unity rested on the condition that an independent commission should be appointed to inquire into the allegation made by Philip Gunawardena, a leader of the LSSP, against a leading member of the Bolshevik Samasamaja section, and that the

25. Contesting the by-election at Gampaha in July 1949, the two fraternal parties clashed with each other despite some attempts at preventing a split left vote. Election competition here even led to physical clashes between members of the two groups. The other notable clash occurred in contesting a town council by-election in Dehivela-Mount Lavinia, where two leading members of the two parties competed with each other.

26. The Communist Party did its best to divide the Samasamajist forces. On several occasions it allied with the Bolsheviks and worked against the LSSP, and this association was to become a bone of contention between the LSSP and the Bolsheviks.

decision of the commission should be final.[27] During this period of unity, the Samasamajists were able to agree on a common list of candidates for the impending elections, but this unity was not to last long. The commission[28] found Philip Gunawardena guilty of making the said allegation, and decreed that he should make a public apology to Doric de Sousa. Philip Gunawardena, known for his independent ways, refused to make any public apology to a person who was almost unknown outside a small circle of Samasamajists. However, he was willing to make an apology in front of the party. The dispute over this eventually disrupted the unity that had lasted almost three months. There were no moves in this direction during the whole of 1947. Attempts were made in early 1948 to hold joint May Day rallies by the two groups of Samasamajists, but these had little success. After these setbacks, the Bolsheviks called the LSSP and the Communist Party for a conference primarily aimed at avoiding clashes at elections. The LSSP refused to attend on the grounds of its disagreement on the methods proposed to avoid clashes. It also expressed misgivings about the usefulness of such conferences in terms of attaining unity. No further attempts were made by either group to establish unity until 1949.

The annual conference of the LSSP held at the beginning of 1949 made a call for unity with the Bolsheviks. However, the stand on the establishment of unity taken by the LSSP, both at the conference and for some time afterwards, was not at all inviting. Its call was more for a total surrender by the BSP, rather than for negotiations to establish unity. Referring to the case of the Indian remnants of the old BLPI joining the Socialist Party of India after dissolving their own organisation, the LSSP conference called upon the Ceylonese Bolsheviks to join the LSSP in the same manner.[29] The LSSP considered that there was no need for negotiations, except to make arrangements to allow the individual members of the BSP to join the LSSP. In a letter that embodied the spirit of the conference resolution on unity, the BSP was informed of this position.[30] The letter demanded that before any discussions could take place, the BSP should terminate its associations with the 'Stalinists'. In a reply to a proposal by the BSP that called

27. At one of the first rallies the LSSP held after the war, Philip Gunawardena alleged that Doric de Sousa was a police spy, and this was repeated several times by Gunawardena, and was later taken up by his supporters.
28. Kamalesh Bannerjee, a Trotskyist from Calcutta who worked with the Samasamajists, was appointed as the one-man commission.
29. The conference called on all those who 'split away from the party and are now known as Bolsheviks to enter the party immediately just as much as the Bolsheviks of India in pursuance of the line advocated by the LSSP entered the Socialist Party of India' (*Times of Ceylon*, 7 January 1949).
30. *Times of Ceylon*, 9 February 1949.

for full negotiations on the basis of a comprehensive plan, the LSSP reiterated the same position.[31]

Though keen to unite forces with the much larger LSSP, the Bolsheviks were not prepared to give themselves over to the LSSP bound hand and foot. They wanted a change in the structure and the constitution of the LSSP before they would join it. They also wanted to have positions of power for their own leaders in a future united Samasamaja party. And they denounced the LSSP's demand for the dissolution of their party as being hostile in intent. Instead of the absorption of one party by the other, the Bolsheviks demanded the fusion of the two parties on the basis of mutual negotiations.[32] For several months this impasse continued, and the two parties failed even to come close enough to hold a joint May Day rally.

However, by the end of the year a breakthrough appeared when the second-rank leadership of the LSSP took the initiative into their own hands. It was widely known that the clash of personalities of the two leaderships was a major obstacle for the conduct of successful negotiations. This factor was apparently taken into account by the second-rankers, who dominated the conference held in January 1950. They initiated a resolution calling for negotiations to be resumed immediately with the BSP with a view to forming a united Samasamaja party. The resolution further required that these negotiations should be conducted by a new set of negotiators; it also proposed that the two most important leaders, Philip Gunawardena and NM Perera, whose personal differences with the leaders of the BSP were thought to have hindered the arrival of any agreement in the past, be kept out of the unity talks.[33] The general membership was so enthusiastic about breaking the deadlock that the second-rankers' resolution succeeded, notwithstanding the opposition of the two important party leaders. Philip Gunawardena, who was largely responsible by his intransigence for the stalemate that existed between the two parties, was replaced as Secretary by one of the younger members, TB Subasinghe. Now in the hands of a new team of negotiators, DF Hettiarachchy, Robert Gunawardena and TB Subasinghe, whose perspective was not prejudiced by personal considerations, the unity talks progressed very rapidly. In January itself the two parties cooperated in sponsoring joint candidates for the high offices in the Co-

31. *Times of Ceylon*, 24 February 1949.
32. Letter from Leslie Goonewardene, Secretary of the BSP, to Philip Gunawardena, Secretary of the LSSP, *Times of Ceylon*, 21 February 1949.
33. Statement by TB Subasinghe, Secretary of the LSSP, *Times of Ceylon*, 2 June 1950.

lombo Municipal Council.[34] This cooperation was extended to cover several by-elections of the Municipal Council that were due to be held shortly. By the end of the month, the negotiators of the two parties were able to announce some concrete developments on the road to establishing a unified Samasamaja party. They announced the setting up of joint LSSP-BSP councils at all levels of organisation and operations.

Another outcome of the negotiations was the establishment of a period of trial unity as a means of testing the ability of the two parties to arrive at full unity. This time the trial unity worked, and after a period of close cooperation the final scene of this long drawn out affair of Samasamaja unity, the establishment of a single united party, came in June 1950. The successful achievement of this, however, was to cost the party an important member and a segment of the LSSP's membership.

As has been already mentioned, Philip Gunawardena was not very enthusiastic about unity with the Bolsheviks. Ostensibly, his position was that the return of the dissident Samasamajists of the BSP to the LSSP was desirable, but there was no need for any constitutional or structural changes in the latter organisation in order to facilitate such a return.[35] He always refused to recognise the BSP as a separate Samasamaja party, and saw the BSP merely as a group of individuals without a base of support in the country or in the trade union movement. The unification arrangements adopted by the party — with a big majority — were seen as being tantamount to a 'dissolution of the revolutionary LSSP', and he refused to support it.[36] However, it is widely held that his objections were mainly due to personal considerations. Because of Philip Gunawardena's objections, there was much interest in the final conference of the LSSP, which was to decide finally the fusion of the two Trotskyist parties.

After reviewing the progress made since the previous conference in January, this conference, held on 14 May 1950, decided by an overwhelming majority to unite with the Bolsheviks with immediate effect. Not unexpectedly, Philip Gunawardena objected to the whole plan. In addition to alleging that the new set-up was incompatible with preserving continuity with the LSSP of 1935, Philip Gunawardena walked out of the conference, and, as it happened, out of the party as well, followed by his supporters, thus creating a minor

34. An independent left winger and an LSSPer were sponsored for mayor and deputy mayor respectively.
35. Statement after leaving the LSSP, *Ceylon Daily News*, 15 May 1950.
36. The final arrangement was for the LSSP and the BSP to fuse to form a new LSSP distinct from either organisation. It would be a new organisation with a new constitution.

split amongst the Samasamajists whilst a major one was being healed.[37]

Once the LSSP's conference approved the fusion of the two Trotskyist parties, the actual formation of a single party was to follow immediately.

A joint 'unification conference' of the members of the LSSP and BSP was called for 3 June 1950, and this conference was to mark the beginning of the LSSP that existed until 1964. This LSSP came to be known as the Nava (New) LSSP, a name given by Philip Gunawardena and publicised by the press: this tag was widely used in describing the LSSP right up to the disappearance of Philip Gunawardena's VLSSP in 1959. The unification conference adopted a new programme[38] and a new party constitution. It also elected a Central Committee and a Secretary for the party. In the new set-up the important posts were filled by the key leaders of the two parties.[39]

The unification gave a new fillip to the whole Samasamaja movement, and it was in a spirit of great enthusiasm that the united LSSP entered the decade that began in 1950.

37. A total of 42 members, including two members of Parliament and the deputy mayor of Colombo, left the conference with Philip Gunawardena. He went on to form another party, the Viplavakari (Revolutionary) LSSP. The founding conference of the VLSSP was held in early June 1950, and was attended by about 75 former LSSP members and candidates, and a new committee was also elected. Although started with the intention of competing for the broader Samasamaja following, Philip Gunawardena's new party found difficulty in establishing itself as a firm left wing party. Within a year it had allied itself with the Communist Party to form a united front, and there was very close cooperation with the Communists for about four years before the front broke down. After that the VLSSP cooperated very briefly with the LSSP in mid-1955, only to part company swiftly to join SWRD Bandaranaike's SLFP to form the MEP. After the collapse of the MEP in 1959, Philip Gunawardena went before the electorate as the 'new' MEP with the symbols of the old party. Since he left the LSSP he has never pretended to be a Trotskyist, and whilst he was associated with the Communist Party he denounced Trotskyism as a 'dead' ideology (*Times of Ceylon*, 31 October 1953).
38. *Programme of Action, Programme and Resolutions of the Unity Conference*, LSSP, Colombo, 1950.
39. Leslie Goonewardene, Secretary of the BSP, was elected Secretary of the new party. The two other leaders of this section, Colvin R de Silva and William Silva, were elected Deputy Leader and Chief Whip respectively. NM Perera, the leader of the old LSSP after the departure of Philip Gunawardena, was elected the leader of the Samasamajist parliamentary group; this made it easy for him to be elected Leader of the Opposition in Parliament.

Philip Gunawardena
The Bolshevik-Leninist Party of India
A Sectarian Dead-End

' A LIEN TO sectarian self-immersion, the revolutionary worker-Marxists must actively participate in the work of the trade unions, educational societies, the Congress Socialist Party and, in general, all mass organisations. Everywhere they remain as the extreme left wing; everywhere they set the example of courage in action; everywhere in a patient and comradely manner they explain their programme to the workers, peasants and revolutionary intellectuals.' (The concluding paragraph of Leon Trotsky's 'Open Letter to the Workers of India', 25 July 1939)

This sound and timely advice was given to the revolutionaries of India by Comrade Trotsky. But they heeded not his advice. The Trotskyists of India were determined to set up as quickly as possible their political party, seek affiliation to the Fourth International, publish the programme of the party, and flatter themselves that a party had come into existence.

The Bolshevik-Leninist Party of India was launched with insufficient preparation by immature and unreliable political elements in May 1942. Its godfathers were Formalism, Bureaucratism and Sectarianism. From its birth this trinity has held the party in their grip and prevented its healthy growth. The leaders of the Bolshevik-Leninist Party of India believed that the publication of the party programme and affiliation to the Fourth International would make all revolutionaries leave their parties and groups to join the new proletarian revolutionary party, and that the toiling masses would rally under the banner of the new party. Trotskyists in India were no more than romantics at the time. It is a pity that the more experienced leaders of the LSSP, who took the initiative in launching the party, advised a propagandist group to believe and act as if it were a fully-fledged party. This initial blunder has made the Bolshevik-Leninist Party of India a cripple from birth...

Had Trotskyists, Fourth Internationalists, Bolshevik-Leninists followed the advice of the founder of the Fourth International, Comrade Trotsky, today Trotskyism, the Fourth International movement, would not be a tiny sect isolated from the mass revolutionary movement of the toilers in India. The Trotskyists of India did not follow Trotsky's advice and enter the Congress Socialist Party and other mass organisations. Had they joined the CSP and other mass organisations, then during the 1942-43 struggle we could have popularised the principles and programme of Trotskyism, and won to the banner of the Fourth International all genuine revolutionaries in the CSP and other mass organisations. We could have participated along with the Congress Socialists in the mass activities of that struggle. The Congress Socialist Party gained in influence as a result of its participation and leadership of mass actions. The Trotskyists of India would have gained invaluable experience and connections among revolutionaries, and won their trust and confidence... That opportunity we missed in 1942.

Colvin R de Silva and Leslie Goonewardene

A Statement

WE WOULD be obliged if you will publish this letter, as we owe it to the party to which we belong to make clear to the public our position in regard to the split-away of Messrs NM Perera and Philip Gunawardena, together with a small group of the Lanka Sama Samaja Party, Ceylon Unit of the Bolshevik-Leninist Party of India, Section of the Fourth International.

We wish to make it clear that we unhesitatingly stand on the side of the party, and within it, as opposed to this group which has split, and which, moreover, is falsely claiming to be the Lanka Sama Samaja Party.

It is our opinion that if Messrs NM Perera and Philip Gunawardena had any differences, real or imaginary, it was their duty to raise the question within the party, and loyally abide by its verdict. This anyhow is the only course open to serious-minded Bolsheviks. For otherwise it is impossible to build the party which is the indispensable instrument of the working class in the revolution.

Further, even if Messrs NM Perera and Philip Gunawardena, for reasons best known to themselves, had decided to reject this course and split away, none can deny that it was still their duty to make

clear to the public that they were now a distinct and separate grouping which was working independently of the LSSP and opposed to it.

Resolution Adopted by the Central Committee of the Bolshevik-Leninist Party of India

WE HAVE stated that Comrades Philip Gunawardena and NM
Perera have split away from the party for no discernible principled reasons. But reasons there are. These relate to differences on
the question of party organisation, and on the concept of the party
itself. At the end of 1943 these two comrades wrote a brochure in jail
in India entitled *The Indian Struggle: The Next Phase*, which was released by them for circulation both within and outside the party.

The Provisional Central Committee of the party was compelled in
a resolution in July 1944 sharply to criticise in detail the ideas set
forth in this brochure. Both the brochure and the criticism have been
freely circulated in the party. The Provisional Central Committee's
criticism demonstrated that the proposals contained in the brochure,
if adopted, must lead to the creation of a loose, petit-bourgeois party
in contradistinction to a well-knit disciplined party integrated with
the proletariat. In other words, from the end of 1943 these comrades
displayed a tendency to reject the Bolshevik, proletarian conception
of the party in favour of a loose, petit-bourgeois one. It is worthy of
note that, despite the fact that the Provisional Central Committee's
criticism of their brochure was conveyed to them long ago, these
comrades have neither made any attempt to reply to the criticism,
nor clearly repudiated the positions they had taken...

After their recent release from detention in Ceylon, they joined in
a move for creating what they called a 'Left Front', in cooperation
with several petit-bourgeois opportunist politicians... The claim of
Comrades Philip Gunawardena and NM Perera and their followers to function in the name of the Lanka Sama Samaja Party is a
false claim which we repudiate... In the face of this situation it remains for us to formalise the split, and thus aid in clarifying the position before the masses. Accordingly we expel Comrades Philip
Gunawardena and NM Perera from the party, and leave the question
of disciplinary action against those of their followers who may be

members of the party in the hands of the Regional Committee of the Ceylon Unit.

Philip Gunawardena and NM Perera

A Statement

A LETTER under the names of Mr Leslie Goonewardene and Dr Colvin R de Silva appeared in your issue of the 18th. In fairness to us, therefore, please spare us a little space for this reply.

We are surprised at the indecent haste with which Mr Leslie Goonewardene and Dr Colvin R de Silva have rushed to the press to denounce us and what they believe to be our politics. That we followed a false political line, that we are in favour of a loose organisation of the party, that we attempted to form a 'Left Front' are only figments of their imagination, an imagination, no doubt, warped under the strenuous conditions of underground life. Mr Leslie Goonewardene and Dr Colvin R de Silva have demonstrated that political exiles feed on gossip and listen to the poisonous tongue of slander of disrupters and saboteurs of the revolutionary movement.

What exactly is their charge against us? We are accused of 'splitting away from the Lanka Sama Samaja Party with a small group of our followers', and of 'falsely claiming to be the LSSP'. What precisely are the facts? It was known to everyone interested in the LSSP, including Mr Leslie Goonewardene and Dr Colvin R de Silva, that since 1942 the LSSP had ceased to exist as an organised party. The Sama Samaja movement, however, continued to exist and develop. The party was split into scattered groups, which carried on an internecine war.

A small group of university assistant lecturers and students, calling themselves the party centre, attempted to pose as the mentors and practical leaders of the Sama Samaja Party. This faction endeavoured systematically to transform the party from a living and growing entity, with its roots deeply based in the masses, into a narrow conspiratorial sect entirely cut off from the masses. Indeed this dangerous position had already arisen under the leadership of their faction.

In October 1942 Dr Colvin R de Silva characterised this faction in the following terms:

'Falsifying party history to support their literary thesis, this faction slanders the party with the utterly false allegation that it has not yet rid itself completely of all the incubus of the old LSSP. Anxious to cover up the unprincipled nature of their intrigues and manoeuvres, they seek to impose on those who criticise them the odium of a false political line, which their critics neither believe in, express, nor manifest. Posing as the custodians of the party's future, which they persuade themselves depends on their own factional dominance, they have betrayed every healthy tradition of the party, brought it to the verge of ruin, and endangered its very continuance as the vanguard of the revolutionary proletariat.

'We denounce this faction, its methods and outlook and the reactionary tendencies which it represents. We declare that the party cannot be restored to health, unity and effectiveness unless this faction is smashed, the tendencies it represents uprooted, and the control it has acquired snatched away from it. Only thus can the party be preserved from the extinction with which it is otherwise threatened, and only thus can the party once more return to that revolutionary purpose and work, and freedom from personal squabbles, which enabled it in the past to win the unchallenged leadership of the toiling masses of Ceylon.' (*Platform of the Workers Opposition*, October 1942, signed by Dr Colvin R de Silva, Comrades Philip Gunawardena, NM Perera and six other comrades)

Since 1942 the situation in the party deteriorated further. When we came out of prison in June this year, we found the rank and file membership of the party hostile to this so-called centre of parlour Bolsheviks. Due to the abject neglect into which party work had fallen, the organised section of the party had no trade union following; the politically advanced workers within the party had begun to drift away from this so-called centre and organise on their own.

This was the situation in the LSSP which we had to face. We felt it was our revolutionary duty to knit together the shredded bits of the party and weld them into an organisation with 'health, unity and effectiveness'. For the accomplishment of this task we sought the cooperation of even the bureaucratic clique — the parlour Bolsheviks. They refused to negotiate with us except on their own terms. We visited party groups and even individuals for the purpose of discussing with them the situation within the party and the urgent question of party unity. Finally, when we were assured of the support of the vast majority of the 1942 membership of the party, we took the only step open to serious Sama Samajists.

Perhaps legalistic minds such as Dr Colvin R de Silva's and worshippers of formalism such as Mr Leslie Goonewardene, in their anxiety to prove that they are seriously-minded Bolsheviks, would have hesitated to take the bold and constitutionally somewhat unorthodox step that we have taken of appealing to the rank and file membership of the party to set up the governing organs of the party by smashing the bureaucratic faction, by uprooting the tendencies which it represented, and by snatching away from it the control it had acquired over the party machine. Of course, Dr Colvin R de Silva conveniently forgets that he gave precisely this advice to the rank and file membership of the party. 'For the attainment of these objectives', he stated, 'two preliminary measures are essential. These are the overthrow of the reactionary rôle of the 13, and the democratic election of a new RC and other directing organs which will command the confidence of the party.'

Accordingly in August 1945 a conference of delegates from groups representing the 1942 membership of the party met and elected the directing organs of the party. Since that date the LSSP has functioned in accordance with the constitution and programme adopted by the 1941 conference of the party. After a lapse of 36 months, since 7 September 1945 the party organ in Sinhalese, the *Sama Samajaya*, has come out regularly every week. Soon party organs in English, Tamil and Malayali will be published. 'The proof of the pudding is in the eating', said our teacher Engels, once. This is our answer to the charge that we have 'split away from the LSSP with a small group of followers'.

Well! Today the party commands the active allegiance of the vast majority of the membership of the LSSP. We are not worried about the bureaucratic clique, the parlour Bolsheviks. They can spin their sterile theories in the boudoirs and salons of Cinnamon Gardens and Bambalapitiya. These Bohemians will never command the confidence of the working class — the toiling masses generally. That is why they have sought to discredit Mr Leslie Goonewardene and Dr Colvin R de Silva by dragging their names to bolster up their tottering cause in this country. We extend our sympathies to our erstwhile comrades in the revolutionary movement. After all, have they not been away from the masses of the island for three to four long years? They cannot distinguish facts from fiction.

We are not 'a separate and distinct grouping which is working independently of the LSSP and opposed to it'. The party with which we are associated is the genuine Lanka Sama Samaja Party. It will continue the revolutionary tradition of the LSSP. Mr Leslie Goonewardene and Dr Colvin R de Silva are endeavouring to support a coterie of disrupters and saboteurs of the LSSP. 'The party, the indispensable instrument of the working class in the revolution' cannot be built in a vacuum. We have built and are continuing to strengthen the

LSSP, the party of the revolutionary proletariat among the toiling masses of Ceylon.

The BLPI and the Petit-Bourgeois Grouping Calling Themselves Samasamajists

WE COME before the public and the working class with a new paper, and a new (or partly new) name. Our party itself, however, is not a new one, but is the same Lanka Sama Samaja Party that in 1942 became a unit of the Bolshevik-Leninist Party of India. The resolution of the Central Committee makes this clear beyond doubt. We seek here to supplement the material of that resolution on some important points, including: firstly, especially the nature of the changes which have taken place in the LSSP during its illegal existence in the war years; secondly, the character of the split-away grouping calling themselves 'Samasamajists'; and thirdly, the reasons why it is now necessary for the party unit in Ceylon to drop the name LSSP and use only the title of BLPI (Ceylon Unit).

The CC resolution describes the LSSP at its inception in 1935 as a 'loose mass party with a vague petit-bourgeois programme'. Let us explain this more fully. Parties are the instruments of social classes, or of significant sections of these, in the political arena. Those who recognise the class struggle as the main motive force of politics will understand that no party can develop without rapidly acquiring a more or less distinct class character, however it may seek to disguise this. The character of a party cannot be judged from its own claims, but must be inferred among other things from: (a) its programme, (b) its form of organisation and its membership, (c) the sources of its broad mass support, and (d) its policies, and the class interests served by these.

The LSSP at its inception had a vague petit-bourgeois programme. Its fundamental aims were 'independence and Socialism'. This seems very well. But the programme did not breathe the spirit of internationalism which characterises proletarian documents of this kind. It was silent regarding Stalinism. It did not pose the dictatorship of the proletariat as its fundamental aim, only the guarantee of 'independence and Socialism'. It failed to recognise that the revolutionary struggle in Ceylon is inextricably bound up with the Indian revolution in all its stages. It did not make clear that no isolated 'national' revolution faced Ceylon, and that the revolutionary struggle in Ceylon will bear a provincial character in relation to the Indian revolution as a whole. Finally, it did not base itself on the conception of Permanent Revolution, on the central thesis that the working class alone can lead the toiling masses of the colonies to 'independence and Socialism'.

Membership of the LSSP was open to all who subscribed to this vague programme and paid a small subscription. The form of organisation of the LSSP did not bear the smallest resemblance to that of a proletarian (Bolshevik) party. The complexion of its membership was overwhelmingly petit-bourgeois.

The main mass support of the party came from the same petit-bourgeois source. This class gave its decisive support to most of the 'immediate demands' included in the programme. Moreover, they read the party's newspapers in the greatest numbers, they attended its meetings and supported its day-to-day policies. This was not accidental, since the policies of the party, and many of its activities, were directed to advance the interests of the petit-bourgeoisie. This applies to a great deal of the work done by the Samasamajist members in the [State] Council, to the agitation for the abolition of the headman system, for free seed paddy, free meals for school children, for lowering taxation of the peasantry, etc. The pressure and support of the petit-bourgeoisie were sufficient to swing the policy of the LSSP on the question of immigrant labour away from an internationalist and proletarian position.

In spite of the influence of the petit-bourgeoisie on the LSSP, a section of the party developed from the beginning rapidly in the direction of proletarian politics. They aimed at the transformation of the LSSP into a proletarian party, integrated with this class, organised on classic Bolshevik lines, and fighting for clear, revolutionary objectives.

This policy was in the end successful, but called for many far-reaching changes in the LSSP. The LSSP linked itself with the Fourth International, and expelled from its ranks those who owed allegiance to Stalinism. It adopted in 1941 a more realistic (though still limited) programme. It progressively reorganised its membership along proper lines, and threw off many passengers and fellow travellers from the petit-bourgeoisie. (Many of these are now, in a less difficult period, coming into politics again and are making a bee-line for the Norris Road Samasamajists.) Finally, recognising that no independent 'national' revolutionary perspectives faced Ceylon, the LSSP set to work to help in the building of a single all-India party, which is the indispensable condition of victory in the coming revolution. The party was set up in 1942, and the LSSP became a constituent unit of the BLPI.

The CC resolution stresses that to all these developments, which led to the formation of the BLPI and the merger therein of the LSSP, NM Perera and DP Gunawardena were parties. But they now appear to have decided to retrace all their steps, and put themselves at the head of all the rubbish left in the wake of the LSSP as it developed into a proletarian organisation. This is the meaning of their attempt to 'reconstruct' an LSSP with all the fellow travellers left behind, and a few new ones like Mr Dahanayake. Their deliberate suppression of the part they themselves played in the formation of the BLPI in 1942, and their disloyal attack on the BLPI (Ceylon Unit) as an 'Indian' party, proves the same thing. The episode of the 'Left Front' which was nothing more, in programme and organisation, than the LSSP of 1935 *without its most genuine elements* confirms this further. Finally, their utilisation of the favourite weapons of the Stalinists' armoury, lies and slanders, accusations of police espionage, etc, made against their political opponents, and their utilisation of pure thuggery as an instrument of political argument (at the Town Hall on Thursday, 25 October, with disastrous results) prove the wide gulf that already separates them from proletarian politics, and the strides they have made towards petit-bourgeois opportunism.

The CC resolution makes it amply clear that the title of LSSP belongs to the Ceylon Unit of the BLPI, and to this alone. The adventurers surrounding NM Perera have no shred of right to it. Nevertheless, the Ceylon Unit of the BLPI has decided to cease to use this name of 'LSSP' for the following reasons.

1. The breakaway grouping, plus all their new-found allies and old followers, who are together in full career down the Gadarene slope that leads to petit-bourgeois politics, are using the name LSSP.

2. They use this name with more plausibility, because the broad masses are relatively ignorant of the developments in the party recounted above, since they took place under conditions of illegality. The petit-bourgeois passengers of the LSSP especially are quite ready now to take up the thread of politics which they left off when it grew dangerous in 1939.

3. In some ways, the 'Samasamajists' led by NM Perera represent more closely than the party itself the policies the LSSP stood for at its inception.

4. It is necessary to make it clear to the workers and broad masses that the LSSP of yesterday is a constituent unit of the BLPI, sec-

tion of the Fourth International. This is not the result of mere good fellowship with Indian revolutionaries, but the corollary of our recognition of the provincial character of the revolutionary struggle in Ceylon. The name LSSP may misleadingly suggest a 'national-revolutionary' grouping, such as the 'Samasamajists' under Perera will possibly turn out to be.

5. It is intolerably confusing for the working class and the public that there should be two parties coming forward with distinct policies, and still more different methods of action, while using the same name. In the recent September strikes, for instance, to have used the same name on our leaflets, etc, as the breakaway group did would have made us, in the eyes of many, responsible for all the clowning they did in that situation.

For these reasons, as stated, the party in Ceylon will only use the title BLPI (Ceylon Unit).

It is not to be expected, of course, that the full implications of all the changes which have taken place in the party since 1939 will be clear from foregoing. Future issues of this paper will be devoted to making these clearer, as well as making more plain the differences of policy and organisation that separate the party from the 'Samasamajists'.

Colvin R de Silva

Whither the New Samasamaja Party?

ONE FEATURE of unprincipled politics is utterly irresponsible attacks upon individuals. At a public meeting Philip Gunawardena, the principal leader of the new Samasamaja Party, has twice accused Doric de Souza of being a police spy. This accusation is an utter falsehood, an absolute lie. The devotion that comrade Doric de Souza has shown and the service he has rendered to the working class revolutionary movement in India and Ceylon is an adequate reply to such a false accusation.

Another despicable example should be cited, because the comrades against whom charges have been made, Hector Abeyawardena and Selina Perera, are not in Ceylon. It is not necessary to mention the devotion they have shown and the service they have rendered to the revolutionary working class movement in India and Ceylon. All this the members of the new Samasamaja Party know as we do.

About six weeks back, two emissaries carried a lengthy document from a person who called himself the Secretary of the new Samasamaja Party to comrades Hector and Selina. This document contained the conclusions of the new Samasamaja Party relating to the breakaway. Hector and Selina promptly addressed a letter to the *Samasamajaya* (the Sinhala newspaper of the new Samasamaja Party) as a reply to this document. In that letter the two comrades not only completely rejected the statements of the new Lanka Samasamaja Party, but also endorsed the decisions made by the Central Committee of the Bolshevik Leninist Party to protect the party from the breakaway group of Philip Gunawardena and NM Perera. I am absolutely certain of these facts, since comrades Hector and Selina as disciplined comrades handed all documents to the Secretary of our Central Committee.

The leaders of the new Samasamaja Party were flabbergasted because of this reply. They could not publish the letter, as by that means they would have received a political blow like a thunderbolt. On the other hand, they could not suppress the letter, since they knew that we had a copy of the letter. After contemplating for several weeks, the editor of the *Samasamajaya* has come forward to resolve this question, which was a puzzle to him, in a most disgraceful manner.

He said that he was not publishing the letter because by doing so the secrets of their organisation would be revealed, and that Hector and Selina were not aware of the facts, and had been misled. But he dishonestly concealed the fact that the letter was a reply to the new Samasamaja Party's account of the breakaway contained in the document addressed to Hector and Selina. He knew that if he did so he would have been the subject of ridicule. Therefore they accused comrades Hector and Selina, of whom they spoke earlier as very valuable comrades, of not knowing even the ABC of secret work.

Lenin has reminded us in a brilliant way that telling the truth to the working class is a principal characteristic of a revolutionary working class party. Therefore leaving others to lie, we will use the truth to reply.

When the leaders of the new Samasamaja Party broke away from our party a few months back, they did not have an adequate reason or principle for so doing. That they did not have an adequate reason or principle to break away is proved by their own actions; namely, that they have to hide from the masses the fact that they broke away, and without mentioning one word about it, they appear as the Lanka

Sama Samaja Party. Our Central Committee has unmasked them, and revealed their dishonesty. Thereby, it was proved that the responsibility of breaking away lay with those who were guilty of breaking away.

With that ended the attempt to show that the new Samasamaja Party was the old Lanka Sama Samaja Party. The masses understood. The breakaway group is a new party that has stolen an old name. All attempts to suppress this fact will be futile.

It serves no purpose to attempt to prove by platform speeches, by issuing statements and by arguments that the new Samasamaja Party is nothing other than the old Lanka Sama Samaja Party; moreover it's a joke to state that that party is the Ceylon Unit of our Bolshevik Leninist Party. It is an utter falsehood and deliberate lie to say that the new Samasamaja Party is the old Lanka Sama Samaja Party. They have come forward to say these things knowing full well that they are false. This is substantiated by their own actions. If not, when they started their newspaper, why did they describe their party as Fourth Internationalist? They did so, although they do not honestly say so now, because they were fully aware that when they left the Bolshevik Leninist Party, by that very step they left the Indian section of the Fourth International, and therefore left the Fourth International itself. They used the words 'Fourth International' as they were convinced that consequent to their setting up a separate organisation opposed to the Bolshevik Leninist Party, they did not have any right whatsoever to call themselves the Ceylon Unit of the Bolshevik Leninist Party. Although they dishonestly attempt to conceal this fact, they still know what they knew then.

The Bolshevik Leninist Party is not merely a supporting party of the Fourth International. It is a part of the international body. Therefore the Ceylon Unit of the Bolshevik Leninist Party is a part of the Fourth International. Those who set forth to be Fourth Internationalist should know that by that means they set themselves apart from the Bolshevik Leninist Party.

They knew. Even now they know. They have indulged in some new thinking, and they lie shamelessly by declaring that they did not set themselves apart from the Bolshevik Leninist Party and that they are the Ceylon Unit. What babes do they intend to mislead by such lies? They should be branded as atrocious liars.

Finally, one thing. It is essential to note that the new Samasamaja Party is not merely composed of the breakaway group from the Bolshevik Leninist Party. Whilst the breakaway group is in the leadership of the new party, it should be remembered that people of diverse political shades have entered the new party. It can be seen that the leadership is already a prey to the pressure of these elements with diverse political characteristics. The leadership is unable to show that there are principled differences between themselves and the Bolshevik Leninists. The result of this will be that the followers will show the leaders what differences they should create with the Bolshevik Leninist Party. The new Samasamaja Party already shows that this is happening. We have already revealed some of these differences, and we shall reveal more in the future.

However, we must now remind ourselves of something which the new Samasamaja Party declares, albeit for a different purpose — that within Ceylon there is no room for two working class parties. We agree. We state further: the apparent Menshevik organisational principles that the new Samasamaja Party is following, the opportunist political activities, and the adventurism displayed in trade union work, all prove that there is no room within Ceylon for two working class revolutionary parties, namely two Bolshevik parties. When these features develop further under the pressure of non-proletarian hostile classes, this will prove that this party is not only a new party, but is a tendency which will clash with the proletarian revolutionary movement operating within the working class. If the working class revolutionaries who are still in the new Samasamaja Party wish to prevent this happening, they should admit their errors, and either disband their organisation, or leave it and return to the revolutionary forces of the Fourth International. This means joining the Ceylon Unit of the Bolshevik Leninist Party, which is a section of the Fourth International. There is no other road for honest revolutionaries.

VIII: The Dispute Over Independence (1948)

The two Trotskyist parties were not only in disagreement over relations with the movement in India, but also over the attitude to be adopted to the type of independence granted to the island in the Soulbury Constitution of 1947. Our first document, *Independence, Real or Fake?*, by Colvin R de Silva (Manifesto of the BLPI, 4 February 1948), represents the views of the Fourth International group (see 'Quelle indépendence pour Ceylan?', *Quatrième Internationale*, Volume 6, nos 1-2, January-February 1948, pp53-4), whereas the statement issued by NM Perera to *The Times of Ceylon* (13 February 1948) gives the very different views of the Samasamajists. The sharpness of this debate is emphasised in our final document, SB Dissanayake's 'Letter from Ceylon', which is taken from the American *Fourth International* (Volume 9, no 5, July 1948, pp158-9).

Further information on the differences between the two groups can be found in the *Manifesto of the Lanka Sama Samaja Party* ('Publication no 1', duplicated pamphlet), and the extracts from the political resolution adopted by the national conference of the Bolshevik Samasamajists published in *Quatrième Internationale* ('Après l'"Independence" des Indes', Volume 6, nos 8-9, August-September 1948, pp32-3).

Colvin R de Silva

Independence Real Or Fake?

Not *Fake* Independence Under the British Flag, but Real Independence *Outside* the British Empire

THE FOURTH of February is being ushered in with Magul Bera.[1] The festivities to follow will conclude with a fireworks display. In the interval the Governor will have become a Governor-General, a Duke will have come and gone, several lakhs of our money will have

1. A Sinhalese festival, a wedding feast.

been frittered away, and Ceylon will have achieved 'fully responsible status within the British Commonwealth of Nations'. Will there be anything for the masses of this country to hail in it all?

The answer of the BLPI to the above question is a clear and unequivocal '*No!*' There is nothing for the masses to enthuse over in the 'new status' which the Senanayake-Monck-Mason Moore[2] combination has brought us. There is nothing for the people to 'rejoice' about in the 'independence' they proclaim. For the new status of their obtaining is not only *not* independence but also actually *a refashioning of the chains of Ceylon's slavery to British imperialism.* It is a *continuation* of British imperialism's *method* of exercising that rule.

Wherein does the continuance of this rule consist? Essentially in the continuance of British imperialism's economic stranglehold over Ceylon. The controllers of our banking system, our plantation system and our system of communications with the outside world are consequently also the controllers of our economy. And whoever controls the economy of a country also controls, in the final analysis, its state. In other words, we would have continued to be subject to British imperialist slavery even if we had been permitted to fly our own flag, sing our own national anthem and declare ourselves (like Burma) an independent state outside the British Empire, *if in the meantime British imperialism's death grip over our economy had been left intact.* The essence of freedom lies in releasing this death-grip.

At the same time, however, it is necessary to stress that the new status consists not only of a continuation of our slavery, but also in a *refashioning* of it. Only fools would contend that there is 'no change' in Ceylon's 'status'. There *is* a change. *But the essence of this change lies not in any passage of Ceylon from colonial status to the status of independence, but in the change-over of British imperialism in Ceylon from methods of direct rule to methods of indirect rule.*

Wherein lies the content of this switch-over? Precisely in this — that *the native exploiting classes of Ceylon have been handed over, well nigh completely, the task of administering British imperialism's interests in Ceylon.* British imperialism has retired into the background, although it has not in any sense abdicated.

It may be asked: what is there to prevent our native exploiters using their power to 'do in' their principals? The answer lies in several factors. There are, first of all, the 'Agreements' which the British government has in fact *imposed* on the Ceylon government. By these, *the military and diplomatic stranglehold of Britain over Ceylon is perpetuated.* There are, again, the *interpenetration of the financial, eco-*

2.   Sir Henry Monck-Mason Moore (1887-1961) was Governor-General of Ceylon during 1944-48.

nomic and political interests of the British and Ceylonese sections of the bourgeoisie *in Ceylon itself*. But over and above them all is the fact that *the general interests of the Ceylon bourgeoisie, especially against the masses of Ceylon, are fundamentally dependent upon the continuance of the link-up, politically, economically and militarily, with British imperialism.* The bourgeoisie of Ceylon have never asked for the independence of Ceylon. They have asked only that they be entrusted with the full responsibility of running Ceylon as part of British imperialism's state and estate. *And now they have got it!*

What are the consequences of the switch-over for the masses of Ceylon and their struggle? In the first place, has the anticipated anti-imperialist struggle ended? To ask the question is to answer it. The struggle to overthrow Britain's economic, military and diplomatic strangle-hold continues, and has to continue. We have, in particular, to fight the slave Agreements which Mr DS Senanayake signed in the name of Ceylon with his own boss, Sir Henry Monck-Mason Moore. The BLPI therefore calls: *On with the struggle against British imperialism! Down with the slave agreements with British imperialism!*

In the development of the struggle against imperialism and the slave Agreements, however, the masses of Ceylon will now come up, *first and foremost*, not against the foreign imperialist bayonets but against the *Swadeshi*[3] capitalists' police and other security forces. *As a result of the new status of Ceylon in the imperial scheme, although British imperialism continues to be the main enemy, our local ruling classes now become the enemy face-to-face.* British imperialism has retired into the background, reserving itself for *open* intervention *only in the last resort*. The task of holding down the oppressed and insurgent masses is left *in the first instance* to Ceylon's 'own' bourgeoisie. Such is the division of labour underlying the rearranged foreign imperialist-native bourgeois alliance.

The struggle against our own bourgeoisie thus comes to the forefront on the road to the overthrow of the continuing imperialist power in Ceylon. 'Down with imperialism!' therefore means, in the first place, 'Down with the imperialist-bourgeois alliance!' And since the basic instrument of this alliance in Ceylon is the Soulbury Constitution (with such changes as it now undergoes and including the Public Services Commission, etc), this means, in turn, that we have to continue our fight for the overthrow of the Soulbury Constitution and its attendant institutions. The BLPI therefore calls: *On with the struggle against the imperialist-bourgeois alliance! Down with the Soulbury constitution and its instruments!*

The struggle against imperialism and the imperialist-bourgeois alli-

3. Independence.

ance cannot be conducted effectively by the masses of this country unless they are organised in appropriate organisations. The trade unions, which rose in power with the rise of the mass movement of the workers in the economic field, have today grown weak with the recession of the mass movement. They have to be reconstituted and rebuilt. The efforts of the rural masses to organise themselves in broad organisations for militant action had only just begun when the slump in the mass movement which followed on the defeat of the June strike overtook them. The effort has to be restarted. There is no other way to stem the *heightening* offensive of the imperialist-bourgeois partnership against the masses (as expressed, for instance, in such laws as the Public Security Bill and in such administrative measures as the regulations denying trade union and civic rights to public servants). The BLPI therefore calls: *Rebuild the mass organisations to meet the imperialist-bourgeois offensive! Down with the Public Security Bill and all other repressive laws and regulations! For the full freedom of speech, press, meeting and organisation!*

The struggle to rebuild the mass organisations and to remove the fetters on their growth and functioning is also the struggle to prepare the toiling masses for the real life and death struggle they face in the coming period. This is the struggle against *growing mass unemployment* and *increasing mass destitution*. The onset of a major economic depression is already apparent. *Dismissals* are taking place in growing numbers. Destitution is spreading anew after the artificial 'prosperity' of wartime. As the only means of advancing the struggle for *work or maintenance* in this situation the BLPI demands: *No dismissals! Reduce hours without reducing earnings! Distribute the available work among the existing labour force! Peg prices down to prewar standards! Tax the rich to relieve the poor! For a sliding scale of wages rising with the cost of living!*

There is only one class in Ceylon that can lead the struggle of *all* the toilers and organise it. This class is the *working class*. But the working class, too, stands disoriented, confused and *disunited* in the general and sharp recession of the mass movement. There is no question but that the *immediate and urgent* task which confronts the working class of Ceylon is to *forge anew its unity in action*. Only thus can it defend itself adequately. Only thus can it draw behind it and unite in action the broad masses of the toilers in Ceylon.

For working class unity in action as the means to toiler unity in action! For working class leadership of the toiling masses of Ceylon!

The road to working class unity lies through the forging of a means for the working class parties to unite in action even while they maintain and continue their *necessary* struggle among themselves over programme and policy. *The rivalry of working class parties must not be a means to disuniting the working class mass in action.* Unless the road is opened in the coming period to a *BLPI-LSSP-CP United Front,* the working class will be sorely weakened in its effort to regroup itself in face of the heightened imperialist-bourgeois offensive. The BLPI therefore calls: *For a BLPI-LSSP-CP United Front as the spearhead of the toilers' struggles in Ceylon! Down with the capitalist UNP Government! On the road to a Workers' and Peasants' Government! Long live the Revolution!*

A Statement by NM Perera

COMRADE JUDD, writing in the *Labor Action*[4] of 1 December 1947, condemned in scathing terms the policy of the Stalinists in France in particular, and in Europe in general: 'A criminal and treacherous campaign of political adventurism and madness whose effect upon the working classes of Italy and France runs the risk of being nothing short of a major disaster.'

At a time when the working class in Europe is on the defensive, thanks to the opportunist policy of the Stalinists ever since the termination of the war, subordinating the interests of the European, and therefore of the international, proletariat to the exigencies of Stalin's foreign policy, a policy of artificial counter-offensive is a criminal sacrifice of the best elements of the proletariat.

That the Stalinists in Ceylon should blindly ape their master in Moscow is neither unusual nor strange. But that the Parlour Bolsheviks who pretend to be revolutionary Marxists should follow in the wake of the Stalinists and sponsor similar adventuristic moves in Ceylon leaves us a little amazed, but we are not entirely surprised. Exhibitionism, ultra-leftism and adventurism are but facets of the same thing: opportunism.

None but opportunists and the purblind will deny that the masses in Ceylon are faced with a period of reaction. The flag-waving and syncopated jingoism of the Senanayakas and Kotelawalas have thrown to the surface the worst kind of ultra-nationalist sentiments. The petit-bourgeois masses are beginning to rally round these sentiments, pushing to the background the weakened proletariat, weakened after the May-June General Strike of 1947. Class issues have temporarily got blurred.

4.　Henry Judd was the pseudonym of Stanley Plastrik (1915-1981), the expert on Indian affairs in Max Shachtman's Workers Party. *Labor Action* was the Workers Party's weekly paper.

It is in this setting, when the working class is on the defensive, that the Parlour Bolsheviks and the Stalinists are organising a counter-demonstration to the independence celebrations of the Senanayakas. The LSSP has refused to be a party to any such stupid adventurism. The Stalinists are not Marxists, and to them the proletariat is so much pawns in a game; the Bolsheviks have no mass backing, and therefore adventures are what they live for. For us the revolutionary movement is much more fundamental. It has to be carefully nurtured and built along scientific revolutionary lines. A revolutionary movement should not be jeopardised by any desires for cheap adventures and snobbish exhibitionism.

SB Dissanayake

A Letter From Ceylon

THIS LETTER is written in the very midst of the great 'independence' racket in Ceylon, and just after its climax at both the official and mass ends. The Fourth of February was the 'appointed day' on which Ceylon was to attain its new status. But the celebrations connected with them were really due for the period from the 9th, when the Duke of Gloucester, brother of the King of England, was due to arrive for the biggest *tamasha* (shindig) planned by the sycophantic bourgeoisie of Ceylon.

The highlight of the Duke's visit was to be the ceremonial opening of the 'Dominion' Parliament of Ceylon on the 10th. A special assembly hall was fitted out in an old RAF hanger. Twenty thousand spectators were to sit around and behind the 101 members of the House of Representatives and the 30 members of the Senate, while the Duke intoned the 'King's speech'. And once the plaintive strains of 'God Save the King' had been wailed, the Prime Minister was to *unfurl* (not *hoist* — note the delicate distinction) a Sinhalese flag just outside the building.

Such were the plans. But everything went awry before and during the event. To begin with, the BLPI contingent in Parliament called the bluff about the flag business. What our new imperialist-agency holders had promised the masses was that the Duke himself would haul down the British flag and run up the Sinhalese flag! A little adroit parliamentary questioning, along with a hard fight over the flag question, forced out the truth. The question was shown to be not whether the Sinhalese flag was to fly over all, but whether it was to have the exclusive right to fly *below the Union Jack*. In other words, Ceylon was to continue under the British flag, and the whole question of the national flag was only so much eye-wash. Thus was the BLPI's stand on this question fully vindicated, and the emptiness of dissident LSSP abstentionism once more shown up.

Then came the question of the ceremonial attendance at the King's speech. That the BLPI parliamentarians would not attend was expected, for the simple reason that they alone had boycotted the King's speech on the previous occasion when it was delivered by the Governor (now Governor General). The CP, too, soon announced their decision not to attend, because this flowed from their having joined us in voting against the fake independence motion of the government. The question was the LSSP (which had *abstained* at the voting on the independence motion). What would they do? The whole working class of Ceylon was glad to hear their announcement that, despite their abstention from voting, they would abstain from attending the King's speech ceremony. We can assure our readers that we did not in the circumstances enquire from them how abstention on this occasion was not 'exhibitionism' as they had alleged our boycott of the Governor's visit to have been!

It is necessary to say that on this occasion we proposed that the boycott should proceed beyond mere abstention from attending at the Assembly Hall, and take some more positive form, for example, a public meeting. The CP was agreeable. The LSSP left the impression of being agreed, though its leader, Dr NM Perera, was none too specific. But in the meantime, after the decision of the other sections of the Opposition not to attend the ceremony got known, the government decided to snipe at the boycott.

A few days before the 10th, the Speaker suddenly communicated with the working class party members in the House of Representatives, demanding that they declare their intention to attend before he provided seats for them in the Assembly Hall. The intent behind this move was to prevent there being empty chairs to greet the Duke, and apprise him (and the host of international observers who would be present) of the boycott. But the Speaker was counting without his BLPI hosts. The leader of our parliamentary fraction, Comrade Colvin R de Silva, immediately wrote back demanding the unconditional provision of the seats under threat of a demonstration at the Assembly Hall itself! The Speaker scuttled — and 25 empty chairs duly protested [against] the independence racket to the Duke of Gloucester! (Seven BLPI, 10 LSSP, six CP — including a senator each — and two independents.) Incidentally, the *Times* carried a photo distinctly showing the empty seats.

In the meantime, the BLPI took the initiative in addressing the LSSP and CP for a united front meeting *during the celebrations*, against this fake independence and for real independence. The CP agreed, and so did the LSSP at the first joint meeting of the three parties' delegates. However, *the LSSP recoiled from its agreement within 24 hours!* The illuminating reason given by Dr NM Perera was 'theoretical differences'.

It is necessary to say that this allegation of Dr NM Perera was *correct*. The LSSP and its theoreticians hold a novel dualistic theory of independence. According to them Ceylon has got 'internal' independence but not 'external' (whatever that may mean), or again, political independence but not economic. The British government's 'Independence Bill', it would seem, takes us forward towards independence, while, presumably, the Defence and other Agreements (which preceded it and were the precondition for it) drag us back part of the way again! That the agreements were the precondition for the passage of the Bill is apparently irrelevant; and the analysis of the class relationships *as a whole* is seemingly unnecessary to these neo-Marxists. They prefer to work with the vulgar theory of a gradualistic progress towards independence, instead of the Marxist conception of the 'dialectical leap' from colonial status to independence. The net result is that they cannot effectively protest [against] the fakery of the 'Independence' that has been 'granted' to Ceylon, and indeed fall into the position of having to persuade the masses that there actually is some 'progress' to enthuse about.

That the above remark about the LSSP is correct will be shown by the outcome of our plans. Although we were let down by them, we went ahead with the CP with our plans for a meeting. The police refused us permission for any day on which the Duke was in Colombo. We could not therefore arrange for a meeting on the 10th as originally contemplated, but had to make do with the 11th. But what an 11th it proved to be!

The meeting was fixed for 4.30pm. Several thousands had already gathered at the Galle Face Green by that time, despite the burning afternoon sun and although many a workplace was not yet closed. But the crowds kept streaming in; and even the bourgeois *Times of Ceylon* was compelled to state next day that over 35 000 attended the meeting. The Sinhalese *Lanka Dipa* estimated the attendance at over 50 000. Such was the mighty demonstration which the Colombo masses made against fake independence in the very midst of the celebrations which had been planned in order to lull them and dull the edge of their hostility.

The meeting found the LSSP in a fix. 'Theoretical differences' being too hot a potato to carry in public, they had shifted their emphasis to 'untimeliness' as their reason for not participating in the meeting. Indeed, they actually set going rumours that the meeting would be wrecked by our opponents — the wish being father to the thought, as was shown by a scurrilous article they circulated at the meeting itself. The position they took was: this was 'a period of reaction' in which the flag-waving of the bourgeoisie had 'thrown to the surface the worst kind of ultra-nationalist sentiments'. Class issues had 'temporarily got blurred'. To organise a 'counter-demonstration' to the Senanayake celebrations 'in this setting', said they, was therefore 'stupid adventurism' to which 'the LSSP had refused to be a party'. 'A revolutionary movement [don't you see?] should not be jeopardised by any desires for cheap adventurism and snobbish exhibitionism.'

The sheer spite of the phraseology we have quoted is a measure of their chagrin when over 35 000 of the people who were alleged to be drugged by patriotic propaganda attended the meeting, and applauded enthusiastically every attack on Senanayaka's fake independence. The truth, of course, was that they were foisting their own idea that this 'independence' constituted considerable 'progress' even though it did not amount to 'complete independence'. The masses looked on it otherwise. This was apparent to us at every stage, and especially when, in the very midst of the Assembly Hall *tamasha* and after, we went down the streets selling a pamphlet denouncing both the fake independence and the celebration. Fully 8000 copies were sold in two days, despite the high price of 10 cents for five pages! Besides, even little children had been heard remarking that there was a notable lack of cheering for the Duke. Only the LSSP discerned in the inevitable sightseers at a pageant a drugged mass, and that was because they had drugged themselves with a false theoretical position. What a remarkably instructive example of the importance of a correct theory as a guide to action!

Despite the rank provocations of the LSSP, both the CP and BLPI speakers at this meeting took care, while repudiating this nonsense, to repeat their call to the LSSP even now to join the united front. In fact, our line calling for a *united front of the working class parties* was rapturously received. The Stalinist Democratic Front was not only not understood but actually got lost on the way — their chairman, Dr Wickremasinghe, who spoke last, virtually followed our line in his speech!

All Colombo, if not all Ceylon, was openly hostile to the action of the LSSP. Mass pressure on them to come into the demonstrations became irresistible. Their own rank and filers had been seen at the meeting denouncing their leaders' mistakes. The result was that *the LSSP had to go back on its position within 24 hours!* Their top leader, theoretician and mass speaker, Philip Gunawardena, himself appeared at a meeting organised by the United Youth Front on the 12th to ask apologetically whether they 'really believed' that the LSSP, 'which had always been with them in their struggles since 1936', would desert them in this struggle?

What a plea! And what a confession! And this, ironically enough, at the very moment when a letter from his twin, Dr NM Perera, appeared in the bourgeois *Times* denouncing the meeting as 'adventurist', 'exhibitionist', etc, etc. The LSSP's attempt to sabotage the demonstration had failed. The BLPI had succeeded in mobilising mass pressure on these recalcitrants and dissidents. A long step had been taken towards the *BLPI-LSSP-CP united front* for which the masses in the process of a regroupment after the June strike defeat patently thirst. Trotskyism had triumphed over sectarianism and ultimatism once more!

IX: The Unification of the LSSP in 1950

The split in the Ceylonese Trotskyist movement and the separate existence and identity of the two groups for much of the 1940s left many issues unresolved. It meant that the reunified LSSP contained two very different political strands, which came to the surface at times of crisis during the years to come. The first item in this section comes from an interview given to Bob Pitt by Prins Rajasooriya (1921-1993) on his visit to Britain in 1990. Although he was a member of the LSSP at the time of the unification congress, he was very critical of its politics. Prins subsequently became the head of the LSSP's trade union organisation. Biographical information about him can be found in the obituaries published at the time of his death: 'Prins Rajasooriya' (*Workers News*, June-July 1993); *Prins Rajasooriya Remembered* (pamphlet issued by the Committee organising the Prins Rajasooriya Commemoration, 15 July 1993); Oscar Pereira, 'Prins Rajasooriya (1921-1993)'; and Peter and Cyril, 'Prins Rajasooriya' (*Revolutionary History*, Volume 5, no 1, Autumn 1993, pp101-3; Volume 5, no 2, Spring 1994, pp179-80); and Ainsley Samarajiwa, *Prins Rajasooriya* (Island, Sri Lanka).

As described in the two reports from the *Ceylon Daily News* of 15 May and 5 June 1950, along with a fellow member of parliament, Philip Gunawardena refused to accept the reunification, although he appears to have attended the Third World Congress of the Fourth International held in August 1951, and to have sat on its Far Eastern Commission. He later formed an organisation for a Peoples' United Front (Mahajana Eksath Peramuna), and entered into a coalition government led by the UNP. The section ends with the *Programme of Action of the Lanka Sama Samaja Party* adopted at the unification congress on 4 June 1950, taken from the party's pamphlet. It accepted affiliation to the Fourth International, and Leslie Goonewardene attended the Third World Congress, sat on several commissions there, and was elected onto the IEC with Colvin R de Silva as an alternate.

The course of the negotiations can be followed in the correspondence between the two organisations on 31 January and 5 February 1949, 'Trotskyist Unity' (Editorial) and 'Organisational Unity of All Trotskyists in the LSSP: Not a United Front Between the LSSP and BSP', published in the *Samasamajist* (Volume 12, no 10, 20 February 1949). The congress itself was reported in *Quatrième Internationale* (Volume 8, nos 5-7, May-July 1950, p70, and nos

9-10, August-October 1950, p46), and its documents are summarised in 'Le Congrès du Lanka Sama Samaja Party' (*Quatrième Internationale*, Volume 9, nos 2-4, February-April 1951, pp53-5). A year later *Fourth International* magazine reported the loss of five parliamentary seats by the party in the general elections of 26-30 May ('Newsletter: The Ceylon Elections', Volume 13, no 3, May-June 1952, p95). HA Peiris, *Political Parties in Sri Lanka Since Independence: A Bibliography* (Navrang, New Delhi, 1988) contains a summary outline sketch (pp19-22) that can serve as an introduction to the period.

Interview with Prins Rajasooriya

How did you come to join the movement in Ceylon?

My first job was as a clerk in the permanent government service in Sri Lanka, and not very long after I joined there occurred the general strike in 1947. I was by that time the Secretary of my union branch, and naturally I organised not only my branch, but also workers in the surrounding government offices. After the strike, I did not think that government service was suitable for me, and decided on trying my hand at teaching. Where I lived was close to the headquarters of what was then called the Bolshevik Samasamaja Party, and many of my friends frequented the office and read their literature, and I was naturally drawn into it. So that by the time I resigned from government service my inclination was to work for the Trotskyist movement. I decided that the best place for me to go and work was among the plantation workers, who were, and still are, the most deprived community in the country. Paid poor wages, they are treated as aliens, even though they produce most of the wealth of our country. So I went to a place called Nawalapitiya, away from Kandy, and about 80 miles from the city of Colombo, and started work with the Trotskyists who were there. Most of my connections before I left Colombo were with the BSP, but in the area where I decided to teach and work, in Nawalapitiya, there was no BSP. But there was a group of the LSSP. I joined that group, and I was very active in trying to get the two groups together.

What were the differences between the two groups?

The greater — if I may use such a term — intellectual content was in the BSP. People who were more interested in theory, in reading books, in finding out what was Trotskyism, were in the BSP, whereas Philip Gunawardena was a man of a certain amount of dynamism, a forceful personality, and Dr NM Perera was a very practical man. So there were various political differences between them; it was even apparent at that time. They had split during the war. Now if I was going to deal with the split, it might take the whole morning, the various splits! I think there were a number of reasons for it. One was the attitude towards the national bourgeoisie. Now, in the 1947 strike Philip Gunawardena called for a national government, which is completely unacceptable. So there were basic differences.

I wonder what the consequences of the unity in 1950 were? I remember reading a pamphlet by Karlo, V Karalasingham, in which he argued that there was always a petit-bourgeois nationalist element to the LSSP, and he argued that this was very much concentrated in the Philip-NM Perera wing of the Samasamaja movement. He argued that the way in which that merger was carried out very much left elements like that in dominant positions in the organisation. I don't know if you'd have any comments on that?

You see, I was in the LSSP. It was recognised that there were political differences. I participated in the conference of the LSSP which decided on the merger. But I must say this, that I agree with most of Karlo's criticisms that you mentioned. Now it was true that both of them called themselves Trotskyists, but there were political differences, that is why they were split. The unity should not have taken place without adequate preparation, without bringing those differences up to the surface, without examining them and finding out whether, in spite of those differences, unity was possible. Now none of that was done. The leaderships of the two groups decided that there should be unity, and before uniting they decided that a conference should be held of each group, and resolutions should be passed. Therefore there was inadequate preparation for unity. It would have been far better to have postponed unity, for there to have been a preparation of documents by each group, and maybe even tendencies in each group, and for there to have been a complete circulation of those documents inside the group and between the groups, and unity after a discussion. But I must say that that was not done.

Philip Gunawardena Splits from the LSSP

A CONFERENCE of the Lanka Sama Samaja Party, convened last evening to discuss proposals for unification with the other Trotskyist party, the Bolshevik Samasamaja Party, ended in a fiasco when Mr Philip Gunawardena walked out accompanied by some of his supporters. Mr Gunawardena told a *Daily News* representative last night that 44 members present joined him in the walk-out as 'a protest against the undemocratic attitude of Dr NM Perera, who was chairman of the conference'. Dr NM Perera, on the other hand, claims that the majority of the members present were in favour of the unification formula, which had been placed before the conference. It is understood that among those who walked out were Mrs Kusuma Gunawardena MP[1] and MS Abu Bakr, Mayor of Colombo. Mr Philip Gunawardena emphasised the fact that he took that step in order to ensure the 'preservation and continuity of the party which certain people were bent on destroying'.

It is understood that the main difference arose over the question of whether a new organisation should be started, or whether the BSP should be amalgamated with the LSSP as it is at present. The view that is understood to be held by Dr NM Perera and his supporters is that both the organisations, the LSSP and the BSP, should cease to function and an entirely new organisation with the name LSSP should be formed, whereas Mr Philip Gunawardena and his supporters insist on the continuation of the present LSSP organisation without any change in its programme, constitution or organisational basis.

The Bolshevik Samasamaja Party at a separate conference held yesterday ratified the proposal to amalgamate with the LSSP.

The LSSP and BSP Unite

'THE PROCESS of unification of the Trotskyist forces in this country was successfully and triumphantly concluded yesterday at the Colombo Town Hall', states Dr NM Perera. At a joint conference, members of the LSSP and BSP resolved to merge into one party called the Lanka Sama Samaja Party, he adds in a statement. The conference, which was presided over by Dr Perera, adopted the programme and constitution of the party. A new Central Committee of 15 was elected. The statement says: 'To the handful who chose to stand out of the party and the Fourth International, the conference addressed a resolution expressing its regret at their action in keeping out of the unification. It appealed to them to rejoin the party and instructed the Central Committee to admit forthwith whosoever so desired.'

At the end of the conference the participants came to the Colpetty

1. Kusuma Siri Gunawardena (1912-1985), the wife of Philip Gunawardena, was MP for Avissawella, and then for Kiriella.

office in procession, and Dr NM Perera opened the doors of the office, which were closed since Saturday when it was feared that a clash might occur, as it was stated that Mr Philip Gunawardena's section intended holding their conference there.

Meanwhile, at a conference held on Saturday at Kolonnawa Vidyaiaya, a section of the party led by Mr Philip Gunawardena maintained that they were the LSSP, and passed a resolution stating that all those members of the LSSP who attended the 'so-called unity conference' would cease to be members of the LSSP. At the Kolonnawa conference, which was attended by about 75 party members and candidate members, Mr Philip Gunawardena was elected General Secretary and Mrs Florence Senanayake MP, party Treasurer.[2] A Central Committee was also elected.

Dr SA Wickremasinghe, Communist Party leader, addressing a public meeting at Slave Island yesterday evening, said: 'The Trotskyites will go on splitting until they are kicked out of the working class movement. Their rôle in the world working class movement has always been that of disrupters. The very people who declared that Socialism in one country was not possible, today defend the renegade Tito for defending Socialism in Yugoslavia. This is the opportunism that goes under the name of Trotskyism.'

Programme of Action of the Lanka Sama Samaja Party

Adopted at the Unity Conference, 4 June 1950

Part I. Fundamental Aims

The fundamental aims of the party are:

1. The overthrow of the capitalist state maintained in Ceylon through the political alliance of the British imperialists and the Ceylonese bourgeoisie.
2. The seizure of political power by the working class at the head of the toiling masses and the establishment of a democratic workers' and peasants' (soviet) government (the dictatorship of the proletariat supported by the urban and rural poor).

2.   Daisy Marian Florence Senanayake (1903-1988) was a pioneer of the Suriya Mal movement, and as MP for Kiriella (1947-52) was Ceylon's first woman MP.

3. The achievement of real national independence. The severance of all political ties with the British Empire. The ending of all forms of colonial subjection to foreign finance capital (imperialism).
4. The confiscation by the workers' state without compensation of all banks, factories, plantations, big commercial concerns, means of transport, mines, etc, which will be run and developed as state-owned enterprises for the public benefit, and not for private profit.
5. The nationalisation of the land. The transfer of all land (excluding large-scale modernised agricultural enterprises) for use to the toiling peasantry. The development of collective forms in peasant agriculture.
6. On the political and economic basis outlined above, the forward development of the productive forces in a Socialist direction. The establishment of Socialism in cooperation with the victorious proletariat of India, South-East Asia, and of the world.

NB: The above fundamental aims cannot be realised through bourgeois parliaments. The inevitable resistance of the bourgeoisie to their achievement necessarily calls for mass revolutionary action as the only means of realising the will of the majority.

Ceylon is for British imperialism not merely a field for profitable investment, but a strategic military bastion, in defence of which its fullest power would be exerted. The prospects of revolutionary victory are greatly advanced, however, by the fact that the toiling masses of Ceylon will have the opportunity to struggle for the overthrow of British imperialism not in isolation, but by participating in the wider and more powerful revolutionary struggles that develop in India and South East Asia. The realisation of this historic opportunity demands the building of the closest ties with the movements in India and South East Asia with which Ceylon is linked.

Part II. The Transitional Programme

The party does not advance any programme of 'minimum demands' which can be separated from its fundamental aims. Decaying world imperialism cannot concede the 'minimum demands' of the masses, least of all in a colonial country. Reformist perspectives are today completely excluded for the proletariat.

The task of the present pre-revolutionary period is to bridge the gulf between the objective maturity of world conditions for the Socialist revolution, and the subjective weakness of the consciousness and organisation of the working class.

The party takes part in every real struggle of the masses, however limited the objectives for the moment (for example, the defence of democratic rights, against wage cuts, etc). But its propaganda and agitation will give these day-to-day struggles their real (that is, revolutionary) perspective, and bring home to the masses the necessity to end colonial subjection and the capitalist order itself, if their most elementary demands are to be effectively realised.

For this purpose, the party advances the following *programme of transitional demands*. These demands spring directly from the immediate situation confronting the masses. But they are posed so as to dispel reformist illusions, and so that the fight around them serves to mobilise the masses for the revolutionary tasks that face them.

The Transitional Demands

1. Cancellation of all agreements made by the Ceylon bourgeoisie with the British imperialists, which serve to maintain semi-colonial subjection. Withdrawal from the Commonwealth, and the setting up of a republic.
2. Full employment. Distribution of available work among all workers. Sliding scale of working hours in relation to the above, without reduction of wages. Public works under trade union control to absorb the unemployed.
3. Decent living standards. A guaranteed minimum according to the real cost of living, with wages increasing according to the rising prices.
4. Freezing of foreign assets. Prohibition of export of dividends.
5. Nationalisation of key industries and public utilities without compensation and under workers' control.
6. Income tax of 100 per cent over a fixed ceiling.
7. Confiscation of all lands owned by absentee landlords, and their transfer to working peasants.
8. Inspection of books of all capitalist concerns by trade unions.

Organisational Slogans

The party takes full part in the day-to-day work of trade unions and the other mass organisations. At the same time, it fights constantly for the *democratisation of trade unions* as a safeguard against bureaucratism, which stifles the energies of the organised workers, and leads them into paths of class collaboration with the bourgeoisie.

As the tempo of mass struggle heightens, trade unions and similar organisations progressively show their limitations, and often act as a retarding force. Under such conditions, the party will agitate for ad hoc organisations which give room for the revolutionary initiative of the masses to develop, including *strike committees, factory committees, workers' defence guards, peasant committees*, etc.

As the struggle assumes revolutionary proportions, the party will agitate for the formation of *soviets*, in order to draw the broadest masses of the toilers into the arena in an organised and democratic manner, and to organise the proletariat as a class for the revolutionary tasks. Under revolutionary conditions the party will agitate for the *arming of the proletariat*, the formation of workers' militias, etc.

The Party

1. Stands uncompromisingly opposed to all forms of chauvinism, and defends the international solidarity of the working class. At the same time, it recognises the democratic right of self-determination for nations.
2. Stands opposed to imperialist war, which it meets with the Leninist tactic of revolutionary defeatism. It rejects as illusory all aims of realising world peace under imperialism, and condemns the UNO as the thieves' kitchen of the imperialists designed to maintain the rule of world imperialism, which can only lead humanity into the catastrophe of a new world war.
3. Unconditionally defends the Soviet Union as a workers' state against imperialist attack, despite the bureaucratic degeneration. At the same time, it stands completely opposed to the Stalinist bureaucracy of the Soviet Union, which has expropriated the Soviet workers politically, and (in its own narrow caste interests) follows a reactionary policy, and subordinates the international revolutionary movement to the temporary aims of its shifting foreign policies, thereby betraying the international revolutionary movement and the real defence of the Soviet Union against imperialist attack.
4. Condemns outright the Stalinist parties of Ceylon and the world, which, having already a long record of shameless betrayals of proletarian struggles, can only lead the workers of the whole world to new catastrophes if their influence is not destroyed in time by the international working class under the leadership of the Fourth International. The 'right turns' (Popular Frontism, Democratic Fronts, collaboration in bourgeois governments, support of imperialist war, sabotage of national and revolutionary struggles), and the 'left turns' (adventurist 'Third Period' tactics) of these parties proceed alike in their aim of exploiting the international working class and its revolutionary struggles solely as a make-weight for the reactionary foreign policies of the Stalinist bureaucracy of the Soviet Union, whose servile agencies these parties are.

5. Condemns outright the false programmatic aim of the 'democratic dictatorship of the proletariat and peasantry' advanced by the Stalinists in Ceylon and other colonial countries, as one which masks the betrayal of the colonial workers to the counter-revolutionary national bourgeoisie.

Trotskyist ISSUE 22 ★ JUNE-DECEMBER 1997

INTERNATIONAL

INCORPORATING PERMANENT REVOLUTION

English language journal of the League for a Revolutionary Communist International

Articles include

Russia: the death agony of a degenerated workers' state
Che Guevara: a revolutionary life?
China's road to capitalism ● Australia under National
Scotland, Wales and self-determination
France, Germany and Italy; workers versus Maastricht II

Subscription rates (3 issues)
Individual: £8 Europe; £11 rest of the world
Institutions: £12 Europe; £20 rest of the world
Cheques to Trotskyist International BCM Box 7750 London WC1N 3XX

Jim Higgins

More Years for the Locust
The Origins of the SWP

This book details the founding of the Socialist Review Group, charts its development into the International Socialists, and its apotheosis into the Socialist Workers Party. No member of the SWP, especially those on its Central Committee, should be without a copy of this seminal work. Others will find it a charming gift for their loved ones, or, suitably rolled, a formidable ideological weapon against their factional opponents.

£5.99 + 66p p+p (UK, £1.50 Europe, £2.50 elsewhere) from PO Box 13824, London SW1P 2ZL, cheques payable to The Assassin.

X: The Great Hartal of 1953

Controversy has always surrounded the events of the Great Hartal, a national strike which convulsed Ceylon in August 1953 in which the LSSP played the leading part, for some sections of the Trotskyist movement abroad regarded it as a missed opportunity for a bid for power. Our extracts here have been selected to illustrate the different views about its significance that developed among the members of the party who were on the spot.

The first is an article written by Bala Tampoe, the head of the Ceylon Mercantile Union, for the *Samasamajist* on 7 October 1956. Tampoe was one of the leaders of the left of the party who split with the LSSP in 1964 to form the LSSP(R) along with Edmund Samarakkody, Meryl Fernando, Prins Rajasooriya and V Karalasingham, which later disintegrated into several tendencies. The history of the CMU up to 1964 is well covered by Roshan Peiris, 'On the History of the Ceylon Mercantile Union', *InterContinental Press*, Volume 9, no 15, 23 April 1973, pp478-80.

Then follows a short extract from Edmund Samarakkody's 'The Struggle for Trotskyism in Ceylon' (*Spartacist*, no 22, Winter 1973-74, p7). Edmund was a founder member and later an MP of the LSSP, and subsequently General Secretary of the LSSP(R) when the left split away from the party in 1964. His biography can be followed in the spate of obituaries that followed his death, 'Edmund Samarakkody (1912-1992): An Appreciation' (*Workers News*, February 1992); Al Richardson, 'Edmund Samarakkody, 1914-1992' (*Workers Power*, February 1992); 'In Memory of Comrade Edmund Samarakkody', 15 January 1992 (*International Trotskyist Correspondence*, new series, no 1, March 1992); Prins Rajasooriya, 'Edmund Samarakkody (1914-1992)' (*Revolutionary History*, Volume 4, no 3, Summer 1992, pp138-41); Paolo Casciola, *Edmund Samarakkody (1912-1992)* (Centro Studi Pietro Tresso, June 1992; *Revolutionary History*, Volume 4, no 4, Spring 1993, pp214-5); and 'Edmund Samarakkody (1914-1992)' (*Cahiers Léon Trotsky*, no 49, January 1993, p125).

The third extract represents the view of the majority of the party, and is taken from Leslie Goonewardene's *The History of the LSSP in Perspective*, 1978, p16. Further narrative treatments of the great August strike along similar lines include those of Colvin R de Silva, *Hartal!* (LSSP publication, September 1953; see *Revolutionary History*, Volume 2, no 1, Spring

1989, pp38-43); and Sydney Wanasinghe, 'The Hartal of 1953' (Ceylonese *Young Socialist*, new series, no 2, June 1980, pp19-27).

Our fourth extract is taken from an interview granted by Prins Raja-sooriya to Bob Pitt in London in August 1990. Since Prins was for a long time the General Secretary of the Ceylon Federation of Labour, his opinion on this subject carries some weight.

Bala Tampoe

Some Lessons of the Hartal

THE CAPITALIST UNP government was returned to power with a large majority of seats in September 1952, though not with a majority of votes over all its opponents in the general election. To those people, even in our own party, whose political thinking is conditioned by parliamentary politics, the stability of the UNP government seemed assured for a further five years at least, and the parties opposed to it seemed to have no hope for the future, unless they got together in a broad 'anti-UNP Front' with a common minimum programme. Yet, in one day, on 12 August 1953, the masses stepped into the political arena and taught the people a lesson in class politics that they will never forget.

The government raised the price of rice in the confidence that this measure would meet with no real resistance from the people, even though they might protest against it. The left parties and leading trade union organisations called for a Hartal. The government and the capitalist press in turn pooh-poohed the idea, and threatened to resort to the use of force against any who dared to challenge its decision by direct action.

The toilers of town and village, particularly in the thickly-populated Western, Southern and Sabaragamuwa Provinces, were not deceived or frightened. On 12 August the workers and rural poor took to the streets, smashed buses, uprooted railway lines and telegraph posts, stopped railway trains, blocked roads, fought the police in numerous places, and demonstrated their power and anger in a hundred other ways. The government, struck with terror, proclaimed a State of Emergency, and then sent the price of rice tumbling down. This was not all. Prime Minister Dudley Senanayake, shaken out of his senses, resigned soon after. The Great Hartal had proved the emptiness of Dudley's majority!

The Hartal taught other and no less important lessons. It taught the urban working class that their brothers and sisters of the village are indeed mighty allies in any direct struggle. It taught both the workers and the rural poor that, together, they are fully capable of challenging and even smashing the forces of the capitalist state. Never again will the police force hold any terror for them, when they have decided to meet it in direct struggle. The day of 12 August 1953 will be remembered as the day when hardly a policeman was seen in Maharagama, Boralesgamuwa and other places; whilst such police as did appear in other places were either put to rout or treated with open contempt, despite their batons, rifles and steel helmets! The masses now know that the police and military, together even, are too few to withstand them, when they are ready to die, as did more than one Hartal hero.

The Hartal has also taught very concrete lessons regarding the nature of the *political leadership* that is necessary for any successful mass action. Before the Hartal, the Stalinist Front had declared a hundred times that the masses were doomed to stagnation unless a 'comprehensive United Front' was formed between the left parties, 'under the leadership of the Soviet Union and New China'. The LSSP, on the other hand, had stressed the need for a United Front *in action* on concrete issues. The Hartal proved the LSSP to be correct. There was no United Front between the LSSP and the Stalinist Front 'under the leadership of the Soviet Union and New China' on 12 August 1953. What was created was a joint committee of the parties and the bigger trade unions for a Hartal, that is for mass *action* on a specific issue. The joint committee made the call, and the response of the masses was immediate and terrific. This is one reason why it is the LSSP and not the Stalinist Front which has advanced from strength to strength after the Hartal. There is another and more important reason.

The CP, no doubt, made the call for the Hartal jointly with the LSSP. But the events of the Hartal proved beyond a shadow of doubt that it was the LSSP which actually *mobilised and led* the masses *in action*. Wherever there were Sama Samaja Youth Leagues functioning — and there were hundreds of them — there was Hartal action. Wherever Samasamajism was deepest rooted, there the Hartal reached its greatest heights. That is why the State of Emergency was maintained longest in the Samasamaja-dominated Western, Southern and Sabaragamuwa Provinces. That, too, is why of the hundreds of persons charged in the courts with 'Hartal offences', nearly all of them were LSSP members, including prominent ones, LSSP Youth Leaguers or supporters.

Significant, in contrast, is the fact that *not a single Communist*

Party member or 'Democratic' Youth Leaguer was charged with a *Hartal* offence in any court! One CPer, Victor Silva of Borella, was charged with spreading rumours *after* the Hartal. Another, Tudawe of Matara, was charged with a *curfew* offence. A third, Nadunge of Kandy, was charged with a having a document in his drawer! This was the CP's case record! Significant, too, is the fact that apart from the strike in the harbour, which was led by ex-Samasamajist Philip Gunawardena's group, every Hartal strike, either in government or non-government workplaces, was brought about by the LSSP and its allied trade union organisations. The Hartal proved that it is the LSSP alone which is capable not only of *calling* the masses to action, but also of *rallying and organising* them *for* action and *leading* them *in* action.

The so-called 'anti-UNP' parties that did not participate in the Hartal should not be forgotten. The part played by the Sri Lanka Freedom Party and the Ceylon Indian Congress (now Ceylon Democratic Congress) was not only inglorious but instructive. Both these parties claim to be 'democratic' and not 'revolutionary'. Both uphold 'Law and Order', that is, *capitalist* law and order, and discourage any form of action that threatens the foundations of capitalist society. Both, therefore, backed out of the Hartal, though both had participated in the discussions with the left parties that had preceded it. This shameful withdrawal teaches that no party that aims to avoid the *class struggle* is ever to be relied on to support, let alone lead, a mass action that challenges the forces of the capitalist state. The withdrawal of the CIC also teaches a special lesson to the lakhs of estate workers of Indian origin in our country. It teaches them that so long as they continue under the CIC leadership, they will be prevented from joining forces with the Ceylonese working class in any showdown with their common enemy, the capitalist class and its government.

The Emergency Regulations introduced after the Hartal and the amendment of the Public Security Act to provide for the proclamation of a State of Emergency even in anticipation of an emergency, make it clear that the capitalist UNP government has drawn its own lessons from the Hartal. In future, the government will not permit the kind of widescale public agitation which the LSSP, in particular, carried on before the Hartal, in open preparation for it.

The masses will enter the next great struggle with the confidence they have gained from the Hartal. But the next struggle will be against a more experienced and better prepared enemy. In such a situation, a single-minded leadership, in which the masses have the fullest confidence, and a firmly-knit network of mass organisations will be essential. The Lanka Sama Samaja Party stands before the

masses, vindicated and strengthened by the Hartal, as the party that
has the leadership and the will to *organise* and *conquer!*

Edmund Samarakkody

1953: A Missed Opportunity?

THE LSSP was confronted [in 1953] with the opportunity of leading the masses in Ceylon's first revolutionary mass struggle
against the government and the capitalist class reaching to the level of
a semi-insurrection.

With the end of the Korean [War] boom and the fall in the prices
of the main exports, tea and rubber, the capitalist UNP government
decided to maintain the profit levels of the capitalist and vested interests by imposing drastic cuts on social services and by the increase in
price of rationed rice. While the price of rice was raised from 25 cents
to 70 cents per measure, the government withdrew the free midday
meal to school children, and increased postal charges and train fares.

The LSSP took the lead in developing mass agitation on these issues. But even while the mass movement was visibly growing around
these issues, the leaders of the LSSP, who had empirically moved into
a struggle situation, failed to see the revolutionary possibilities in the
situation. Their perspectives did not go beyond mass protest action
against the actions and the policies of the government. In this context, the LSSP leaders were taken by surprise by the response of the
masses to the one-day protest action that was decided upon.

Though acting empirically, the LSSP correctly applied the tactic of
the united front. The Philip Gunawardena group (VLSSP), the Stalinists and even the Federal Party were pushed into becoming the co-
sponsors of the Hartal action.

The withdrawal of work by the workers, supported by the closing
of business, and the stoppage of work by peasants and other self-
employed people, all of whom resorted to direct action struggle by
barricading roads, cutting down trees and telephone poles, stopping
buses and trains — all this turned into a real confrontation with the
armed forces of the government. What occurred was a semi-
insurrection in which the masses fought the police and the army with
stones and clubs and whatever they found by way of weapons. Nine
persons were killed by police shooting.

What the working class and the masses that were in the struggle
looked forward to was not a mere one-day protest action and a return

to work the following day. They were in readiness for a struggle to overthrow the hated UNP government. In fact, this direct action of the masses continued on the next day also. There were clear possibilities of this Hartal action being continued for several days thereafter. But the LSSP leadership, despite the unmistakable moods of the workers and other sections of the masses, decided to keep to their plan of a mere protest action and called off the Hartal, and prevented the masses from continuing the struggle.

Leslie Goonewardene

1953 in Perspective

THERE IS the criticism that the LSSP should not have allowed the Hartal of 12 August 1953 to be confined to one day, but should have continued it to bring about the downfall of the government. People who make this kind of criticism are often unaware of the situation that existed at the time, and of the nature of the action itself. In the first place, it should be borne in mind that the one-day Hartal became possible at all because the government of the day permitted the publicising of the call for the Hartal both by publications and meetings and the very date for which it was fixed, weeks ahead of 12 August. (Let us remember that Mr Dudley Senanayake, having learned from experience, clamped down an Emergency simultaneously with his cutting down of the rice ration in 1966.)

Secondly, only three organisations were prepared to issue a call for the one-day Hartal, namely the LSSP, the VLSSP-CP United Front and the Federal Party. The SLFP considered that the masses had not yet reached a degree of political consciousness to justify such a call, while the Ceylon Indian Congress, led by Mr Thondaman,[1] decided to confine themselves to public meetings of protest on that day. Is it suggested by the critics of the LSSP that the LSSP should unilaterally, without consulting the other parties with whom it had jointly called for a one-day Hartal, called for a continuation of the Hartal on the second day?

Finally, and most important of all, it was the considered view of the LSSP (as well as, we believe, of the VLSSP-CP United Front) that the mass movement had reached only a stage of protest against the action of the government in imposing the burdens it did on the

1. Savumiamoorthy Thondaman (1913-) was the leader of the Ceylon Workers Congress, which represented the Tamil workers in the plantations.

masses, and not a stage where it was aiming at the overthrow of the government.

In some places, police action continued after the 12th. But to the best of our knowledge, nowhere in the country did the masses attempt to continue the Hartal on the second day. This bears out the correctness of the LSSP's estimate of the mass situation.

Prins Rajasooriya

A Purely LSSP Affair

Edmund Samarakkody argues that the 1953 Hartal was a missed opportunity, and that there was a possibility of launching a struggle for power. Leslie Goonewardene, on the other hand, argues that the masses were at far too low a level, and it really wasn't on. On the basis of your experiences, what would your evaluation of that be?

I was a member of the Central Committee of the LSSP at that time, and I was also one of the organisers in the field. The LSSP had set up secret headquarters, so I was one of the people chosen to have contact between the headquarters and the field. Now I don't agree that the Hartal could have been taken beyond what happened. There were a number of factors.

First of all, the Stalinists were making every attempt to stab the Hartal in the back. All the parties in opposition to the government got together to organise and take the Hartal forward. The Stalinists held a meeting in Galle Face, in spite of being part of that unity, calling for the Hartal a number of days earlier than had been decided, to create confusion and so on. Then SWRD Bandaranaike was chairman of one of the largest meetings that Sri Lanka has seen on Galle Face Green. After the meeting, it ended in some stone throwing by people who had listened to the speakers and got worked up, and clashed with the police. That was, if my memory is right, a few days before the date of the Hartal. SWRD Bandaranaike saw the size of the meeting, and then withdrew from that front of opposition parties, withdrew from the Hartal.

Then the main plantation proletariat never participated in the Hartal. How were you going to stage a working class uprising without the main bulk of the plantation proletariat participating in the Hartal? The plantation workers are all working in the hills, in the tea country. That tea country is strategically situated, and comprises the main central mountain mass of the country. Nothing was done there.

The Hartal occurred entirely in the areas controlled by the LSSP, that is the coastal belt, the western coastal belt, the city of Colombo and those areas where the LSSP had Youth Leagues, or groups, or influence. That is on the whole concentrated in about one-third of the country, or even less. So when two-thirds or three-fourths of the country is dormant, how are you going to extend it to the rest of the country? You see, ultimately it became a purely LSSP affair. And even the LSSP cadres were organised and prepared for a one-day Hartal. Now it is true that it reached a very high level, in this coastal belt. Now on what basis and under what conditions and how do you take it forward from there when your own ranks are not prepared for any further action, not because they are not willing, but they are not prepared? Nobody expected it to reach that level at that time.

It's just that even if you read Colvin's account, which is very uncritical of the LSSP leadership, there does seem to be a clear gulf between the ferocity of the clashes with the state forces, with workers rooting up railway lines and rolling boulders down blocking roads, and the response of the LSSP. There seems to have been, by his account, a semi-insurrectionary quality to this, which seems to be somewhat in contrast to the fact that the next day everyone was sent back to work.

It was not exactly like that. It is true that that is a fairly factual account of Colvin's. But all of this occurred in a certain concentrated area, you see. Now I think it is true that the extent of the action completely surprised everybody, and therefore there was a grave miscalculation about the real situation that existed. But then how can Edmund criticise? Because Edmund himself was in the leadership at that time, and he did not make any different assessment.

XI: Tamil Rights: The LSSP Against Sinhala Only (1955-56)

The background to the difficult question of the relations between the two communities in Ceylon, which ended in the bloody conflict of recent times, can be studied from a Socialist point of view in Vaithianathan Karalasingham's *The Way Out for the Tamil Speaking People* (first published as a series of articles in the Ceylonese *Young Socialist*, nos 6, 7 and 10, July 1962-September 1963); Sydney Wanasinghe's 'From Marxism to Communalism', and 'The Failure of Communalist Politics' (*Young Socialist*, no 13, June 1965, pp113-25; no 15, April 1966, pp210-25); Vickramabahu Karunaratne's *The Lanka Samasamaja Party and the Tamil Speaking People* (Samasamaja publications no 1, Colombo, 1979); and *Tribe, Nation and Assimilation of Nations* (World Publications, Colombo, 1987); and Shanthi Satchithananthan's *The Politics of Communalism and the Tamil Electorate* (V Karalasingham Memorial Lecture, 27 October 1990, LSSP pamphlet). The Revolutionary Workers Party has issued two pamphlets on this issue, *The Tamil Minority Question and the Revolutionary Workers Party* (1978), and *Tamil Liberation Struggle* (June 1990).

The LSSP had always been a supporter of the rights of the Tamils, and indeed was the only party largely from the South that could address mass meetings in Tamil-speaking areas of the country. As early as 1948 the BLPI and the LSSP had opposed the Citizenship Bill and the Immigrants and Emigrants Bill, the first attempts made to remove the citizenship of Tamil workers on the tea and rubber estates (see Colvin R de Silva, *Against Helotry*, two speeches, pamphlet of the Bolshevik-Leninist Party, Ceylon Unit, August 1948; *The Failure of Communalist Politics*, a speech in parliament, LSSP pamphlet, August 1958). The agitation of the newly-formed SLFP for the adoption of Sinhala only as the language of state led inevitably to communalist violence (see 'Ceylan: Les emeutés communalistes', *Quatrième Internationale*, sixteenth year, no 3, July 1958, pp90-2), which the party bravely opposed.

The introduction to this section is extracted from Leslie Goonewardene's *A Short History of the Lanka Sama Samaja Party*, December 1960, pp52-4. This is followed by a number of excerpts from *The State Language Question: A Declaration of the LSSP* (LSSP pamphlet, October 1955), and is rounded off by a number of extracts from a speech made by NM Perera to the Ceylon House of Representatives on 19 October 1955.

Dr Nanayakkarapathirage Martin Perera (1905-1979) was the most popular spokesman for the LSSP. He was a faithful student of Harold Laski, and served as finance minister in the first LSSP-SLFP coalition government. His career can be followed from EP de Silva's *A Short Biography of Dr NM Perera* (Colombo, June 1975), and the obituaries published at the time of his death, Colvin R de Silva, 'NM Perera: Apostle of Social Change' (*Young Socialist*, new series, no 1, March 1980, pp9-10); and 'Obituary of a Traitor' (*Class Struggle*, Volume 1, no 1, February 1980, pp18-21).

Leslie Goonewardene

The Language Question

THE YEAR 1956 saw the dawn of a new era. This new period was characterised not only by an increased consciousness among the masses with regard to their economic rights, but even more by a cultural renaissance among the Sinhalese. This renaissance took the form principally of an effort to elevate the position of the Sinhala language in the state and society, and also of an attempt to revive the customs, traditions and arts of the Sinhalese and to restore Buddhism to the place it had occupied in past history. Unfortunately, however, on the question of the Sinhala language, which was the most important question, the demand took the form of a movement to make Sinhala the sole official language, to the exclusion of Tamil, which is spoken by a quite considerable minority.

In April 1955 the political resolution adopted at the party conference had stated as follows: 'The potentiality of this new factor in our politics (the language problem) has not in fact been grasped by our party thus far. We have no doubt seen the *swabasha*[1] question as a question of national unity, but we have not sufficiently grasped the necessity, or the potentialities, of advocating it in the form and as a means of the struggle for the completion of our national independence. The party will certainly have to take up the *swabasha* weapon much more as its own, instead of leaving it in wrong and reactionary hands.'

True, even after the conference the party did not sufficiently grasp

1. Native language.

the importance of the question and make a determined effort to work according to the spirit of this resolution. But even if it had done so, to put it at its lowest, it is extremely doubtful that the party could have altered the course of subsequent events. For the movement represented by 'Sinhala Only' became not only a movement for raising the status of the Sinhala language to the status of an official language, but also a movement against the Tamil minority. This movement was fed not only by historical factors, but also by economic competition between the two communities, particularly in relation to jobs. The fact that no mass struggle for independence had taken place, fostering a common bond of Ceylonese consciousness in the two communities, made such a development all the easier.

The natural leadership of this movement of cultural renaissance among the Sinhalese went to the SLFP, which in 1955 changed its language policy from Sinhalese and Tamil as state languages to one of Sinhala as the sole official language. The leadership was further consolidated when, shortly before the general election of 1956, the SLFP combined with the LSSP of Philip Gunawardena to form the Mahajana Eksath Peramuna (MEP).

The Lanka Sama Samaja Party was the only party with a base among the Sinhalese that stood firmly right to the end by its policy of both Sinhala and Tamil as official languages. Even the Communist Party latterly changed its position on this question. In October 1955 a public meeting held by the party on this question at the Colombo Town Hall was attacked by a hostile crowd with brickbats and bombs, while the police stood by. The police finally moved into action only to baton-charge and disperse those who were leaving the meeting after it had concluded. Both friend and foe expressed their admiration of the party's devotion to principle. But there is no gainsaying that the party has paid a heavy price for its stand. It lost heavily among the Sinhalese masses. And although it has won the sympathy of the minorities, this has far from compensated for the losses.

The party's position on the question of the citizenship of the workers of Indian origin on the plantations has also cost the party a price, but the effect of this has been principally in the up-country areas. However, the party has never ceased its opposition to the unjust citizenship laws, and has adhered to its position that those who are permanent residents who desire to make Ceylon their home should be granted citizenship. (The corollary of this is, of course, that the others should become Indian citizens, so that there is no category of 'stateless' people left.)

As a revolutionary Socialist party, the Lanka Sama Samaja party could not have acted otherwise. For, as distinct from opportunist politicians to whom power is an end in itself, to the LSSP power is only a means to an end. That is Socialism. And it knows that Socialism cannot be built except on the basis of the unity and willing cooperation of all the communities that inhabit Ceylon. And that unity and cooperation can only be achieved by a correct attitude to the problem of the minorities.

The State Language Question
A Declaration of the LSSP (excerpts)

THE LANKA Sama Samaja Party has always stood for the administration of the country in Sinhalese and Tamil, which are the languages of the vast majority of the people of Ceylon. It will be remembered that as far back as 1937, as a first step in this direction, the party's representatives in the then State Council moved resolutions demanding that proceedings in the lower courts should be conducted in Sinhalese and Tamil, and that facilities be provided for the making of entries in police stations in these languages. These resolutions were an effort to implement in the legislature of the country the following 'immediate demand' which the party made in its very first manifesto in 1935 when the party was founded: 'Use of the vernaculars in the lower courts of law and in entries and recorded statements of police stations, and the extension of this use to all government departments.' Looking back in retrospect, it is impossible not to ask oneself how much simpler the transition to a *swabasha* administration would have been today, if these early suggestions had been accepted and acted upon at the time.

It is the imperative necessity that the people should be governed in a language they understand that makes the LSSP demand that the state languages of Ceylon should be Sinhalese and Tamil. For, while the majority know only the Sinhalese language, a large minority know only Tamil. It is only with the carrying out of this change that the people can come into their own.

The ruling United National Party has today been compelled to accept the justice of the demand that the state languages of Ceylon should be Sinhalese and Tamil. But as the party of the capitalists, it is tied to vested interests on the one hand, and on the other hand is fearful of the masses, who will certainly play a more vigorous rôle in politics when the administration [of the country] is conducted in a language which they understand. Consequently, the UNP government pays only lip-service to the cause of making Sinhalese and Tamil the state languages of the country. It takes no decisive step which will bring about, or even seriously prepare, this transition, but instead follows a vacillating and planless policy which will result in the indefinite postponement of the day of such a change.

Comrade NM Perera's motion, therefore, demanding that an amendment be made to the constitution providing for the recognition of Sinhalese and Tamil as the state languages of the country calls the bluff of the UNP. If the UNP is indeed for Sinhalese and Tamil as the state languages, and not for the status quo, then there is no reason why they should object to the inclusion of such a clause in the constitution. The inclusion of such a clause in the constitution will at least have the effect of helping to allay the suspicions of the Tamil-speaking minority that Tamil will not be accorded the same status as Sinhalese as a state language.

There has, however, recently arisen another section of politicians in Ceylon, such as the SLFP and the party of Mr Philip Gunawardena, who stand for Sinhalese alone as the language of Ceylon, with Tamil as a regional language in Tamil-speaking areas (and also, according to the SLFP, as a language permissible in parliament). This is a new proposal in the area of Ceylon politics, and the main purpose of this statement is to make public the views of the LSSP in relation to this proposal.

It is necessary to point out that this question of whether the state language should be Sinhalese, or Sinhalese and Tamil, has already ceased to be simply a question of which proposal is more practicable or suitable, and it would be completely unrealistic to view it simply as a state language question. It has already become a communal question, in which is involved the bigger question of the welding of the different races of Ceylon into a single Ceylonese nation.

We are living in a period in which a Ceylonese nation is being born. This process represents a natural and progressive step forward in our development. However, this process is being impeded and endangered by communalism, both Sinhalese and Tamil. It must be said that, as was to be expected, communal sentiments have in particular gathered force; among the Tamil-speaking sections, because they constitute a minority, communal and separatist leaders have been able successfully to sow the fear among these sections of Sinhalese domination. It is indeed true that there is a section of influential Ceylonese politicians who in fact aim at such domination. Nevertheless, the important point is not to consider whether these fears are justified and if they are justified to what extent they are justified, but to discover how these fears can be removed, and the process of the growth of a Ceylonese nation can proceed unimpeded.

We should never forget that the Sinhalese and Tamil languages are also the languages of different races, and further that these races occupy different and separate parts of our country. Therefore, separatist tendencies, once allowed to arise and develop, can culminate readily in the division of the country into two separate states.

That is why the state language question is not simply a language question, but a question which involves the building of a Ceylonese nation, and specifically the fusion of the Sinhalese and Tamil-speaking sections into the Ceylonese nation that is coming into being. This process can only be accomplished by the adoption of Sinhalese and Tamil as the state languages of Ceylon with parity of status throughout the country.

What, we would ask the Sinhalese-as-the-state-language protagonists, is really lost by granting this status to the Tamil language? Why, for their part, are they so insistent on Sinhalese alone enjoying this status, particularly when the process of the formation of a Ceylonese nation is thereby so seriously jeopardised? The only meaning

𝕭ooks 𝖂anted

𝔓lease write to us if you can provide us with any of these

Tariq Ali, *Redemption*
Belfort Bax, *The Legal Subjection of Men*
Mika Etchebehere, *Ma Guerre D'Espagne a Moi*
Peter Kropotkin, *Memoirs*
VI Lenin, *Collected Works*, part ii of index
Sidney Lens, *Unrepentant Radical*
James Malloy, *Bolivia: The Uncompleted Revolution*
Grigori Maximov, *The Guillotine at Work*, Volume 2
Ivan Maistrenko, *Borotbism: A Chapter in the History of Ukrainian Communism*
J Moneta, *La Politique coloniale du PCF (1921-1965)*
Peter Petrov, *The Secrets of Hitler's Victory*
John Reed, *The War in Eastern Europe*
Arthur Rosenberg, *The History of the Weimar Republic*
David Rousset, *The Other Kingdom*
Jorge Semprun, *The Second Death of Ramón Mercader*
Léon Trotsky, *Oeuvres* (French), first series, volumes 22 to end; new series covering 1928 onwards, all volumes.
Albert Weisbord, *The Conquest of Power*, Volume 1
Robert Werth, *Leon Trotsky*

that we can attribute to their actions is that they really stand, not for a Ceylonese nation, but for a Sinhalese nation.

The LSSP, which stands for the emancipation of all the toilers in Ceylon regardless of race, caste or creed, stands also for the building of a Ceylonese nation. It will continue to oppose communalism, whether it be of the minority, or of the majority variety. It points out that the growth of communalism in Ceylon, seven years after the transfer of power by the imperialists, is proof of the inability of the capitalist class to build a Ceylonese nation, and is a testimony to the bankruptcy of capitalist leadership. This task too, namely, that of building a Ceylonese nation, along with the other social and political tasks before the people of Ceylon, will only be solved under the leadership of the working class and its party, the Lanka Sama Samaja Party.

NM Perera

For Parity of Status

Speech in the Ceylon House of Representatives, 19 October 1955 (excerpts)

Dr NM Perera: I move: 'That in the opinion of this House the Ceylon (Constitution) Order in Council should be amended further to provide for the Sinhalese and Tamil languages to be state languages of Ceylon with parity of status throughout the Island.' This motion is in my own name as being sponsored by the Lanka Sama Samaja Party, but the government will realise that this is a motion of paramount importance to every section of the people of this country. I have no hesitation in saying, Mr Speaker, that a correct solution to this problem will make it easy for this country to continue as one united nation. But if we take a wrong step, I think we will be courting disaster. I say that with all the solemnity I can command. I am gravely conscious of the importance of the situation.

It would have been easy for me, and the members of my party, to have sponsored the very popular idea, Sinhalese only, and we would have been acclaimed as heroes, as a good many others have been. But our party has taken up a consistent attitude. Ever since our party was launched, we have never faltered or wavered from that position, because we felt that was the correct line to take. That position we still adhere to. However unpopular that line of action might be, I am convinced myself of the correctness of our attitude. It might mean going into the political wilderness for some time, but still we, the members of the Lanka Sama Samaja Party, are prepared to face that. Let there be no mistake about it. For a just cause, for correct principles, for a correct political line, I think, it is fully worth it. The membership of this House is not the be-all and end-all of a political party.

If all of us are agreed that we must endeavour to build up a united nation in this country — notwithstanding the diverse cultures we have, notwithstanding the diversities of language we have — that we want to build up unity in diversity; if that is our objective, then I say in all earnestness that we must take a course of action which will enable us to achieve that object. I sincerely hope that there are no members here, or people outside, who are not wedded to that object.

I dare say there is a section that does not view it in that light. I refer to an organisation called the Tri Sinhala Peramuna.

Mr DBR Gunawardena: Headed by Mr JR Jayawardene.

Dr Perera: There is that so-called organisation which, apparently, thinks of building a nation only out of the Sinhalese. Sinhala alone will form not a Ceylonese nation, but a Sinhalese nation; all the other minorities are to be left outside. I have no doubt that there are important members of the government who are apparently associated with that organisation. I know a good number of people outside, good capitalists — I do not want to mention names — good supporters also of the United National Party, who are sponsoring that organisation. We had a taste of their activities last Sunday at the Town Hall.

This matter has agitated the minds of a large number of people outside, people of political organisations of one type or another, except of course the members of the Cabinet. Most politicians of one hue or another have expressed their opinions, whatever they may be, except the one category of people who are or should be most concerned about this issue. It would appear that they are the most silent on this issue. They have buried their heads in the political sand and refuse to look at the question.

In the process of considering this matter, all these gentlemen have referred to and drawn analogies from various countries. Some of them have gone to Soviet Russia, and others to countries like India, England, Switzerland, Finland, Ireland, Belgium, Canada and so on. I think it would be entirely wrong to draw conclusions from the historical experience of those countries and say that the present position in Ceylon must necessarily be analogous. Whether we like it or not, we are conditioned by certain historical facts, confronted with particular historical situations.

I think we ought to recognise that if we had never been a colony, if we never came under the British, or for the matter of that even the Portuguese or the Dutch, we may never have had such a problem at all. The Portuguese were all out to create dissension in the country, to keep the people apart as much as possible. They forced their language, their religion and their customs on the people of this country. The Dutch did the same. They also created artificial distinctions and fostered them, setting up one community or one racial group against another, and created a great deal of dissension. Not only that, these new colonial masters brought new elements into the country, established them here, and created fresh problems for us. The British did the same.

The Right Honourable Sir J Kotelawala: What about Keuneman? The Dutch brought Keuneman, and created a problem for us.[2]

Mr Keuneman: That is the only good thing that the Dutch did for Ceylon.

Dr Perera: In that connection, Sir, I am fully inclined to believe that we owe a deep debt of gratitude to the Dutch for giving us my good friend the Honourable First Member for Colombo Central. All that I am pointing out is this. The British people did create a lot of trouble. The fact is that we were a colony, and the biggest problem of the moment is that they imposed their language on us. That was thrust down upon us, whether we liked it or not. A good number of people — maybe my own ancestors — willingly embraced English, learned English; a good deal of people, mainly from the upper classes, learned English, and, in point of fact, absorbed it as part of their home language, to the detriment of the Sinhalese language or even, in certain cases, the Tamil language. The mother tongue became a sort of domestic language confined to the hearths, the homes and no more; but nevertheless the Sinhalese language flourished in the villages, where the British connection did not penetrate so deeply, where it was not felt very much.

We are now confronted with the question of replacing the official language, which is the English language, by another language or languages. Mr Speaker, with your permission I shall read a small paragraph from the statement issued by the Lanka Sama Samaja Party about two or three days ago:

2. Pieter Keuneman (1917-) was the veteran leader of the Communist Party in Ceylon.

'The Lanka Sama Samaja Party's demand for Sinhalese and Tamil as the state languages, it should be made clear at the outset, flows from a very real concern for the interests of the people who speak these languages, and not from some merely academic interest in these languages. The state language in Ceylon continues to be English, despite the fact that barely seven per cent of the inhabitants have any knowledge of this language. Practically the entire remaining 93 per cent speak only Sinhalese or Tamil. These people are not only impeded in their day-to-day lives, but are prevented from intelligently following how they are being governed, as a result of the administration of the country being in a language which they do not understand. To speak of democracy in such a situation is a farce. To perpetuate such a situation seven years after the transfer of political power by the British imperialists is outrageous.'[3]

That sums up the attitude that we have taken. We have been for *swabasha*, that is, for Sinhalese and Tamil, ever since we started in 1935. That was one of the items in our first programme issued by the Lanka Sama Samaja Party, that the administration of the country should be in Sinhalese and Tamil. Consequent to that attitude, in 1936 the then member for Avissawella [Philip Gunawardena] introduced a motion in this House that as a beginning the work in the Police Courts and Municipal Courts should be conducted, as it was termed, in the vernacular, in Sinhalese and Tamil.

I want now to nail that lie — because I have heard it said — that those who are asking for parity are really in disguise asking for English. That charge has been made — a thoroughly undeserved charge, because not one of these people who have now suddenly become vociferous about the national languages raised his voice. We were the only people who were fighting against the English language at that time. The charge should be levelled against the Cabinet. The real charge against them is that while they are paying lip service to Sinhalese and Tamil being the official languages, they are really thinking of English as the only official language and continuing it.

The Honourable JR Jayawardene: You are speaking in English.

Dr Perera: You have not made arrangements for the use of the national languages even here. If there is provision for simultaneous translation the position will be different.

My good friend, the Right Honourable Gentleman [Sir John Kotelawala], went to Jaffna recently where he had more garlands than he could carry. I do not know whether he was overwhelmed by those

3.   From *The State Language Question: A Declaration of the LSSP.*

garlands, or inebriated by the warmth of the welcome he was given there, but he made a promise to the people of Jaffna that he would be prepared to amend the constitution to provide for both languages as official languages. My good friend changed his mind after he came back from Jaffna. He came down to Colombo, and said that he did not make such a promise. I ask you, what is wrong about that promise which he made? Although the Right Honourable Gentleman may have been carried away by his emotions on that occasion it is the correct thing that he did, the only correct thing he has done in his life so far as the political future of this country is concerned. It is my charge against him that he has failed to do it.

Ever since then there have been vague statements, but I want to ask in all seriousness, can any one Sinhalese minister on the front benches get up in this House and say that at any particular place in Colombo, or anywhere in this country, he has openly declared that they are for Sinhalese and Tamil as the official languages? Is there one such single minister, barring the Right Honourable Gentleman? The other ministers, the Tamil members of the cabinet, have gone about trying to plead on behalf of the government, trying to interpret the policy of the Cabinet, in Jaffna and elsewhere; and of course there are some minor fry, like junior ministers, who have become very vocal about it. These are the people who are propagating the so-called policy, but, I ask you, what amount of confidence can the people of Jaffna and the Tamil-speaking people in the East and elsewhere have in this matter, when the other Sinhalese ministers of the cabinet are not prepared unequivocally to state in the country that they are in favour of both Sinhalese and Tamil as official languages? What conclusion can they come to but that you are not playing fair by them, and that at the end you will fall back on Sinhalese as the only official language? That is the fear they have, and that is the fear that we must throw out of their minds.

Everything that this government has done vis-à-vis some of the minority communities, particularly the Tamil community, has been wrong. You have aggravated feelings, exacerbated feelings. Most of the recent actions of the government have tended to create more bitterness among the Tamil community than anything that has been done in the past. Even some of the administrative acts that have been done have had that effect. I say that by your conduct you have strengthened the communalists in Jaffna, the people whom you do not want to strengthen in Jaffna.

All this is due to your short-sighted policy. It is necessary to foster the most progressive elements who are prepared to work with the majority community harmoniously and make Ceylon a united country, but what are you doing? It is a tragic situation. Honourable Members must realise this. In the process what are you doing? You are fanning the worst of sentimental flames. We can fight on political ideologies, on economic principles, but when it comes to rousing people to a state of mass hysteria on issues like religion, language and race, there is no knowing where it will end. If Honourable Members had seen the spectacle I witnessed on Sunday at the Town Hall grounds, they would have been ashamed of themselves. They would have felt sorry for the future of this country.

I was trying to point out to Honourable Members that it is not enough for us merely to mouth phrases and say that the minority communities have nothing to fear from the majority community; that in the past we have all got on well, and that we will get on in the same old way. That is not enough today. Today, the situation has gone beyond that. Today, we have to do something positive in order to allay these fears that are increasing. What is worse, if we do not take a positive stand, we will continue to give room for Sinhalese chauvinists to do what damage they can.

The Honourable JR Jayawardene: He is on your left![4]

Dr Perera: I am not referring to any one person. There are people on the other side who do the same thing, who say one thing here and a different thing in their constituencies, and who are really for Sinhalese and Sinhalese alone. There are a good number of members at the back. It is my contention that parity will be the answer to this, meaning that there is equal status for both Sinhalese and Tamil — and the only reason I am asking that the constitution be amended is that it will allay all these fears once and for all.

Let us get down to the meaning of 'equality of status'. All that this motion urges is that equality of status should be given not merely a formal recognition, but that it should be recognised in a tangible way. The minorities must be made to feel that there is something positive in the assurances we give them, that they have nothing to fear at all, that their interests will be safeguarded for good. That is necessary in view of the chauvinistic attitude that is growing up in certain quarters.

Some time back these positive assurances may not have been necessary, but today the position is different. Today we find it difficult even to hold an ordinary meeting to explain the position to the public because the other — the chauvinistic — attitude has got the better of them.

When I use the words 'parity of status', all that I am concerned to

4. Presumably a reference to Philip Gunawardena

ensure is that when a Tamil, wherever he may be, writes a letter in Tamil, say, to the local *kacheri*,[5] or to a department in that area, he should receive a reply in Tamil as of right — not merely as a concession — as of right due to a member of the Ceylonese nation. In the same way, a Sinhalese living, say, in Jaffna should be able to get a reply in Sinhalese, whether it be in Jaffna or Batticaloa. He must be able to get his birth certificate, or any other official document, if he so wants it, in Sinhalese. A Tamil should get a reply in Tamil, and a Sinhalese should be able to get a reply in Sinhalese.

This is not seriously objected to by anyone, and yet they say: 'We cannot amend the constitution to provide for this.' Why not, if such an amendment to the constitution will create harmony in the country? Some Honourable Members are opposed to an amendment of the constitution because at the back of their minds there is an unwillingness to recognise the official status of Tamil. They want to have only Sinhalese. At some stage or other they feel that they can ram Sinhalese down the throats of the minority. That is why they take up this position.

I was trying to explain the implications of parity of status as I understand it. It does not necessarily mean that in predominantly Tamil areas or in predominantly Sinhalese areas every person should know both languages. The real fundamental position is that a Tamil-speaking person will have the right to go before a court and get his case heard in a language which he understands. It may mean the use of an interpreter in a particular case. It is a right that he has. That is important.

What 'parity of status' means is a recognition of a right that each individual has to be governed in the language which he understands, so that all his dealings with the government are in a language that he understands. It also means legislatively that a person who comes to this House can speak either in Sinhalese or in Tamil. He will not be entitled to speak in Tamil if Sinhalese is the official language. If Sinhalese is the only official language, no member from a Tamil-speaking area will be in a position to work in this House, because amendments cannot be moved in Tamil. That is what Sinhalese as the only official language means.

I have seen a statement in the local press that their [the government's] reluctance to accept this motion is because they feel that it is not seriously meant, that it is an election stunt. I want to ask Honourable Members if they really understand the meaning of words when they use words like 'election stunt'. It would have been an election stunt if we said that Sinhalese should be the only official lan-

5. A government office for records.

guage, because that is running with the current. We do swim against the current. If it is an election stunt, there is no need to stand all the abuse, and brave all the stones and the hand-grenades, and to lose your limbs. If you say that Sinhalese should be the only language, then you are popular. But to state that both languages must be given official status is not an election stunt. It is the contrary. It is fighting for a principle.

There are some Honourable Members who say that to give equality of status to both languages is undemocratic, that the vast majority of the people are Sinhalese and therefore they are entitled to have Sinhalese as the official language, and the idea of giving equality of status to a language which is spoken by a small minority — on their own admission the figures are about 58 lakhs Sinhalese-speaking to about 23 lakhs Tamil-speaking — is a denial of democracy. All I can say is that this is a very strange concept of democracy. Democracy, apparently, is purely a counting of heads.

If democracy is to be treated as an arithmetical concept, that whatever the majority decides must be accepted, then, if the majority decides that the majority religion must prevail, it must be accepted merely because they have got superiority in numbers. That is not democracy. In a democracy where you have different communities, where you have different religions, the sovereignty of the majority is automatically checked by those inalienable rights that the minorities have, which cannot be overridden by the mere whim and fancy of a majority.

That is what democracy means; it is not merely a counting of heads. If that were so, if democracy is to be interpreted in that way, it will be the simplest thing for the majority of this House to pass a resolution that in future only Sinhalese-speaking people will get jobs in government service. Would that be democracy? That would be a denial, a travesty of democracy. When put in that particular way, Honourable Members might be against the idea of a majority passing a resolution to that effect. But is it not the same thing? In point of fact, if you insist on Sinhalese as the only official language, does it not come to the same thing in the end, namely that those who do not speak Sinhalese will automatically get weeded out by virtue of the fact that they cannot speak the Sinhalese language? Does it not mean that?

It will mean, if Sinhalese is the only official language, that all people must carry out their business, and carry out their transactions with the government, in Sinhalese. No other language will be permitted, no other language will have official status. A Tamil person will not be able to obtain from the government a reply in Tamil to a letter that he writes; he will not be able to get a document in Tamil. It will be true also of this parliament: a member cannot make a speech in Tamil; he will not be in a position to introduce amendments or motions in Tamil. That is the implication of having Sinhalese as the sole official language of this country.

Do Honourable Members seriously believe that we can compel the minority community to accept that position, and that we can force them to that position? Of course, if they are willing to accept that position, it is a different matter. But the present position is that they, the Tamil-speaking people, are not disposed to accept it. We can certainly try to persuade them, but if they do not like to do it, are Honourable Members prepared to compel them to do everything in Sinhalese, even as the British compelled us to do everything in English? Are we to continue the exploitation that the British and other imperialist powers carried out in this country? After a struggle for freedom apparently from exploitation, are we to exploit and oppress the minorities? No, Mr Speaker.

The answer to this question apparently is given in a different way: of course, Tamil can be a regional language confined to the areas where there are predominantly Tamil-speaking people — the Northern and Eastern Provinces — and the rest of the country will have Sinhalese as the official language. However, the important point still is that Sinhalese will be the state language throughout the country, which means, therefore, that a Sinhalese person in Jaffna will have the right to have his business transacted in Sinhalese, but a Tamil person in Colombo will not have the right to have his business transacted in Tamil, because Tamil, as a regional language, will be confined only to the Northern and Eastern Provinces; and in the rest of the Island any non-Sinhalese person will still be compelled to have his business transacted through the Sinhalese language.

In point of fact, therefore, it also means that those who are at present in employment and who cannot speak Sinhalese will have to leave, will have to migrate, or will be pushed on to the Northern and Eastern Provinces. You are, therefore, forcing all this non-Sinhalese-speaking element, that is the Tamil-speaking element, to the Northern and Eastern Provinces. That will be the logical conclusion if Sinhalese is made the only official language.

There are political parties who advocate this in Ceylon. Well, Sir, if this is the position, what is the logical step? Those people who advocate this are really advocating the federalism of Mr Chelvanayakam.[6] Nobody can deny that. Precisely that is what Mr Chelvanay-

6.   Samuel James Velupillai Chelvanayakam (1898-1977), the MP for Kankesanturai, and one of the leaders of the Tamil Congress, later set up the Tamil Federal Party.

akam has been arguing for, over and over again. Having Tamil as a regional language in the Northern and Eastern Provinces would mean having federalism in this country. They will have a separate government. Is there any earthly reason why they should agree to be a portion of Ceylon if they are to be confined to those areas? In point of fact, therefore, if that argument is advanced, we are recognising the right, we are recognising the justice of the claim made by Mr Chelvanayakam, that federalism is the only solution to the present language problem in Ceylon.

Now, I wonder how many Honourable Members here consider the implications of that. Ceylon is a small country. Even if we concede that the other portions of the Island can exist by themselves, the Northern and Eastern Provinces are certainly not viable: they cannot live; they will not last a few months. They have one or two alternatives. For instance, we should prepare to accept them as a federation, and give them all the assistance to make them viable and have a federated state for Ceylon, small as it is. That is thoroughly unworkable, and I am certain they will go away with so much disharmony and ill-feeling that the rest of Ceylon will not be prepared to do that.

Then what is the other alternative left for the Northern and Eastern Provinces? They must break away and join somebody else. Certainly that is what is likely to happen. That will be the logical sequence of compelling the Tamil minority to swallow Sinhalese, and enforcing Tamil as the regional language for those areas. They will either look to India, or, as is likely to happen, other imperialist countries will be fishing in troubled waters. The United States has done that more than once. Any big country will find this a convenient fish to swallow. And let us not forget that the British still have got their bases in this country. Let it also not be forgotten by Honourable Members that it is still possible within this constitution for the government to hand them over to the British, because — it is one of the alternative possibilities, of course — you can send an army from the South to the Northern and Eastern Provinces, and compel them by force of arms to accept Sinhalese as the official language and Tamil as the regional language, and be within Ceylon. Does any person in his senses seriously contemplate that possibility of sending an army of occupation? If you compel these people in the Northern and Eastern Provinces to accept Sinhalese only as the state language and Tamil as a regional language, it will lead to so much rioting, bloodshed and civil war. That will give the imperialists the one chance they have been waiting for for so long, with all their bases here, to come and occupy this place because we are incapable of governing ourselves.

Those are the alternatives to which we are being pushed by the short-sighted policy that has been advocated by various people. There are a large number of people who in the backwoods did not hesitate to advocate Sinhalese being made the only state language. That is my charge, and that is why it has become necessary for me to bring this motion before the House. That is why I am asking Honourable Members to support this motion. Why I am pleading with Honourable Members is to make them realise the dangers of the situation. We are playing with fire. We are creating a tense situation outside by our failure to meet these arguments. The arguments that have been advanced are short-sighted, ill-thought-out and ill-conceived, in order to foster this claim for Sinhalese only as the official language. There is a tremendous amount of opinion for that. Why are Honourable Members so blind to the situation that is developing in the country outside? They are not raising one finger to meet that situation, instead they are encouraging it. It is not too late for us to make amends.

We cannot in all conscience compel the minority communities to accept a language which they do not want to accept. We must try to allay their suspicions, make them realise that we have nothing but goodwill for them, and that we want to treat them as equals. Otherwise, the alternative will be disastrous for the welfare of this country. We shall have a perpetual division of the country, we shall never get a united Ceylon, and we shall have a tremendous amount of bloodshed which will lead us nowhere, and, in the end, this country will either become a colony or a plaything of interested big powers. That is what we must try and avoid. We may have our differences on economic grounds and on other political grounds, but surely on questions of religion, race and language we must have one united policy that will harmonise the various diverse factors and bring them together as one nation. It is in that spirit that I place this motion before the House.

George Orwell and the Left

I am working on a fairly substantial work on the manner in which the legacy of George Orwell has been claimed by commentators of nearly all political persuasions. Part of this project will involve investigating the attitudes of left wing activists towards Orwell and his writings, and in particular his political works. If readers who were around during Orwell's lifetime, or who have studied Orwell's writings, would like to help me in this project, please contact me c/o *Revolutionary History*, BCM 7646, London WC1N 3XX. Thanks to all those who have helped me so far.

Paul Flewers

XII: The LSSP Against the People's Front (1956-1960)

This was a period of general instability in Ceylon. It was marked by new alignments in politics, including an increase in communalism, the accession to office of the Sri Lanka Freedom Party that had been recently founded by Solomon West Ridgeway Dias Bandaranaike (1899-1959), who was Prime Minister from 1956 until his assassination in 1959, plots from the right, and a rising tide of industrial militancy.

Some grasp of the atmosphere at the time can be gained from 'Ceylon: May Day Resolution Moved by the Lanka Sama Samaja Party', 'Our Special Colombo Correspondent', and 'The Strikes of 23 April' (*Information Bulletin* of the International Secretariat of the Fourth International, Volume 1, no 7, 15 May 1958, pp6-8); 'Ceylon: The Recent Strike Wave in the Private Sector' (*Fourth International*, no 2, Spring 1958, p70), and a speech made by Colvin R de Silva at Jaffna on 18 October 1958, *On the Present Situation in Ceylon* (duplicated pamphlet produced by the LSSP Student Union in Great Britain).

The LSSP launched an optimistic campaign for the following elections ('Conference of the Lanka Sama Samaja Party: Political Resolution', *Fourth International*, no 7, Autumn 1959, pp69-76; 'Pour un gouvernement du LSSP', *Quatrième Internationale*, seventeeth year, no 7, September-October 1959, pp86-96; 'Ceylon: LSSP Warns Against Rightist Coup, Demands Workers' Government', *Fourth International*, no 8, Winter 1959-60, pp61-2; 'Our Ceylonese Correspondent', 'The Coming Elections', *The Internationalist*, Volume 4, no 4, 15 February 1960, p2).

It is clear that at this time some of the LSSP's leaders believed that it was even possible for the party to come to power via the ballot box. As reported by G Selvarajatnan in 1978: 'In this connection it is interesting to note a conversation which Leslie Goonewardene had in Soho Square with John Fairhead, Sam Bornstein and G Selvarajatnan in September 1959 on the day of the assassination of Mr Bandaranaike. He wanted to cancel his trip to Europe and return to Sri Lanka the same day. His argument was: "The masses believed in the UNP and became disillusioned. Then they believed in the SLFP, which did not deliver the goods. Now inevitably they are bound to turn to us. I want to be there to conduct operations and form the government. I must go back!"' ('British Friends of the Sri Lankan Trot-

skyists', *A Strange Alliance: The British Militant and the 'Vama'
Samasamajists*, 22 August 1978, p4, n1)
   The two pieces we have selected to illustrate the party's hopes and attitudes at this time are M Grannum, 'Ceylon Trotskyists Double Parliamentary Strength', *Fourth International*, no 4, July-August 1956, pp7-8 (a duplicated magazine produced in London); and 'Behind Bandaranaike's
Assassination', an article by Edmund Samarakkody published in the Socialist Labour League's *Newsletter*, 24 October 1959. 'Grannum' is an
obvious pseudonym, and may stand for Vaithianathan Karalasingham,
who represented the LSSP on the IEC of the International Secretariat at this
time.

M Grannum
The 1956 General Election

A T THE recent general election in Ceylon the Lanka Sama
Samaja Party, section of the Fourth International, increased its
parliamentary strength from seven to 14 seats. Its candidates polled 25
per cent more votes than in the general election of 1952. The party is
now the largest single group in the Opposition, having six more seats
than the former government party (Sir John Kotelawala's United National Party) and 11 more than the Communist Party.
   The sweeping victory of the Popular Front coalition, led by Mr
SWRD Bandaranaike, has immeasurably raised the whole level of
political awakening in Ceylon. With one conclusive kick, the Ceylon
workers and peasants have discarded British imperialism's open and
undisguised big capitalist and feudal agents — the UNP. Unlike their
opposite numbers in India, the bourgeoisie in Ceylon never played so
much as an oppositional rôle to imperialism in the days before the
granting of the façade of 'independence' in 1947. *Whatever measure of
power the Ceylonese bourgeoisie received at the hands of imperialism was
the result of the national struggle of the Indian masses, and not of their
own efforts.* In the whole continent of Asia, one searches in vain for a
colonial bourgeoisie equal in cowardice and treachery to the Sinhalese
capitalists; even in China, in the days of Sun Yat Sen, the bourgeoisie
did better. It was this record of comprador complicity before 1948,
and smug servility after it, which the masses rejected in last month's
election.
   What is the record of the new Prime Minister, and whom does he
represent? SWRD Bandaranaike was a faithful pillar of the UNP un-

til, after the death of Don Stephen Senanayake, he was superseded in the leadership of the party, first by Dudley Senanayake, and later by Sir John. *Bandaranaike's 'opposition' to imperialism dates only from then.* Like the Kisan Mazdoor Praja Party in India, the Ceylonese Sri Lanka Freedom Party (SLFP), which Bandaranaike broke from the UNP, was an extraordinary hodgepodge of bourgeois liberals, religious revivalists, communal traditionalists and pseudo-Socialist phrasemongers. Its guiding philosophy an eclectic ragbag ranging from the Gautama through Gandhi to Bernstein and European revisionism, *its political programme had nonetheless a definite appeal for the discontented petit-bourgeois masses of town and countryside who, while not yet ready to accept working class leadership, were thoroughly discontented with the UNP.* This was the basis upon which the SLFP prospered; yet it was aided from another source.

Unlike the KMPP in India, which in several states fought the 1951 election in harness with the Communist Party of India, Bandaranaike from the start rejected an alliance with the weak Ceylon Communist Party. The hand of uncritical friendship proffered so pathetically and so often by Pieter Keuneman, the Stalinist leader, was contemptuously spurned. Bandaranaike was shrewd enough to realise that the proletariat of Ceylon, in so far as it was consciously organised as a class, was grouped under the banner of the LSSP, the party of the Fourth International. With them — and only with them — was he prepared to consider an 'anti-UNP front'.

Taking its stand on the principled position of world Communism on the question of the People's Front, the LSSP, backed by the International Executive Committee, rejected this approach, *posing instead the need for an anti-capitalist front of workers' parties: the LSSP, the CP and the Philip group.* This the CP rejected, condemning the LSSP leaders as splitters and disrupters.

It was at this stage that a group of the LSSP leadership, Cochranites before Cochran,[1] began to waver beneath the pressure of the CP's accusations. After being given every opportunity to state their case to the membership and failing to convince a majority of the party, this group (William Silva, Henry Peiris, Reggie Perera and a small group of their supporters) left the party and entered into an unprincipled alliance with the Stalinists. Observing, however, that the Stalinists were in themselves persona non grata with Bandaranaike, William Silva and his supporters entered into direct relations with the latter; he has accepted the post of Minister of Industry and Fisheries in the

---

1. Bert Cochran (1917-1984) led a split from the US Socialist Workers Party in support of Pablo in 1953. He subsequently left the Trotskyist movement, and became an academic.

new government. *History will vindicate, not them, but the principled Marxist stand taken up by the overwhelming majority of Ceylonese Trotskyists.* Meanwhile, it is necessary to clarify the situation to our fellow workers in the British labour movement who may have been misled by reports (such as that appearing in the *News Chronicle*) that the new government contained a 'Trotskyist' minister.

For it is certain that the Popular Front leaders, embarrassed by the completeness of their victory and staggering under the weight of the fruits of office so suddenly shaken into their laps, will hesitate and prevaricate before the solution of their tasks: national independence, the public ownership of basic industry, the giving of the land to those who till it. Already the new leaders are drawing back from the thorny problems which confront them: the closing of the British base at Trincomalee, parity of the Tamil tongue with Sinhalese (with which the whole question of Indian labour is bound up), the nationalisation of the tea and rubber estates. In the wings, the disappointed Sir John must already be consoling himself by muttering the rebuke he made famous in his passage with the Eastcheap teabrokers: 'Damned ridiculous!'

In truth, these problems can be solved only by the strength of the organised and united working class. Against the false 'People's Front' of Bandaranaike, the LSSP demands a real united front of workers' parties! In place of timid tinkering, nationalisation of the land and industry under workers' control. Instead of 'neutralism', a bold alignment with the people of India and the colonies and semi-colonies, with the workers of the metropolitan countries and with the workers' states in China and Eastern Europe. That is the only hope of the Ceylonese workers. That is the *real* voice of Trotskyism in Ceylon.

Edmund Samarakkody
Behind Bandaranaike's Assassination

TO ASCERTAIN and understand the forces behind the assassination of Mr Bandaranaike, it is necessary to recapitulate some facts about the Mahajana Eksath Peramuna (People's United Front) government which came into existence in April 1956. The MEP was a petit-bourgeois front with a programme of bourgeois reforms. This front received a Socialist coloration by the presence of two ex-Marxists — Philip Gunawardena and William Silva — in the cabinet.

The Front comprised a number of groups. One led by Dahanayake called itself the Language (Sinhalese) Front. The largest group was the Sri Lanka Freedom Party (SLFP) of Bandaranaike — a party of the small capitalists. From the outset a militant Sinhalese Buddhist group, backed by a section of the monks, sought in a determined manner to influence and control the government.

Within two months of the formation of the government, this group, led by a parliamentary secretary and a university lecturer, together with certain prominent Buddhist monks, resorted to direct action by staging a hunger strike to prevent the Prime Minister from granting 'concessions' to the Tamils on the language question. This passive resistance was developed by them into open active resistance in anti-Tamil riots in June 1956 when the Sinhalese Only Bill was introduced in parliament.

On the economic front this same group, with recruits from others, sought to oppose nationalisation proposals and the limited land reform of the government — the Paddy Lands Act introduced by the former food minister, Gunawardena. With their minds firmly set against the economic reconstruction of the country in a progressive direction, they sought to prevent Bandaranaike from passing any measures that appeared as concessions to the working class and the peasantry.

The first concession to working class pressure was in October 1957, when Bandaranaike gave in to the government workers' strike of 80 000 led by the Lanka Sama Samaja Party. With the forward movement of the working class, the Sinhalese Buddhist group combined to fan the flames of communal hatred. The language issue was once again taken up. Bandaranaike sought a solution of the communal question within the framework of his own policy. He was ready for compromise and concessions. But the racialists in the government opposed any concessions.

In the government parliamentary party, ministers Dahanayake and Marikkar[2] took the lead, while the Bhikkus (Buddhist monks) of the MEP came out in full force in this anti-Tamil campaign. The petit-bourgeois opportunist group of Philip Gunawardena came into action, and the communal reactionary forces outside the People's United Front also played their part in the campaign.

2.   CAS Marikkar (1911-1970), a Sinhalese chauvinist popularly known as 'Sinhala Marikkar', was a member of the SLFP and Minister for Posts, Broadcasting and Information.

The result was an unprecedented communal conflagration. Over 1000 people lost their lives. There was widespread looting and burning of property. The Public Security Act was brought into operation, and a state of emergency declared which lasted 10 months, till February 1959. The serious rupture of communal relations and the virtual break-up of society into Sinhalese and Tamil areas was a victory for the extreme racialist group. Prime Minister Bandaranaike sought to resist the pressure of the united group of extreme communalists by encouraging the rival petit-bourgeois grouping of Gunawardena and William Silva.

The mass situation did not permit him to flirt any more with the so-called left. In spite of the serious communal riots and the 10 months of emergency, which restricted democratic and trade union rights, the strike movement spread extensively. The strikes since October 1957 are unprecedented in the history of Ceylon. The first mass political strike since the government was set up took place in March 1959. The racialist reactionary group now decided on firm action. They demanded the ending of Bandaranaike's balancing tactics. They would no longer tolerate even Socialist phrase-mongering. This group decided to fight the Philip Gunawardena group to a finish.

May 1959 brought the biggest government crisis since 1956. The racialists utilised the situation arising out of the controversial Cooperative Bank Bill to demand the removal of the Gunawardena group from the cabinet. The Prime Minister sought to continue his balancing act as before. But this time it was impossible. To do so would have meant the resignation of nine ministers, and the possibility of losing the presidency of his own party. At the threat of Dahanayake being made the President of his party, the Prime Minister yielded and threw out the 'Marxists' from the cabinet. The right wing communal group won the day. At last it appeared as if Bandaranaike were under their control.

But the tendency of Bandaranaike to yield to mass pressure was very strong. The last Colombo port strike in August, which lasted 26 days, showed that he was still unreliable. It was the determined and continued pressure of the Dahanayake-Stanley de Zoysa[3] group that prevented the Prime Minister from giving in to the strikers. The reactionary group could not take the bold steps needed to save capitalism with Bandaranaike as Prime Minister. He had to be removed if the working class and the peasants were to be effectively controlled. The assassin brought victory to these forces. The Prime Minister was shot,

3.   Stanley de Zoysa (1907-1970), a pioneer of the Suriya Mal movement, was MP for Ja-Ela in 1950, then Minister for Home Affairs, and later Ambassador to Indonesia.

killed and buried with the biggest funeral ever. When the weeping and the government ceremonies were over, one fact emerged in bold relief — that racialist, capitalist reactionary forces through former education minister Dahanayake had usurped the power.

The Dahanayake government will not make any concessions to the masses. On the contrary, the general economic conditions in the country and the present financial situation of the government will push it to an immediate head-on collision with the working class, to pave the way for a military dictatorship, if necessary. It is clear that a revolutionary situation is maturing in Ceylon. If the working class led by the LSSP is equal to its task, the setting up of a workers' and peasants' government is a real possibility.

Magazines Wanted

Please write to us if you can provide us with any of these

Fourth International (USA)

Whole numbers 1, 5, 35, 110, 112, 115, 117, 129, 132.

New International (USA)

Volume 1, nos 1, 3; Volume 2, nos 2, 3, 5, 6; Volume 3, nos 1; whole numbers 16, 18, 40-63, 65-69, 71, 73-75, 77-82, 85-88, 90, 92, 93, 107, 132, 177, 178.

La Vérité (France, PCI/OCI, magazine format)

Nos 1, 2, 4, 6- 513; 517, 518, 558, 571, 621.

Quatrième Internationale (France)

Nos 1-3, 8-19, December 1945-April 1947, July-December 1947, November-December 1950, November-December 1951, November-December 1952, February 1953-May 1955, July-September 1955, January-February 1956, April-May 1956, August 1956, January-February 1957, December 1957, January 1958, August-December 1960, August-October 1961, December 1961, May-November 1962, January 1963-January 1964, December 1965-May 1966, May-October 1968, November-December 1971, Summer 1975-September 1980, January 1982-May 1983, September 1984-March 1990, all after November 1993.

Sous le Drapeau du Socialisme (France)

Nos 1-17, 19-22, 25-36, 60, 62, 63, 74, 76, 81, 117, 120, 122 onwards.

XIII: The Years of Crisis
(1960-1964)

The following description of how the LSSP took the decision to conclude an electoral pact with the SLFP, the Communist Party and the MEP, and then enter the government of Mrs Sirimavo Ratwatte Dias Bandaranaike (1916-), the widow of the former Prime Minister, comes to us from Yodage Ranjith Amarasinghe's thesis *Trotskyism in Ceylon* (pp193-248), to whom we offer our thanks. It is followed by an analysis of the historical reasons for this unprecedented step taken from the third chapter of Vaithianathan Karalasingham's *Politics of Coalition* (International Publishers, October 1964, pp63-75), a pamphlet dedicated to Sam and Doris Bornstein.

Karalasingham joined the LSSP in 1937, and during the war he edited the BLPI's magazine *Permanent Revolution* until his arrest in Bombay in 1945. He continued to work for the movement in India for a while in the postwar period, representing the Indian group at the Third World Congress of the Fourth International in 1951 (see 'The War in Korea', in *The Origins of the International Socialists*, London, 1971, pp76-8). He studied law in Britain between 1952 and 1958, and after a violent altercation with Mike Banda he left the Healy organisation and joined the group around Sam Bornstein in London that remained loyal to the International Secretariat after the split of 1953. He returned to Ceylon to contest the Kankesanturai constituency in the North on behalf of the LSSP in the 1960 general election. When the decision was taken to enter the government he split from the party with the left wing to set up the LSSP(R) in 1964. Karlo's later break with the LSSP(R) over its decision to allow its MPs to vote with the right to bring down the coalition is explained in full in *Senile Leftism: A Reply to Edmund Samarakkody* (International Publishers, December 1966). He returned to the LSSP, and ended his career as a director of the national carrier, Air Ceylon.

The documentation explaining how the LSSP passed over to a coalition with the SLFP is very rich, and only a part of it can be summarised here. The initial decision of the party to conclude a no-contest pact and support a government with the SLFP in 1960 is fully covered in 'Documents on the Ceylon Question' (*Internal Bulletin* of the International Secretariat of the Fourth International, October 1960). The short and rather mild public criticism issued by the International Secretariat at this time is to be found in 'On Ceylon: Declaration of the ISFI of 10 September 1960' (*Fourth International*, no 11, Autumn 1960, pp53-4; 'Déclaration du SI sur Ceylan', *Quatrième Internationale*, eighteenth year, no 11, October-November 1960, p90).

The resulting ferment within the party produced the 'National Political Resolution' signed by Bernard Zoysa, Edmund Samarakkody, Sydney Wanasinghe, DS Mallawaratchi, Reggie Mendis, Desmond Wickremasuriya, RS Baghavan, Bala Tampoe, V Karalasingham, Prins Rajasooriya, Meryl Fernando, etc, in the LSSP's *Internal Bulletin* in December 1961. The alarm of the LSSP at the events of early 1962 is well reflected in 'Ceylon: The General Strike of 5 January'; 'On the Political Situation in Ceylon' (extracts from a resolution of the working committee of the LSSP); 'Ceylon Coup D'état', in the *International Bulletin* of the International group, Volume 1, no 10, 8 February 1962; and 'Ceylon: Statement by the Lanka Sama Samaja Party on the Recent Attempted Coup', *International Bulletin* of the International Group, Volume 1, no 13, 3 March 1962. *The General and Immediate Programme of the United Left Front of Ceylon* signed by the LSSP, CP and MEP was put out as a small duplicated pamphlet in 1963. Edmund Samarakkody puts the case against it in *Whither the LSSP?*, an undated duplicated internal document of the party (probably 1963).

The letter sent by the United Secretariat to the Central Committee of the LSSP on 23 April 1964 opposing the coalition is reprinted in 'Fourth International's Warning Against Trap of Posts in Ceylonese Bourgeois Government', *InterContinental Press*, 22 September 1975, pp1261-2, and the letter of the USFI supporting the Emergency Conference of the LSSP(R) in 1964 appears in *Revolutionary Marxism vs Class Collaboration in Sri Lanka*, New York, 1975. The resolutions of the Majority, the Centre group, and the Revolutionary Minority to the LSSP Congress of 6 and 7 June 1964 that took the decision to enter the government, along with the IEC's letter of 25 May 1964, appear in *Fourth International*, Volume 1, no 2, Summer 1964, pp86-92, and are most easily consulted in Cliff Slaughter (ed), *The International Committee Against Liquidationism*, Volume 4 of *Trotskyism versus Revisionism*, London, 1974, pp253-66. The 'Decision of the Special Conference of the LSSP(R)' of July 1964 and the 'Statement of the LSSP(R) on the Fall of the Coalition' of December 1964 appear in Mike Banda's *The Logic of Coalition Politics*, SLL Pamphlet, 1975, and *Fourth International*, Volume 1, no 3, Autumn-Winter 1964, pp156-8.

The main accounts by the supporters of the United Secretariat of the political defection of their Ceylonese section are collected together in *Revolutionary Marxism vs Class Collaboration in Sri Lanka* ('Towards a

History of the Fourth International', part 6, *Education for Socialists* series, New York, August 1975). Additional matter can be gleaned from 'The Balance Sheet of the Whole Experience of the LSSP' (*Internal Bulletin* of the USFI, 1966), Peter Green, 'Balance Sheet of the LSSP's Betrayal' (*InterContinental Press*, Volume 13, no 34, 29 September 1975, pp1286-94), and Pierre Frank, 'The Degeneration of the Ceylonese Section', in *The Fourth International: The Long March of the Trotskyists*, London, 1979, pp112-7.

The views of the supporters of Michel Pablo, who were then in the process of breaking with the United Secretariat to set up their own organisation, the AMR, are represented by *The Crisis in Ceylon* ('Documents of the African Commission of the Fourth International on the Crisis in the LSSP', November 1964); 'Ceylon: A New Situation' (*Under the Banner of Socialism*, no 4, February-March 1965, p20), and Mohan Thampoo, 'Ceylon: The Elections and After', written on 15 May 1965 (*Under the Banner of Socialism*, no 6, June-July 1965, pp13-15; cf the criticism by Nihal Goonatilake, 'Pablo Woos the Reformist LSSP', in the *Newsletter*, 19 June 1965). The Minutes of the United Secretariat of 25-26 January 1964 contain the motion on Ceylon submitted by Dennis Freney on behalf of the Pablo grouping and a 'Statement by the USFI' in reply to it (pp18-20).

The International Committee's critique of these events is contained in Wilfred Pereira, 'The Strategy of Betrayal: From Permanent Revolution to Permanent Betrayal', *Young Socialist*, no 12, 1964, pp60-8; Gerry Healy, *Ceylon: The Great Betrayal*, Newsletter pamphlet, 1964; 'Coalition Ghost Haunts Ceylon Centrists' (*Newsletter*, 16 May 1964); Mike Banda, 'Ceylon Coalition Plans New Burdens for Workers' (*Newsletter*, 25 July 1964); and *The Logic of Coalition Politics* (SLL pamphlet, 1965); Michael Ross, *The Struggle for Trotskyism in Ceylon* (*Bulletin* Pamphlet Series no 9, February 1972); and Cliff Slaughter (ed), 'The LSSP and the International Secretariat', Appendix to *Trotskyism Versus Revisionism*, Volume 2, London, 1974, pp206-15; and 'Ceylon and the Fruits of Betrayal', op cit, Volume 4, chapter 6, pp224-66.

Criticisms made by other Trotskyist currents include 'Ceylon: Hunting With the Hounds' (Editorial no 5 of *International Socialism*, no 18, Autumn 1964, p5); 'SWP Rewrites History of Betrayal by Ceylonese LSSP' (*Workers Vanguard*, 3 October 1975); the correspondence between James Robertson and Edmund Samarakkody in the 'Exchange of Views Between the SL/US and the RWP of Ceylon' (*International Discussion Bulletin* of the Spartacist League, May 1974); Workers Power/Irish Workers Group, *The Death Agony of the Fourth International*, London, 1983, pp44-6; and David North, 'The Historic Betrayal in Ceylon', in *The Heritage We Defend*, Detroit, 1988, pp394-402. To these should be added

Vijaya Samaraweera's 'Sri Lankan Marxists in Electoral Politics' (*Journal of Commonwealth and Comparative Politics*, November 1980, pp308-24), which argues that the pact of the working class parties with the SLFP had a detrimental effect upon their electoral progress, to the benefit of Mrs Bandaranaike's party.

YR Amarasinghe

From Independent Party to Coalition Partner

The Aftermath of March 1960

IMMEDIATELY FOLLOWING the elections of March 1960, the Central Committee of the LSSP decided to work towards the defeat of the minority government of the United National Party that came into being as a result of the inconclusive nature of the election results. In parliament the LSSP group closely associated with other anti-UNP groups, and endeavoured to bring down the government with the intention of assisting the Sri Lanka Freedom Party to form an alternative government. This acceptance of the lead of the SLFP did not secure a consensus within the party, even though the leadership explained that this was the only viable strategy at the time for the LSSP. The party's proven incapacity to present itself as the alternative to the UNP was given as the main reason for the acceptance of this line. As a spokesman of the LSSP explained, it was the SLFP that the masses accepted as the alternative to the UNP; he thought that a majority of the 'Sinhalese petit-bourgeoisie' still had faith in the SLFP.[1] It was correctly anticipated that the government, which was without allies in parliament and about 20 members short of a majority, could be brought down without delay. A special conference of the party was convened to sanction the new line of, firstly, taking every possible step to bring down the UNP government, and, secondly, to assist in the formation of a government of the SLFP in the event of a defeat of the UNP government.[2] The party, however, underlined the fact that the SLFP was still considered to be a 'capitalist party',[3] indicating

1. *Samasamajist*, 1 April 1960.
2. *Samasamajist*, 22 April 1960.
3. The press release issued after the conference stated that the party decided to support the formation of a government of the SLFP in the 'concrete situation' that

that the new line was only a change of tactics rather than of the party's sanctioned and accepted policy. Even then, the resolution was accepted only amidst much opposition[4] from those members who believed that the party should not offer any kind of support to the SLFP. NM Perera, who led the tendency that campaigned for the extension of assistance to the SLFP to form a government, also wanted the party to support all progressive measures of a future SLFP government. The reason for the party's decision to support the SLFP, as given by the editor of the official party organ, was the view that the masses had about the character of the SLFP. He said that because the masses saw the SLFP as a party of the left and as a Socialist party, it was the LSSP's duty to go with them until the masses themselves shed these illusions.[5] However, upon the defeat of the UNP minority government,[6] parliament was dissolved and fresh elections called for July, and the chance to form an alternative government was not given to the SLFP.

The experience at the March elections demonstrated to the parties the consequences of multi-party competition: the anti-UNP parties were convinced that the UNP was able to win the number of seats that it actually did win in March because of a split in the anti-UNP vote. The defeat of the UNP in parliament also highlighted the value of their united action. When the parliament was dissolved, these parties, having as their primary aim prevention at any cost of a UNP comeback, started negotiations to eliminate contests amongst themselves. Although they failed to agree on a three party no-contest pact, agreement was separately reached between the LSSP, the Communist Party and the SLFP.[7] The no-contest pacts showed that both the LSSP and the Communist Party had agreed upon the superiority of

existed at the time; the statement reiterated that the SLFP was a 'capitalist party' (*Samasamajist*, 22 April 1960).

4. According to a press report, only about 260 out of over 300 approved the new line; amongst the minority that opposed it were leading members such as Colvin R de Silva, Edmund Samarakkody, Doric de Sousa, Bala Tampoe and Robert Gunawardena (*Ceylon News*, 5 May 1960).

5. *Samasamajist*, 22 April 1960. The editor also reiterated the party's accepted position vis-à-vis the SLFP. He stated: 'The LSSP has no illusions about the character of the SLFP... Although it is not the instrument of big capital like the UNP, the SLFP is nevertheless a capitalist party which will strive to maintain the capitalist system in Ceylon.'

6. The minority government of the UNP resigned after losing the vote on the common amendment of the opposition by 25 votes. See House of Representatives, *Debates*, Volume 38, 1960, column 898.

7. The no-contest pact between the LSSP and the SLFP was signed on 17 May 1960. The agreement pledged to eliminate all contests between them (*Samasamajist*, 20 May 1960).

the SLFP as the main anti-UNP contender. The final allocation gave the LSSP 21 contests as against the 101 that it fought in March, and seven to the Communist Party, which had contested 53 at the previous election. The SLFP was assigned 98 electorates.[8] The signing of an electoral pact with the SLFP was not a departure for the LSSP, as this had been done twice in the past; however, before the elections actually took place, the LSSP was to reconsider its attitude regarding the SLFP. As this was done in relation to the party's general strategy for the coming period, the LSSP's new line regarding the SLFP was a very important indicator of its impending, and rapid, transformation.

In May 1960 a party conference was convened to decide on the short-term strategy; the decisions approved by the conference were also to have a lasting effect on the party's long-term policy. The conference, which the party's left wing spokesmen alleged was forced upon them by the 'reformist' leaders,[9] approved the 'no-contest and mutual support' pact the party had entered into the month before. It also approved by a majority vote a resolution that called upon the party to accept office, if the need arose, in an SLFP government on an agreed programme; such an agreed programme would include the nationalisation of insurance companies and the import and export trade, and the state take-over of all schools in the country.[10] This was a momentous decision; the LSSP that had not contemplated entering into front agreements even with parties that were normally accepted by it as based on the working class, now decided to work in harness with a party that it had identified as a capitalist party only two months earlier. The moment the conference voted for the acceptance of this perspective the entire Central Committee resigned, apparently because it felt that the approval of the proposal to accept office in an SLFP government was tantamount to a vote of no-confidence in it, as the Central Committee had previously rejected the same proposal when brought forward by NM Perera.[11] The newly-adopted line was to harden the opposition of the left wing Samasamajists towards the established 'reformist' leadership, and they were to continue this opposition more vigorously. The opposition of the left wing Samasamajists[12] was to continue right up to the culmination of June 1964, when

8. These three parties were to contest all the elections that followed as partners of no-contest agreements, and the LSSP's allocation remained around 20.
9. See 'Platform of the Left Opposition (LSSP)', LSSP *Internal Bulletin*, nd [after August 1963?], p8.
10. The voting was 269 for taking office and 128 against.
11. Amongst the leading members who opposed the new line were Edmund Samarakkody, Colvin R de Silva and Leslie Goonewardene.
12. The term 'left wing Samasamajists' is used here to describe the leaders (and members) who uncompromisingly campaigned to steer the party away from its parliamentarian position to a revolutionary position. In 1960 leaders like Colvin

there was a split away of a large number of them from the party; until then the party was rent with almost continual dissension.

The new strategy adopted by the May conference speaks much for the party's changed policy line; a document that justified the new line of action gave an unambiguous explanation of the reasons behind the changing of the party's line, and an insight into the thinking of the leader of the majority group, NM Perera, who wrote the document, and initiated the new line. The document, circulated before the conference was convened, embodied the main proposals that were later to be accepted by the May conference. It also made a strong case for the LSSP to change its policies and tactics.[13]

The document at the outset surveyed the party's history, and came to the conclusion that the LSSP was 'unique in the history of the revolutionary movements', in that it had succeeded in achieving the position of being a major political organisation in the country, even reaching a position of being able to make a serious challenge for power. The LSSP was seen as a revolutionary party that had gone a long way along the parliamentary road, but had now reached a point where it was unlikely to succeed 'within the conceivable future in getting its policy and programme accepted by a sufficient number of people to enable it to attain power through parliamentary means'. The radicalism of the party's programme with its stand on the important issues of language and citizenship were given as the main reasons for this retardation of its progress. In this situation, the document saw only two options open to the party: either to 'retrace its steps [along the parliamentary road], forswear the position to which historical factors have brought it and confine itself mainly to the extra-parliamentary struggle', or to 'persist along the path of obtaining power through parliament with somewhat different tactics'.[14]

R de Silva, Leslie Goonewardene and Doric de Sousa also opposed the line proposed by NM Perera, but they were not attempting to change the course of the party completely; in fact those leaders were to emerge as the leading campaigners to form and strengthen a 'united left front' of all the left wing parties that would make a serious bid for a parliamentary majority. Edmund Samarakkody and Bala Tampoe were the two leaders who continually opposed the parliamentarian line, and attempted to steer the party to adopt a revolutionary line.

13. This mimeographed and untitled document does not give the identity of the author, but there is irrefutable evidence that NM Perera was the author. Referring to the contents of this document, Edmund Samarakkody has attributed its authorship to NM Perera on two occasions; in 1964 he referred to this in a speech in the House of Representatives, see House of Representatives, *Debates*, Volume 56, 1964, column 833. In 1963 NM Perera was identified as the author of this document in the famous critique of the right wing tendency issued by the left wing Samasamajists, 'The Platform of the Left Opposition', op cit, p8. This was not denied by Perera.

14. Untitled document, p1.

The author saw the class situation in Ceylon as unfavourable to extra-parliamentary action, and thought that even in the conditions of deteriorating economic circumstances it would be difficult to 'evoke that degree of militancy amongst the workers necessary for extra-parliamentary action'. This left no choice but to take the parliamentary road. The main tactic the author proposed was that of a close alliance with the SLFP. Alliance with the SLFP was thought to have become possible because of its changed character, and the author saw the SLFP as a 'reformist petit-bourgeois party' that cannot be categorised as a capitalist party in view of 'the interests that it subserves'. The SLFP was 'capitalist only in the sense that its ultimate objective is not the overthrow of capitalism'. An alliance with it was thought to facilitate the achievement of 'the anti-capitalist struggle by smashing the UNP; the removal of the isolation of the LSSP from the rural masses by creating a favourable atmosphere for the reception of a Socialist programme; and the prevention of the consolidation of the right by driving a wedge into the rightist forces'. As preliminary measures, the author proposed signing a no-contest pact with the SLFP, and taking steps to bring about programmatic agreement with it with a view to forming a joint government.[15]

The new orientation also reflects the victory of the tendency led by the author of the document, NM Perera. It further marks an important stage in the history of the LSSP. Now, for the first time in its history, the official line of the LSSP became, firstly, to rule out the viability of the revolutionary strategy for Ceylon, at least for the conceivable future; secondly, to accept the possibility of establishing a Socialist state in Ceylon through parliamentary means; and thirdly, to consider the SLFP as a party qualitatively different from the UNP, and a party with a progressive rôle that could be associated with the movement towards the establishment of a Socialist state. The significance of this document was all the greater because the LSSP was to follow the line advocated in it in the years that followed, with no more than minor modifications, right through to the present day.

The elections of July 1960 brought a clear victory for the SLFP, assisted greatly by the no-contest pacts it had with the two left parties, the LSSP and the Communist Party. The LSSP, contesting 21 seats and with no direct conflict with its left wing rival, the Communist Party, and with only one such contest with the SLFP,[16] had 12 of its number returned; but its total poll was reduced by 100 000 to

15. Op cit, pp1,2.
16. The LSSP and the SLFP clashed in the constituency of Kesbewa. Here, the contest by all the three parties of the three-member constituency of Colombo Central is not taken into account.

214 693. The programme put forward by the LSSP for the July elections was identical with its March programme. With 75 of its members elected, the SLFP was in a position to form a government on its own, and as a result the prospect for an SLFP-LSSP coalition disappeared, at least for the time being.[17] The LSSP declared that it would extend 'general support' to the new government in parliament, and in a press release issued after the elections the LSSP's Secretary stated that his party 'would cooperate with the SLFP government as an independent party in every activity which carries the country along progressive lines'.[18] Putting its pledge of general support into practice, the LSSP group in parliament supported the SLFP's first major policy declaration, the Throne Speech.

The left wing Samasamajists, however, were to express in parliament their disagreement with the party's new line on the SLFP government. In the course of the debate on the Throne Speech, Edmund Samarakkody categorised the government as a 'Centre Party' that had no prospects of solving problems in a 'backward capitalist country like Ceylon'.[19] Samarakkody and another left Samasamajist member in the House of Representatives joined several opposition members against the wishes of their group leader in proposing an amendment to the Throne Speech.[20] Apparently, the right wing of the LSSP had desired closer cooperation with the SLFP than merely supporting it inside parliament. It was later revealed that a letter had been written by this section to the SLFP seeking agreement for the LSSP's parliamentary group to participate in the meetings of the government's parliamentary group.[21] The LSSP was to maintain the attitude of general support to the SLFP government for some time, in spite of both the opposition of the left wing group and advice given by the International Secretariat of the Fourth International.[22]

17. Under the 1947 Constitution, which was in force until May 1972 in Ceylon, there was provision for the nomination of up to six members, by the Governor General on the advice of the Prime Minister, to the House of Representatives to represent under-represented minority interests. In 1960 the total number of elected members in the House was 151.
18. *Ceylon Observer*, 31 July 1960.
19. House of Representatives, *Debates*, Volume 39, 1960, columns 607-608.
20. Op cit, column 931. The other LSSP members declined to vote on this.
21. See the speech by Edmund Samarakkody, House of Representatives, *Debates*, Volume 56, 1964, column 825. The request had been refused on grounds that such participation was 'not necessary'.
22. The LSSP's attitude of general support to the SLFP government was considered as incorrect by the International headquarters, and the party was even censured by the World Congress of the Fourth International.

From Electoral Alliance to 'Frontism', 1961-1963

The LSSP's attitude of general support for the government was to change after about a year, and by the end of 1961 it had in fact become one of the main critics of the government. At the same time the LSSP drew nearer to its rivals on the left, a trend that was eventually to culminate in the establishment of a 'United Left Front'. This change of attitude towards the government was caused more by the circumstances of the years 1961-63, those of labour unrest, the increased discontentment amongst the minority groups, and the general economic deterioration, than by a radical change in the LSSP's understanding of the character of the SLFP as a political organisation.

Early in 1961, when the government set out to implement measures to change the language in the courts from English to Sinhalese, the traditional protest of the Tamils reached a new height. The major Tamil communal party, the Federal Party, launched a *Satyagraha*, or a passive resistance campaign, in the two provinces which had a high concentration of Tamils, aimed at the prevention of the implementation of new government regulations regarding language. The *Satyagrahis* sat and squatted in the streets and entrances to government offices, bringing the administration of the two provinces to a virtual halt. This protest campaign was supported by the plantation workers of Tamil origin in the central highland districts; this act of solidarity, significant because of the rarity of such actions between the two communities, was instanced by the events leading up to the one-day strike of 25 February 1961. When the Federal Party, carrying its acts of civil disobedience to a higher level, violated the inland revenue and postal laws by setting up its own post offices and issuing 'Federal stamps', the government took a very stern course of action to bring the situation under control. The Federal Party was proscribed, and its leaders, amongst whose numbers were about a dozen parliamentarians, were detained. A state of emergency was declared, and troops were despatched to the two provinces. In the face of firm government action, the *Satyagraha* worked itself out within weeks, but it was to revive Tamil hostility against the SLFP, which even at the best of times did not enjoy much confidence amongst the Tamils. The Federal Party leaders were kept in detention for about six months, and the proscription order on their party remained valid for a year. The state of emergency thus declared was to remain a common feature virtually throughout the period of the SLFP's rule.

The issue of minority rights aroused afresh by the Languages of the Courts Bill was also to set the LSSP against the government. In a statement, the Secretary of the LSSP, Leslie Goonewardene, whilst emphasising the party's full agreement for changing the language of the courts to Sinhalese, stated that it would be iniquitous to use Sinhalese in the courts in the Northern and the Eastern provinces where the vast majority of the population speak Tamil.[23] In parliament the LSSP introduced an amendment to the government's bill, and called for the adoption of Sinhalese and Tamil as languages of the courts 'where facilities were available'. On this the LSSP was also to vote against the government. On the particular issue of the Satyagraha the party spokesmen urged the government to use negotiation rather than the wielding of the 'big stick'.[24]

The LSSP was also to blame the government for the events that led to the Satyagraha. At the same time, the LSSP started a campaign to have the state of emergency withdrawn. It claimed that the main purpose behind the imposition and the maintenance of the state of emergency was the restriction of legitimate protests of the trade unions. It was in this arena that the LSSP was next to conflict with the government.

The first labour dispute in which the LSSP came into direct conflict with the government was the bank employees' strike, in which the LSSP-led trade union centre, the Continuing Committee of Trade Union Organisations, was involved. When the emergency was declared, amidst protests by the LSSP, the bank employees' strike was made illegal by the government. The more the government took up inflexible positions regarding labour disputes and other matters in which the LSSP had direct interests, the more readily the LSSP tended to dissociate itself from the government, and the support of the LSSP for the government increasingly became qualified. The sentiments expressed at the party's traditional May Day rally reflected this very clearly; the party's spokesmen emphasised that the party would support the government against 'reaction' led by the UNP, and for all 'progressive measures' the government might take, but explained in unmistakable terms that the LSSP was against the policy of the government towards the trade unions and the minorities. The LSSP also attacked the government's 'general incompetence'.[25] At the time of the SLFP's general policy statement for 1961, the LSSP was not prepared to support it as in the previous year, and in the voting on the government's Throne Speech, the LSSP (and the Communist Party) abstained. The budget that followed contained several new taxes, and increased indirect taxes and the prices of several essential

23. *Ceylon News*, 5 January 1961.
24. See the statement by NM Perera (*Ceylon News*, 9 March 1961).
25. See the report of the rally, *Ceylon News*, 4 May 1961, particularly the speech by Colvin R de Silva.

foods. Several of the direct taxes were thought to affect key support groups of the LSSP, namely, secretarial grade civil servants and some grades of skilled workers.[26] The budget proposals and the government's general economic perspective came in for severe criticism from the leaders of the LSSP. NM Perera, who was also the party's chief spokesman on economic affairs, criticised the budget for its non-adherence to a larger developmental plan.[27] Colvin R de Silva saw the budget as one which 'moved completely with the capitalist framework with a bias in favour of the capitalist class', in spite of the government's many claims to the contrary.[28] It was also thought that the budget of 1961, like many previous economic measures of the SLFP, had a 'rural bias', that is, an implicit tendency to favour the rural dwellers.[29] It was not a complete condemnation, but an expression of general disagreement with the government's economic policies. In view of the price increases and the new taxes, the LSSP would not have been able to support the budget without jeopardising its own support in the country. It was not very surprising that the party's Central Committee decided against supporting the budget proposals; the government's lack of a developmental plan, lack of an integrated project for industrialisation, and the new taxes and price increases were given as reasons for the decision. However, the party was to emphasise that it would 'continue its line of supporting all progressive acts of the government and of defending it against saboteur activities of reactionary forces'.[30] Following the decision of the Central Committee, the party also took part in a limited campaign to force the government to withdraw all price increases and taxes that affected lower income groups.

Towards the end of 1961 increased dissatisfaction caused mainly by the rise in prices, the government's policy of wage freeze, and the widespread scarcities, gave rise to a wave of trade union protests amongst the workers. The operations of the government-controlled Ceylon Transport Board were paralysed by a six-day strike. Though it started as an unplanned protest against the management, the LSSP's All-Ceylon United Motor Workers Union came to the support of the

26. The price of flour was increased by about 15 per cent, sugar by about eight per cent, matches by about 20 per cent, and cigarettes by between 10 and 15 per cent.

27. NM Perera, 'Felix's Second Budget', Young Socialist, Colombo, no 2 (Special Budget Issue), 1961, pp73-80.

28. Colvin R de Silva, 'The Politics of the Budget', Young Socialist, no 2 (Special Budget Issue), 1961, pp80-9.

29. See Colvin R de Silva, 'The Politics of the Budget', p87; and also Edmund Samarakkody, 'Budgetary Policy and the Working Class', Young Socialist, no 2 (Special Budget Issue), 1961, pp66-73.

30. Ceylon News, 17 August 1961.

workers once the strike started. The government at first stood very firm, but eventually conceded the main demands. The labour disputes also spread to the port of Colombo, and by the end of the year there were about 17 000 men on strike there. Soon the port workers were to be joined by the bank clerks, workers in the petroleum and gas industry, and in one of the government factories. Again the government resorted to a hard line, and the army and navy were moved to operate the port and other disrupted services. The use of the military in intimidating workers and breaking the strikes, something against which the LSSP had consistently fought, further aided the deterioration of the relationship between the government and the LSSP. By this time, the government's credibility amongst the organised working class movement was so low that at the end of the year the Communist Party, which was earlier following a policy of support for the government more consistently than the LSSP, joined the LSSP to make a joint protest. The two parties, with the support of some independent trade unions and Philip Gunawardena's Mahajana Eksath Peramuna, called a general strike for 5 January 1962, on the demand for the withdrawal of military personnel from the port of Colombo, and the settlement of the dispute.[31]

The general strike proved to be a great success for the left wing parties. It was a success in terms of effectiveness. In spite of stern measures taken by the government to disrupt the strike plan,[32] there was widespread support given to the strike. Several branches of services and industries were brought to a halt by the strike; telecommunications, road and rail transportation, the government factories, the distribution of oil and gas, and the plantations and banks were amongst the most affected. The strike was a success from another point of view as well — the preparations that preceded the strike and the reactions of the government[33] to it were to bring the left wing parties, the LSSP, the Communist Party and the MEP, onto one platform after several years of separation and mutual hostility. The last occasion on which all these parties had acted together was in 1953 on

31. See the statement issued by the two Secretaries of the trade union centres of the LSSP and the Communist Party and the Secretary of the powerful Government Clerical Services Union (*Ceylon News*, 4 January 1962). Philip Gunawardena's party did not join the anti-UNP camp in 1960; it was fiercely anti-SLFP at the time. When the other two left wing parties, particularly the LSSP, began to move away from the SLFP, the MEP's relations with them also improved.

32. The government had a full military alert, military patrols and air surveillance were also used, and the key points in Colombo were guarded. It also tried to induce the workers to come to work on the day of the strike by advancing the day on which salary advances are normally paid.

33. The government reacted by imposing still more restrictions. Public meetings were banned, and strict censorship was introduced.

the occasion of the *hartal*, but unlike in 1953 this unity achieved in trade union action was to develop into a unity that took a more co-hesive and wider-ranging organised form. This was not to happen immediately. The parties were in agreement about the need for and the value of joint action, but still there were differences concerning the form of unity that should be achieved. Moreover, the Communist Party was still wary of joining in a venture that would inevitably be a challenge to the SLFP, towards which it still maintained an attitude of support on many political issues. In fact, at this early stage the Communist Party desired the establishment of a front of all progres-sive forces in order to influence the government to move to the left.[34]

The MEP, on the other hand, was not so favourably disposed to assist in strengthening the SLFP government. It desired a united left front that could work to replace the government.[35] The LSSP was nearer to the position of the MEP, but was not decided as yet; how-ever, when the attempted coup d'état conspiracy was discovered the situation was to change. Towards the end of January 1962, a plot to overthrow the government, initiated by several high-ranking army and police officers, was uncovered a day before it was due to take ef-fect. About two dozen officers of the security forces and some civil-ians were taken into custody and charged. The coup's plan entailed the arrest of several members of the government and leading left wingers. The LSSP and the other left parties condemned the coup attempt, and offered help to the government to defeat the 'reactionary forces' behind it.[36] The support offered by the MEP and the Communist Party to the government went very much further than that of the LSSP. As a show of goodwill to the government, the Communist Party and the MEP called off the strike led by them in the harbour, without even consulting the LSSP.[37] The MEP, hitherto the least sympathetic to the government of the left wing parties, of-fered it and the people 'every assistance possible to rid the country finally and totally of all the conspiratorial elements'.[38] The Commu-nist Party also promised full support to the government to deal with the 'reactionary elements behind the coup'.[39] The LSSP's position was a little ambiguous; it did condemn the coup as a 'rightist plot', em-phasising the social background of the coup suspects, who were

34. See the speech by Pieter Keuneman, the General Secretary of the Communist Party (*Ceylon News*, 27 November 1961).
35. See the statement by Philip Gunawardena (*Ceylon Daily News*, 25 December 1961).
36. *Ceylon News*, 8 February, 1962.
37. 'Editorial Notes', *Young Socialist*, Colombo, no 5, April-June 1962, p233.
38. *Ceylon Daily News*, 31 January 1962.
39. *Ceylon Daily News*, 30 January 1962.

mostly Catholics from established families. But at the same time the LSSP's spokesmen alleged that there were two coups ('a coup within a coup') — one aimed at the leaders of the left wing movement and the other aimed at the government. They implied that the government, in fear of a rising working class movement, had planned to arrest its leaders. They suggested that the security forces that were detailed to make the arrests went one step further and planned the detention of some members of the government as well.[40] The LSSP also expressed fears that the government might use the attempted coup d'état as a cover to establish its own dictatorship. The government's past reliance on the military, and the remarks of the powerful Minister of Finance, Felix Dias Bandaranaike, to the effect that 'a little bit of totalitarianism' was desirable for Ceylon, served only to reinforce the suspicions and attitudes harboured by the LSSP. Because of these misgivings following the coup, the LSSP was to be isolated from the other two left wing parties for some time. When the government introduced a bill facilitating the setting up of a special court to try the coup suspects, the LSSP along with the Federal Party and the UNP voted against, whereas the MEP and the Communist Party supported it. The emergency created by the coup generated some sympathy towards the government; it was also to retard the nascent movement towards cooperation amongst the left wingers.

Despite the early setbacks, by the middle of the year, the unity of the left again became the talking point. The separate May Day rallies of all the three parties expressed the value of unity amongst the 'progressive forces'. For instance, the main May Day resolution of the LSSP called for the workers and peasants to 'fight jointly against repression and anti-working class measures'.[41] Philip Gunawardena repeated the call for the formation of a 'Socialist government of the united progressive forces'.[42] And in early May the three party leaders, NM Perera of the LSSP, Philip Gunawardena of the MEP, and SA

40. See the speech by NM Perera, House of Representatives, *Debates*, Volume 46, 1962, columns 1272-1308; the statement by Doric de Sousa, Ceylon Senate, *Debates*, Volume 17, 1962, columns 1574-1601; and 'Editorial Notes', *Young Socialist*, Colombo, no 5, April-June 1962, pp227-34. Writing in a special article on the subject, Edmund Samarakkody expressed the extreme position of the LSSP's thinking on the subject. He finds no reason for the 'reactionaries and vested interests' to overthrow the government of Mrs Bandaranaike, because, according to him, that government would not take any measure that 'endangers capitalism'. And he adds: 'But what moved the coup forces into action was mainly the conviction that immediate and drastic action was called for against the working classes and the masses if capitalism was to be saved.' (*Young Socialist*, April-June 1962, p254)
41. *Ceylon Daily News*, 28 April 1962.
42. *Ceylon Daily News*, 28 April 1962.

Wickremasinghe of the Communist Party appeared on the same platform on the occasion of a solidarity rally held in support of the 'people of Indonesia in their fight to liberate West Irian from the hands of Dutch imperialism'.[43] The spirit of left unity within all the three parties concerned was kept going by these moves; more importantly, it was to generate a popular enthusiasm towards establishing some kind of unity amongst the parties of the left. These feelings were to grow to new heights by the beginning of the next year.

During this period, the LSSP was to move from the position of extending qualified support to the SLFP to a position of opposition. As a first step, the LSSP's Working Committee decided in June 1962 not to support the SLFP's candidate at a by-election that was to be held at the end of the month. It was explained that this decision was taken in view of the non-progressive nature of the policies of the government, and because of the repressive legislation it introduced in the aftermath of the attempted coup.[44] A month later the party decided to oppose the Throne Speech, and the amendment brought by the LSSP expressed dissatisfaction with the government's policies, and took the form of a motion of no-confidence in the government. From this point onwards until the coalition talks began more than a year later, the LSSP was to assume a position of general opposition to the SLFP. The LSSP conference that met towards the end of July was to sanction this new attitude.

This conference, attended by over 200 delegates, not only confirmed the party's new line towards the SLFP, but was also to indicate the party's general strategy for the coming period. The main political resolution adopted by the conference reviewed the record of the government over the two years that it had been in power, and declared that its 'governing aim had been the capitalist development of Ceylon's economy'; it went on to state that 'the middle way of the SLFP government was nearing a dead end'. The government's alleged anti-working class policy was denounced, whilst expressing the party's dissatisfaction over the SLFP's lack of 'trust in the masses'. The resolution called for 'the defence of people's living standards and democratic rights' by going along 'mass lines and mass methods'. The new line towards the government was described as one of general opposition: 'The coming struggle will not be simply against this or that measure of the SLFP government, but against the SLFP government's entire policies.' The resolution envisaged that such struggles would

43. *Ceylon Daily News*, 7 May 1962.
44. This was the by-election of Anuradhapura. The party's stand was to end effectively the validity of the 'no-contest and mutual support' agreement signed between the two parties two years previously (*Ceylon Daily News*, 15 June 1962).

soon 'acquire the aim of replacing the SLFP government itself with a government which is responsive to the demands of the masses'. The slogan 'Forward to a Genuine Socialist Government' was thought to be the most appropriate to the circumstances of the day, and it was also expected that such a slogan would 'help to unite in action the broadest progressive forces'.[45] The LSSP in its opposition to the government thus did not counterpose the slogan of 'a government of the LSSP' as it did in the past, rather it signalled for the unity of the progressive forces. The movement towards achieving unity amongst the left wingers was assisted by the government's own weakness and failures. The more the government adopted unpopular measures, whether in economic management or in the trade union field, the more scant became the support of the parties of the left.

In August 1962, when the government proposed the reduction by 50 per cent of the subsidised rice ration, the left joined in protest and demanded its withdrawal.[46] Whilst the left wingers took the protest to the country, the government was also threatened from amongst its own ranks.[47] Eventually the proposal was withdrawn, but at the price of the resignation of the Minister of Finance.[48]

In the meantime the movement for left unity was gathering momentum. In November the Communist Party and the LSSP signed a 'no-contest and mutual support' agreement to contest the impending elections for the Colombo Municipal Council, the first such agreement to be signed between them.[49] By March 1963 talks for establish-

---

45. The extracts of the conference resolution were taken from the press release issued by the Secretary of the party following the conference (*Ceylon Daily News*, 24 July 1962).
46. *Ceylon Daily News*, 15 August 1962. A joint LSSP-Communist Party-MEP rally was held on 24 August (*Ceylon Daily News*, 25 August 1962).
47. Several back bench members of the government parliamentary group expressed their opposition in public. The move also caused the crossing over of one member, and the resignation of the Junior Minister of Finance.
48. The government was to change the Minister of Finance twice more before the SLFP-LSSP coalition was formed in June 1964.
49. See the statement issued by representatives of the two parties (*Ceylon Daily News*, 7 November 1962). Notwithstanding the agreement, the LSSP (and the Communist Party) failed to make any gains in Colombo. Of the 17 wards it contested the LSSP lost in 14, and its representation in the new Municipal Council was reduced from eight in the previous one to three. The Communist Party failed to win all but one of the wards it contested. The LSSP's poor performance reflected glaringly by the Colombo Municipal Council elections appeared to be the general trend: in Panadura Urban Council, situated in the constituency of the party's Secretary, the LSSP lost all the seats it contested. In another coastal stronghold of the LSSP, Ambalangoda, the party lost all the seats it contested at the Urban Council elections, and in Moratuwa Urban Council the LSSP won only two against 10 by the UNP. Its considerable failure in these local council contests would have strengthened the LSSP's desire for establishing a joint front

ing close cooperation between the three left wing parties were well under way.[50] These moves received a great boost by the joint action these parties were to take on the occasion of the stoppage of aid by the United States; this was intended as a punitive measure for the alleged non-payment of full compensation by the government of Ceylon for the nationalised American oil companies. The continuing close cooperation[51] led to the preparations for holding a joint May Day rally by the three parties. In March the Central Committee of the LSSP approved, albeit in guarded terms, a resolution to seek unity with the other left wing parties and working class organisations. The resolution saw a marked tendency amongst the petit-bourgeoisie to turn to the right with the deterioration of the economic situation. It was also thought that there was a 'genuine desire amongst a large section of the population' for united activity by the left wingers. In view of this, the Central Committee approved four lines of action: united action of the three left wing parties on political issues as they arose; the drawing in of organisations such as the plantation workers' unions, the Ceylon Workers Congress and the Democratic Workers Congress; discussions, based on a list of demands, with the Communist Party and the MEP 'for the purpose of seeking to build a fighting centre of the three parties'; and to build a joint consultative committee of the three parties if the discussions were successful, for the purpose of coordinating united left wing activities. The Central Committee dismissed suggestions for a merger of the three parties as 'incorrect' and 'unreal'.[52] It appears as if the Central Committee's decision was a compromise between the right wing that wanted the establishment of a united left front with the perspective of forming a joint government of the three parties, and the left wing that wanted all working class organisations — the political parties and trade unions — to act in unison on issues of common interest, with no joint governmental perspective. However, the decision of the Central

with the other two left wing parties.
50. All the three parties expressed their preparation to join hands. See also the special article by Pieter Keuneman, the General Secretary of the Communist Party (*Ceylon Daily News*, 4 February 1963).
51. United rallies of the left wing parties became a common feature during the second quarter of 1963. The joint rallies held in places varying as Colombo (Western Province), Badulla (Uva Province), Ratnapura (Sabaragamuva), Polonnaruwa (North Central Province) would have gone a long way to create a widespread mass enthusiasm for a united left front. As a result of this obvious cooperation amongst the left wing comrades in place of the squabbles and mutual hostility in the past, the united front of the left wing parties had become a reality — at least in the eyes of the public — before it was formally established.
52. *Samasamajaya*, 29 March 1963. See also *Ceylon Daily News*, 10 April 1963, for the main Central Committee resolution.

Committee was to pave the way for commencing formal negotiations with the other left wing parties, and the first step of these formal negotiations was concerned with holding a united May Day rally. After several rounds of discussions, the parties agreed to hold a joint rally, the first such rally of the left wingers for about 24 years.[53] Several joint committees were set up to take charge of the different aspects of the rally. In the course of the preparations comradeship was to develop. Soon the trade unions affiliated to these parties and some unaffiliated ones were also to decide to join the united May Day rally. The two big plantation workers' unions, however, were not amongst these, and this was later to become a bone of contention between the right and left wings of the LSSP. The left wing alleged that the LSSP's leadership acquiesced in this (and also to the dropping of the party's traditional stand of parity of status for Tamil and Sinhalese as official languages) in order to satisfy its partners in the alliance, particularly the MEP which did not wish to associate either with the Tamil unions or with the move to give equal language rights to the Tamils.[54]

The joint May Day rally was a great show of unity and strength by the left. Even the normally hostile national press admitted that it was the biggest rally ever to be held in Ceylon. The problem of chairing the rally was temporarily solved by having a 'presidium' consisting of the three main leaders of the parties, NM Perera (the leader of the LSSP's parliamentary group), Philip Gunawardena and SA Wickremasinghe (the Presidents of the MEP and the Communist Party respectively). The call that was repeatedly made at the rally was 'left unity', and after the success of the May Day rally it was only a matter of time before the left wingers formally signed a unity agreement. On 8 August the parties formally committed themselves to a United Left Front, and its statement declared that 'the three parties agreed to form a United Left Front on the basis of a general programme and a programme of immediate demands'.[55] Four days later, on 12 August 1963, on the day of the tenth anniversary of the *hartal* (the last big occasion when these three parties acted together), the United Left Front agreement was signed amidst much pomp and ceremony.

The United Left Front

The signing of the agreement formalised the United Left Front (ULF), which was already a fait accompli. The agreement, embody-

53. The May Day rally of the old LSSP in 1939 was the last occasion when these left wingers participated in a single rally.
54. *Ceylon Daily News*, 29 April 1963. See also 'The Platform of the Left Opposition', op cit.
55. *Ceylon Daily News*, 9 August 1963.

ing a preface reviewing the current political situation and stating the tasks of left wingers in the circumstances, was a general programme of 16 items and an immediate programme of 10 items.[56] The preface also saw the continuing threat of the 'resurrection of the UNP' as a result of the failures of the SLFP government; in order to face the threat coming from imperialism and the UNP, to protect democratic rights in full, to solve the burning economic problems of the people, and to consolidate national independence in every sphere, it was thought that a new lead was required. The preface of the ULF agreement declared that in view of this situation, 'the three parties, the Communist Party of Ceylon, the Lanka Sama Samaja Party and the Mahajana Eksath Peramuna have agreed to establish a United Left Front in order to fight for the formation of a government that can implement the programme (given below) and to unite and lead the anti-imperialist, anti-feudalist and Socialist forces of Ceylon'.[57]

The 16-point general programme included in the ULF agreement did not differ very much from the accepted LSSP programme, at least in foreign policy, social services and economic planning. But it differed quite noticeably in areas such as the proposals for economic reform, and the language and citizenship rights of the minorities.[58] In its policies for radical economic reforms, the ULF's programme proposed 'the nationalisation of all estates owned by foreigners and the big estates owned by Ceylonese',[59] whereas the LSSP stood for 'the confiscation and running as state enterprises' of *all* estates over 250 acres.[60] In the field of constitutional reforms, the LSSP's own programme pledged the 'scrapping of the Soulbury Constitution', and the drafting of a new democratic constitution by summoning a constitutional assembly. The ULF merely proposed the democratisation of the existing Soulbury constitution by making amendments.[61]

Regarding the crucial issue of language, the position of the ULF did not differ fundamentally from that held by the SLFP at the time. This entailed the recognition of the position given to the Sinhalese language under the Official Languages Act (1956), that is to say, mak-

56. *Vámánsika Eksat Peramunu Givisuma (The ULF Agreement)*, 12 August 1963, Lanka Press, Colombo, 1963.
57. Op cit, p3. The agreement had no provision for setting up an organisation for the ULF as such, and after the signing a 'Joint Central Committee' was set up to coordinate the affairs of the three parties, which was basically a meeting of their leading members.
58. Here the LSSP's programme that is used for comparison is its *14-Point Programme*.
59. Item 5 of the General Programme of the ULF agreement, *Vámánsika Eksat Peramunu Givisuma*, op cit, p5.
60. Item 6 of the *14-Point Programme*, op cit.
61. Item 2 of *Vámánsika Eksat Peramunu Givisuma*, op cit, p4.

ing Sinhalese the official language, and the position given to the Tamil language under the Tamil Language Special Provisions Act (1958), which facilitated the restricted use of Tamil. In addition, the ULF agreement pledged to remove all administrative difficulties and other discriminatory measures against the use of Tamil for official purposes as decreed under the above mentioned Act. It also laid down that Tamil would be one of the languages used for administrative and judicial work in the two Tamil majority provinces. The traditional policy of the LSSP regarding this issue had been the grant of 'parity of status' to both languages.[62] Even when this was altered in the party's manifesto for the March 1960 elections, the LSSP spokesmen maintained that the party had not moved from its earlier position of conferring equal status on both languages.[63] On the question of citizenship rights to the recent immigrant Tamils, the basic policy of the ULF was to solve the problem by means of negotiations between the governments of Ceylon and India, a procedure that had been rejected by the LSSP time and time again.[64] The ULF expected to solve the problem, firstly, by obtaining the agreement of the Indian government to remove obstacles it had placed against the registration of the Indian immigrants in Ceylon as Indian citizens; and secondly, by conferring Ceylonese citizenship on all those whose origin was in India and whose permanency of residence in Ceylon was accepted by the governments of India and Ceylon, and by granting Indian citizenship to the rest.[65] This is radically different from the position the LSSP held up to March 1960, but it was in accordance with the party's election manifesto of March 1960.[66]

On the whole, the LSSP appeared to have conceded some ground for the sake of achieving unity, but its acceptance of the ULF agreement is more a confirmation of the change of policy that commenced with the party's preparations for the elections of March 1960 rather than a completely new departure. These changes were a logical outcome of the changes that had occurred in the party's strategy during the first three years of the 1960s. Once the party accepted the electoral path, in alliance with either the SLFP or the other left wing parties, as the only viable path to power, as it did in 1960, these policy changes were inevitable.

62. Item 3 of the *14-Point Programme*, op cit.
63. See the statement made by the LSSP's Secretary on the party's attitude to the language question (*Ceylon News*, 2 June 1960).
64. Item 4 of the *14-Point Programme*, op cit. See also the reaffirmation of this made eight years after the *14-Point Programme* was drafted by Colvin R de Silva (House of Representatives, *Debates*, Volume 35, 1959, column 588).
65. Item 16, *Vámánsika Eksat Peramunu Givisuma*, op cit, p10.
66. 'LSSP Election Manifesto', item D(3), *Samasamajist*, 12 January 1960.

No success could have been made along the electoral path without winning over the rural masses, 'the umpire' in Ceylon politics, to employ the term used by an LSSP theoretician, albeit in a different context.[67] Though very egalitarian, the continuation of the LSSP's traditional stand of conferring parity status on the Tamil language as an official language and the granting of citizenship to all recent Indian immigrants who had lived in Ceylon for a period of more than five years may not have been very fruitful in electoral terms. The citizenship bills passed in the late 1940s made the vast majority of the Indian immigrants 'stateless', and with no right to vote they were pushed effectively out of the arena of competitive electoral politics in the country. Furthermore, the growth of Sinhalese nationalism made the Indian and other Tamils reject the leadership of Sinhalese-led parties, and accept the Tamil communal parties. This situation may well have at least been partially instrumental in shaping the policy of the LSSP in this period.

The formation of the ULF and the movement towards it was to reinforce the ideological battle between members of the left and the right within the LSSP. Two of the leading opponents of the alliance strategy put forward by NM Perera in 1960, Colvin R de Silva and Leslie Goonewardene, were in the forefront in the campaign for establishing unity amongst the three left wing parties. However, two other leaders of Political Bureau level, Edmund Samarakkody and Bala Tampoe, were to continue with their left wing opposition to the party's new line. For the left wingers of the LSSP, the party's participation in forming the ULF was another manifestation of its departure from revolutionary Marxist practice. The left wingers did not completely rule out cooperation with other working class-based parties; they acknowledged the suitability of, and the need for, united action with such parties on specific issues. But the left wing Samasamajists held that their party should not enter into programmatic agreements which put forward the prospects of forming a joint government. The fact that the ULF was seeking to attain power solely by parliamentary means, and the exclusion of the unions of the plantation workers, the country's biggest working class organisations, from the activities of the ULF only made this opposition more bitter.

Apparently, the LSSP's original strategy had been to seek the establishment of a 'fighting centre' to coordinate the action of the left wing parties on common issues,[68] rather than forming a united front

67. Doric de Sousa, 'Parliamentary Democracy', *Ceylon News*, 7 September 1961.
68. Edmund Samarakkody, 'Whither the LSSP? (The implications of the ULF), Confidential and Members Only', LSSP *Internal Bulletin*, nd [1963, after August?], p2.

under a common programme. Edmund Samarakkody alleged that the party's three top leaders, NM Perera, Colvin R de Silva and Leslie Goonewardene, conspiratorially changed this original position to one of seeking the establishment of a united front of the three political parties.[69] When the moves for the formation of the ULF got under way, the left wingers openly criticised the path the party had taken.[70] But they were in a minority, and were unable to prevent the ULF, as desired by the right wing majority leaders, from becoming a reality. Once it was formed, almost every aspect of the ULF came in for criticism by the left wing Samasamajists. The programme of the ULF was condemned as one designed to '*protect and promote the development of capitalism in Ceylon*'. Pin-pointing the implicit and the explicit differences between that programme and the programme of the LSSP, Edmund Samarakkody called the acceptance of the ULF programme by the party a 'surrendering' of the party's cherished principles. It was stated that a government of the ULF based on such a programme would 'continue bourgeois class rule and the protection of capitalist property, institutions and relations. The ULF government would further protect and preserve the oppression of the Tamil minority and support the denial of citizenship to nearly seven lakhs of plantation workers.' Asking the question of whether the ULF, despite its limitations, was a step forward in the anti-capitalist struggle, Samarakkody answered that 'it was inconceivable as to how the ULF could take the masses a step forward in the direction of the realisation of the Marxist programme'. He thought that such a formation 'must lead to class collaboration, anti-working class attitudes... and further strengthening of the hold of the reformist and communalist unions of the plantation workers'. Samarakkody thought that the LSSP was embarking upon 'popular frontism' pure and simple, a tactic against which 'the Trotskyist movement had repeatedly warned and fought'. He called upon the party to take an independent stand within the ULF if it was not possible to withdraw from it completely, without losing the party's credibility. The left wingers desired the party to follow its own programme and to highlight the differences between the LSSP and its partners in the ULF, a policy that would have brought it to a speedy end.[71]

69. Samarakkody alleged that this change was made without even notifying the Political Bureau which approved the original line on left wing cooperation ('Whither the LSSP?', op cit, p2).
70. See, for instance, the report on the special lecture given by Samarakkody entitled 'Coming Ceylon Revolution' (*Ceylon Daily News*, 7 August 1963).
71. 'Whither the LSSP?', op cit, pp4, 6, 8-10. See also the speeches made at the University of Ceylon, Peradeniya by Edmund Samarakkody and Bala Tampoe (*Ceylon Daily News*, 19 and 24 August 1963).

In the controversy the left wingers appeared as the guardians of the 'revolutionary quality' of the LSSP. They seemed oblivious to the fact that the LSSP had removed itself from the position of a revolutionary party. The widespread support the ULF received from the general membership of the LSSP, the important achievement of uniting a broad section of the organised workers under the leadership of the ULF, and its apparent potentialities in the contemporary political situation, made the attempts of the left wingers to steer the party away from the ULF impossible. The ULF also received the blessings of the Trotskyist headquarters in Paris, as it was thought to be a tactic better than the LSSP's earlier line of alliance with the SLFP.

From the signing of the agreement, ULF activities thrived in the country for a brief period. The ULF exhibited much dynamism and potential, particularly in view of the fact that the weak government was beset with inner-party and general problems. In many areas, trade union work, political protests, local government elections and in parliamentary activities, the partners in the ULF were to work in close cooperation. The evolution of the Joint Committee of Trade Unions linking all the major trade unions in the country was an important development of the period immediately following the establishment of the ULF. After continued negotiations in which the unions affiliated with the left wing parties took the lead, the JCTU took effect in September; a conference representing a majority of the organised trade unions was held. This represented the highest level of unity that the country's trade union movement was able to achieve. The high water mark of the trade union activities was the drafting of a list of 21 demands around which all the unions associated with the JCTU could organise united action. This list included demands such as all-round wage increases of Rs1/- per day or Rs30/- per month, monthly pay for all, a 45-hour week, increased paid leave, permanency for all temporary employees, trade union rights for public servants, a unified public service, and better compensation schemes. The list of demands approved by the unions that were represented in the JCTU was formally presented to the government and the private sector employers, but the changed political circumstances in the second quarter of 1964 put paid to any further progress. The ULF, which had formed the JCTU and brought about the general enthusiasm in the left wing movement, did not last long, and when new factors, unforeseen by many at the time of the establishment of the ULF, came into play, it was to crumble. The process in which the ULF reached the end of its short life and the developments that followed, in all of which the LSSP figures very centrally, will be the subject of the next section.

The LSSP in 1964: The End of an Era

The year of 1964 was a very significant period in the history of the LSSP, and also in the development of Ceylon's left wing movement. It saw the formalisation of the factional dispute in the Communist Party, leading to the rise of a second Communist Party in Ceylon. It also witnessed the breakdown of the United Left Front that was launched with great enthusiasm the year before. Closely connected with the fate of the ULF was the LSSP's joining a coalition government with the SLFP, thereby attaining the position of sharing governmental power, if only for a short period. The coalition decision was to cost the party a considerable segment of its membership. The split in the LSSP was to give birth to another Lanka Sama Samaja Party, which also robbed the main organisation of its affiliation to the Fourth International, thus ending a 22-year-old association. The partnership that the LSSP established with the SLFP in government was to last out of office as well, right to the present day. The year of 1964 marked the end of a distinctive period for the LSSP.

The rise to prominence of the ULF, which provided an organisational focal point for broad sections of the population, added to the problems of the government. Poor performance in managing the economy, almost total failure with the organised sections of the working class, and acute hostility from the minority groups, were beginning to have an effect on the ranks of the government itself. By early 1964 several defections had melted the governing party's majority to a precariously low level. The apparent revival of the UNP as reflected by the rapid growth of its youth movement and widespread success in local government elections, was to worry the SLFP much more than the left wing parties.

The new year started with a series of major labour disputes. The strikes, starting in December in the port of Colombo, continued through to the new year, and these strikes were supported by an island-wide general strike of the powerful Ceylon Mercantile Union. Despite the government's attempts to defeat them, the strikers stood firm and made several gains. January also brought electoral gains to the government's rivals: at a by-election the government lost to the UNP a constituency it had held since 1956, whilst the LSSP won at another by-election contesting on behalf of the ULF.[72] In the same period, whilst the trade unions organised in the JCTU were finalising arrangements for a major confrontation with the government and the private employers on the '21 Demands', the political wing of the

---

72. The UNP won Nikaweratiya in the North-Western Province, and the ULF candidate won Borella in Colombo.

ULF, by way of highlighting the country's economic problems, launched a campaign to sign a mammoth petition demanding that the government bring down the cost of living. There was also a growing demand for the abolition of the press commission appointed by the government to look into the behaviour of the press monopolies in Ceylon; on this demand both the right and left wing opponents of the government were in agreement.

On top of these troubles came more trade union disputes: a go-slow by the postal workers, and strikes by the electrical engineers and the government medical officers. In desperation, the government re-introduced a state of emergency, coupled with strict press censorship and an essential services order that covered all the major services and industries in the country. The new action of the government brought a flood of protests from other political organisations. Within days of the declaration of a state of emergency, the parliamentary group of the ULF gave notice of a no-confidence motion against the government, aimed mainly at the press commission, an issue on which the other parties in opposition and a section of the government party itself, disagreed with the policy of the government. Perhaps avoiding a possible set-back inside parliament, the government took the rather unusual step of proroguing parliament several weeks before the current session was due to end. Having ended any possible manoeuvring within parliament, the SLFP leadership embarked on a new line of action. A move to associate the parties of the ULF with the government, a move that was soon to change relationships amongst the different political groups and the course of political development as a whole, was initiated by the government. The question of cooperation between the government and the left wingers became the primary issue, and the ULF went into the background, soon to disappear altogether.

By the end of March vague speculation about informal talks between leading members of the government and the leaders of the left wing parties towards establishing some form of cooperation between the SLFP and the parties of the ULF gave way to substantial news about moves in such directions.[73] On 28 March, at a public rally, the Prime Minister invited the left wingers to cooperate with the government in order to carry forward the 'fight against reactionary forces'.[74] Although initial talks held by leading members of the gov-

73. *Ceylon Daily News* reported on 17 March 1964 that a Minister met NM Perera to discuss the possibility of establishing some form of cooperation between the SLFP and the LSSP. Two days later the same newspaper reported that the Cabinet also discussed the matter, apparently guided by the Prime Minister herself, and unanimously agreed to explore the possibilities of forming a 'national government'.
74. *Ceylon Daily News*, 30 March 1964.

ernment were with individual leaders of the left, particularly NM Perera and Philip Gunawardena, the ULF attempted to develop a common strategy in offering cooperation to the government. Three days after the Prime Minister's announcement, the Joint Central Committee of the ULF issued a statement stating that 'the ULF stands ready to cooperate with the leftward-moving forces of the SLFP' for the purpose of 'mobilising the resistance to the UNP-led reaction and for a leftward solution of the present crisis.'[75] After this, the leaders were to canvass the new line inside their respective parties. The leadership of the LSSP managed to obtain the consent of the Central Committee to conduct negotiations with the government, but not without much difficulty. The Seventh Congress of the Communist Party that met in April welcomed the idea, and described the development as a bright sign in the prevailing crisis situation.[76] The MEP, whose attitude was expressed by Philip Gunawardena, was also very enthusiastic about the prospect of forming a joint left-SLFP government, but his support was hedged with the condition that the 'reactionary and corrupt elements' in the SLFP government must be expelled if such a joint government were to become possible.[77] Philip Gunawardena specified two members of the government who were in the faction of the Cabinet that opposed him, as his colleagues in the old MEP government of 1956-59.[78] In view of the changed political atmosphere, the ULF stalled all trade union protests that were in the making;[79] understandably anticipating a regroupment of forces in the government that could include members of the ULF, the left wingers were careful not to embarrass their prospective partner. Negotiations went on throughout April, and as NM Perera, who

75. *Ceylon Daily News*, 1 April 1964.
76. *Ceylon Daily News*, 17 April 1964. See also the Communist Party of Ceylon, *Visipas Vasarak (Twenty-Five Years)*, People's Publishers, Colombo, 1968, p95.
77. However, the other important leader of the MEP, Robert Gunawardena, objected to the establishment of any kind of association with the SLFP; he wanted the strengthening of the ULF as an alternative to the SLFP. The differences of opinion centred around this issue, perhaps fostered by personal differences, led eventually to the separation of the two brothers in May. Robert later formed a party called the United Left Front Party, and contested the 1965 elections in isolation from the other left wing as well as the rightist party groupings, resulting in a complete rout of the few candidates he supported, and his own defeat. The new government of the UNP-led coalition formed in March 1965, in which Philip Gunawardena was a Minister, appointed Robert as Ceylon's Ambassador to the People's Republic of China.
78. The two Ministers whose removal Philip Gunawardena demanded were CP de Silva (Minister of Lands and Land Development and the Leader of the House of Representatives) and Maithripala Senanayake (Minister of Public Works).
79. During April NM Perera, in his capacity as the President of the JCTU, persuaded the trade union representatives to postpone action on two occasions.

worked as the chief negotiator on the side of the ULF, declared at a May Day rally, the forming of a joint 'ULF and SLFP government' was a certainty before the end of May.[80] However, when the joint government with the SLFP was actually formed, though a little later than Perera predicted, not all of the ULF took part in its formation.

For obvious reasons, the Prime Minister was not prepared to concede the demands made by Philip Gunawardena. This she expressed in public, and also conveyed to the ULF delegation that met her later in May. Moreover, the making of such a demand created stiff opposition within the government party against admitting Philip Gunawardena into the Cabinet; in this the senior Ministers whom Gunawardena disliked were joined by many others. Therefore, even when talks were continued with the MEP, it was clear from a very early stage that the MEP was not going to be a partner in government, at least for the time being. Sections of the SLFP also objected to giving cabinet positions to members of the Communist Party. It is also possible, as the Prime Minister was reported to have informed the ULF delegation that she met, that the international repercussions of admitting a Communist Party that was closely associated with the Soviet Union could have been an obstacle to including the Communists in the government. Ceylon's special relationship with China and the government's declared policy of neutrality in the Sino-Soviet dispute may have influenced this decision. It is also possible that in view of the Communist Party's almost consistent support for SLFP governments in the past, that the offer of Ministerial portfolios was thought unnecessary to sustain that support. Whatever the reasons, by the end of May the indicators were that at least for the time being, the joint government was going to be one between the SLFP and the LSSP, and this was to create tension within the ULF. Despite the possibility of their exclusion, both the Communist Party and the MEP continued to campaign for a joint government that would include the entire ULF. The Central Committee of the Communist Party approved a resolution which called on the left wing movement not to allow the SLFP to 'split the left and pick and choose as it pleases'.[81] After the meeting between the Prime Minister and the ULF delegation, NM Perera was accused by Philip Gunawardena of representing his own personal interests rather than the common interests of the ULF in his capacity as the chief ULF negotiator. Two days before the LSSP's conference met to sanction definitely the party's line of forming a coalition, the Secretaries of the three left wing parties sent a letter to the Prime Minister, evidently in response to the latter's stand of sup-

80. *Ceylon Daily News*, 2 May 1964.
81. *Ceylon Daily News*, 30 May 1964.

porting the setting up of a coalition between the SLFP and the LSSP; here it was stated that a 'coalition was not possible' along the lines the Prime Minister had indicated.[82] However, individually the LSSP was to decide otherwise.

The LSSP Special Conference met on 6-7 June amidst severe inner-party rivalries. This conference was crucial because of the importance of the decision that it was called upon to make. The divisiveness of the issues involved was so great that the party split even before the conference was actually over. There were three resolutions put forward by different groupings of Central Committee members: two of these favoured a coalition with the SLFP, although they differed on the composition; the other opposed all forms of coalition and collaboration. One of the pro-coalition resolutions, initiated by eight Central Committee members including Colvin R de Silva, Leslie Goonewardene and Doric de Sousa, called upon the conference to authorise the party to work towards establishing a 'progressive government' subject to three conditions: an agreement on measures that would enthuse the masses and secure their active participation, capable of being implemented in one year; that the government should be between the SLFP and the ULF; and that the LSSP should obtain the three portfolios of Finance, Nationalised Services and Internal and External Trade.[83] The single anti-coalition resolution supported by 14 members of the Central Committee, including Edmund Samarakkody, Bala Tampoe and V Karalasingham, called upon the conference to 'reject categorically all proposals for coalition with the SLFP on any basis whatsoever'. It counterposed to this the task of defeating the attempt to divide the working class, and the task of 'carrying forward the class struggle against the capitalist class and the SLFP government'. This resolution saw the attempts of the SLFP government to coalesce with the parties of the working class as a desperate measure taken by an unpopular and weak bourgeois government faced with a mounting 'tide of working class and mass discontent against it'. The left wingers argued that 'the entry of the LSSP into the SLFP government will result in open class collaboration, the disorientation of the masses, the division of the working class and the abandonment of the struggle perspective, which will lead to the disruption of the working class movement and the elimination of the independent revolutionary axis of the left. In the result, the forces of capitalist reaction, far from being weakened or thwarted, will be ultimately strengthened.'[84]

82. The letter was signed by Leslie Goonewardene (LSSP), KD Perera (MEP) and Pieter Keuneman (Communist Party) (*Ceylon Daily News*, 4 June 1964).
83. *LSSP Special Conference, 6 and 7 June 1964: Agenda and Resolutions*, 1964, p14.
84. Op cit, pp12-13.

The third resolution, sponsored by 21 members led by NM Perera, called upon the conference to approve the formation of a coalition government between the ULF and the SLFP, or, if the negotiations failed, the setting up of a coalition between the LSSP and the SLFP. This resolution saw, as did the ULF agreement a year earlier, the government of the SLFP as a weakened, inefficient and unpopular one; if the government were not supported in the circumstances the result could be a right wing dictatorship. It admitted that the rise of the ULF generated tremendous mass enthusiasm, but doubted the capacity of the ULF to mobilise that support. The opposition that came from within the LSSP and the lack of cooperation from Philip Gunawardena were given as two of the reasons for doubting the future potentialities of the ULF. By way of defending the proposed tactic of coalition against being criticised as 'class collaboration', the resolution made a concerted effort to highlight the 'progressive character' of the SLFP; it was said that the SLFP was based on the 'radical petit-bourgeoisie and the lower middle class'. The 'overall drive' of the SLFP was seen as a 'steady movement leftwards'. After enumerating the many measures of social and economic reform undertaken by the two SLFP governments in the past, the resolution declared that 'when the cumulative effect of these measures is considered it will be quite apparent that *the SLFP is not a capitalist party*. The fact that it is functioning within the capitalist framework does not necessarily make it a party of the capitalist class.' It was also thought that a coalition government between the LSSP and the SLFP would further increase the 'progressive content' of the SLFP. The resolution, in addition to proposing negotiations with the SLFP government with a view to forming a coalition, urged that such a government should agree to the list of demands that the resolution enumerated, and allow three ministerial portfolios to go to the LSSP — Finance, Nationalised Services and Trade. The proposed list of demands for immediate implementation included the conferring of a banking monopoly on the two state commercial banks, the control of agency houses, the restriction of the export of capital, profits and dividends, an increase in the efficiency of the administration, the taking over of the import of all essential goods, the handing over of the wholesale distribution of goods to the state-sponsored Cooperative Wholesale Establishment, the ending of the 'press monopoly', the setting up of 'people's boards', and the association of the trade unions in making the planning machinery more efficient.[85] It was this resolution that the conference approved; within four days the LSSP became a partner in government, obtaining three portfolios, Finance (NM Perera),

85. Op cit, pp1-8, my emphasis.

Communications (Anil Moonesinghe), and Public Works (Cholmondely Goonewardene). After nearly 30 years of existence, the LSSP achieved the sharing of governmental power. The new coalition government adopted a 14-point programme closely following the proposals put forward by the majority group of the LSSP at the party's conference. Although the coalition government was not to last long,[86] the partnership thus established between the LSSP and the SLFP was to remain to the present day.

The majority of the left wing Samasamajists who opposed their party taking part in any form of coalition government walked out of the conference, and, as it happened, out of the party as well, immediately following the adoption of the 'pro-LSSP/SLFP coalition' resolution. Gathering in conference, they formed into a party under the name of the Lanka Sama Samaja Party (Revolutionary Section), with Edmund Samarakkody as the Secretary of the Provisional Central Committee of the new party.[87]

86. The government was brought down on 3 December 1964 on the voting of an amendment to the new government's Throne Speech, because 14 members of the SLFP led by the Leader of the House, CP de Silva, defected to the side of the opposition.

87. The breakaway group carried with it sections from the radical LSSP groups in Colombo harbour, the universities, and the constituencies of the group's two Members of Parliament, Edmund Samarakkody and Meryl Fernando. It also gained control of the *Samasamajaya*, the party's Sinhalese organ; the group's trade union link was through Bala Tampoe, who was the Secretary of the Ceylon Mercantile Union. Although the leading figures of the LSSP(R) worked together as the 'left opposition' within the LSSP, they failed to maintain that unity in their own party, and the LSSP(R) was soon rent with dissension. This took the form of considerable differences of opinion on such fundamental questions as attitudes towards the Communist Party and the LSSP, forms of organisation, and attitudes towards the International movement. The party's isolation from the larger left wing movement in the country (at the 1965 elections the LSSP(R) contested independently four constituencies; it lost deposits in all these contests) only fostered the ideological and tactical differences, leading to several splits in 1967-69. One group, led by V Karalasingham returned to the mother party, and another under Samarakkody separated to form the Revolutionary LSSP. Bala Tampoe, assisted no doubt by his base in the CMU, consolidated himself as the leader of the now depleted LSSP(R); in 1969 some of his younger militants, drawn mainly from the universities, separated to organise as the Revolutionary Communist League, the only Ceylonese Trotskyist splinter group not to take the name of the LSSP. In another respect they also differed from the rest: this group allied with the newly-emerged London-based International Committee of the Fourth International, adding another dimension to the dissension within the Ceylonese Trotskyist movement. For further details of the dissension and some aspects of the new developments since June 1964, see V Karalasingham, *Senile Leftism: A Reply to Edmund Samarakkody*, International Publishers, Colombo, 1966; Jaya Vithana, 'Ceylon and the Healy School of Falsification', *InterContinental Press*, New York, Volume 11, no 10, March 1973, pp307-15; 'Ceylon: The

In the meantime, the Executive of the United Secretariat of the Fourth International, meeting in Paris on 22 June, expelled the three Samasamajists who had accepted ministerial portfolios, and suspended all the rest who voted with them to enter into a coalition.[88] The United Secretariat, which supported the left wing Samasamajists who broke away from the party, disaffiliated the LSSP and accepted the new LSSP (Revolutionary Section) as the body representing the Trotskyist movement in Ceylon in the world organisation,[89] thus ending the LSSP's 22-year-old organisational link with the world Trotskyist movement. A definite period in the life of the LSSP had come to an end.

V Karalasingham
The Collapse of the Old Leadership

EVEN BEFORE the Special Conference, all sections of opinion within the party were agreed that the right wing group of Dr Perera would get a majority in favour of its line of forming a coalition government with the capitalist SLFP. But the actual voting figures on the three resolutions, that is the resolutions of the Right, Centre and the Left, showed an overwhelming support for the resolution of the Perera faction, which received over 500 of the 700 votes.[90] This disproportionately large vote in favour of an openly and nakedly revisionist position reveals that the LSSP as it was constituted at the time of the conference was clearly not what it claimed to be, namely, the vanguard organisation of the revolutionary working class.

It would be idle to blame the party rank and file who in such

Centrism of Bala Tampoe', *Fourth International*, London, Volume 8, no 2, Spring 1973, pp53-61.

88. G Healy, *Ceylon: The Great Betrayal*, Socialist Labour League, London, 1964, p1.
89. Letter of the United Secretariat, 10 July 1964, reproduced in Ernest Germain, 'People's Frontism in Ceylon: From Wavering to Capitulation', *International Socialist Review*, Fall 1964, p114.
90. The Right's resolution, prepared by NM Perera, Jack Kotelawala, Anil Moonesinghe and others, gained 501 votes (65 per cent). The Centre's resolution, proposed by Colvin R de Silva, Leslie Goonewardene, Doric de Souza and Bernard Zoysa, gained 75 votes (10 per cent). The Left's resolution, proposed by Edmund Samarakkody, Meryl Fernando, V Karalasingham, Prins Rajasooriya, P Bala Tampoe, RS Baghavan, Sidney Wanasinghe, DS Mallawarachchi and Reggie Mendis gained 159 votes (25 per cent).

numbers voted for the resolution of Dr Perera. To the best of their ability they thought out the problems before them in the limited time, and voted for the resolution which promised them an opening to 'Socialism'. It is no fault of theirs that these votes added to give the revisionists an absolute majority. What is unfortunate is that they were called to vote on a fundamental theoretical Marxist question, though in the specific form of a coalition with the SLFP. For this, the blame entirely rests on the leadership of Leslie, who was mainly responsible for their recruitment into the party and their continuance as members on an abysmally low political level. The leadership made no attempts to raise the political level of these new members, and an ignorant membership was looked on as a distinct advantage in the fight against the Left, since loyalty to the established leadership was the test of admission. So long as the political leadership of Leslie-Colvin was accepted by NM Perera, both groups happily went along, utterly indifferent to the political education of the party's rank and file, the Youth Leagues, the trade unions, and the party periphery generally. It was not only a matter of the Marxist education of the membership. Even political discussions on current questions were discouraged, and, in the last few years, new forms of activity were specially devised in order to avoid political discussion, even on occasions when it was traditional to hold them. Thus, commencing with the Anuradhapura session of the Youth Leagues in 1961, the farce of *Shramadhana* [community service] was introduced, and several hours were sliced off political debate, and delegates were physically exhausted in labour not profitable either to the party or to the movement as a whole. The disease of *Shramadhana* spread down the line. At the next session of the Youth Leagues, at Balapitiya, the leadership shamelessly avoided all political discussions by organising a meaningless 50 mile march, which did not even take the form of a demonstration against the government. It is no accident that all this commenced after the LSSP decided on close collaboration with the government of Mrs Bandaranaike, following the general election of July 1960 when the party leadership voted to support the budget and the throne speech of the SLFP government.

In this manner, the entirety of the post-1960 party members was denied the political inner life of the party which is sustained through education, discussion, debates, internal bulletins, etc. Out of the new recruits, a docile membership distinguished only by its obedience to the leadership of Leslie was sought to be created. But history plays funny tricks with the best laid plans of mice and men. Leslie Goonewardene, who built up an organisation to keep the Left in a perpetual minority, was soon to be crushed and demoralised by the very members whom he brought into the LSSP. When NM Perera showed his pro-coalitionist stand, the entire membership which Leslie nursed to life turned against him to support a coalition of the LSSP and SLFP. For whatever the conference showed, it revealed with absolute clearness the wholesale rejection of the politics of the Leslie-Colvin group.

Till recently, Dr Perera never claimed to provide political leadership to the LSSP. In the early days of the party, it was Philip Gunawardena who played this rôle, and after the latter's defection, Leslie and Colvin constituted the political leadership of the party. During all these years, NM Perera dutifully accepted the political line as determined by the leadership. However much he and his cohorts may sneer at their revolutionary past, with its alleged 'sectarianism', it was precisely the Marxist character of the old political leadership of Colvin-Leslie which made of NM Perera the revolutionary public figure so familiar till his absorption into the cabinet of Mrs Bandaranaike. It is an open secret that Dr NM Perera was far from being a Marxist — he was, and is, at best a Laskian in politics and a Keynesian in economics. This fatal combination of Laski and Keynes in a backward country like Ceylon would have long ago ruined Dr Perera. But thanks to the Marxist orientation of the LSSP given by Philip Gunawardena, and later by Colvin and Leslie, Dr Perera not merely averted a premature political death, but was able, on the very back of that revolutionary Marxist movement (today labelled by him as 'sectarian, doctrinaire, sterile, ingrown' etc), to scale the 'heights' of Mrs Bandaranaike's cabinet.

The first time Dr Perera ventured to political leadership was at the party conference in May 1960. And, significantly, on the first occasion he sought to act independently, either of Philip Gunawardena or of Colvin-Leslie, it was to propose a coalition with the SLFP! The party conference accepted his proposal, but subsequent events, particularly the return of the SLFP with an absolute majority, saved the party. Never before had History given a warning signal so sharp and, what is more important, so timely — to avert an impending catastrophe. The lesson of NM's revisionist victory was not altogether lost on the leadership of Leslie-Colvin, since the latter, too, met the opposition elements to discuss the new danger represented by the emergence of NM Perera with his independent political line, based not on Marxism and Trotskyism, but on petit-bourgeois and bourgeois theorists like Harold Laski and Maynard Keynes. After the July 1960 elections, Colvin and Leslie lost all interest in saving the LSSP from the pestilence of NM Perera's open espousal of basically anti-working class ideas. Actually they were themselves moving closer to the capitalist SLFP government — relentlessly driven to that course by the

1956 policy of responsive cooperation. They made out, however, that they were adapting themselves to NM Perera's revisionism in order to save him from the final and irretrievable debâcle of open class collaboration. But all to no avail. A scientist must be strictly objective, and, if he tries to cheat himself on imagined facts and phenomena, he can only blame himself if he is later overcome by a crisis which he could have avoided through a proper, honest and objective appreciation of facts. Every science is a terrible discipline, and the science of Marxism is no different. Leslie and Colvin disregarded all the storm signals, and now they are caught up in the deluge of NM Perera's revisionism.

But startling though it may appear, the fact is that bourgeois reformism is their habitat. That is why, within a few weeks of the formation of the coalition government, these men are already doing the dirty work for their new mistress and masters with zest. Mr Leslie Goonewardene, displaying a new burst of initiative, is attempting to muzzle the opposition in parliament, while his colleague, Dr Colvin R de Silva, is the principal public relations officer of the government, and together they are the shadow advisers of two 'Socialist' ministers. These men and Dr Perera did not come into the revolutionary Socialist movement — they drifted into it, drawn by the force exerted by Mr Philip Gunawardena. The latter alone, of the early pioneers of the LSSP, was a Marxist, and, what is most important of all, he alone was an active and serious participant in the revolutionary movement abroad, in the United States and the United Kingdom. The others, while abroad, settled into their academic routine so diligently that they surfaced to political life only after their professional examinations and university doctorates. And the politics to which they took was the harmless Fabianism of the early 1930s, or the equally gentle radicalism of an Intourist visitor to the Soviet Union, or to a variety of Christian Socialism. These were the puny heights of their Socialist accomplishment. And that, too, in the impetuosity of their youth, and in the England of the depression years with its heightened class struggles, and most important of all a Communist Party that for all the errors of the ultra-leftism of the Third Period was aggressively militant! The organic conservatism of their politics is clearly brought out in the fact that in this turbulent period they came nowhere near even the fringe of the English labour movement. In sharp contrast was Mr Philip Gunawardena, who, abandoning his academic pursuits, was active in colonial student circles, and within the British Communist Party had moved to open support of the International Left Opposition. The contrast was to persist through the years, but the association of the Marxist Philip Gunawardena with the *Herr Doktors* of the London University soon rescued the latter from the rut of conventional bourgeois learning and opened them to new horizons. Under his powerful influence, the more talented among them moved from 'Popular Frontism' while even the Fabian traits of others receded to the background. And, together with Philip Gunawardena, they constituted a formidable team which has left its imprint on history in what is the 'heroic period' of the LSSP (1935-47). But the effervescence of their revolutionary activity lasted as long as Mr Philip Gunawardena himself was in the organised Marxist movement. True, in the years of the latter's independent existence as a Marxist outside the LSSP, the leadership of Leslie-Colvin maintained their Marxist orientation, but competition with Mr Philip Gunawardena's rival Trotskyist organisation left them with no other choice. But once Mr Philip Gunawardena broke with Marxism and joined the late Mr Bandaranaike, the bell tolled for the Leslies and Colvins. Within a few months of Mr Philip Gunawardena's final defection from the revolutionary movement, the Leslies and Colvins, in their own way, broke with Marxism with their policy of 'responsive cooperation' with the capitalist government of Mr Bandaranaike. They were, in fact, beginning to find a road back to the respectable politics of their youth.

But the poor calibre of the leadership is only one aspect, and a subordinate one at that. The LSSP ever since its inception carried within it two sharply defined tendencies, a petit-bourgeois nationalist and a proletarian Marxist, and the factional struggles and splits which have punctuated its history reflected the struggle of these tendencies. In the early years of the party, its loose mass character gave a weightage to petit-bourgeois nationalist elements, but the unity of the leadership, under the Marxist Philip Gunawardena, was sufficient to hold the alien elements under control. The adoption of a Marxist programme and the Bolshevik principle of party organisation, without adequate and proper preparation, did not do away with the old conflict, but brought it to a head when, in 1945, two Trotskyist organisations functioned. But the bifurcation at least had the distinct merit of reducing the pressure of the petit-bourgeois masses on the genuine Marxist tendency represented by the Bolshevik-Leninist Party. The Sama Samaja Party of NM Perera was the natural haven for these elements. But the unification of the two organisations in 1950 revived the old struggle, and in 1953 over one-third of the unified organisation led by Henry Peiris and others demanded that the party should line up with Mr Bandaranaike to form a 'democratic government'. Leslie and Colvin gave battle. The proposal was defeated, but the victors were soon to be vanquished. In less than three years the very men who fought the revisionism of Henry Peiris offered 'responsive cooperation' to the government of Mr Bandaranaike, thereby conceding the basic positions of the 1953 revisionists. The capitulation of the Leslie-Colvin leadership to the politics of Henry Peiris is as much proof of their fundamental incapacity to provide revolutionary leadership, as of the tremendous pressure on the party of non-proletarian elements in a predominantly petit-bourgeois country.

While the party successfully withstood this pressure during the next onslaught (the Sinhala Only agitation), the impact of the fury of the petit-bourgeois masses no doubt left a deep impression on the weak leadership. The formation in 1939 by Pandit Nehru of the Ceylon Indian Congress — which later divided to form the Ceylon Workers Congress and the Democratic Workers Congress — and its growth as the principal organisation of the plantation workers — and that, too, outside the influence of the LSSP — and the emergence of the reactionary Federal Party as the spokesman of the Tamil-speaking people of the North and East, further isolated the LSSP from the two groups whose direct influence on the party would have counteracted to some extent at least the pressures of the chauvinist middle classes. Thondaman and Chelvanayakam, each for his own class reason, successfully held back the masses supporting them from the LSSP. The healthy mass influences on the party were restricted entirely to the advanced sections among the urban working class. A revolutionary party no less than any other organisation is ultimately a part of society. The successful containment of the class pressures of the plantation working class in an exclusive organisation under reactionary leadership and the quarantining of the oppressed Tamil-speaking people in the communal Tamil Federal Party exposed the LSSP, almost wholly, to middle class influences that were far from healthy.

A leadership of exceptional dedication and strength was required to stand up to the mounting new pressures, which increased tenfold once the SLFP itself had twice dashed the hopes of the petit-bourgeois masses who had supported it in April 1956 and July 1960. This the leadership of Colvin-Leslie was not. But thanks to the deep-seated revolutionary tradition in the LSSP, it took over eight years before the leadership could move further from 'responsive cooperation' to actual participation in an SLFP government.

But the transformation of the LSSP from the vanguard of the working class into a bourgeois agency within the working class got under way. The first steps were so innocuous that only in retrospect have they significance. Thus the SLFP, which was originally denounced as the alternative capitalist party, was no longer so characterised, and, what is more, neither was the old characterisation withdrawn; on the plea that the SLFP is not the UNP, the party leadership patronised state *tamashas*, and soon commenced to fraternise with the class enemy and ingratiate itself with 'official' society; the emphasis of party propaganda gradually shifted from the class to the 'nation', from revolution to parliament, from science to witchcraft; new virtues were discovered in Mr Bandaranaike as 'the champion of the common man', although only a few years previously he was rightly branded as 'that principal crusader against the Indian workers, who is a declared anti-Marxist, anti-Communist and anti-Soviet politician'. Soon the pace quickened, and after the return to earth in March 1960 the party became virtually the fifth wheel of the SLFP bandwagon. Under cover of fraction work, the parliamentary group attempted to join the government parliamentary party; the Budget and Throne Speech of the Sirima Bandaranaike government received the support of the leadership, while the members of the Left who opposed it were censured; the principal defenders of the government were NM Perera, Colvin R de Silva and others; where criticism of the government was unavoidable, it was done in the spirit of a loyal opposition, and soon criticism degenerated into an anti-Felix Diaz diatribe; the door opened to the ideas of the Moscow wing of the Communist Party, and the leadership became receptive to Popular Frontist policies; the defence of the Chinese Revolution was quietly abandoned, and on the Sino-Indian conflict the well-known Trotskyist position was jettisoned in favour of the thoroughly petit-bourgeois appeal to an International Court for arbitration; Soviet diplomacy received open support, and the Nuclear Test Ban Treaty, which was directed at China, won the approval of the leadership; in the Sino-Soviet ideological dispute, the first major theoretical debate since Trotsky's own theoretical struggles within the Comintern, the party leadership took up no position, no doubt out of deference to its new allies, the Moscow wing of the Communist Party. The trade union policy of the party, too, underwent a gradual change, and strikes were no longer what Engels called 'the schools wherein the proletariat is prepared for entry into the great struggle which is inevitable', but a source of acute embarrassment; in the mighty strike action of the CTB in January 1963, the party leadership intervened only to work out a formula for a 'return to work'; later that year, it openly condemned the strike of government electricians in language so worthy of the extreme right that even Felix Diaz raised his hands in horror.

While extra-parliamentary action was avoided like the plague, parliamentary manoeuvring proceeded at great intensity. Exploiting the mass urge for unity in action and for the centralisation of their struggles, the reformists of the party, the CP and Mr Philip Gunawardena formed the ULF, a caricature of a united front, in that it was expressly conceived for the purpose of parliamentary and electoral jockeying. This was soon apparent when on the initiative of the CTUF, the trade union centre of the Communist Party (Peking wing), the Joint Committee of Trade Unions convened to formulate working class demands, and soon geared the class to action; for a time the revisionists performed the impossible feat of running with the hare and hunting with the hounds. Then, with a cynicism that would even have embarrassed Ramsay MacDonald, Dr NM Perera, behind the back of his own party, opened up negotiations with the government of Mrs Bandaranaike, just as the agitation of the working class on its 21 demands was mounting to a decisive climax. In the language of class war, this was high treason, both against the party and the class. But Leslie Goonewardene and Colvin R de Silva stepped in to defend a self-confessed Quisling, and to pave the way for the final act. The votes of the Leslie-Colvin faction in the Central Committee enabled NM Perera to summon a conference at a bare four weeks notice in order to give constitutional propriety to his shameful treachery. Thus by their very distortion of the principal of democratic centralism — rigid centralism against the revolutionary Left, and full democracy for the revisionist Right — the leaders of the Centre betrayed their real rôle. They did more. They also hastened their doom, because in the events which followed the Special Conference, it was not

NM Perera who was exposed — he had long proclaimed from the house-top his bourgeois coalitionist politics. At last events caught up with Colvin and Leslie, and there was no retreat for them — either with or against the bourgeois coalition. And no sooner was it formed than they promptly lined up behind the bourgeois coalition. In her own way, history now humiliated them for the many liberties they had taken in the past — their own votes not only gave 'legality' to NM Perera's capitulation, but these same votes, finally, stripped away their seventh veil, to reveal this time the hideousness of their bourgeois politics.

Of course our enemies are rejoicing. And, from the standpoint of their class, what a resounding victory! Despite all the severe limitations to which we have made reference, this was in the context of Ceylon the incorruptible leadership, feared by the class enemy, and looked upon by the masses as their leadership. Its collapse gives the bourgeoisie of Ceylon an unexpected breathing spell, at least till such time as the new revolutionary leadership wins the confidence of the masses. No wonder the bourgeoisie, whether organised in the UNP, or the SLFP, or the Federal Party, now takes comfort in the general disarray in the left, since they know well that they now have a new lease of life. And not only the bourgeoisie, even their petit-bourgeois hangers-on have shown a new spurt of activity. The cynics and sceptics, the pessimists and confusionists, the Middle Way preachers and the Bandaranaike apostles are already pulling out their old copybooks, prescriptions and universal panaceas. With a new defiance, all the old deserters and cowards who left the movement because they could not keep pace with the tempo of its advance and found solace in Koestler and Burnham,[91] now ask: 'Did we not tell you so — they are all alike. Three decades of sweat and toil, and what have you to show?' With a malicious grin, they themselves reply: 'Three senior and two junior scavengers of the bourgeois state!' Despite the grain of truth in their rhetorical answer, they are all wrong, hopelessly wrong, including the misanthropes who chirp in: 'You will do the same, when you are older.'

All alike have no understanding of the inner spring of *development*, that is, they have not comprehended the dialectic of the historic process which Hegel so elegantly expressed, even though within the frame and in the language of his idealist philosophy:

91. Arthur Koestler (1905-83), the well-known author, was a Stalinist until 1938, and his repudiation of his views later appeared in *The God That Failed*. James Burnham (1905-1987) left the US Socialist Workers Party with Max Shachtman's group, then split from that, wrote *The Managerial Revolution*, and soon became an extreme anti-Communist.

'The general thought — the category which first presents itself in this restless mutation of individuals and peoples, existing for a time and then vanishing — is that of *change* at large. The sight of the ruins of some ancient sovereignty directly leads us to contemplate this thought of change in its negative aspect. What traveller among the ruins of Carthage, of Palmyra, Persepolis or Rome has not been stimulated to reflections on the transiency of kingdoms and men, and to sadness at the thought of a vigorous and rich life now departed — a sadness which does not expend itself on personal losses and the uncertainty of one's own undertakings, but is a disinterested sorrow at the decay of a splendid and highly cultured national life! But the next consideration which allies itself with that of change, is that change, while it imports dissolution, involves at the same time the rise of a *new life* — that while death is the issue of life, life is also the issue of death. That is a grand conception; one which the Oriental thinkers attained, and which is perhaps the highest in their metaphysics. In the idea of *Metempsychosis* we find it evolved in its relation to individual existence; but a myth more generally known is that of the *Phoenix* as a type of the Life of *Nature*; eternally preparing for itself a funeral pile, and consuming itself upon it; but so that from its ashes is produced the new, renovated, fresh life. But this image is only Asiatic; oriental not occidental. Spirit — consuming the envelope of its existence — does not merely pass into another envelope, nor rise rejuvenescent from the ashes of its previous form; it comes forth exalted, glorified, a purer spirit. It certainly makes war upon itself — consumes its own existence; *but in this very destruction it works up that existence into a new form, and each successive phase becomes in its turn a material, working on which it exalts itself to a new grade.*'

Much as the living ruins now languishing in the ranks of the government evoke our 'disinterested sorrow', the fact is that in conformity with the very law of *development*, the new life has already arisen out of the disintegration of the old leadership of the LSSP — revolutionary Marxists from the ranks of the *swabasha*, in particular the Sinhala-educated intelligentsia in the Universities of Peradiniya, Vidyalankara and Vidyodaya, and the *Privenas*[92] of Ceylon. These are the elements who take over from now, and they do so on the higher plane of the positive achievements and enduring conquests already made. This is the guarantee that the new revolutionary leadership shall take the movement to its historic goal.

---

92. Buddhist teaching schools.

Charles Wesley Ervin
Trotskyism in India, 1942-48

We are greatly indebted to Charles Wesley Ervin for providing us with the
second part of his account of the Trotskyist movement in India. The first
part, 'Trotskyism in India: Origins Through World War II (1935-45)', appeared in *Revolutionary History*, Volume 1, no 4, Winter 1988-89, pp22-
34, and was translated into French in order to appear in *Cahiers Léon
Trotsky*, no 39, September 1989, pp77-111. Another issue of the *Cahiers
Léon Trotsky* (no 21, March 1985) was devoted to the history of the Trotskyist movement in India.

THE HISTORY of the Trotskyist movement in India has never
been adequately recorded. For the most part, the Bolshevik Leninist Party of India (BLPI), the section of the Fourth International
from 1942 to 1948, is treated as a minor episode in the history of the
Lanka Sama Samaja Party (LSSP) of Ceylon (now Sri Lanka). If one
goes back to the publications of the international Trotskyist movement, there is enough material from the BLPI at least to dispel the
myth that it was simply an appendage of the LSSP. In fact, the
Fourth International was quite proud and enthusiastic about the
achievements of the BLPI.

Though a tiny party in a vast multinational country, the BLPI was
well-endowed with brilliant writers and capable mass leaders. It
turned out a stream of sophisticated pamphlets, a high-quality Eng-
lish-language newspaper, and several papers in native languages aimed
at workers.[1] The Indian secret police noted that the volume of BLPI
propaganda gave the impression of a much larger party.[2] Trotskyist
trade unionists led one of the largest general strikes in the immediate
postwar period, and in South India the BLPI attracted thousands to
its rallies. But suddenly, in late 1948, the BLPI disappeared into the

---

1. The BLPI's main newspaper was *Spark* and *New Spark*, which appeared from
early 1946 to late 1948. The BLPI also put out *Purogami Kamgar* (*Radical
Worker*) in Marathi, *Thi Pori* (*Spark*) in Tamil, and *Inquilab* (*Revolution*) in Bengali.
2. Police file, Home (Pol) File 7/7/47-Poll (1), p3, National Archives of India, New
Delhi.

petit-bourgeois Socialist Party. It has always been an enigma how and why such a promising, growing party was shipwrecked. The first part of this article, published in *Revolutionary History* (Volume 1, no 4, Winter 1988-89), covered the origins of Indian Trotskyism in the late 1930s, the launching of the BLPI in 1942 on the eve of the historic 'Quit India' revolt, and the struggle to build the party under conditions of wartime repression. This article focuses on the eventful years immediately following the Second World War, when India's struggle for independence reached its climax. It seeks to answer these questions: what was the BLPI, and why did it collapse?

It is fitting that this article appears in an issue of *Revolutionary History* devoted to Ceylonese Trotskyism, for the two movements were intimately linked. One cannot really understand what happened to Ceylonese Trotskyism without knowing the story of the BLPI, and vice versa.

For the most part, this article is based on primary sources. I was fortunate enough to have begun this quest in India and Ceylon back in 1973, when many former leaders and members of the old BLPI were still alive. I gained access to leaflets and newspapers available nowhere else. I again wish to thank everyone who helped me to piece together the hidden history of Indian Trotskyism.

The BLPI and the Congress Left

The Indian National Congress — the political party of the Indian bourgeoisie — dominated the independence movement. Most of the Indian left supported Gandhi's Congress. So, the main obstacle to building a revolutionary party in India was the Congress Left, in particular the Congress Socialist Party, which formed a broad left wing within Gandhi's Congress. The Congress Socialists had been in the vanguard of the violent 'Quit India' protest of 1942-43, which the Stalinists opposed and actively betrayed. When the nationalist movement revived at the end of the war, the Congress Socialists grew and made inroads in the trade union movement, often at the direct expense of the Communist Party of India, which was widely despised.

In a sense, the history of the BLPI was defined by its attempts to split the Congress Socialists, and win over their best militants. From the very outset, there were sharp differences over how best to accomplish that task. As recounted in the first part of this article, Philip Gunawardena and NM Perera, the two most senior leaders of the LSSP, opposed forming a Leninist party in India in favour of work within the Congress Socialist Party.[3] Remember that Philip Guna-

---

3.   So did Leon Trotsky! [Editor's note]

wardena personally knew many Indian Socialist leaders. But when the British arrested the top leadership of the LSSP at the start of the war, the younger Samasamajists pressed ahead with plans to unify the Indian Trotskyist groups.[4] The imprisoned Samasamajists jumped jail in 1942 and made tracks for India.[5] But by then the BLPI had just been launched.

In August 1942 the top leadership of the old LSSP formed a 'Workers Opposition' faction. At first, their main objection was precisely the fact that the LSSP back in Ceylon was being turned into a tight, democratic-centralist party subordinate to the BLPI.[6] In the *Platform of the Workers Opposition*, Colvin de Silva called the Bolshevik Leninist faction in Ceylon 'reactionary', and declared that 'the party cannot be restored to health, unity and effectiveness unless this faction is smashed'.[7] Philip Gunawardena and NM Perera denounced their 'attempt to transform the party from a living and growing entity with its deep roots in the masses into a narrow conspiratorial sect entirely cut off from the masses'.

In 1943 the Workers Opposition advocated merging the BLPI into the Congress Left (that is to say, what Gunawardena and Perera had wanted all along). They used the fresh experience of the 'Quit India' revolt to argue that it was a waste of precious time to try to build a Trotskyist party: 'We are convinced that the future is with us; but the time factor is all important. While we perfect our organisation, the deluge will be upon us.'[8]

Gunawardena and Perera basically had a scheme to broker a broad regroupment of Congress Socialists and other nationalist parties which had played a prominent rôle in the 'Quit India' struggle.[9] Their opportunist proposal was couched in terms of 'tactics', a ploy

4. The BLPI was a top-down merger of the Revolutionary Socialist League of Bengal, led by Kamalesh Bannerjee and Indra Sen; the Bolshevik-Leninist Party of the United Provinces and Bihar, led by Onkarnath Shastri; and the Bolshevik Mazdoor Party of Chandravadan Shukla. A fourth group, the Mazdoor Trotskyist Party, created in Bombay by the ultra-leftist adventurer Murray Gow Purdy, refused to join the BLPI.
5. The leading Samasamajists in Bombay at this point were Philip Gunawardena (party name 'Guruswami'), his brother Robert ('Vaidya' and 'Prakash'), NM Perera ('Vishvanath'), his wife Selina Perera, Colvin R de Silva ('Govindan' and 'Lily Roy'), Leslie Goonewardene ('Tilak') and Lionel Cooray.
6. The Ceylon Unit of the BLPI was led by Edmund Samarakkody, Doric de Souza and Bernard Soysa.
7. *Platform of the Workers Opposition*, August 1942.
8. *Indian Struggle: Next Phase*, quoted in YR Amarasinghe, *Trotskyism in Ceylon: A Study of the Development, Ideology and Political Rôle of the Lanka Sama Samaja Party, 1935-1964*, PhD Thesis, University of London (1974), p105.
9. This new party should include 'the genuine revolutionaries of the Congress Socialist Party, the Forward Bloc, the Revolutionary Communist Party of India, the group of Datta Majumdar and the BLPI, at least to begin with'.

which these slick revisionists would repeat over the next several decades. The Indians in the BLPI underground were opposed. Colvin R de Silva backed off from the Workers Opposition. Here, in embryo, were what would become the main tendencies of the BLPI: Philip Gunawardena and NM Perera on the right, the Indians and younger Samasamajists on the left, and Colvin R de Silva and Leslie Goonewardene vacillating in between.[10]

The fight was aborted when Philip Gunawardena and NM Perera were arrested in a police raid and returned to prison in Ceylon. Colvin R de Silva and Leslie Goonewardene escaped arrest, thus giving the Bolshevik Leninist faction the upper hand.[11] The BLPI's Provisional Central Committee meeting in July 1944 rejected the Workers Opposition's resolution for merger with the Congress Socialists, noting that 'if adopted, this resolution would lead to the creation of a loose, petit-bourgeois party in contradistinction to a well-knit disciplined party integrated with the proletariat'.[12] Gunawardena and Perera represented 'a tendency to reject the Bolshevik proletarian concept of the party in favour of a loose petit-bourgeois one', akin to the soft, Menshevik LSSP of the 1930s. In any case, the liquidationist proposal had become muted, as most of the Indian left was in jail.

With the end of the war, the burning question in Indian politics was whether Gandhi's Congress would resume open opposition, or pursue negotiations with British imperialism. The British, war-weary and weakened, wanted to avoid having to station a large military force in India to put down renewed unrest. The electoral victory of the Labour Party set the wheels moving for renewed negotiations. Congress heatedly debated the issue of 'struggle' versus 'negotiations'. Gandhi emphatically disowned the August Struggle (as the violent phase of the 'Quit India' protest became known), while the Congress Socialists glorified it. 'Struggle' became their mantra. A section of the Congress Socialists even called for launching a new 'Augusters Party' — the line of Philip Gunawardena!

The BLPI's propaganda hammered away at the contradictions of the Congress Socialists: 'Every left group (and not only the CSP) that has remained within Congress to capture the leadership has ended up by giving up its struggle and supporting the bourgeois leadership.'[13]

10. At the time, one of the Indian leaders, Chandravadan Shukla, alleged that initially Leslie Goonewardene played a somewhat centrist rôle between the Workers Opposition and the Bolshevik Leninist factions. See DG [Douglas Garbutt], 'Report on the Fourth International Movement in India', typescript [late 1946].
11. After 1943, the leadership was based on Colvin R de Silva, Leslie Goonewardene, Hector Abhayavardhana ['HR Vardan'], and Indra Sen ['Suresh'?].
12. Quoted in Amarasinghe, op cit, p105.
13. G Selvarajatnam, *The Meaning of the Simla Surrender* [late 1945?], p25.

The party challenged the Congress Left to join an 'Anti-Imperialist Left Front' based on a series of specific demands, including opposition to the acceptance of office, release of political prisoners, and opposition to a Congress takeover of trade unions and peasant councils.[14]

The British proposed elections to the Central Legislative Assembly in late 1945, and for Provincial Legislatures in 1946. When Gandhi's Congress decided to contest, the BLPI had to formulate a line on the election. The BLPI's Central Committee met in September 1945, but couldn't reach agreement. Two position papers were circulated for discussion within the party. One was by the top party leaders, 'Govindan' (Colvin R de Silva) and 'Tilak' (Leslie Goonewardene), who advocated trying to transform the election into a demonstration of support for the August Struggle: 'The question is, therefore, what is the way the masses can show *through their vote* their endorsement of the August Struggle and the path of struggle *without falling into the position of support for Congress*... Let each *candidate who runs... be judged on one issue... What part did he take in, what attitude did he take to the August Struggle?*'[15] This was almost pure Congress Socialism. At that very moment, the Socialists were loudly proclaiming that the elections should only be a form of preparation for revolutionary struggle!

The second proposal, by 'Comrade Gu' [?] accepted the Govindan/Tilak position, but added a call for a vote to the CPI's candidates in working class constituencies. The CPI was nominally independent of Congress, having been driven out in late 1945, and was trying to regain credibility through leading student and labour actions.

These drafts were discussed at Unit Conferences of the party. At the Calcutta Unit conference, a majority favoured combining the Govindan/Tilak line with a class criterion, adding that the candidate must also oppose the Congress Party's fake unions and its 'Constructive Programme'. At a special expanded Central Committee meeting in December 1945, three lines were put forward: the original Govindan/Tilak position, the position of the Calcutta majority, and a position of outright support for Congress candidates advocated by the United Provinces Unit. After two days of debate, the Central Committee adopted a position which was essentially the Calcutta majority line.

The BLPI's position was incorporated into an election pamphlet translated into Bengali, Marathi, Tamil and Hindi.[16] It provided an

14. *For an Anti-Imperialist Left Front*, 20 May 1945.
15. Quoted in Garbutt, op cit, original emphasis.
16. *Vote for August, Vote for Struggle* [December 1945].

excellent analysis of the situation, presented the programme of the BLPI, and pointed out the limitations of the August Struggle:

'It is impossible to vote for struggle in these elections by supporting any of the major political parties... There are, however, individual Congressmen who give full political support to the August mass struggle. In token of our solidarity with the mass struggle of August '42 we lend our support to them, Congressmen though they be. We vote *not for Congress but for struggle.*'

In the new line-up of tendencies, the right wing was the group in the United Provinces around Raj Narayan Arya, which had called for outright support to Congress. The left wing was the Calcutta Unit, which had groped around for some kind of class criterion. And the centrists were (again) the top Ceylonese leaders, Colvin R de Silva and Leslie Goonewardene, who tried to find a clever way to give Congress Leftists backhanded support without demanding that they break from Congress.

The Spectre of Revolution

As it turned out, Philip Gunawardena's prediction of the imminent 'deluge' was quite correct (though his conclusions were opportunist). Starting in November 1945 and peaking in February 1946, the nationalist struggle roared into life, drowning out the electioneering. This was the most serious challenge to British rule since the Indian Mutiny of 1857. But the BLPI, indeed, was too weak to take the leadership, even on a local scale.

At the end of the Second World War, the BLPI was a tiny, fragile organisation. It had no more than a few dozen cadres, who were concentrated in the major cities (Calcutta, Bombay, Madras), separated by thousands of miles. The BLPI was starved for resources. It couldn't resume its press until early in 1946, nor convene an all-India convention until mid-1947. In a sense, the BLPI wasn't really a party yet. Formed clandestinely in 1942, it hadn't had the opportunity to cohere. The party had been hit several times during the war by the police. Many members were imprisoned in Indian hell-holes, or deported back to Ceylon. Contact between the underground party centres and local units was risky and difficult. The remnants of the party carried on admirably under conditions that were little better than in occupied Europe.

In November 1945 the British provoked demonstrations around the country by putting officers of the Indian National Army on trial for treason. The INA, which had been created by former Congress

President Subhas Chandra Bose, fought alongside the Japanese against Allied forces. The British miscalculated the depth of popular support for Bose. Moreover, by putting a Hindu, a Muslim and a Sikh in the dock, the British caused Congress and the Muslim League to close ranks for the first time.

Mass student demonstrations clashed with the police for two days in Calcutta. Workers demonstrated in solidarity. The military was called out. The BLPI's student activists in the Muslim Students League and the All-Bengal Students Federation distributed leaflets calling on the students to fraternise with the workers, and vice versa.[17] Unrest spread to the Indian armed forces. Airmen refused orders in January 1946.

The British inflamed this already volatile situation by proceeding with a second INA trial in February 1946. Militant students in Calcutta again clashed with the police, sparking off a *hartal* (general strike) and solidarity strikes by workers in the huge textile factories that stretched up the river from the city for 30 miles. Half a million people carrying Congress, Muslim League and red flags flooded central Calcutta, chanting 'Down with British Imperialism!' and 'Hindus, Muslims, unite!' British troops were called in to replace the Indian police and soldiers, who had began to waver. While British soldiers were shooting down hundreds of unarmed teenagers, Congress leaders, both of the right and left, blamed '*goonda* [hooligan] elements' for rioting in Calcutta! A military report vividly described the situation: 'Riots are very serious. Railway lines have been torn up at Naihati and Chalegar... Kankinara Station and Tollygunj Tram Depôt [were] set on fire. All English shops had their windows smashed, military lorries burnt. Bodies still lying around Chowringhee area. North Calcutta is isolated.'[18]

The BLPI group showed the right instincts in seeking a united front 'from below' with the Stalinists' student federation, which was in the vanguard of the struggle.[19] Initially, the Calcutta CPI had tailed behind events, but after an urgent telegram from the party's General Secretary, the Stalinist youth jumped into the fray.[20] But the CPI kept

17. The BLPI provided an account of its participation in a pamphlet, *The Inside Story of the Calcutta Events*. See also 'Les Fusillades Policières de Calcutta', *Quatrième Internationale*, August-September 1946, pp57-60. BLPI member UA Zuberi was Secretary of the All-Bengal Muslim Students League. Satyen Koley, Kamalesh Bannerjee and Dhiresh Sanyal were active in the All-Bengal Students Congress.
18. Quoted in Gautam Chattopadhyaya, 'The Almost Revolution: India in February 1946', *Indian Left Review*, April 1974, p37.
19. Garbutt, op cit.
20. CPI Secretary PC Joshi called for the flip-flop: 'Get all wartime understanding out of your heads. Postwar revolutionary situation developing fast. New tactical line needed. Be with the people.' (Quoted in Chattopadhyaya, op cit)

the workers at a safe distance. BLPI leaflets stated: 'The students can only have a correct policy by linking themselves with the proletarian class struggle and breaking with the bourgeois Congress.'[21]

Less than one week after the Calcutta student protests, a mutiny broke out in the Royal Indian Navy in Bombay. Indian ratings on 20 ships in Bombay mutinied on 18 February 1946, and the revolt quickly spread to Karachi and far-flung ships in the Bay of Bengal and Bahrain. The BLPI led walkouts from factories and painted '*hartal*' [strike] on sidewalks.[22] The Bombay *Evening News* blamed 'Trotskyist rowdies' for instigating the general strike of 300 000 textile workers! Within four days, general strikes gripped cities and towns all over India. In Bombay, police and military units opened fire on demonstrators, culminating in an eight-hour battle at Castle Barracks. In Karachi, rebel sailors bombarded British forces.

Lacking a revolutionary leadership, the Royal Indian Navy Central Strike Committee put their trust in Congress and the Muslim League, who betrayed them. On cue, the Stalinists formed 'peace brigades' to calm the situation, and help clear the streets.[23] Echoing Gandhi, the CPI denounced 'mob violence', and preached: 'What is most essential is that the whole campaign based on the glorification of "August" and the INA heroes should now stop.'[24]

India teetered on the brink of a pre-revolutionary crisis in February 1946. The revolt was spreading in the armed forces; in late February, two Indian pioneer units in the Eastern Command refused to obey orders. A Labour MP rushed back to London to warn Prime Minister Attlee: 'We must quit India quickly. If we don't, we shall be kicked out.'[25] Within a few days, the British announced a new Cabinet Mission, which brought a new plan.

Trotsky once remarked that if a revolutionary situation becomes over-ripe, it begins to rot. Indeed, only a few months after Hindus and Muslims united at the barricades, Calcutta was again a battlefield, but this time it was Hindus and Muslims slaughtering each other. On 16 August 1946 the feudalist-reactionary Muslim League's 'Direct Ac-

21. *Spark*, no 3 [late March 1946].
22. This account is based on interviews with many of the former BLPI militants who participated in the events: Indra Sen (Calcutta, 1 February 1974), Tulsi Boda (Bombay, 17 December 1973), Dulal Bose (Calcutta, 2 February 1974), SP Udyawar (Bombay, 24 December 1973). See also the accounts in the BLPI press, *Spark*, no 3 [late March 1946]; *New Spark*, 14 February and 6 March 1948; and *Fourth International*, October 1946, pp310-12.
23. In Karachi, the government issued a statement which revealed: 'Every facility was given to [Communist] Party members to pacify the mobs.' Quoted in *Spark*, no 3 [late March 1946].
24. 'Mob Violence and After', *National Front*, 3 March 1946.
25. Quoted in Chattopadhyaya, op cit.

tion Day' in Calcutta erupted in an orgy of communal rioting which left more than 5000 dead.[26] Virtually overnight, Hindu-Muslim unity was shattered. A general strike which had been mounting in Bengal collapsed. The killing quickly spread to East Bengal, Bihar and the United Provinces, and westward into the Punjab. A Sikh leader warned: 'The Punjab is drifting towards a civil war.'[27]

Tragically, events proved that the Indian bourgeoisie was incapable of carrying through the tasks of the democratic revolution, not the least of which was unifying the country. It feared the masses more than the prospect of partition. The British ripped apart India in their final act of 'divide and conquer'. In this 'freedom at midnight', hundreds of thousands perished in communal riots and forced population transfers, which uprooted more than 14 million people.

The Fight for the Party

As the storm clouds gathered, the BLPI was still a tiny propaganda group struggling to become a Leninist party. None of the Indian leaders had ever functioned in a truly democratic-centralist party, nor had most of the Ceylonese leaders. It is not surprising that under the extremely difficult conditions of underground work, the BLPI had suffered several splits, each motivated by 'organisational' or 'personal' differences. With the end of the war, the party tried to heal the splits and win back militants which it so desperately needed.

The two Indian leaders who split during and right after the war were Chandravadan Shukla in Bombay and Onkarnath Shastri in the United Provinces. Both had been schooled in the Stalinist CPI, and it is understandable that the Trotskyist groups, each of which had developed in complete isolation in the late 1930s, were hardly democratic-centralist organisations. Both had accumulated essentially personal followings. Even inside the BLPI, both Shukla and Shastri continued to be very protective of 'their' followers, and resisted the attempts of the Ceylonese to impose the elementary norms of Leninist functioning.

Shukla became editor of the party's journal, *Bolshevik Leninist*. Trouble started when the escaped Samasamajists came to Bombay in 1942. Evidently, Shukla opposed the Workers Opposition (to his credit). In turn, the Ceylonese criticised his handling of the press, and blamed him for the party's slow growth. So intense was the animosity that at one meeting the hot-headed Philip Gunawardena slapped Shukla. When the party voted to take control of the press, Shukla

26. The Mayor of Calcutta, a leader of the Muslim League, issued a statement which exhorted: 'By fighting you will go to heaven in the holy war.'
27. Quoted in L Gordon, *Brothers Against the Raj*, 1990, p577.

took it as a personal insult and withdrew, taking the press with him. After the police smashed the Bombay unit in 1943, Shukla in effect set up a rival party. He continued the *Bolshevik Leninist*, rallied his supporters in Ahmedabad and Bhauvnagar (Gujarat), and reverted to his pre-merger name, the Bolshevik Mazdoor Party, which claimed to be the Indian Section of the Fourth International.[28]

Shastri likewise defected from the BLPI for egotistical reasons. When he was released from jail in 1945, he was piqued that the party centre in Calcutta had re-established contact with 'his' followers in Kanpur and Allahabad.[29] Shastri argued that he alone should lead and decide for his followers. When the party centre in Calcutta rejected this federalist (or guru/devotee) notion of a party, Shastri denounced the Ceylonese, and continued independently as the BLPI.[30]

In both cases, the BLPI was able to win back some of the rank and file. A section of Shukla's group favoured reunification, and despite Shukla's opposition, rejoined the BLPI in early 1946.[31] Likewise, Shastri's student followers in Allahabad rejoined the party, and helped develop a small circle in Kanpur. Shastri joined Shukla's BMP in December 1946, but broke away and formed the Revolutionary Workers Party (Trotskyist) after he developed differences on the issue of the linguistic reorganisation of the states.[32] Shastri started a paper, *Jivan (Life)* in early 1948, while Shukla revived *Age Kadam (Forward March)* in January 1949.

In Ceylon, the split was much more serious and spectacular. Gunawardena and Perera had simply refused to accept the decisions of the BLPI's Central Committee to support the Bolshevik Leninist faction, which they contemptuously dismissed as irresponsible, arrogant 'parlour Bolsheviks'. In September 1945, after their release from jail, they did exactly what the BLPI Central Committee had predicted: revive the old LSSP! The BLPI had no choice but to expel them from the BLPI.[33] The split soon got nasty; Philip Gunawardena accused the Ceylon Unit's leader, Doric de Souza, of being a police spy.

28. Twenty-four delegates attended the BMP national conference held on 26-31 December 1945. See *Bolshevik Leninist*, April 1946.
29. As Shastri put it in personal correspondence to the author in June 1974: 'I found that they [the Ceylonese leaders of the BLPI] had done sufficient mischief in my absence, and had tried to win over some of my recruits.'
30. One of Shastri's leaflets stated: 'We have nothing to do with the Lanka Samasamajists or a brand of Calcutta "Bolshevik Leninists".'
31. The pro-BLPI group was led by Tulsi Boda and Shanta Patel. Shukla continued the BMP, and put out *Age Kadam (Forward March)*.
32. Shastri opposed this democratic demand. See *Jivan*, no 1, 6 February 1948.
33. 'Splitaway from the Lanka Samasamaja Party, Ceylon Unit of the Bolshevik-Leninist Party of India (Section of the Fourth International)', Resolution of the Central Committee of the BLPI, 8 October 1945.

The defection to the right of Gunawardena and Perera cleared the way for the BLPI and its Ceylon Unit to develop in a healthy, revolutionary direction. But it also took a toll of the BLPI. It stretched the BLPI's Ceylonese leadership even thinner, as they had to travel back and forth between India and Ceylon. Colvin R de Silva eventually remained in Ceylon to lead the Bolshevik Samasamaja Party (the Ceylon Unit). In mid-1947 one of the two Indian leaders of the BLPI, Kamalesh Bannerjee, left to attend the Fourth International's World Congress, and to join in the International Secretariat in Paris.

Over the next couple of years, the rival groups in Ceylon alternated between war and truce. From afar, the Fourth International tried to mediate and mend. But in hindsight, it is crystal clear that the differences represented more than personality clashes and organisational squabbles. Gunawardena and Perera were opportunist hustlers who were hostile to the BLPI precisely because it was trying, as best it could, to become a hard, democratic-centralist, internationalist party.

Work in the Labour Movement

Held back by the CPI during the war, the labour movement revived with a vengeance. In many unions, the CPI faced a rank and file revolt. As a CPI leader later lamented: 'Right wing Socialists, or Trotskyites and other elements stole the leadership, as in the case of the Madras Binny strike.'[34]

Indeed, the BLPI made its biggest gains in the trade union movement in Madras Province. During the war, the BLPI worked in the textile factories of Madras and Madura and the MSM Railway workshop at Perambur.[35] Tamil-speaking Samasamajists, including Balasingham and SCC Anthonipillai, were instrumental in this preparatory work. In Madras, the party developed a fraction in the Buckingham and Carnatic Mills, the largest textile mill in India, employing 14 000 workers. From this base, the BLPI was able to capture the leadership of the Madras Labour Union, the strongest union in the South, and the oldest union in all of India. The MLU owned a three-story union headquarters, ran its own printing press, and put out the newspaper, *The Indian Labourer*.

As the story goes, Anthonipillai was elected President of the MLU in 1946 through a coup. The MLU Executive Committee elected the

34. SA Dange, *On the Trade Union Movement: Reports to a Convention of Communist Party Members Working in the Trade Union Movement*, Calcutta, 20-22 May 1952.
35. Ground breaking work in the mills was done by SCC Anthonipillai, Muthiah and G Selvarajatnan.

President. The incumbent, a Congressman and Theosophist, wanted to check the influence of the Stalinists. He respected the work that the Trotskyists had done during the war, and backed Anthonipillai. If this account were true, it wouldn't be surprising. Most Indian trade unions were created and run by political parties. Bureaucratic practices and careerism were a disease, fostered by social conditions in which most workers were penniless, malnourished, often illiterate, and housed in dreadful slums.

On the other hand, the BLPI openly routed the CPI in the powerful MSM Railway Employees Union. Based on the Trotskyists' leadership of a successful 48-day strike at the B&C Mills, the rail workers elected Anthonipillai President of the union branch in Perambur, representing 8000 workers.[36] This was an important prize, as the Railway Union was a powerful force in the All-India Railwaymen's Federation.

In March 1947 the MLU called another strike at the B&C Mills. When Anthonipillai was arrested, over 100 000 workers responded to the MLU's call for a general strike, including the entire Perambur railway workshop. The Congress Ministers in the provincial government called in the Malabar Special Police. As described by a local newspaper: 'Beside stationing mobile units at all main police stations, patrol parties were sent on foot and lorries to almost every important road. Armed pickets were posted at all strategic points and in front of banks, courts, electric substations, pumping stations and similar places.'[37] Police dispersed crowds with baton charges and tear gas. When 50 000 turned out for a MLU rally, the Congress Ministry banned all gatherings, and arrested strike leaders and BLPI leaders, including the party Secretary, Colvin R de Silva, and the Madras Unit Secretary, M Muthiah.

Nehru sent his Cabinet Minister for Industries to Madras. A crowd of 150 000 gathered, pelted him, and chanted: 'Grant the demands of the B&C workers!', 'Release Anthonipillai immediately!' Anthonipillai, who had been held in solitary confinement, was released but expelled from Madras Province.

Anthonipillai returned to address a mammoth rally, in the middle of which police arrived, fired shots, beat workers, and rearrested Anthonipillai. Ten thousand Malabar Special Police terrorised the worker's slums in nightly raids, arresting 1000 in a single sweep. Police seized the MLU's building, its funds, its press, and jailed 49 militants as 'men of the Fourth International'.[38] The strike was broken

36. See *Spark*, no 2 [early March 1946].
37. *The Hindu*, quoted in *New Spark*, 26 April 1947.
38. BLPI militants who were arrested included Elumalai, Murugesan and Ganesan

after more than 100 days. The MLU was made semi-legal by the government. In March 1948 the MLU's Volunteer Corps, a form of workers' militia, led by the Trotskyist S Amarnath, was banned as a 'Communist organisation', and 13 volunteers were arrested.

In Madura, also in Madras Province, the BLPI had developed trade union work in the railway and textile unions.[39] Once in 1946, when the BLPI called a meeting in connection with a small textile union of 1000 members, several thousand people showed up 'to hear what the Trotskyists were saying'.[40] The BLPI in Madura was almost wholly proletarian in composition. The BLPI also had influence in the textile mills at Tuticorin, and in a peasant union in Sholavandam.[41]

In Bengal, the party's first success came in 1946 when it won an 11-day strike of the Calcutta fire-fighters' union, which it had helped to build during the war.[42] In 1946 and 1947, the party led two long strikes of clerical workers at Cox & Kings. This work was carried out by one of the BLPI's energetic, dedicated young recruits, Haradhan Chatterjee. He had joined the BLPI at the age of 21, dedicated himself to full-time party work, for which he was arrested 10 times, and died before he reached the age of 30.

In the Calcutta industrial belt, the BLPI built fractions in the paper and jute mills at Titaghur and Kankimara, captured the Titaghur Paper Mills union from the CPI, and led a 72-day strike in early 1947. The BLPI also became a force in the coal mines, paper mills, oil mills and pottery works of Raniganj and Purulia, near the Bihar border. The Raniganj Local of the BLPI could attract thousands of workers to its public meetings and processions under the banner of the Fourth International. The BLPI also worked among the peasants in Hariharpur and Sogardighi.[43]

The BLPI was less successful in Bombay, the Petrograd of India. The party hadn't been able to establish a base in the labour movement during the war because of the police smashes, the factionalism, and Shukla's defection. The Bombay Unit, which only had about a dozen members by the end of 1946, was also handicapped by a group

from the Perambur railway workshop; Nagiah, the MLU Treasurer; Duraisamy from the B&C mill; and Anthonipillai's wife, Caroline.

39. Appan Raj was the Chairman of the Madura Unit.
40. Garbutt, op cit.
41. This work was led by BLPI cadres, Appan Raj and Venkatachalam.
42. BLPI cadres in Bengal included Kamalesh Bannerjee, PK Roy, Karuna Kant Roy, Sitanshu Das, Zahrul Hasan Khan, Dulal Bose, Haradhan Chatterjee, Jagadish Jha, Satyen Koley, Robin Sen, Anil Pala, GS Choubey, Amal Bagchi, Naren Ghosh and Biman Sur Roy.
43. This work was carried out by Naren Biswas, a recognised peasant leader in Murshidabad.

of demoralised members who tied up the party in endless internal discussions of trade union strategy.[44]

In 1947, thanks to the work of its young organiser, Anant Mandekar, the party led a strike of 6000 workers at the New Kaiser-i-Hind Mills in Bombay.[45] Mandekar was elected President of the Mill Committee, and was imprisoned by the Congress government as a 'C' class convict in Worli Jail for over six months.[46] The BLPI also scored gains in the silk and wool mills.[47] Based on their work at the India Woollen Mills and the Usha Woollen Mills, BLPI militants took the leadership from Congress, and formed a new, militant union of textile workers, the Bombay Woollen Mill Kamgar Union.[48]

Orthodoxy and Opportunism

The BLPI upheld Trotsky's theory of Permanent Revolution, stating that in India the native bourgeoisie could not carry out the tasks of the belated democratic revolution (independence, national unification, abolition of feudalism, etc). In 1945 the BLPI flatly denied that the British would quit India short of a revolution. But just two years later, the Union Jack was lowered for the last time over Delhi's Red Fort. How could this happen? Where was the revolution? The answer of the BLPI and the Fourth International was that independence was 'fake', merely a shifting from 'direct' to 'indirect' rule. Unfortunately, the Trotskyists tried to preserve orthodoxy by denying reality.

No wonder the BLPI stumbled politically in this period. In 1946, when the sham 'Constituent Assembly' was convened, the BLPI pooh-poohed the importance of democratic demands, arguing that 'the Constituent has not been a rallying cry for the masses of people'. The following year, the party's Convention went to the opposite extreme, making this purely democratic demand the BLPI's *central transitional slogan!* This was then reversed at the 1948 Convention, which resolved that 'the party is entitled to raise the Constituent Assembly slogan independently, when circumstances warrant it, in a suitable form and manner'.[49] In the internal struggle over this slogan, the BLPI polarised along familiar lines. On the right, the Morrowite tendency represented by Raj Narayan Arya advocated making it the

44. A Central Committee Commission had to be convened in Bombay in June 1946 to clean house.
45. See *New Spark*, 26 April, 10 and 24 May, 7 June, 5 July and 16 August 1947.
46. A BLPI defence campaign leaflet is reprinted in *New Spark*, 8 November 1947. See also *New Spark*, 6 December 1947.
47. See *New Spark*, 20 March 1948.
48. See *New Spark*, 8 November 1947.
49. *New Spark*, 31 July 1948.

central transitional demand.[50] On the left, the Bengal group took the ultra-left position that it should not be part of a transitional programme.[51]

On the critical issue of Pakistan, the BLPI recognised that India's Muslims were not a nation in the Leninist sense, and strongly opposed the reactionary partition of the country. With partition, it called for Revolutionary Constituent Assemblies in both Pakistan and India, making it clear that these could only be achieved through revolution. But when it came to the issue of Hyderabad, the BLPI lost its Marxist bearings. Hyderabad was one of hundreds of feudal states sprinkled over India which were ruled by autocratic Hindu and Muslim dynasties. After partition, most of these 'Princely States' cast in their lot with either the Indian Union or Pakistan. But Hyderabad, a vast state in South India larger than most European countries, rebuffed Nehru's overtures. The Nizam of Hyderabad also faced an armed peasant insurgency in Telengana led by the CPI. The BLPI denounced the CPI's struggle as a 'communal fifth-column against the people', and demanded that the Nehru government '*immediately arm the people of Hyderabad!*'.[52] In a bout of wishful thinking, the BLPI portrayed the Indian army as a revolutionary-democratic force:

'An invasion of Hyderabad by the armed forces of the Indian Union would have consequences far more far-reaching than the accomplishments of the military operations alone... It will act as a spark to light a conflagration which will proceed to burn to ashes every relic and remnant of feudalism in the state. It would be our clear duty to support the military action undertaken by the Indian Union Government against Hyderabad.'[53]

In fact, the Indian army did invade Hyderabad in September 1948, not to arm the people, but to disarm the CPI, and partition the state.

Regroupment Opportunities

In 1947-48 the Indian far left was in turmoil, as both the Socialists and the CPI capitulated to partition and supported the new government. The BLPI recognised the opportunities for revolutionary regroupment, starting with the Revolutionary Communist Party of India, led by the veteran Indian Communist, Saumyendranath Tagore. The

50. Raj Narain, 'Slogan of RCA', *Internal Bulletin*, Volume 3, no 1, 1 March 1948, pp1-3.
51. 'Resolution of the Calcutta District Committee, Unanimously Adopted on 29 September 1947.'
52. *New Spark*, 15 May 1948.
53. *New Spark*, 31 July 1948.

RCPI was an eclectic hodge-podge of former Stalinists, terrorists, and a small group of Trotskyist sympathisers. Tagore had been one of the early leaders of the Communist movement in India. He had criticised the German Communist Party's disastrous ultra-left policy and the Comintern's subsequent turn to the Popular Front.[54] At odds with the CPI, he split away and claimed to be the true Communist Party. However, Tagore didn't really break with the Comintern until 1942, after which he took the name RCPI.

The RCPI had two distinct tendencies. On the one hand, there was Tagore and a Trotskyist-influenced group around Sudarshan Chatterji. Tagore was familiar with Trotsky's writings, but wanted nothing to do with the organised Trotskyist movement. In 1944 he concocted his own muddled theory of Permanent Revolution.[55] On the other hand, there was a Narodnik-like tendency around Pannalal Das Gupta, consisting of former terrorists who had joined during the 'Quit India' movement. It should be added that the RCPI had a strong Hindu chauvinist streak; one pamphlet described Hindus as 'pioneers of a new civilisation', while Muslims were 'a degenerated people', with 'neither vision nor greatness'.[56]

In 1947 delegations from the BLPI and RCPI met in Calcutta to discuss unity. But there were two major differences: the Russian question, and the assessment of the Indian situation. The RCPI had a deliberately fuzzy line on the Russian question. Sometimes it described the USSR in Shachtmanite terms, other times it paraphrased the Trotskyist position.[57] The BLPI polemicised with the RCPI on this question.[58] The second difference concerned the issue of soviets. During the INA demonstrations in Calcutta, the RCPI had raised the slogan: '*Panchayats* [soviets] must be formed.' The RCPI saw this violent nationalist protest as 'revolution which has placed seizure of power on the order of the day'. The RCPI created its own soviets, which were nothing more than discussion groups, or, worse, sectarian substitutes for trade unions. The BLPI aptly characterised the RCPI's line as adventurist voluntarism, akin to Stalin's artificial, belated creation of the Canton Soviet in the Chinese Revolution of 1925-27.[59]

54. See SN Tagore, *Hitlerism: The Aryan Rule in Germany*, 1934, and *United Front or Betrayal*, 1938.
55. See SN Tagore, *Permanent Revolution*, 1944.
56. SM Jaffar, *An Outline of Leftism in India*, 1944.
57. SM Jaffar, *An Outline of Leftism in India*, describes the USSR as 'dominated by a class of bureaucrats and parasites'. Sudarshan Chatterji reiterated the Trotskyist position in 'USSR and Ourselves', *Toilers Front*, 22 September 1947.
58. 'Marxism on the USSR: What We Attack and What We Defend', *Spark*, no 4 [early April 1946].
59. See 'Opportunism on the Question of Revolution and Soviets', *Spark*, nos 2 and 3 (1946); and K Tilak [Leslie Goonewardene], 'Saumyendranath Tagore and So-

The BLPI and RCPI in a sense shared the same false assumption, but drew different conclusions. The RCPI reasoned that if a revolution was necessary for independence, and power was now being transferred, then a democratic (February) revolution must have happened, and October was next. The BLPI drew the opposite conclusion: if there had been no revolution, then India could not really be independent, and thus still awaited its February.

In September 1947 the RCPI and BLPI collaborated in forming a Workers United Front to promote unity in the trade union movement, and to oppose the Congress Party's company unions. In January 1948 both also joined a United Left Front, a dubious propaganda bloc of left parties, based on a full political programme which had to be kept vague and amenable to the Stalinists. The BLPI refused to ratify the Front's programme, and insisted on the right of participating parties to raise criticism. However, the BLPI's press in effect endorsed the whole concept of the strategic united front: 'If the programme which the signatory parties have agreed to were realised, it would mean the end of landlordism and capitalism. It would usher in the beginning of a Socialist party.'[60] Similar logic was later to be used by the LSSP to rationalise its United Left Front, which was the precursor of outright Popular Frontism.

In any case, the BLPI-RCPI regroupment initiative went nowhere. The RCPI ended up by splitting into its terrorist and anti-Communist components. In February 1949 the majority around the ex-terrorist Pannalal Das Gupta tried to 'galvanise the masses' by attacking police stations, a gun factory and the Dum Dum airport. The Tagore cult soon consolidated around a plagiarised version of Max Shachtman's 'bureaucratic collectivist' position, and took a Third Camp position on the Korean War, claiming that 'Stalinist expansionism is as great a menace as the imperialist expansionism of the USA and Great Britain'.[61]

During this period, the BLPI also pursued the Kerala Socialist Party, which had split to the left from the Congress Socialists in August 1947. Even though the KSP was silent on the nature of Congress, the BLPI gave it *unconditional* support in the Travancore general elections.[62] The KSP leaders regarded the Trotskyists as hairsplitters, and the BLPI's overture fell flat.

viets', *New Spark*, 10 May 1947. Tagore and Sudarshan Chatterji both defended the RCPI's line, in *Toilers Front*, 14 April, 26 May and 16 June 1947.
60. *New Spark*, 14 February 1948.
61. See SN Tagore, *Revolutionary Communism: The World and India*, 1951; and *Stalin, Truman, Hands Off Korea*, 1951.
62. *New Spark*, 3 and 31 January 1948.

Entryism and the Crisis of Leadership

The BLPI was haunted by the ghost of Philip Gunawardena. In 1947, the BLPI's General Secretary, Hector Abhayavardhana, revived Philip's proposal that the BLPI execute an 'entry' into the Congress Socialist Party. The 'entry' strategy was defeated at the BLPI's convention in May 1947.[63] But four months later an 'Entry Group' faction was formed, met in Bombay, and circulated the minutes of the meeting.[64] As is clear from the minutes, the Entry Group had no single, coherent argument. The common denominator was the belief that the Socialist Party would mushroom and become radicalised. The rationalisations reflected the disorientation over the nature of the period ('fake' independence, etc). The entry proposal was endorsed by Raj Narayan Arya in Kanpur, who openly voiced a defeatist mood within the party. He argued that because the BLPI was small and isolated, the only way it could ever hope to attract the masses was 'to appear before them dressed up as they like'.[65]

The main opposition to the 'entry-wallahs' (entryists) came from the party's left wing, the Bengal Unit.[66] V Karalasingham authored the main, and best, anti-entry document.[67] Karalasingham characterised the Entry Group as 'a tendency of petit-bourgeois liquidationism', noting its direct kinship with the position fathered by Philip Gunawardena:

'We seem to remember a document written in 1943 or 1944, to which certain sponsors of this faction were signatory, in which the same charges [the immaturity of the BLPI] were laid. Then it was Philip and NM who were the leading lights. Unless our memory fails us... the reasons adduced were that Bolshevik-Leninism was too advanced a doctrine for the Indian masses. This showed the way Philip and NM were heading. And we all know what happened to them!'

As Karalasingham pointed out, the entry proposal reflected a defeat-

---

63. *Militant* (USA), 21 July 1947. Abhayavardhana is sometimes spelled as 'Abeyawardena'.
64. The Entry Group consisted of Hector Abhayavardhana, VS Shastri, Sitanshu Das, Vinayak Purohit, Prabhakar More and Ambalal. See 'Minutes of the First Meeting of the Entry Group of the Bombay Unit held on 7 September 1947' [internal document].
65. Raj Narain, 'SP Entry', *Internal Bulletin* (BLPI), Volume 3, no 1, 1 March 1948, pp19-20.
66. The main anti-entrists were PK (Netai) Roy, Dulal Bose and Hiranand Mishra.
67. V Chester [V Karalasingham], 'The Grave-Diggers of the BLPI', *Internal Bulletin* (BLPI), Volume 3, no 1, 1 March 1948, pp13-19.

ist, impatient mood within the party. Support for entryism was strong precisely where the party was weakest: Bombay and Kanpur. Likewise, opposition to entryism was strong where the Socialists were weakest: Calcutta, Madras and Madura. The entry-wallahs pointed to the successes of the Socialists in Bombay as proof that the Social Democrats would become the main left party. The Socialists had captured the main textile union in Bombay from the CPI, and in the 1947 Bombay municipal elections, the Socialists won what the BLPI called 'a veritable landslide of the masses in the direction of the Socialist Party'.[68]

However, it is important to note that the BLPI's fraction in the Bombay Socialist Party *opposed* the entry proposal. The two rank and file BLPI cadres working in the Bombay Socialist Party reported that prospects for recruitment were meagre, and criticism of the party leadership was not well received.[69]

Nevertheless, support for the entry position gained momentum in 1948, especially after the Socialists left Congress, and welcomed non-Stalinist parties to join. The decisive change, however, was when Leslie Goonewardene suddenly cast in his lot with the entry-wallahs, and recruited two more Central Committee members, Ajit Roy and SCC Anthonipillai. Another key Central Committee member, Indra Sen, who initially endorsed the Karalasingham document, began to waver. According to Sen, he told Leslie Goonewardene that if the entryist position were to be viable, it had to be based on the model of 'deep entry' into the British Labour Party, because there was no great internal crisis providing the basis for a 'shallow' (French Turn) entry. Sen and Goonewardene jointly drafted a revised entry perspective. When Goonewardene introduced it in the Central Committee, Sen declared that he would support it only if Leslie Goonewardene promised to remain in India and take responsibility. Leslie Goonewardene refused, and Sen abstained on the resolution.[70]

By 1948 the BLPI was split right down the middle. The 'entry-wallahs' had the Bombay Unit, while the Bengal Unit was narrowly divided, with a number of the trade unionists in Raniganj and Titagarh in favour of entry. It took a series of close votes to decide the

68. *New Spark*, 6 March 1948. The BLPI ran one candidate, the strike leader Anant Mandekar, in the working class district of Ghorup Deo, who lost to a Socialist by 641 to 3136 votes.

69. Appaswami [P Bhaskaran] and Shapptram [SR Rao], 'Memorandum to the BLPI from the Members of the Party Fraction Inside the Socialist Party on the Question of Entering the Socialist Party', 12 September 1947, *Internal Bulletin* (BLPI), Volume 3, no 1, 1 March 1948, pp9-10.

70. Interview with Indra Sen (Calcutta, 5 February 1974). Sen told the author that up to then he had only related this story to one other person, his BLPI comrade, Tulsi Boda.

issue. In an extended Central Committee meeting, entry was defeated 7-5. But in a second vote, G Selvarajatnan, an anti-entry delegate from Madras, crossed over, producing a 6-6 tie. The entry proposal was finally adopted in late 1948 at a conference held at ZH Khan's house in Calcutta. The Bengal group, at Karalasingham's urging, accepted the majority decision, and agreed to give the tactic a try.

It has often been said that in adopting entryism, the BLPI was just following the line of the Fourth International. Actually, the godfather of entry in India was Philip Gunawardena. No doubt, the entryists in the British RCP also played a role. Two British Revolutionary Communist Party leaders, Ajit Roy and VS Shastri, returned to India in this period, and joined the BLPI.[71] As is clear from the Entry Group's first meeting in Bombay, VS Shastri was a leading light. Ajit Roy seems to have been recruited a bit later. But the point is that the entry proposal had independent roots in the BLPI. As for the Fourth International, Kamalesh Bannerjee in Paris opposed entry, proposing a compromise in which the majority would enter the Socialist Party, while the minority remained independent. The only other intervention seems to have been a letter from Cannon's American Socialist Workers Party, which asked the BLPI to reconsider entryism after it was rejected by the 1947 party convention.[72] A right wing leader of the Congress Socialists, Yusuf Meherally, had visited New York and met with the SWP leaders, who obviously took his left talk for good coin.

In Ceylon, Philip Gunawardena gleefully cheered the entry-wallahs, since he wanted to be rid of the BLPI for purely factional reasons.[73] His nemesis, Colvin R de Silva, almost had to oppose entry. But in deeds, he didn't risk his parliamentary career by coming to the rescue of the BLPI in its hour of greatest need. As the late Edmund Samarakkody recalled:

'As for the BSP (Colvin, Leslie, Bernard, Edmund, etc), we were simply immersed in election politics. The struggle of the Indian comrades of the BLPI against the entry-wallahs was not even sufficiently known. The BLPI was allowed unceremoniously to disappear from our consciousness. The importance of the Indian revolution for the Socialist revolution in Ceylon and that the Indian and Ceylon revolutions are aspects of a single and unified revolutionary process, went

71. Neither Roy or Shastri were supporters of the entry faction around Gerry Healy in the RCP. [Editor's note]
72. Letter from William F Warde, 24 November 1947, *Internal Bulletin* (BLPI), Volume 3, no 1, 1 March 1948, pp23-4.
73. DPR Gunawardena, 'Bolshevik-Leninists Should Enter Immediately the Socialist Party of India (CSP)', *Internal Bulletin* (LSSP), Volume 1, no 2, March 1947, p2.

out of our perspectives...The "BLPI days" became an unhappy ghost of the past.[74]

In years to come, it would often be said that Leslie Goonewardene became an 'entry-wallah' because he wanted to return home to Ceylon. As Goonewardene admitted much later, he was torn between standing at his post in India or rejoining his wife, Vivienne, who had returned to Ceylon. After negotiating the merger of the BLPI with the Socialist Party, he reluctantly went home. Perhaps entry was Goonewardene's rationalisation, but about all that can be said for certain is that the BLPI had a terminal crisis of leadership, and there were Samasamajists on both sides.

Shipwreck of the BLPI

In late 1948 the BLPI dissolved and its members, including the Bengal minority, joined the Socialist Party as individuals.[75] The Congress Socialists would not tolerate an organised faction; they had been badly burned by the entry tactics of the Communist Party in the late 1930s.

The BLPI's leadership knew that the attempt at entry was fraught with risks. Anthonipillai had never done political work in his unions, and wasn't reliable; so Hector Abhayavardhana was sent to Madras. The Bengal anti-entryists were sectarian; so V Karalasingham was brought to Calcutta. Ajit Roy wasn't dependable; so the guiding centre was supposed to keep him in check. But there was no organised fractional activity or coordinated central leadership. The strategy was to maximise impact as Trotskyist individuals, and to avoid being baited by the rightist Socialist Party leadership.

The Socialist Party gave the Trotskyist leaders their share of prizes. Ajit Roy was coopted onto the Socialist Party's National Executive. Indra Sen became joint editor of *Janata*, the Socialist Party's press. BLPI trade unionists in Bombay and Madras were given positions in the Socialist Party's new labour federation. Indeed, the Socialist Party looked to the Trotskyists to help them produce more sophisticated propaganda, and to expand into the labour movement in Bengal and the South. In Bombay, the BLPIers served the Socialist Party well, recruiting and training a layer of union leaders.[76]

The entryists had no success in pushing the Socialist Party to the

74. Letter from Edmund Samarakkody to Charles W Ervin, 1 April 1979.
75. See '"Bolsheviks" to Merge with the Socialist Party', *Janata*, 24 October 1948. Also *Janata*, 22 May 1949.
76. The leading Trotskyists in Bombay included Indra Sen, Prabhakar More, TR Rao, SR Rao and Tulsi Panchal.

left. In 1948 the Socialist Party opened a discussion on the nature of the party. The Socialist Party leaders wanted a 'mass party'.[77] The Trotskyists argued for a cadre organisation, with rights for minorities. At the 1949 party conference, the Socialist Party adopted a new constitution that declared it a mass party with no special minority rights. By 1950 the Socialist Party had banned all organised groups, which paved the way for a purge of the left wing elements in Bombay.[78] In the September of that year the Socialist Party's General Council resolved that 'only democratic means lead to Socialism'.[79] In Calcutta, Sheila Perera was brought up on charges for teaching new recruits that a revolutionary insurrection was not inconsistent with the party's programme.

As the Cold War heated up, the 'Third Camp' Socialist Party moved sharply to the right. With the Korean war, the anti-Communist Socialist Party adopted a pro-US line. At the party's Madras conference in 1950, the ex-BLPIers called for no support for either side and for Korean independence, an outright Shachtmanite line. Even this was too much for JP Narayan, who attacked the Trotskyists as saboteurs. Indra Sen was dismissed as *Janata* editor after writing an article mildly critical of the Socialist Party.[80]

The entry was a disaster. Ajit Roy quickly became a right wing Social Democrat; at the Socialist Party's conference in 1950 he declared: 'Democratic Socialism should be the article of faith of the party, and nobody who did not believe in it should have room in the party.'[81] In Madras, Anthonipillai built his trade union empire, became a municipal councillor, and joined the reformist Indian trade union establishment in New Delhi.[82] The anti-entry Bengal group went into hibernation, except for Sheila Perera, who became a loyal left Socialist. V Karalasingham, the staunch opponent of entry into the Socialist Party, became a 'state capitalist', and returned to Ceylon in 1951.[83]

As the Trotskyists foundered and capitulated, the International Secretariat was of no help, because it was now the biggest partisan of liquidationism. In 1950 it sent Kamalesh Bannerjee back to India to help the entryists.[84] Bannerjee remained in India less than a year, and

77. *Janata*, 21 November 1948.
78. *Janata*, 1 May 1950.
79. *Janata*, 9 and 16 October 1949.
80. Indra Sen, 'More Militant Policy, Need of the Hour', *Janata*, 2 July 1950.
81. Quoted in *Janata*, 16 July 1950.
82. See *Quatrième Internationale*, October-November 1948, p56.
83. See *Janata*, 9 July 1950.
84. Leslie Goonewardene came to Delhi for a meeting with Kamalesh Bannerjee, Indra Sen and Tulsi Boda. Evidently, nothing much came out of it.

then returned on his own to Paris, where he degenerated into alcoholism.[85]

The whole perspective upon which the entry had been based proved wrong. The Socialists didn't become the mass left opposition. On the contrary, after the CPI's left turn in 1948 and the victory of the Chinese Revolution, Stalinism revived stronger than ever. Nehru launched his 'Socialist' Five Year Plans, while whipping up chauvinism against Pakistan. In the country's first general elections in 1952, the Socialist Party was buried in the Congress landslide. Traumatised, it dissolved, and merged with a petit-bourgeois party.

But what happened to the Trotskyists after the shipwreck of the BLPI is another story.

Conclusion

The late Edmund Samarakkody, who wrote the best single balance sheet of the LSSP, summed up his view of the BLPI in a personal letter:

'It has been clear to me for a long time that the decision of the LSSP leaders to go over to India between 1940 and 1942 had very little to do with intervening in the Indian revolution and for the building of a revolutionary party there. It was really a question of escaping from the Ceylon police in wartime when the LSSP was made illegal. And that is why, no sooner was the war over and legal conditions prevailed, the internationalism of the LSSP leaders vanished.

'That the orientation of the "left wing LSSP" leaders who stood for the formation of the BLPI had only slender roots is shown by their capitulation to petit-bourgeois and Social Democratic pressures as soon as the war was over. When the "entry into the CSP" question came up again (1947-48), Leslie Goonewardene and the Secretary Hector Abeyawardena were strongly advocating entry. Only the Indian comrades of the BLPI were fighting desperately against the liquidationists, who were in the main the LSSP leaders. And it was without doubt the decision of the LSSP leaders to abandon the BLPI that brought about its demise.'[86]

While this is oversimplified, Samarakkody speaks wisely. The whole picture comes into sharp focus as soon as you look at Trotskyism in

85. Bannerjee's articles appeared in *Janata* from April 1950 to March 1951. [Bannerjee, a relative of Sam Bornstein, rejoined the Stalinists at the time of the Korean War. Editor's note]

86. Letter from Edmund Samarakkody to Charles W Ervin, 1 April 1979. Samarakkody's 'The Struggle for Trotskyism in Ceylon' was printed in the journal *Spartacist*, no 22, Winter 1973-74.

Ceylon and India together. As long as Philip Gunawardena and NM Perera occupied their old political niche on the right, Colvin de Silva and Leslie Goonewardene steered left. When Colvin and Leslie listed to the right, they were kept in check by the Indians and the younger Ceylonese militants. But when the Indian leadership collapsed, Colvin and Leslie lost their leftist moorings, and began to drift back into the swamp of insular, parliamentary politics — 'Trotskyism in one island.'

Philip Gunawardena was always one step ahead of the rest. He always wanted the Indian Trotskyists to cosy up to his friends in the Indian Social Democracy. Colvin R de Silva and Leslie Goonewardene went on an odyssey to India to build a Trotskyist party. But they eventually returned having accomplished Philip Gunawardena's original goal.

In hindsight, the BLPI fought for Trotskyism as best it could. Virtually alone on the Indian left, the BLPI called for the independence of the workers and toiling peoples from the bourgeois Congress. It pointed to India's urban working class, concentrated in huge textile mills and railway workshops, as the only force capable of carrying out the tasks of the belated democratic revolution — driving out British imperialism, shattering the class power of the rural exploiters, purging caste slavery, and unifying the many peoples of the vast sub-continent.

Fifty years after independence, India is proof of the Trotskyist truth that the bourgeoisie can no longer carry out the historic tasks of their own democratic revolution, not to mention the 'Socialism' which Nehru and his heirs promised. India remains mired in poverty and caste. Pakistan has broken in two, and separatist movements tug at India. The original programme of the BLPI has lost none of its relevance and power.

Obituaries

Alec Acheson (1912-1996)

ANOTHER SAD loss to our journal has been the death of Alec
Acheson from cancer in hospital on 5 May 1996. Coming from a
Marxist background, he gave the movement 65 years of unbroken
service with quiet courage as a secularist, a Labour Party activist and a
Trotskyist.

His father was a Northern Irish Protestant who came over to England, joined the Social Democratic Federation, and supported the suf-
fragettes. Alec came up to London from Bedford for a job, and soon
began to frequent Hyde Park and the 'bomb shop' in Charing Cross
Road, where he first encountered the *Red Flag* of the Communist
League and *Quatrième Internationale*. In 1931 he joined the Socialist
Propaganda Group, a split-off from the Socialist Party of Great Britain led by Harry Martin, who had seen Engels and worked with William Morris. He left this organisation in 1936 when it supported the
line of the Stalinists during the Spanish Civil War.

After hearing CLR James demolish the Stalinists at meetings on
the Moscow Trials, Alec joined the Marxist Group, began to sell
Fight, and became a delegate to the London Trades Council. He became a member of the Revolutionary Socialist League, the British
Section of the Fourth International set up in 1938, but supported the
split of the Revolutionary Workers League of Bill Duncan and Hilda
Lane in the February of the following year, moving to Leicester two
months later. Disgusted at their lack of courage when war came, he
left them and rejoined the parent organisation. As he described it:

'When the war came I disagreed with Hilda Lane and Bill Duncan,
because they said it would not be fair to issue an anti-war proclamation and involve members who might be opposed to it, and those like
Hilda, who had a family. It would be unfair if they were imprisoned
for anti-war activity, and their children suffered. I was so incensed by
this, possibly because I didn't fully appreciate the dangers of anti-war
activity, and when I got home I used an old hectograph — the old
jelly duplicator — and produced an anti-war leaflet, and the Trotskyist position on the imperialist war was made public. My wife, who
was non-political, helped me to produce it. She had the courage that

some of my comrades hadn't.' (Interview with Sam Bornstein and Al Richardson, 12 June 1986)

Alec was largely responsible for organising the successful Leicester anti-war conference of January 1940. It was typical of him that after his call-up he should risk his neck further by revolutionary agitation in the armed forces during the Second World War (S Bornstein and A Richardson, *War and the International*, London, 1986, pp26, 246-7).

After his discharge from the army in 1945, Alec trained as a teacher. He supported the Healy Minority in the Revolutionary Communist Party, and joined the Leicester City Labour Party. Alienated by Healy's authoritarianism and manipulation, he sided with John Lawrence and Hilda Lane during the split of 1953, but after they dropped out of the Trotskyist movement Alec rejoined the new section, the Revolutionary Socialist League, in 1957. His loyalty to the idea of a Fourth International led him from there into the International Group in 1964, and via the International Marxist Group into the present International Socialist Group.

Alec was an atypical headmaster, for he had not the slightest trace of authoritarianism, and humanity counted for a great deal with him. He invariably conducted himself with civility and reason in argument, and was always unhappy about expulsions. And he was no conformist, to the extent of standing as a secularist in the local elections against the local Labour Party's concessions to 'ethnic' religious services in schools, a stance that brought him into bad odour with his organisation. He always retained the highest regard of those of us who were privileged to know him.

Al Richardson

Nils Kaare Dahl (1909-1996)

I ONLY knew Nils Dahl for the last seven years of his life, but what I learned about him and what he told me made a lasting impression. He came from a very privileged Norwegian family. His great grandfather had been the Governor of Halden under the Danish Crown when Bernadotte invaded in 1814, and when Halden opened it gates. He was thus one of the 'Men of Eidsvoll', the leading Norwegian citizens who called on the Swedish King to accept the crown of a constitutional Norway. Like those who signed the American Constitution, the 'Men of Eidsvoll' are the Founding Fathers of Norway. Nils was educated at the Royal Military Academy, and, with his family firm being involved in surveying, he trained as a civil engineer. He became a reserve officer in the Norwegian army. In

1929 he joined both the Norwegian Communist Party, from which he was soon expelled as an oppositionist, and the quite unique association of intellectuals around the journal *Mot Dag* (*Towards the Dawn*). Originally set up to draw students and intellectuals around the Labour Party, from 1926 to 1929 it was linked to the NKP, but with the ultra-left turn against 'right-wingers' the *Mot Dag* association became associated with the IVKO (the international opposition inspired by Brandler and Thalheimer). It was a group with very progressive and advanced ideas for its time in many areas of social and political life.

He disagreed violently with the Labour government's defence policy. From the late 1920s the bourgeoisie assumed greater control of the armed forces, which became more useless for national defence, as the officers feared and hated the workers more than any possible aggressor. Parts of all the guns in the barracks were removed and kept in separate secret places to prevent the workers arming themselves. This did not help when the Germans invaded in 1940. The Labour government built up the state's defences, and dissolved the labour movement's own defence organisations. The Workers Defence, which was set up after a decision by the Trade Union Congress in 1931 to defend the workers against 'any violent illegal attack', to defend labour movement properties and to prevent a Fascist coup, was dissolved, together with the Workers Athletic League, which had on occasion been mobilised for street fighting against Fascists. Nils thought all of this was evidence that the labour movement was abandoning class struggle for class collaboration, and more recently was to criticise the present generation of young comrades as not sufficiently accustomed to arms.

In 1931-33 he went to Berlin to train in the specialised area of photographic aerial surveying, which was the 'coming thing'. There he represented *Mot Dag* within the IVKO, to which they had affiliated in 1929, and he became a bodyguard for Brandler and Thalheimer. Even when he was 80 he was a tall, fine-looking man, and when he was younger he must have been a splendid and powerful figure reminiscent of the Vikings of old, while his knowledge of arms would have been a further deterrent. He fell ill and returned to Norway just before Hitler's accession to power. In Norway he became a full-timer for *Mot Dag* and eventually a trade union official in the Building Workers Union, one of the biggest in Norway, a key centre of debate within the unions, where he helped to establish a progressive team-working system for pricing building works controlled by the union members, which is still in use. He played a major rôle in the production of a six volume *Workers Encyclopædia* with contributions from many of the foremost Norwegian intellectuals and academics of the day, which popularised and made available Marxist ideas in that language. When Leon Trotsky was forced to leave France in 1935, he was given refuge in Norway. There Nils, who was one of the few sympathisers to own a car and who had come under the influence of Walter Held (Heinz Epe), helped the exiles, and he stayed with Trotsky for two periods, having long discussions with him.

During the Moscow Trials, he attempted to defend the accused in left wing papers, for which the Stalinists tried to get him expelled from his union and the Labour Party. He and all of Trotsky's supporters were really tested, for both the NKP, the right wing conservatives and Quisling's Fascistic party were all in agreement that Trotsky should be deported. In his words: 'It was confusing, as one didn't know where the main enemy was. Blows came from so many and unexpected places.' After Trotsky's expulsion from Norway in 1936, Nils played a rôle among the many highly talented refugees from Nazism who had come to Norway, including Held and Daniel Guérin, as well as Willy Brandt. When the war broke out in 1939, Norway was neutral, but none of the Norwegian Trotskyists supported the line of the Fourth International during the Russo-Finnish Winter War, so though they defended the local Communist Party against bans and proscriptions, they also upheld the right of the Finns to nationhood. Walter Held and Nils Dahl seem to have supported Max Shachtman's view on Finland, but not his actual split. Alas, we in *Revolutionary History* never really discussed this point with him. In the opinion of this writer, history has decisively shown that Held, Dahl and the Danish Trotskyists were correct on Finland, as opposed to Trotsky.

When the Germans invaded Norway in April 1940, all the Trotskyists there regarded the situation as that of a non-imperialist country invaded by the Nazis, and insofar as the Quisling government was immediately proclaimed, they also considered the conflict to be a civil war against the Fascists. They did not even know if the British had joined in for three or four days. He deals very fully with this short and critical period in his two books, some of which is summarised below. Nils did not hesitate but joined the mobilised forces at Hønefoss, bringing with him some anti-Fascist refugees, including veterans of the Spanish Civil War. They formed part of a column of troops in central Norway that was forced back into the mountains, and eventually had to surrender at Segelstag Bridge. The exiled friends of Nils, however, would certainly have been shot, as they would not have been covered by surrender terms, so, with the refugees, he skied off into the mountains, buried the uniforms, weapons and documents that they had on an isolated farm, and, coming down into another valley unoccupied by the enemy, hired a car and pretended that they were civilian Norwegian refugees returning to their homes in Oslo as the Germans had ordered. There the foreign comrades could be hidden, and eventually smuggled across to Sweden.

All the Norwegian troops who surrendered were sent back to their homes, and the officers had to give their parole not to continue the fighting. But Nils contacted some smugglers, and crossed by boat to Strömstad in Sweden. He took care to be arrested by the Swedish police rather than the army, who would have sent him straight back to the Germans, and got their permission to telephone a relation, a cousin of his father's, in the Embassy in Stockholm. He had with him the documents that he had saved. After giving a talk to the Swedish General Staff on the recent fighting, he secretly left Stockholm and travelled north on the railways towards Narvik until two stops before a station near the border with Norway, where he had learnt that there would be police checks on people. He made off into the mountains on his skis, and crossing the ranges came down among the Norwegian, French and British troops who were still fighting in the far north of the country near Tromsø. Looking at the map, it seems he must have been a very hard man. There he commanded a battery of artillery and liaised with the French Army, the Chasseurs Alpins. But when France surrendered in June, the French and British forces were withdrawn. Nils again refused to surrender, took off his uniform, and pretended to be a civilian going home with a boatload of others to Trondheim. He got back to Oslo from that place by train, where he found he was in trouble with the Norwegian army for taking money from the regimental chest when he had escaped with his anti-Fascist friends, and for not keeping proper accounts. He made a tremendous fuss, saying his honour was impugned, and said that he would retrace every step and give an absolutely full account of his expenditure. This gave him the cover and opportunity to find his cache, get hold of all his hidden documents to take eventually to Sweden, and to hide the arms more conveniently elsewhere. After the war he gave a full account of his view of the period in *Stormaktenes kamp om Norge og Skandinavia 1939-40: en militærpolitisk studie. I. Det tyske angrep på Norden* (*The Great Power Struggle over Norway 1939-40: A Politico-Military Study, 1: The German Attack on the Nordic Countries*, Oslo, 1948). This deals with the first few days after the German attack. An interesting and unusual point that he makes was that the young officers and NCOs in this conscript force were mostly ex-students who had often been influenced by the Socialist ideas of *Mot Dag*. German military reports of the time that he cites refer to these as 'young fanatics'. They were much keener on resisting the Nazis than many of their elders. Alas, since the book was totally ignored at the time, he never followed it up with any further study.

In the early months of the Occupation, Nils took an active part in preparing the labour movement for the repression which he knew would come. He went back to Sweden legally in October 1940, and collaborated with the Swedish High Command by building a network to supply information about the Germans. He was flown out of that country to Britain in 1943. He had left a piece to be published by a Swedish Syndicalist trade union publisher under a pseudonym (Harald K Johansen, *Den norska tragedien*, Federativs, Stockholm, 1943, published from a Norwegian manuscript). As it gave an account of the first 48 hours of the German invasion in 1940, when the government and King got away to Elverum just north of Oslo, and had to decide what to do, this caused a row, and he was threatened with a court-martial. In the confusion the young reserve officer and Trotskyist was present, and spoke in the discussion. To his amazement, and quite contradicting his Marxist preconceptions, though the right wing wanted to make a deal with the Nazis, the King and Crown Prince were determined to fight it out. The King broadcast to the nation to resist, and furiously denounced the Luftwaffe for its 'unchivalrous' behaviour in bombing civilians. From that moment sabotage started. In England he met an activist from the Polish Bund, Lucjan Blit, and sought to find out what had happened in Russia to his friend Walter Held.

In an article in the paper of the Norwegian International Socialists, Nils commented that the October Group of Norwegian Trotskyists did not survive after the war, and stated that 'the long years of underground work under the Nazi regime resulted in the comrades being unable to carry out political work under normal circumstances'. In the postwar world he took an active part in Scandinavian anti-imperialist struggles, including defending the rights of the Samish people (Lapps) of Norway, was a supporter of the United Secretariat — he had attended the Fourth International cadre school of 1947 — and later represented Norway at many of their international conferences. He also took part in re-establishing a revolutionary organisation when it finally became possible in the 1970s. Young people on the left remember him vigorously defending a book stall at the university against a Maoist assault while in his 70s. Latterly he participated in the meetings of the IS group in Norway, and, as long as his health permitted, always attended the 'Marxism' conference of the SWP in London. It was there that I introduced him to Harry Wicks, but alas by then he was already becoming deaf, and found it difficult to communicate with this fellow veteran. He married for the second time Mildred Gordon MP, the widow of an eminent member of the United Secretariat of the Fourth International, Sam Gordon, who looked after him devotedly despite the heavy burden of her parliamentary duties. The last few years of his life were not so happy, as he became unable to read, and his deafness cut him off from people. He died in a nursing home in Norway, and the IS comrades there were very kind and supportive of him in his last illness, frequently visiting him, and greatly helping Mildred at that difficult time. After his death when Mildred went to clear up the house, to her amazement she found a light machine gun and a dozen rifles, all in good order, boxes and boxes of ammunition, uniforms and gas masks carefully hidden — just in case. It seems that Nils was always serious about preparing for a workers' insurrection, even if that possibility appeared remote.

As a small tribute *Revolutionary History* intends to publish something on Scandinavia in a future issue, and, if we can, some extracts from, or perhaps a summary of, his main works (a summary of his book in Swedish is printed below). Their aim was to rebuff the attempt by the bourgeoisie to blame the labour movement for the war. At the time that his last book was published in 1948 — he had to do it himself — and with the onset of the Cold War, no-one took any notice of it, and it was only in the last few years that scholars started to recognise his important testimony. By then, of course, the political dangers to the ruling class of telling people what respectable right wing people had been doing in 1940 had disappeared.

In other circumstances Nils Dahl might have played a considerable and distinguished rôle as a commander — perhaps *the* commander — in a revolutionary army, but history was to judge otherwise. He could have done so much in the right circumstances. He lacked neither the brains, nor the heart — nor the courage. At the Nazi invasion many would have wrung their hands, gone underground, or made for the border. He was no sectarian, thought coolly in a difficult situation, and with great bravery carried out what history would later call the Proletarian Military Policy. Had things turned out differently, and had revolutionary upheavals occurred as everyone expected, he would by his actions have aligned himself with the best elements of the working class who sought to struggle against Nazism.

We have lost a great revolutionary fighter and friend whose rôle and true worth few in the broad Trotskyist movement recognised.

He is survived by his wife, Mildred Gordon MP, his daughter Kari Petrie, and his son Johan Jacob Dahl.

Much of the information in this obituary has been culled from *Revolutionary History*, Volume 1, no 2, pp9-11; Volume 1, no 4, pp39-43; and Volume 2, no 2, pp33-42, where much more can be found on his discussions with Trotsky and his researches on the fate of Walter Held. Our warm thanks go to Magne Svendsen of the Norwegian TUC and Solveig Halvorsen of the Norwegian Labour Movement Archive for providing precise details of his publications, and also to the Norwegian International Socialists, who sent us a collection of their material. We still seek further information on articles that he may have written.

Ted Crawford

Nils Kaare Dahl
The Norwegian Tragedy

THE TEXT below is a summary by Mike Jones of *Den norska tragedien* (*The Norwegian Tragedy*) by Harald K Johansen (pseudonym of Nils Kaare Dahl) published in Swedish in Stockholm by Federativs (a Syndicalist body) in 1943.[1] Notes by Ted Crawford have been added. Many of the judgements made at the time by Nils Dahl on the individuals and events have been proved correct, but what is remarkable is that this was written at the time with little documentation to go on, except the current newspapers and what Nils had taken out of Norway. His own shrewd views on the people that he knew and the analytical weapons of Marxism are responsible. Copies of this Swedish book are now rare.

This is an account of Norwegian events as they unfolded from the German invasion on 9 April 1940 until the Allies decamped by sea along with the Norwegian government, King and Crown Prince. It was written almost immediately after the events that he described, and many of his judgements have been confirmed by much later historical research. Dahl starts by discussing the Great Powers' attitude to and plans for Scandinavia up to the attack. Initially, the Allies wanted to cross Norway and Sweden to help Finland during the Winter War against Soviet Russia, and a force was assembled to do this, though it was later dispersed. Norway only refused transit rights to Finland after the Swedes had already done so. The Allied plan was to hold the Swedish ore fields by force, as well as Narvik. Not all Swedish ore left by Narvik, and Dahl asks if the British did not really know that. A large part was taken by train to Central Sweden and smelted there, and then shipped by sea through the Baltic, and this

1. The standard works in English on the campaign in Norway are official history: TK Derry, *The Campaign in Norway*, 1962; JL Moulton, *The Norwegian Campaign of 1940*, 1966; and François Kersaudy, *Norway 1940*, 1990 (first published in French in 1987).

continued to be so after the defeat, so Dahl questioned as to whether the whole policy was designed to draw both Norway and Sweden into the war on the Allied side.[2] Dahl asserts that the Swedes were very badly armed, as they had sent all their spare munitions to Finland. Dahl states that Narvik and the ore seem to have been a pretext, and when the Winter War ended in March 1940 Chamberlain needed to appear as if he was really waging war, while the French government was under political pressure as well.[3] Dahl argues that any attempt by Britain to involve Norway in the war seemed quite irrational. Germany's need of Norway (Denmark was only important as a stepping stone) involved not so much Swedish ore, but the need to break out of the British blockade of the North Sea.

On the Winter War itself, Dahl was very clear that the Finns had the right to defend themselves, thus totally rejecting the orthodox Trotskyist view. Germany was worried that as the war went on the Allies would intervene militarily, and so Hitler needed it finished, particularly as the Red Army was not doing very well. Dahl believed that the Germans sent instructors and organisational help for the big Soviet offensive on the Karelian isthmus in March 1940 which broke the Finnish defences and advanced to Viborg (Viipuri) so that the Finns were exhausted and had to ask for terms.[4] Germany put huge diplomatic pressure on the Swedes not to aid the Finns, thus helping the Soviet Union, and the Swedish Foreign Minister was replaced under German pressure. After Finland had made peace, and during the fighting in Norway, the Finnish radio stations in their Norwegian broadcasts supported Norway against Hitler. It is clear that claims that Finland was a 'Fascist' country and a German ally at this point were nonsense.

Dahl criticises the Norwegian Labour Party for a lack of bold leadership and decision at the moment of the German attack. However, he thought that this was not because the Labour Party leaders were 'bad men' and had personal flaws, but because they were reformists and parliamentarians. The Storting (parliament) left Oslo together with the state apparatus, which soon returned to Oslo as it was a reactionary stratum. Parliamentary sessions were held in the still unconquered parts of Norway, and the Labour Party was keen to maintain democratic norms. Dahl argues that the constitution al-

2. All modern commentators find the allied diplomacy and strategy totally muddled and badly thought out, but do not say that it arose from their right wing political attitudes and sympathy among some of their members for some of Hitler's policies.
3. The French were even keener to involve the Allies in Scandinavia.
4. There seems to be no evidence for this, though it was believed at the time, and there is a cartoon in Punch to this effect in January 1940.

lowed for a temporary dictatorship in time of war, but Norway had no military tradition, while some ministers had even been in prison for militant pacifist activity in the 1920s. Norway had next to no foreign policy experts, but it was so tied to Britain through its shipping and trading links that it has always followed the UK in such matters. The leading foreign policy expert was Mowinckel, a ship owner, though he never foresaw quite how things were going to unfold, and bourgeois figures like Hambro had an international outlook with their better education, language skills and money. The Labour Party leaders came from a municipal background, and were capable in town hall politics, but foreign affairs were a closed book. Once the Winter War in Finland was over, many people in the government thought that the crisis was past. Dahl goes into the behaviour of the Labour Party in great detail.

The book was published in 1943, but the introduction says that it was delayed for some time owing to the author's references to sensitive matters such as the 'elastic neutrality' of the Swedes. The main reason why he was regarded with great disfavour by the Norwegian bourgeoisie becomes clear from the book. He pointed out that after the invasion during the night of 8-9 April, though the Norwegian government published on the 10th a declaration to the people signed by Johan Nygaardsvold, to which the King appended two sentences giving his total support, and which was broadcast on the 11th, this text lacked clarity on what kind of resistance it was calling for, and whether this was military or merely passive. It was not a declaration of war. Dahl saw it as simply a call for further negotiations, which was also the view of the Oslo bourgeoisie and the Germans. The bourgeoisie worked to get the Germans to drop that part of their ultimatum that Quisling be recognised as part of the government. Dahl saw this as ambiguous, and as an indication that not all bridges had been burnt.

Immediately he heard the broadcast, Hambro went on the radio in Stockholm to declare that Norway was at war with Germany, but German diplomatic pressure forthwith barred him from broadcasting in Sweden, while their embassy issued a statement that Germany was not at war with Norway.

Meanwhile, an intermediary went to see the King at Nybergsund, but he refused to negotiate. Later that day both Nybergsund and Elverum were bombed and machine gunned by the Luftwaffe; 54 civilians being killed in Elverum, and another 110 wounded. Dahl cites Hambro's book as hinting that the mediator gave away the King's whereabouts to the Germans, who then tried to murder him. On 13 April the King issued a new declaration calling upon all Norwegian men and women to do everything they could to regain freedom for 'our dear country', and denouncing the 'unchivalrous' German attacks on peaceful civilians. He thanked those who had stayed with him and the government at their posts in the fight for Norwegian independence and freedom, and asked everyone to remember those who had died for the country.

Dahl saw this statement as the basis for a real national uprising, which was the only way that the Germans could be defeated. Military resistance should have been quickly organised within the country, and linked with resistance in the German-occupied area to hit the enemy behind the lines. The government should have called for a people's war, mass mobilisation and active resistance, though not individual terror. Legal limits should have been disregarded by virtue of the higher principle of human rights and the right of the oppressed to rebel. He believed there were elements of this in the King's speech, but that it was too abstract and needed to be far more concrete, such as an appeal to transport workers not to move German supplies, building workers not to repair damage to airfields, and that the people should obstruct the invaders as much as possible. These kind of mass actions would, he thought, have eventually developed into armed formations of workers and street fighting. Dahl drew a comparison with Marshal Timoshenko's appeal to the Soviet population in the occupied areas, and regretted that the Norwegian government never went that far, and confined itself to abstract slogans in that key period at the beginning of April. A Major Sunde, a liberal and a lawyer, did send out such an appeal on the radio from London on 24 April, but by then it was far too late.

By insisting on Norwegian acceptance of a Quisling government and thus putting a traitor and Nazi at the helm, the Germans created the possibility of a revolutionary civil war, and the limited and abstract appeals of the government of 11-13 April were enough to start the process. Some students tried to blow up a bridge between Oslo and Fornebu airfields, and a few armed groups were formed. The Germans greatly feared such a development, and warned on 12 April that 'franc-tireurs' and saboteurs would be shot. The Oslo bourgeoisie, although bitter, as from being the boss they were reduced to being German subordinates, were also terrified at this possibility. Hambro seems to suggest this situation in his book when he recounts that a delegation of industrialists met the German Ambassador, Dr Bräuer, and explained that if Quisling was not removed there would be trouble. Bräuer understood and promised to remove him, while the industrialists promised to try to prevent the war turning into a national uprising.

Of course, such a popular uprising, although directed against the Germans in the first instance, would, once the masses were armed and aware of their power, probably turn against the ruling class, and there was no guarantee that after victory the bourgeoisie would remain in power, since in the course of struggle respect for bourgeois law and order would break down. It was no coincidence, therefore, that the leaders of the apparatus of ideological oppression, Paal Berg (Chief Justice of the High Court, or Justicarius) and Bishop Berggrav (Head of the state Lutheran church) were the chief spokesmen of the tendency that wanted a deal with the Germans. The result was the so-called Administrative Council.

From an abstract nationalist viewpoint both Quisling and the Administrative Council were traitors, as both wanted to end the war and subordinate Norway to Germany, but whereas Quisling was prepared for Norway to be totally subordinate, the Administrative Council wanted the bourgeoisie to keep control of industry, law and order, and so forth. They wanted to deal with the Germans as equals so that the oppression would be exercised through them, but indirectly, while Quisling was an open traitor and tried to hinder and sabotage Norwegian military resistance. Paal Berg and Berggrav simply discouraged people from going through the lines to join up, and encouraged people to work for the Germans on the docks, by clearing airfields and so on, while confusing people with speeches about German chivalry and decency. Thus their rôle was more passive than that of Quisling.

On 15 April Quisling left office, and was thanked by Berg for his work on Norway's behalf and his patriotic attitude, while the Administrative Council took over responsibility for law and order in the occupied areas. A proclamation was issued explaining that the High Court had appointed the Council, and the Norwegian people were called upon to go about their business as usual and to act legally, while sabotage was denounced as counter-productive. The various bosses' organisations and a section of the TUC backed up this appeal. (Paal Berg later became a 'resistance' leader, so Dahl might not be thanked in 1943 for pointing all this out.)

Dahl believed that this non-Nazi, non-pro-German government could have been accepted by the Nygaardsvold government on 10 April, but by the 15th it was too late. An Anglo-Norwegian military alliance had commenced, and the first British troops had landed in Norway, while Norwegian soldiers had engaged both the Germans and the Quisling youth groups. Mobilisation was complete, and contact between the Oslo bourgeoisie and the military command was almost non-existent. After the confusion and contradictory orders of the first 48 hours, the troops were now in action, and would not have believed an order to stop fighting. What is more, after the German air attack on Elverum and Nybergsund, all talk of and belief in German respect for human rights and international law had disappeared, together with any faith in German promises.

In response to the creation of the Administrative Council, the legal government issued on 17 April a statement welcoming the fall of the Quisling government, pointing out that Norway had only one legal government, appointed by the King and unanimously approved by the Storting. It regarded the Administrative Council as an emergency measure for the occupied areas, which had of necessity to take orders from the Germans, but it was not an alternative to the real government, as it neither represented the will of the Norwegian people, nor had any basis in Norwegian law. It existed purely to give some protection to the rights of Norwegian citizens when Norway was occupied, and would have to step aside when the legal government regained power. The statement went on to affirm that the King and government would do everything possible to liberate Norway and regain its independence as soon as feasible. It added that 'all Norwegians must help this liberation struggle as they want to be, and want to be called, Norwegians'.

The declaration showed that the government had understood very little. The statement that the government wanted to do all that it could to push the Germans out of the country was in fact a call for civil war — precisely the result that the Administrative Council wanted to avoid. Dahl saw this as the inevitable result of five years in government, when the Labour Party saw its main aim as the collaboration between classes, and had thus lost sight of class contradictions. And, though it stated that the Administrative Council lacked all basis in Norwegian law, it failed to take a clear line against it. To illustrate this point, Dahl describes how Berg sent a telegram to the King, apparently assuming that he would see the class nature of the situation more easily than the Labour politicians and so, by by-passing the elected government, solve the tricky legal situation of the illegal Administrative Council. The letter mentions that the Germans had offered to negotiate with the government, but that this had been rejected. It stressed that 'the initiative must now come from the Norwegian side', and asked the King to persuade the Crown Prince to make an appeal on the radio to the people in the occupied areas to refrain from sabotage and destructive behaviour. On the 19th the Germans finally told the Norwegian Ambassador in Berlin to leave, and the gloves were off.

In the war itself, 10 000 Norwegians soldiers took part in the fighting in the south, and all were volunteer reservists who had reported to the local depôts in the hope of being given arms.[5] Because of

5. A total of 1355 Norwegian servicemen were killed and wounded (together with

the very confused situation and the lack of clarity in calls to resist by the government, only about a thousand men from Oslo got through the lines to join the fighting. What prompted them in the confused situation was the existence of the Quisling government, but, apart from these few, most of the urban working class saw no action. The Norwegian TUC and the Norwegian Communist Party did not call for resistance in the initial stages of the invasion, and some trade union bosses returned to Oslo to collaborate. The NKP was neutral in the south, though their members there did not necessarily obey the call to refrain from resisting, striking or carrying out sabotage. In the north the NKP members rallied to the colours and fought. Dahl believes that this was because the Soviet Union had distinct interests in North Norway.

At the start of the war, Dahl thought it important that the open traitors and tentative collaborators were denounced; this was not done. Volunteers turned up to enlist and were sent back home by the officers, which caused demoralisation. Indeed, although the government wanted immediate mobilisation, the high command ordered a normal mobilisation, which meant reporting for duty in two days time. Dahl says the Navy was keener on a fight than the Army, and had alerted ships and shore batteries. The Commander of the Armed Forces, Major-General Laake, after delaying the mobilisation as described, changed into civilian clothes and did a vanishing act, for which he was dismissed by the King.[6] Colonel Ruge, an Inspector of Artillery, was promoted to general and put in charge, but although a brave man and good soldier, he had to take over in the worst circumstances. Once the Allies abandoned Central Norway without telling the Norwegians — which caused great demoralisation and cynicism, above all in the Trondheim area — Dahl believed that the battle for Norway was really over. Northern Norway was sparsely populated, had no industry except the export of primary products such as fish, was partly inhabited by the Lapp (Samish) minority, and could not maintain a resistance for long. The Germans who had landed in Narvik at the start of the war were beaten and penned up near the Swedish frontier in a 'motti' — a Finnish word he uses to compare the cutting up of Russian columns in the Winter War in the northern wastes by the Finns, and they were stuck in isolated strong points that were worn down and eventually overrun. Dahl points out that it was the Norwegian troops rather than the Allies who succeeded

400 civilians killed mostly by bombing) according to Norwegian figures cited by Moulton and Derry.

6.   Technically, he retired, as he had passed the retirement age of 65 the day after the invasion! Unofficially, his behaviour was attributed to incompetence rather than defeatism.

here,[7] but then the Swedes came to the German's rescue after pressure was applied, and the German wounded together with naval survivors from the action in Narvik Fjord, who were not much use as soldiers, were evacuated through Sweden, and fresh German troops arrived.[8] At the time he wrote this, Dahl was uncertain as to whether such troops had come from Central Norway or not, but he reports rumours that they had.

General Ruge was offered the chance of leaving Norway when the Allies evacuated on 7 June 1940, but he chose to remain and surrender with his troops. He then refused to give his parole, which would have meant his release to go back home, as was the case with the rest of the Norwegian troops. His presence in prison in Norway was a beacon for resistance feelings, and he was sent to a fortress in Germany. Dahl had a high opinion of the character of Ruge, who was a soldier not a politician, but who stepped forward in a situation when most Norwegian senior officers were useless.[9] Dahl speaks of the need for a special type of person in the kind of situation that arose when Hitler attacked Norway, individuals who had the ability to see what was happening, and the boldness, decisiveness and courage then to carry out the necessary action.

As for the Norwegian population, it was only after the Norwegian soldiers had been released to return to their homes that the mood changed from one of defeatism to much greater hostility to the Germans. During the war, the majority of the population had been passive, opposed to the war, and this was particularly so in the country districts and, above all, among the more prosperous in the country areas. Efforts at working class resistance, such as the strike in the naval shipyard at Horten, were broken by the Germans with the help of the TUC. Even after the war, the dishonesty about this period continued, as Foreign Minister Koht, who made a speech on the radio from London in early May denouncing Bishop Berggrav, was bitterly attacked in the Oslo papers at the time, and, more significantly, his statement was omitted from the official *White Book* published by the Norwegian government as an account of these events. Koht was never forgiven by the bourgeoisie.

7. Dahl is correct here, though the British and French historians do not emphasise that, even with most of their country occupied, hastily levied Norwegians proved more formidable warriors in the mountains than the Allies' picked troops.

8. Between 19 and 22 April 'a train had crossed Sweden and reached Narvik with both food and medical equipment. On the 25th another train with five wagons also brought 300 "health service personnel"' (Kersaudy, p202). This is not mentioned by Derry or Moulton in earlier accounts.

9. Ruge told his own story in *Krigens Dagbok (War Diary)* Oslo, 1946. He retired after the war with the rank of Lieutenant-General.

Work in Progress

Comintern Archives on Microfiche

BEFORE THE collapse of the USSR, the Comintern archives, which were closed down in 1943, were held in the inaccessible central archive of the CPSU's Central Committee. Following the political and economic reforms in the early 1990s in Russia, these Comintern archives were then made accessible through the Russian Centre for the Preservation and Study of Contemporary Historical Documents (RTsKhIDNI), the former Central Party Archive. In recent years, though, the Inter Documentation Company (IDC) Publishers of The Netherlands has been filming parts of the Comintern archives so as to make this material available on microfiche to a much wider world of researchers.

The last instalment of this microfiche series was due to be completed in April 1997. In its totality, it will include all documents which relate to the seven Congresses and 13 Plenums of the Executive Committee of the Communist International, including the shorthand notes made on the first Comintern congresses, as well as the material from all the preparatory and working commissions.

IDC Publishers is also transforming the complete archive indexes (opisi) into a full-text database format. The database records contain the following fields: fond number, opis number, number of archive folio, description of folio contents, date and year, number of pages, language of publication, and microfiche number of the collection. At the same time they have also translated the text of the opisi from Russian into English, French and German. In a unique approach to micro-publishing of archival material, IDC Publishers together with the International Institute of Social History (IISG) in Amsterdam are also producing a detailed index so that researchers at the IISG will be able to add notes and comments to specific highlights of the collection.

The collection, which comprises approximately 14 000 microfiches, goes some way to preserving long-term the 1.5 million items held in 551 fonds in the RTsKhIDNI; something which is invaluable given that last year the Russians suspended the microfilming project they had been undertaking with the Hoover Institution. If the future does brighten up, though, perhaps the next step will be to add the materials' sections of the various national Communist parties to this electronic preservation and retrieval system.

The price of the entire collection at around 151 000 Guilders is beyond the budget of all except a limited number of specialist libraries and archives, though instalments of the series will be able to be purchased separately. Further information on this work and its availability can be had from Inter Documentation Company Publishers, Hogewoerd 151, PO Box 11205, 2301 EE Leiden, The Netherlands. Their E-mail address is info@idc.nl and they have a website at http://www.idc.nl
Gary Tennant

Useful Websites

We warmly recommend the following Websites

The Marx Archive
<http://csf.colorado.edu/psn/marx/>

Trotsky FAQ (Frequently Asked Questions)
<http://freenet.msp.mn.us/people/ryans/
trotfaqintro.html>

Marxist Sites provide a lead into many interesting areas
<http://www.idbsu.edu/surveyrc/Staff/jaynes/marxism/
websites.htm>

The Marx Archive appreciates help in inputting large or small works of Marx and Engels which are not yet on the Web

CENTRO STUDI PIETRO TRESSO

Archive of the Italian and International Trotskyist Movement

The Centro Studi Pietro Tresso was founded in October 1983 by militants and comrades of different political orientations, to collect and publicise material relevant to the Italian and international Trotskyist movement. The Centro Studi is not an intellectual debating club, but aims to investigate the past in order to help build a revolutionary movement in the present and future.

Write to: Centro Studi Pietro Tresso, c/o Paulo Casciola, Via Firenze, 18-06034 Foligno PG, Italy.

Reviews

George Breitman, Paul LeBlanc and Alan Wald, *Trotskyism in the United States: Historical Essays and Reconsiderations,* Humanities Press, New Jersey, 1996, pp318

I FIRST came across the Trotskyist movement, and that in its Healyite manifestation, in the aftermath of Khrushchev's 'Secret Speech' to the Twentieth Congress of the CPSU. That speech, such a well-kept secret that the full text was in the next issue of the *Observer*, showed beyond dispute that Stalin was not only fallible, but also a mass murderer in the tradition of, and easily surpassing, Ivan the Terrible. The shock of all these revelations was rather like the one you might experience on hearing the Virgin Mary ask the procurator to take her first born into care. In that splintered aftermath of Khrushchev's speech, I, together with thousands of others, came to realise that yesterday's political certainty was but the prelude to today's disillusion.

During that hand-wringing interregnum, where the most oft-heard phrase was 'Oh God, where did it all go wrong?', a few hundred of us were introduced to Trotskyism. The negative aspect was Gerry Healy, who on first, and all subsequent, sight looked as if he had recently been fulfilling an active rôle in the murkier recesses of an apocalyptic work by Hieronymus Bosch. The Healy factor was, however, heavily outweighed by the Trotsky effect, as expressed in his published works. The simple, not to say simple-minded, certainties of Stalinism were no match for the high tensile, armoured certainties of Trotskyism. This was not just any old suit of armour, it came fully equipped with hand-stitched lapels, waistcoat and two pairs of trousers. Not only could this theory answer all your questions, even those you had not the wit to ask, but it was also a complete defence against all the slings and arrows of any outrageous fortune that happened to be lurking about the place.

Ill-favoured Healy might have been, but he had the tremendous advantage of possessing a number of key texts by Leon Trotsky, such as *The Revolution Betrayed*. There are better books by Trotsky, but there are none that could have been more appropriate to the times than *The Revolution Betrayed* in the years 1956-57. These gems from the pen of the master came to us via the good offices of the US Socialist Workers Party. Whatever my subsequent criticism of the SWP, I shall always be grateful for that introduction into a world of grown-up Marxist politics.

Nowadays, I am told, the SWP not only eschews all generosity with Trotsky's texts, they have also eschewed Trotskyism. Under their maximum leader Jack Barnes, the SWP declares itself to be a sister party of the Cuban

Communist Party. Whether the Cubans' own maximum leader entertains similar feelings of sisterhood toward Jack Barnes and his comrades is open to doubt. Holding such views, it is only proper that they should abandon Trotskyism, for even the most egregiously opportunist Trotskyist could not pretend that the working class had moved south, and was surreptitiously carrying through its revolutionary purposes in the disguise of an over-weight, bearded Cuban petit-bourgeois. Whilst this is noted in the book here under review, it does not seem to excite much interest in the authors. This may be because Breitman is dead, and was in any case part of the leadership that first endorsed the assumption of Cuba into the pantheon of 'workers' states', whilst LeBlanc and Wald joined the SWP after this great theoretical breakthrough had been made.

Right at the beginning of this book Paul LeBlanc writes: 'Neither my collaborator Alan Wald and I are satisfied with the modest cross section provided here...' Well, they can add my name to the list as well. For them, Trotskyism in the United States is the Socialist Workers Party, the 18 years of the Workers Party-Independent Socialist League merit only passing reference, and the International Socialists no mention at all. Wald and LeBlanc are American academics, and both of them write in that clotted style which was pioneered by Erlichman and Haldeman, and was not the least of their crimes against humanity. Wald, who has the more interesting thesis, was clearly pulling ahead of LeBlanc in the race for my approval, when he introduced that abomination the verb 'to critique' as in 'he critiqued...'. I subjected him to a great deal of 'critiquing' for that, I can tell you. Breitman, who was self-educated, produces an altogether nicer class of prose.

What the authors do have in common is that they were all expelled from the SWP by Jack Barnes and his camarilla. For Breitman this must have been a particularly bitter experience, because he had been part of the Farrell Dobbs-Tom Kerry leadership that had selected Barnes in the first place. As LeBlanc explains: 'The most serious errors by the SWP "old guard" were made after Cannon's retirement from the central leadership. These were associated, in part, with the selection and grooming of Jack Barnes as the new central leader of the SWP. He was allowed to assemble his own leadership team, and the kind of authority that Cannon, Dobbs and Kerry enjoyed was conferred upon him.' It is LeBlanc's general thesis that, with one or two reservations, the SWP was essentially a sound organisation until Barnes was handed the franchise. Having acquired the job through a pose of ultra-Cannonism, it was not too long before he 'undermined the party democracy that is essential to Leninism'.

Barnes, according to the convincing testimony of our authors, behaved in an undemocratic manner. What seems to have escaped their notice is that there is something amiss in a leadership approaching its sell-by date hand-picking its successor. James P Cannon chose Farrell Dobbs to be his successor, as the man most likely to continue the traditions of Cannonism. To ensure that Dobbs kept to that tradition, Cannon set up a sort of parallel centre in California where he could, with no little embarrassment to Dobbs, correct any deviations from Cannonite rectitude. This is a style of selection that was popular in the Tory party, until it conferred leadership on Alec Douglas Home, which effectively discredited the whole procedure. Unfortunately, when Barnes, through a stunning display of devotion to the living thought of Cannon, acquired the franchise and then proceeded to divest himself of this heritage, there was no way of effectively calling him to order. It was now Jack Barnes' party, and he could give it to Castro, or to anyone else his mean little heart desired.

I have little doubt that Jack Barnes is not the man you would want in charge of your favourite revolutionary party. Frankly, I would advise against having him in for baby-sitting, but it has to be conceded that the constitutional niceties were observed when he got rid of troublesome opponents. He just utilised the draconian rules enacted by the Kerry-Dobbs leadership to rid themselves of Tim Wohlforth and James Robertson. Later, given a little practice, Barnes began to get a bit inventive with his expulsion technique. The Internationalist Tendency were declared to be a separate organisation, and were not allowed to re-register. This cunning ploy ensured that they were not allowed to utilise the appeals procedure.

Lowering over the history of the SWP is the dominating presence of James P Cannon. Of the three authors of the essays in this book, George Breitman is the most dedicated Cannonite. His view is encapsulated in the quote: 'I am very satisfied with Marxism and Leninism and with the American version of that, which came to get the name of "Cannonism" in our movement.'

Alan Wald represents the opposite pole in the volume. He takes the view that Cannon, despite his manifest talents, inculcated a notion in the party that it represented the acme of revolutionary purity, an immaculate organisation, with muscles twangingly poised to lead the workers to power at a moment's notice. This, which we might call self-deluding sectarianism, is beautifully summed up in Cannon's *Theses on the American Revolution* of 1946: 'The revolutionary vanguard party, destined to lead this tumultuous revolutionary movement in the US, does not have to be created. It already exists, and its name is the Socialist Workers Party... The fundamental core of the professional leadership has been assembled... The task of the SWP consists simply in this: to remain true to its program and banner...' This was put even more sharply by Morris Stein (who was National Secretary whilst Cannon was in prison during the war) with the words:

'We are monopolists in the field of politics. We cannot stand any competition. We can tolerate no rivals. The working class, to make the revolution, can do it only through one party and one program... This is why we are out to destroy every single party in the field that makes any pretence of being a working class revolutionary party. Ours is the only correct program that can lead to the revolution. Everything else is deception, treachery.'

If, on reading this, you do not experience something of the cold chill of the Lubyanka cellars, you almost certainly have your central heating turned up expensively high.

The middle ground in all this is occupied by Paul LeBlanc. His view is that the formative years of the SWP were the time when the opposing contenders for leadership in the working class were either Stalinism or Social Democracy. In the 1930s neither of these forces would accept work or discussion with Trotskyists, who were thus alone and must shout very loud to be heard.

Really though, the explicit sectarian vainglory in Stein is implicit in Cannon, because for good or ill he set his stamp on the SWP. Cannon was a native American revolutionary, experienced in working class politics before the founding of the CPUSA, and an influential figure within that party. He learned well and participated freely in the faction fights that enlivened the early years of American Communism, but he was always the junior partner in the combinations he joined. Early in the proceedings he became aware that advancement in the sections of the Communist International depended on choosing the right patron in its leadership. He was less concerned at the fact that Zinoviev and Stalin could impose a minority leadership on the majority of the US party, than that it was not his minority that was chosen. When it came to the much smaller world of Trotskyism, Cannon made sure that he was 110 per cent on the right side of LDT, and, whenever given the chance, operated in the Fourth International like a cut-price Zinoviev.

In the early years of the Left Opposition, if Cannon was the best known figure, he was, at least, associated with some other formidable personalities, the most outstanding being Max Shachtman. These two complemented each other very effectively in those formative years. Shachtman was the brilliant Socialist intellectual; witty, stylish, a ruthless polemicist and debater, and at the same time very funny and highly approachable, especially for the young. Cannon, an altogether more dour character, was given to dark depression when things were not going well, and in those moods was liable to withdraw from the struggle to commune with vast quantities of the hard stuff. Nevertheless, he was an exceptionally talented propagandist, both in print and on the platform. If Cannon was not in the same street as Shachtman intellectually, neither was Shachtman a patch on Cannon in the popular agitation stakes. Later on, others of considerable calibre joined the movement: James Burnham, AJ Muste, Hal Draper, Felix Morrow, CLR James and Raya Dunayevskaya, to name just a few.

The movement has always been plagued by the proliferation of tiny groups, each with its founding guru, whose raison d'être is difficult to fathom, the quality of their cadre not discernible to the naked eye, and whose inevitable passing is unaccompanied by expressions of regret. The SWP, however, was not such an organisation. The people mentioned above would all have had some significant rôle to play in a movement that was infinitely more successful and with many more members than the SWP ever enjoyed. It was their tragedy, as it was for the rest of the Trotskyist movement, that they never connected with the working class in any but the most transitory and peripheral way. Perhaps, in general, it is true that the upper and nether millstones of Stalinism and Social Democracy ground the revolutionaries to dust, but in America Stalinism was never a mass party, and Social Democracy was even smaller. With the exception of the Teamsters, the SWP was hardly involved at all in the great upsurge of the CIO, and during the height of that union organising drive, the Trotskyists were engaged in two years of deep entry in the American Socialist Party.

None of this is to suggest that if they had had an orientation to the CIO it would have been a runaway success, but it is to say that in any set of circumstances where the revolutionary movement has a chance to connect with the workers, it should take it. You will not find the proletarian vanguard in Norman Thomas' back pocket, any more than you will find it in Fidel's beard, although there is at least one large petit-bourgeois behind that. The irony of the Trotskyists' entry into the American Socialist Party is that they came out with more than double their original membership, having taken the Socialist Party's youth movement almost lock, stock and barrel. This splendid young cadre formed the majority of Shachtman's faction — and accompanied him out of the SWP in 1940.

The orientation to the working class is not just some fuddy-duddy old foible, it is the essence of revolutionary Marxism, but it is one of the easiest to forget in the over-heated enthusiasm for a new get-rich-quick theory. You can substitute the peasantry for the revolutionary class. You can witter on about 'centuries of deformed workers' states', or Fabian-Stalinism, like Pablo; you might even see the revolution springing unchained from the junior common room; or you could hymn the praises of youth, and good luck to you mate; but none of that will have anything to do with Marxism. One of the besetting sins of our movement is what might be called 'the Socialism of the peroration'. This is where we affirm our 'undying faith in the working class', and promise to 'storm both heaven and earth' in the very near future. Then we go home and try and think up some short cut that will save us from all the hard work, and frequent failure, of organising in the working class.

It is this sort of thing that Trotsky called substitutionism, that is, a besetting sin. In 1973 the SWP had around 1000 members, and LeBlanc quotes someone called Sheir who reported that at that time it had 120 persons, most of them paid, working at the party HQ, with room for many more. George Novack boasted that the SWP had 'an infrastructure for a party of about 100 000'. During the period in question, SWP branches had local branch offices and full-time organisers, and paid for their own leaflets and propaganda. The subs range was from $5 to $50 per week (with the average much closer to $5 than $50, I should think), and the balance after paying local costs was sent to the party. How the party financed its 120 full-time head office staff and all the associated expenses on this income is difficult to understand. It is even more difficult to understand why the party members kept sending the money when it is recalled that this vast army of party functionaries managed in just 12 months to increase the membership by a pathetic 140. A year later still, Barnes' imaginative expulsion tactics had reduced the membership once more to 1000. You pays your money, and Jack Barnes makes his choice.

Whilst we are discussing membership figures, it is quite interesting to note that the SWP never had a membership of more than 1500, and that was the high point in 1938, as they exited from the Socialist Party. That was the time when they were claiming 2500 at the founding congress of the Fourth International. In 1944 they had just 840 as they set out to arrange the future of the British section and control the Fourth International. The postwar SWP, whose membership was usually in the hundreds and never exceeded 1250, threw its weight about internationally, and presumed to lecture the world on how to make the revolution. It is difficult to say who was the most deluded, the SWP for believing its own vainglory, or the rest of us for accepting it as good coin.

When Trotsky was murdered, Cannon saw himself as the natural successor to lead the forces of the Fourth International. In 1940, of course, the Fourth International had been put into lukewarm storage for the duration, but in 1944 Cannon sent his man Sam Gordon to the UK to sort out the British Trotskyists. This, Cannon's second attempt to unify the British section of the Fourth International, involved setting up Gerry Healy as the opposition to the Haston-Grant leadership of the Revolutionary Communist Party. This silly piece of politicking is alone enough to nullify the picture of the wise leader portrayed in LeBlanc's essays, if the fault had not been further compounded by his selection of Michel Raptis (Pablo) as the man to run the Fourth International when it was returned to Europe.

Neither of these interesting sidelights into Cannon's legacy are mentioned in the book, although LeBlanc does treat us to examples of praise for Cannon and the SWP from ex-members of the Johnson-Forest Tendency. Now this is odd, because LeBlanc is co-editor, along with Scott McLemee, of *CLR James and Revolutionary Marxism*, which suggests that he is familiar with the texts of the Johnson-Forest Tendency including, presumably, *The Balance Sheet Completed* (subtitled *Ten Years of American Trotskyism*), the tendency's final farewell to Trotskyism. Here is what Johnson-Forest had to say, amongst other things, about the SWP:

'Finally there was forced upon us a shocking recognition of the callousness, the brutality, the lack of elementary human decency, far less revolutionary principle and vigilance to which substantial elements of the most highly placed leadership had sunk... As we understood ourselves and where we were, the cry became unanimous: "Let us get out of here at once. It is a political gas chamber. We do not trust this political leadership to carry out its own political line. None of our comrades who is in any difficulty can trust himself to them. Even those who are not degenerate are ready to support those who are when their crimes are discovered. We do not want to discuss with them. Such a discussion can only besmirch us. Let us get out of here as quickly as we can." We hesitated for a moment, but the final, the ultimate certainty came with the discovery that the one with the most brains, authority and experience who had come to the rescue of the politically unstable and fortified the turn to Stalinism, was also at the disposal of any degenerate who might need protection.'

Now all of that, which might put you in mind of the last days of the Roman Empire or of the Weimar Republic — or Gerry Healy — is saying that for Johnson-Forest the SWP was a moral swamp, and one would have expected that an admirer of both James P Cannon and CLR James would, if he must quote Johnson-Forest in this context, have something to say about the tendency's final considered word on the SWP.

Alan Wald, despite his addiction to the noun-verb, does cast a rather more critical eye on the SWP. He pays due homage to the high talents of some of the Trotskyist leaders, but points out that not only were they unsuccessful in their own terms, but were also failures by almost any comparison you like to make. Dogmatism was and is almost always confused with high principle, and this is nowhere more apparent than on the tortured question of the class nature of the Stalinist states. As Wald says in a footnote on page 285: 'None of these theories [state capitalist, bureaucratic collectivism or workers' state — JH] persuasively accounts for all aspects of these societies... Unfortunately, for most Trotskyists, absolute fidelity to their particular interpretation of a specific theory of Soviet-type societies is their political touchstone.' Wald, as you will see from this, has a definite grip on reality. He sums up his final essay: 'Trotskyism!!! is dead. Long live Trotskyism.' I do not mind seconding that particular proposition.

For the rest, this is an inadequate book that will be all but incomprehensible to young would-be Marxists who do not have any great knowledge of Trotskyism in general, or the SWP in particular. This may be because some of the material was originally written by LeBlanc and Wald as internal bulletins in obscure faction fights in the SWP. Whatever the reason, this is a pity, because there is the beginning of a worthwhile critique that might help us all to greater clarity and effectiveness.

Jim Higgins

Workers Fight, *When the Proletariat Rose to Change the World*, Internationalist Communist Forum no 27, London, 1996, pp32, 70p

SURPRISINGLY LITTLE has been produced by the left in Britain in book or in pamphlet form to defend Ken Loach's *Land and Freedom* from the ferocious attacks of the Stalinists. An honourable exception is Bob Pitt's translation of the crucial passages from Hernández's memoirs reviewed elsewhere in this issue, and this pamphlet ranks with it as a valuable summary of the real politics of the Spanish Civil War.

Far from being a conflict of 'Fascism versus democracy', it tells us right at the start that 'the reality was entirely different' (p1), and develops its argument step by step from there. It is clearly written, and crams an amazing amount of accurate material into a few pages. No better guide can be placed in the hands of those approaching the subject for the first time, and it deserves to be sold outside every showing of the film.

There is only one minor factual slip, the assertion that the mass base of the CNT was limited to Catalonia (p3), forgetting the support that it possessed amongst the very poorest peasantry in Andalusia, and indeed else-where in Spain. The CNT was, after all, by far the largest trade union fed-eration, numbering some 1.5 million members to the UGT's one million, and many of the UGT's strongest sections were caught behind the National-ist lines.

More could also have been done to discredit the dishonest and sinister claim dealt with on page 20 that the USSR granted disinterested 'aid' to the Republic. As a matter of fact, every piece of Soviet weaponry that arrived had been paid for several times over, for Spain's gold reserve, one of the largest half dozen in the world, had been shipped into Odessa harbour. Sta-lin's hold over the Republic's wealth not only prevented it from buying any arms elsewhere, but also enabled the Comintern advisors, the Russian dip-lomats and the local Stalinist hierarchy to keep a stranglehold over the war effort and the country. It was for this reason rather than his expansion of the carabineros (p22) that Juan Negrín became prime minister after the Sta-linists had ousted Largo Caballero (p28), for it was he who was responsible for the removal of this gold along with the Russian military attaché, Arthur Stashevsky.

This brings us to this pamphlet's only real weakness, its failure to make much of a distinction between the Socialist left, which Trotsky regarded as centrist, and the Socialist right, which allied wholeheartedly with the Stalin-ists in the counter-revolution. Indeed, it even argues that the defeat of the left was its own fault: 'If the Communist Party was able, in the end, to act as the policeman of the bourgeois order, it was primarily because the vast ma-jority of revolutionary workers remained under the influence of the reform-ist leaders.' (p32) By so placing an equals sign between gangsters like Orlov and muddled old Socialists like Caballero, the Stalinists are let neatly off the hook — and Trotsky placed the main responsibility for the betrayal squarely upon their shoulders. This stems from the strange assumption of *Workers' Fight* and its co-thinkers that Stalinists are always to the left of Socialists, an assumption dubious in Spain, and laughable over here.

But if all the reader learns from this brochure is to watch his back where Stalinists are involved, it will have served a useful purpose.

Al Richardson

Richard Pipes, *The Unknown Lenin*, Yale University Press, London, 1996, pp204, £18.50

HOT ON the heels of his sizeable no-holds-barred volumes on the Russian Revolution and the Soviet regime under Lenin, the leading conservative his-torian Richard Pipes presents a hundred or so assorted documents by Lenin that had been omitted from his *Collected Works* and kept hidden away in the Soviet archives, together with some documents addressed to him along with his comments.

The title itself isn't quite accurate. Some of this material has appeared elsewhere in the English language. Lenin's speech at the Ninth Party Con-ference in 1920 was included in Al Richardson's collection *In Defence of the*

Russian Revolution, and his instructions calling for gold to be confiscated from Orthodox churches appeared years ago in *Religion in Communist Lands* (Volume 7, no 1, Spring 1979). Dmitri Volkogonov's *Lenin: Life and Legacy* and the third volume of Robert Service's Lenin trilogy, *The Iron Ring*, both quote from many of the documents in this book, and, moreover, put them into a much broader context.

Furthermore, the image of Lenin presented in this book is hardly unknown. Anyone with any knowledge of the man knows that he was poor at delegating work and involved himself with things which could have been dealt with at a lower level, went over the top at times in his polemics against political opponents, dealt deviously with foreign governments, was critical of his comrades, called for the exile of hostile intellectuals, and demanded harsh measures against opposition. So why publish a very small proportion of the thousands of documents that are in the archives, a selection which adds little to our knowledge of him?

As we have noted previously in this journal (Volume 5, no 4, pp213-21), Pipes is an historian who allows his political views to influence his writings to the extent that they lose the objectivity that is necessary for a worthwhile historical account. It seems to me that the documents in this selection have been chosen specifically for the purpose of putting Lenin in as bad a light as possible. However, Pipes is fighting yesterday's battles. Nobody these days sees Lenin as a plaster saint, Leninists themselves consider that some of his actions hindered the fight for Socialism, and is anyone going to lose any sleep over whether he had an affair with Inessa Armand? Not surprisingly, *The Unknown Lenin* has a somewhat redundant feel about it.

Some of the documents require more background information than is provided if they are to be fully understood, not least Lenin's draft instructions to Bolsheviks in Ukraine which call for Jews and other urban people to be kept out of the Soviet administration. Although this is published here to infer that Lenin was anti-Semitic, it is much more likely to be in respect of ensuring that more Ukrainians were recruited to the Soviet regime in Ukraine, rather than Russians and Jews, who comprised much of the urban population, and were predominant in the Ukrainian Soviet apparatus. Anti-Semitism or indifference to the fate of the Jews is implied in respect of reports of pogroms to Lenin to which no responses have been found. If no replies can be found to these and other documents sent to him, were they written and then lost or misfiled? (That documents may have been lost is raised in the introduction.) Does marking documents 'for the archives' mean that Lenin did not act on them, as is suggested? Or did he take up the issues informally, without writing anything down? Some documents were also addressed to other leading Bolsheviks, so were they taken up first by them? Short of knowing every minute of Lenin's life, and every word he spoke, something that was beyond the capabilities of even the most pedantic Soviet scholar, can anything categorical be said?

Although there are some interesting documents in this book, particularly Lenin's disposition on Roman Malinovsky, the Tsarist police agent in the Bolsheviks' Duma delegation, and his remarkably prescient warning to

Kamenev about the consequences of removing Trotsky from the Central Committee, I can't help thinking that Pipes has picked these documents in order to bolster his own bitterly hostile attitude towards Lenin. Like Volkogonov in his final years, Pipes seeks to promote a one-dimensional Lenin, a malignant incarnation of evil, and tries to put the clock back a few decades to the times when Cold War demonology was the norm. A less prejudiced investigator could have used the wealth of documentation in the archives in order to produce a worthwhile analysis of the mechanics of the Soviet government. If, as Yuri Baranov says in his introduction, work on unpublished Lenin material is to continue, let us hope that in future it is put in the hands of a scholar who can provide a more objective understanding of Lenin and the Soviet regime than old-fashioned conservatives like Richard Pipes.

Paul Flewers

Bob Pitt, *John Maclean and the CPGB*, Pitt Publications, London, 1995, pp44, £2.00

JOHN MACLEAN is a familiar figure to those with an interest in the politics of the revolutionary left in Britain. A member of the Social Democratic Federation from early 1903, he remained a committed Social Democrat up to the outbreak of the First World War, winning a modest reputation as a tireless propagandist and a skilful Marxist educator. On the outbreak of war, he adopted a position of active opposition to a war which he characterised as imperialist, and he consistently maintained the view that the destruction of the British Empire was an object to be enthusiastically desired and fought for. To that end he gave immediate support to the Dublin Rising of 1916 in terms not dissimilar to Lenin's, and he remained committed to the cause of Irish liberation as a key element in the anti-imperialist project. It also brought him to the attention of Lenin, and, following the October Revolution, assured him an important status in the Third International. However, in 1920-21 Maclean became estranged from those who were forging a British Communist Party, and he never joined the Communist Party of Great Britain. Instead, he criticised those who were initially prominent within it, and found a niche briefly in the Socialist Labour Party, and later the Scottish Workers Republican Party, before he died at the end of 1923, a largely isolated figure.

Bob Pitt has produced a pamphlet dealing with Maclean's relationship with the CPGB, which was a decisive if not *the* decisive moment in his political career. The pamphlet is well and clearly written, and adds new information to that already available on Maclean's rôle in the political debates surrounding the formation of the CPGB. It also contains a reprint of Maclean's 'Open Letter to Lenin', in which he outlined his analysis of the general political situation in Britain, and his particular criticisms of the political manoeuvring then taking place on the revolutionary left.

Pitt's thesis is not new, but is a reformulation of the orthodox Communist Party line that was first developed by Willie Gallacher and Tom Bell. It acknowledges Maclean's courageous rôle during the First World War, which resulted in his imprisonment, and attributes Maclean's estrangement from the developing CPGB in 1920-21 to the consequences of that imprisonment. These consequences are alleged to have undermined Maclean's mental state to the point where paranoia profoundly affected his political judgement. Pitt cites various examples of Maclean's paranoid behaviour, which involved a sense of being followed and watched by government agents, and his suspicious and startling criticisms of important figures within the revolutionary left, most notably Francis Meynell (the editor of *The Communist*), Colonel L'Estrange Malone and Theodore Rothstein, the long-time SDF member and the principal representative of the Bolsheviks in the processes leading to the formation of the CPGB. In addition, Maclean denounced Gallacher for lacking a real basis in Marxism, and for having betrayed him personally by asserting his mental instability in a letter to the SLP.

For Pitt, all this leads to the conclusion that Maclean was 'mad' at the crucial time when the CPGB was formed, and Maclean's criticism of the party and its leaders can thus be safely rejected as the product of an unbalanced mind. Pitt's purpose is not to denigrate Maclean, but 'to set the record straight', and counter those who would use Maclean's criticisms to argue 'that the Bolshevik Revolution and all its consequences were rotten from the start'. This is presumably aimed at someone like Walter Kendall, who has long held that the creation of the CPGB was the product of 'external' pressures, rather than a 'natural' development of the British revolutionary left. Moreover, Kendall sees this forced development as representing an 'historic error on the grand scale' because it effectively cut off the potentially rich tributaries of the left from the mainstream labour movement, leaving the left as a backwater.

It is not necessary to go all the way with Kendall to recognise that Maclean's reservations about the revolutionary potentiality of the CPGB and its early leaders were not so absurd that they could not be shared by others who were no 'madder' than he. Indeed, it is worth noting that of those British left wing organisations specifically invited to the founding of the Third International, almost none lost its identity within the CPGB, but rather opposed its particular configuration. The CPGB did, however, offer prominent positions to Malone, a member of parliament with a history of virulent anti-Socialist outbursts, and Francis Meynell, who, along with Malone, was identified by Maclean as having no background in Marxism. Meynell himself subsequently observed that no revolutionary theoretical journal could have had an editor less theoretically versed in Marxism than he. Yet he was installed by Arthur MacManus.

It is difficult to judge Maclean's 'madness' with any real confidence at this distance in time, and without a medical background. Certainly, as Pitt recognises, people like Maclean on the left were conventionally defined as 'mad' for holding the beliefs they did. But Pitt goes further, and accepts the evidence that Maclean was paranoid in the proper medical sense. For my part, the best evidence is that of Doctor Garrey, the Medical Officer at Peterhead Prison who refused to certify Maclean insane despite pressure from his superiors. The specific evidence of 'madness' related to Maclean's allegations that his prison food was drugged. Since this was patently untrue, the medical practitioners saw this as clear evidence of mental instability. However, Garrey, who had the most contact with Maclean, refused to accept this diagnosis. Pitt's suggestion that Garrey's refusal to certify Maclean insane can be questioned on the grounds that having organised his forced feeding, he was anxious to deny that Maclean suffered ill effects that could have been attributed to his actions, is not a credible explanation. If Garrey had any concerns about how his treatment of Maclean might have been interpreted, the simplest course was to declare him insane. Maclean's criticisms of leading Communists may well have been extreme. He may well have cited the wrong individuals as government agents operating at the highest level of the CPGB (ironically, the support for such a misconception comes from one such agent referred to in the pamphlet). However, there is no short cut to considering the essential criticisms made about the events surrounding the formation of the CPGB, nor about the inherent failings of that party.

Maclean was not an isolated revolutionary 'non-joiner', but was one amongst many. As Raymond Challinor has observed, the CPGB was formed as the result of a series of mergers, and, perhaps uniquely, the product of these mergers was less than the sum of those involved at the outset. Many of those who chose to remain outside did so because they believed it to be dominated by reformists and 'Johnny-come-latelys' to the revolutionary cause. Whilst some of these oppositionists can be seen as ultra-leftists or 'infantile leftists' in the Leninist sense, this is not a charge that could easily be laid at Maclean's door. Maclean was not an ultra-leftist, and right up to the last few months of his life, when worn out, ill and isolated, he lost his sense of political reality, his letters and indeed his *Open Letter to Lenin* show him to be more realistic and balanced in his assessment of the political situation in Britain than the leadership of the CPGB. If you leave aside the vitriolic attacks launched on Maclean by members of the CPGB in language familiarly applied by Trotskyists and Stalinists to Socialists of all hues, then Maclean's criticisms of the emerging and infant CPGB have a powerful ring to them. In taking them seriously, it is not inevitable that you are forced to repudiate the October Revolution, or even the need for a Communist Party in Britain, but maybe to ask whether the CPGB that was formed in 1921 was the only such party available, and if there were not better options.

Copies of this pamphlet can be obtained from the author at 92 Castlehaven Road, London NW1 8PL.

John McHugh

Israel Shahak, *Jewish History, Jewish Religion*, Pluto Press, London, 1994, pp127, £11.99

APART FROM providing a useful supplement to Enzo Traverso's work reviewed in our last issue, few books explain quite so much modern history as this one does. Why is a state professing a universalist religion so ruthlessly racist with its Palestinian victims? Why are more of its governmental crises 'caused by religious reasons, often trivial, than by any other cause' (p98)?

Why do so many studious-looking gentlemen dressed in mid-nineteenth century clothing turn out to stone archaeologists digging up bronze age burials? Why does a people of such small numbers once believed to inhabit an area no larger than Wales harbour such far-reaching plans of conquest? How did the ideals of the later Old Testament prophets give rise to such a frightening and frightful obscurantism, backed by so predatory a state?

Shahak's credentials for his bold exposure of the racist corruption of Israeli politics are impeccable. A retired professor of chemistry who had suffered in Belsen and served in the Israeli army, he turned to civil rights activity when he found to his disgust that rabbis who supported a Jew who refused to call an ambulance for a gentile on the sabbath were acting in accordance with Talmudic law (p1). Although he makes no secret of his 'opposition to Marxism, both in philosophy and as a social theory' (p49), much that is vital to a revolutionary understanding of world politics is crammed into his pages, with a staggering display of erudition, and not a word of it is wasted.

He makes it plain that not all the victims of anti-Semitism have been Jews, for racism breeds racism. Some horrible examples are given of Talmudic hostility to other peoples and creeds, even monotheistic ones (pp20-7, 74-98), and it is with some sadness that we learn that this spirit even infected Maimonides (pp viii, 24-6,80). But there is far more to the book than this.

Its analysis of the main phases in the history of Judaism (pp50-7) places them firmly within the development of the social conditions of its existence, a dimension that is so signally lacking in Traverso's book. He explains our inability to grasp the real mechanism that drives Israel forward today from the fact that whilst knowledge of the Old Testament is widely disseminated, modern Judaism's inheritance from Kabbala and Talmud is almost unknown to outsiders, and it is this fusion of traditional lore that exercises such a fatal influence upon the state (pp36ff). His description of Kabbalism in chapter three as a 'decay of monotheism', and of Jewish society in eighteenth century Germany as 'burning of books, persecution of writers, disputes about the magic powers of amulets' (p16) might be upsetting to many, but it is backed by numerous and telling examples. By this time, he concludes, classical Judaism had degenerated into 'a tribal collection of empty religious and magic superstitions' (p47).

Nowhere was this worse than in Poland, 'the most superstitious and fanatic of all Jewish communities' (p63). It was this population from Eastern Europe, and particularly from Poland and the Ukraine, that set the tone for the politics of modern Israel. It was, as he points out, a community totally without a peasantry and with little sympathy for its predicament, since the rôle of the Jews as bailiffs and tax gatherers on behalf of the nobility in these lands had long exposed it to peasant uprisings and attendant pogroms (pp52-5, 61-6, 72-4, etc). Now the inhabitants of the land whom they displaced were also predominantly peasants. 'Insane as it sounds', he concludes, 'it is nevertheless plain upon close examination of the real motives of the Zionists, that one of the most deep-seated ideological sources of the Zionist establishment's persistent hostility towards the Palestinians is the fact that they are identified in the minds of many East European Jews with the rebellious East European peasants who participated in the Chmielnicki uprising and in similar revolts.' (p72)

And the position of Israel in global politics also condemns it to 'a rôle not unlike that of the Jews in pre-1795 Poland: that of a bailiff to the imperial oppressor' (p73). Only by unlocking this culture can we understand the incredible frenzy in some circles whenever the Israeli government comes to any sort of agreement, however advantageous, with its neighbours. For some rabbinical authorities interpret the poetical flourishes of the Old Testament so as to include within the borders of Biblical Israel all Egypt as far as Cairo, and 'Iraq, Lebanon, Syria, Jordan, etc, as far as the Euphrates (p9), whilst 'in all Talmudic authorities the Land of Israel includes Cyprus' (p90).

I could go further, but to bring out everything of value from this book would be to write a review as long as the book itself. Far better read it instead, and encourage all your friends to read it as well!
Al Richardson

Andres Romero, *Después Del Stalinismo: Los Estados Burocráticos y la revolución socialista*, Antídoto, Buenos Aires, 1995, pp251

Ernesto González (Coordinador), *El trotskismo obrero e internacionalista en la Argentina. Tomo I. Del GOM a la federación Banners Del PORN (1943-1955)*, Antídoto, Buenos Aires, 1995, pp274

THE MORENO tendency produces considerable puzzlement outside Argentina. In the mid-1980s Moreno's party, the MAS, was probably the largest group in the world claiming to be Trotskyist. Nahuel Moreno (Hugo Bressano, 1924-87) was obviously a figure of enormous dynamism, whose ability to build and sustain a group for more than 40 years was an enormous achievement. Yet we have, until now, lacked a detailed history of the tendency, and have had to rely on polemical accounts from political opponents. These two recent books by leading members of the MAS are, therefore, to be welcomed.

El trotskismo obrero..., produced by a committee led by Ernesto González, shows how seriously the MAS takes its history. This first volume covers the period from 1943 until 1955, before the tendency had reached the strength which it was later to achieve. The first two chapters give an account of Trotskyism in Argentina until 1943, which agrees with that in *Revolutionary History*, Volume 2, no 2. It then goes on to describe the beginnings of the MAS tendency when Moreno, a precocious boy who was giving lectures on philosophy when he was 15, founded his own group, the Grupo Obrero Marxista, whilst still in his teens, after breaking with Liborio Justo. Moreno had by 1943 come to the conclusion that the failures of Argentinean Trotskyism stemmed from its poor social composition. Therefore, he and his few young followers moved to activity in working class areas, recruiting some workers of Polish and Jewish origin in the textile industry. The book's access to oral history sources is impressive here. How many groups can call on the memories of workers who were active 50 years earlier? The rich detail of the devoted work in building up trade union activity would be the envy of any university social history department.

The beginnings of the GOM coincided, of course, with the rise of Perón. Here, the book is less informative. In particular, the account of the massive workers' demonstration and strike of 17 October 1945, which freed Perón from prison and brought him to power, is very unsatisfactory. On 17 October, the key date in Argentinean working class history, the Communist and Socialist Parties supported the oligarchy and opposed the strike, thereby condemning themselves to impotence. So did the GOM, although that is not made clear in *El Trotskismo obrero...* Nor is it in González's earlier work, *Qué fue y qué es el Peronismo* (1974). Once in power, Perón encouraged trade unionism, whilst trying to keep it under his own control, and forced through the massive welfare programme which won him the support of most workers. The unions were not merely Labour Fronts on the Fascist model, but they were subject to all kinds of bureaucratic interference. The GOM sensibly worked within these union structures, trying to form broad alliances against the sometimes violent opposition of the Peronist bureaucracy. Much of the latter part of the book is an excessively detailed account of these struggles, to the detriment of any overall analysis, so that it becomes the description of a trade union faction rather than of a political party. In 1948 the GOM became the Partido Obrero Revolucionario. In 1954 it took part in the elections as part of the Partido Socialista de la Revolución Nacional, which was legally entitled to stand. The book describes this tactic as 'entrism', but, in fact, it seems to have been a merger with a splinter of the old Socialist Party. Once again, political analysis is buried under lengthy, if vivid, descriptions of electoral meetings. The PSR opposed the military coup in 1955 which toppled Perón and restored the traditional oligarchy, but this gets less analysis than a description of the crimes of Pabloite revisionism — of which there can never be too much.

The book tells us something about Morenoism, both in its contents and what is left out. Clearly, Moreno directed his efforts in Argentina at the working class, not at rebel officers or an imaginary peasantry. The steady work over years brought results, even if the 'Trotskyism' was, in Moreno's own words, 'barbaric'. In terms of intellectual baggage, Moreno travelled light, and this seems often to have been an advantage. There is much mention of self-criticism, but it is expressed in such general terms as to be uninformative. While Moreno's attitude to non-working class forces seems to be so incompatible with Marxism that opponents have seen him as a chameleon, prepared to adapt to any environment, his working class supporters seem to have accepted his sometimes bizarre alliances. What did they think of their party's turns and twists? The extremely detailed personal reminiscences are of no help here. It is to be hoped that as well as producing further volumes, the MAS will open its archives to independent scholars who might be able to produce the synthesis which has eluded the present authors. Until that happens we are dependent on the works of Moreno's political opponents. There have been detailed criticisms from Workers Power, the Spartacist League and (in Spanish) Politica Obrera. These describe how Moreno's group survived the collapse of Maoism and Castroism, despite having embraced them.

Después Del Stalinismo is a very different book, and marks the formal abandonment by the MAS of Trotskyist positions on the Soviet Union and similar societies. As the subtitle suggests, *Después...* abandons the Trotskyist categories of 'workers' states' in favour of 'bureaucratic states'. (Are not states bureaucratic by definition?) As the Morenoite attitude to the Soviet Union was always hostile, that would seem to be logical, but the change is proclaimed, not argued. Curiously, Romero hardly refers to the extensive polemics within the revolutionary movement on the class nature of those societies. He gives a fairly standard account of the degeneration of the Soviet Union. He describes the evolution of the Soviet Union in recent decades as making the 'degenerated workers' state' label inappropriate, but insists that it was never really suitable. LD Trotsky is treated respectfully, but there is no examination of the ideas of those such as Shachtman which generally form the basis for opposed views of the Soviet Union. Frankly, this is poor stuff.

There are lengthy accounts of how the technology of the Soviet Union lagged behind that of the capitalist world. Most of this is generally accepted. *Después...* has a stylistic resemblance to *El Trotskismo...* in that both are padded with enormously long quotes. Much of Romero's book consists of extracts from academic works and from the bourgeois press, with his own text almost buried in them. If there is a Morenoite style, it is one in which prolixity and silence are the best forms of concealment. Having struggled through the theoretical preliminaries, we get to the practical purpose of the book: extricating the MAS from Moreno's prediction that world capitalism was about to collapse, and differentiating the MAS from other products on the political market. Romero claims that Ted Grant's followers in Russia tag along behind the 'red-black' alliance, the United Secretariat joins Gysi's Social Democratic Party, and the Lambertists everywhere cuddle up to right wing trade union leaders. The Spartacist tendency, amongst others, is criticised for describing the overthrow of Stalinism as a counter-revolution. On the contrary, it was an immense step forward.

These two books describing the early and late stages of Morenoism will leave most non-Argentineans puzzled. A reading of Moreno's own writings ought to cast light on the tendency. However, Nahuel Moreno's *El Partido y la Revolución*, a polemic with Ernest Mandel written in 1973, does little to help our understanding. Usually, when Marxists disagree, they understand what their opponents are saying, but it is difficult to follow Moreno's arguments. Part of the problem may be Moreno's style of writing, influenced perhaps by his early philosophical inclinations, where criteria of logic, evidence and proof are usually absent.

So, was Morenoism a purely Argentinean phenomenon which cannot be understood outside that cultural context? An argument against it is that in the 1980s, Moreno formed an International (the LIT) which had branches in other Latin American countries, and even in Europe. Opponents seem to suggest that Morenoism is the political equivalent of glue sniffing, and that it is a waste of time to seek coherence where none exists. How, then, can his achievement in maintaining a working class group, often working under severe repression, be explained? He obviously inspired great devotion. His pragmatism allowed him to drop one strategy and pick up another, leaving lesser men to bother about justifications. Critics point to his inconsistency in supporting armed struggle throughout Latin America but not in the Argentine, but his followers owe him their lives for refusing to launch them into a suicidal guerrilla war in the 1970s. By contrast, the followers of Ernest Mandel, an outstanding Marxist theoretician, were massacred. Morenoism peaked in the mid-1980s, when he predicted the fall of capitalism and an Argentinean revolution which would lead the rest of the world. Given the fantastic nature of that world-view, dying in January 1987 saved him a lot of embarrassment. Without him, his movement began to fall apart, although there are three substantial groups claiming his inheritance. Like other great men he seems not to have found adequate successors. Perhaps the description of him by Peter Fryer in *Crocodiles in the Streets* as a jovial figure who took his place at the end of the queue in the canteen at party headquarters, provides a clue to the affection his followers felt for him.

John Sullivan

Conor Kostick, *Revolution in Ireland: Popular Militancy 1917-1923*, Pluto Press, London, 1996, pp239

ALL SERIOUS students of Irish history in the present century, all those British Socialists who wish to further the cause of the working class in our sister isle as well as over here, and all those wishing to understand the labour movement in Europe and its course over the last hundred years or so cannot afford to pass over this book. Packed with vital information available in many other separate publications, but never, as far as I know, assembled in quite such a masterly way in a work of less than 250 pages, it must surely deserve pride of place as the authoritative Socialist survey of this turbulent period in Ireland's history.

This review cannot possibly do justice to the wealth of detail conveyed in the work. Instead I will try to trace some dominant themes concerning the achievement of Irish independence, the part played by the successors of Larkin and Connolly as leaders of Irish Labour, the partition of the country, and, in general, the policy and tactics necessary to advance the cause of labour in Ireland in those years.

The central thesis advanced by Kostick concerning the War of Independence begins from a consideration of the military balance of forces in 1921:

'The usual argument given for the reason why, despite their determination to crush the rebellion, the British government were forced to the negotiating table is that they had been worn down by the War of Independence waged by the Irish Republican Army. However an examination of the figures challenges that assumption. According to both unionist and republican figures, approximately 18 policemen were killed by the IRA in 1919. In 1920 around 176 policemen were killed (251 wounded); additionally 54 soldiers were killed (118 wounded). Foster's figures for the whole War of Independence are that 400 policemen and 160 soldiers were killed. This represents about one-fortieth of the police and well under one per cent of the troops in Ireland. If military considerations were the only ones, then the British were far from experiencing difficulties. The IRA numbered between 14 000 and 15 000 volunteers; however, due to shortage of equipment and ammunition only around 5000 were active. Collins later said that "in the whole of Ireland there were not more than 3000 fighting men".' (pp94-5)

Elsewhere in the book Kostick gives figures for the strength of the British Army and police: 'By the end of 1921 the total number of police was 17 000. The number of troops jumped by a third in June of that year, to over 80 000, with the cabinet discussing the possibility for a "decisive and systematic conquest of the country".' (p92)

Clearly on the basis of these figures, other factors were at work pushing the British authorities towards some kind of negotiated settlement. Kostick argues that these were 'the structures of a new Irish state and, far more importantly, the activities of the Irish working class' (p98).

It became more and more difficult for the British to provide effective policing in rural areas, and the local courts began to be replaced de facto in many cases by republican ones. The rural poor began to seize land from the richer farmers, whilst the ITUC began organising agricultural workers. Against these threats wealthy farmers began to turn to the underground republican administration for help. But still more serious was the threat posed by the independent action of Irish workers (see Chapter 6, pp108-38).

Strikes and occupations mushroomed in the period 1918-23. Red flags appeared on numerous occasions, and occupations and other expressions of workers' control occurred, called 'soviets' in obvious response to the momentous events of 1917 in Russia. In April 1919 Limerick City was declared to be under military control by the British authorities; Limerick's workers, already angry at the treatment of republican prisoners in the area, answered with a general strike, and effectively ran the city for a fortnight. A year later, in April 1920, a number of republican prisoners in Mountjoy jail in Dublin went on hunger strike, and large crowds of people began gathering outside the prison. The ITUC, one of whose leaders, William O'Brien, had already been arrested and deported to England on trumped-up charges, issued a call for a general strike, which soon had the authorities reeling as locality after locality passed under the effective control of the strikers. The strike forced the release of republican prisoners in substantial numbers. Kostick argues:

'The strike revealed that Irish workers had the power to defeat British rule. The two days of general strike, threatening to go on even further, did more to undermine British authority than months of armed struggle. Sinn Fein politicians were sidelined by the events, not wanting to be seen to oppose a popular strike against British injustice, but at the same time recognising that the working class' independent activity was an implicit challenge for the leadership of the national movement.' (pp127-8)

Finally, in May 1920 the railway workers decided to block the transport of military cargoes, including bodies of unarmed military in excess of 20 men, an action which lasted until almost the end of the year. Kostick argues — and his conclusions seem plausible given the parallel militancy of British workers up to April 1921 — that this working class resistance was an important factor in persuading the British government to abandon its plans for an all-out onslaught on the Irish rebels:

'Looking back over the period... it is clear that the British government were prepared to sanction an attempt at full military repression of Ireland. That they failed and started to look for a way out from the middle of 1920 was more a response to working class activity than any other force in Irish political life.' (p137)

This working class activity was not only vitally important in bringing the Irish Free State into existence, but also revealed that Irish Labour, given the necessary leadership, could have made a bid for the establishment of a Workers' Republic as desired by James Connolly. Unfortunately the Labour leaders who succeeded Connolly — William O'Brien, Thomas Johnson, Cathal O'Shannon and others — whilst paying lip-service to the goal of a Workers' Republic, in practice lined up behind the apostles of national capital, aspiring to play the rôle of 'loyal opposition' after the manner of our own Ramsay MacDonald, Philip Snowden and similar individuals at the head of the Labour Party in Britain. The treacherous rôle of such people in a revolutionary situation is well documented by Kostick. Time after time, the leadership agreed to issue calls to action, only to seize on every excuse for calling it off as soon as ever they felt they had to and could do so. This was particularly evident in connection with the general strike in support of the republican prisoners in Mountjoy. In vain did Jim Larkin, stranded in America for the duration, urge independent action by the working class leaders, exclaiming: 'I wish O'Brien and the others would declare themselves. Are they all turned Sinn Fein?' (p148)

Such arguments, however, carried no weight with the Irish Labour leaders. As Kostick observes: 'To have followed Larkin's perspective would have been to endanger their own positions in a Socialist revolution. The Labour officials had found a home in their relationship with the nationalists.' (p149) Their 'neutrality' over the 1921 Treaty (in fact it was an undercover pro-Treaty stance) deprived Irish workers of an effective political lead in the difficult situation following the split in Sinn Fein which led to the Civil War of 1922-23. According to Kostick, they even tried to block discussion of the question in trade union branches (p172). In April 1922 they issued a call for a general strike against 'militarism', which duly took place, but it failed to persuade the anti-Treaty republicans to concentrate on political rather than military opposition to the Treaty, and it did not really strengthen the workers either. The book contains abundant additional evidence of the inadequacies of the O'Brien-Johnson leadership, a leadership often denounced by Irish left wingers, yet not often so thoroughly and so convincingly.

Kostick brings out yet another pernicious effect of these misguided policies: their effect on the situation in the North where the Six County regime was attempting to consolidate itself. Here the damage started already in 1918 with the refusal of the Irish Labour Party to stand candidates in the election, the decisive election which resulted in the return of 73 Sinn Fein candidates, six for the Irish Parliamentary Party and 26 Unionists in a total of 105 Irish seats (p46; see Dorothy MacArdle, *The Irish Republic*, p247). The result can only have served to reinforce a laager mentality, a sense of dangerous isolation in Ireland as a whole, felt by large numbers of Protestant workers in Ulster. Yet other political influences were at work in the North, as is shown by the Belfast engineering strike of 1919, to which Kostick devotes a most valuable section of the book (Chapter 3, pp51-69). However, here again the post-Connolly leadership missed the bus:

'The passivity of the Southern leadership was noticeable — they made no protest at the movement of troops to Belfast, nor at their use in breaking the strike. This failure to act, even in a modest way, must have contributed to the feeling that Northern workers and Southern workers had different interests.' (p64)

This made things worse for Socialists in the North, where the recession of 1920-21 led to increasing unemployment and short-time working, events that provided the excuse for a savage blow against the labour movement in Belfast — the shipyard expulsions and the driving of Catholics from other workplaces which occurred in July 1920. According to a contemporary estimate, 12 000 people, a quarter of whom were Protestant trade unionists, lost their jobs (cited, p155). This, said the perpetrators, was the answer to unemployment; however, unemployment persisted and actually rose.

The leaders of Irish Labour failed to learn the lessons of such events. Kostick quotes Thomas Johnson in 1921 as saying that the workers of Ireland were willing to sacrifice their own aspirations for political power if that would further the national cause. His comment is apposite and devastating: 'Partition was inevitable so long as the movement of the Southern workers confined itself to a nationalist agenda.' (p151)

The book's main virtue is the way it hints at the possibilities existing in the period whereby Irish Labour could have increased its influence by standing openly and fighting resolutely for a Workers' Republic of all 32 Irish counties. This is illustrated by a statement issued by Galway Trades Council in April 1920, one of those statements of ringing defiance so characteristic of the Irish revolutionary tradition:

'Well, the Workers' Council is formed in Galway, and it's here to stay. God speed the day when such Councils shall be established all over Erin and the world, control the natural resources of the country, the means of production and distribution, run them as the worker knows how to run them, for the good and welfare of the whole and not for the profits of a few bloated parasites. Up Galway!' (cited, p122)

Such a policy would have involved a campaign in opposition to the 1921 Treaty and for a Workers' Republic on both sides of the border, with no illusions in the anti-Treaty republican faction such as those exhibited by the fledgling Irish Communist Party, or participation in a futile armed struggle for a capitalist rather than a Socialist republic, as displayed in the Civil War. The call for a Workers' Republic retains its relevance today, as Kostick notes in the conclusion to his absorbing study.

Chris Gray

Oleg Dubrovskii with Simon Pirani, *Fighting Back in Ukraine*, Index Books, London, 1996, pp67, £2.00

THIS BOOKLET is based around a series of tape-recorded interviews with Oleg Dubrovskii conducted by Simon Pirani in September 1995. Although much of the material it discusses falls outside the time-span with which *Revolutionary History* concerns itself, Dubrovskii's account of political developments within the Stalinist regimes and the Former Soviet Union illustrates the power of Trotskyist ideas and analyses to a remarkable degree, and consequently it is not inappropriate to review it here.

Dubrovskii is a prime example of a militant worker whose experience spans the period from the Stalinist regime to Yeltsin's attempts to introduce market capitalism, and the disintegration of the Soviet Union. As such, he is of great interest to us in attempting to understand the present state of the workers' movement in the countries of the FSU.

Dubrovskii's political learning began when he studied the reports of the congresses of the CPSU, as part of his preparation for joining the party, during military service in the early 1970s. Here he read the original speeches of Trotsky and the Left Opposition, and, at later congresses, of Bukharin and the Right Opposition. This is very interesting; he became aware of revolutionary positions from material available during the Brezhnev regime. We can reasonably ask ourselves then, why does Dubrovskii seem to be so unusual in responding to it?

By 1975 he had concluded that the Workers Opposition of 1920 best represented the interests of the workers, and he arrived at a position that trade unionism was the form through which the workers could best organise. The 'party', as manifest in the CPSU, was something he rejected.

In the early 1980s Dubrovskii adopted Solidarnosc as the model form of workers' organisation against Stalinism, and moved from the Workers Opposition to a more clearly defined Anarcho-Syndicalist programme. His agitation in the major factories of Dnipropetrovsk (for example, against unpaid

Sunday working) through the Andropov period attracted the attention of the KGB, but he was not arrested.

After 1987 it was possible to state open political disagreements with the regime, and Dubrovskii was able to force his programme onto the agenda of the factory political education class. He was elected to the union committee against party candidates.

After a series of attempts to establish independent trade unions, he and his Anarcho-Syndicalist comrades concluded that the key strategy was to work in the official unions, to transform them from tools of management into being weapons of working class struggle. Whatever the logic of this shift, it put Dubrovskii in a position where he was elected Chairman of a strike committee to protest against price increases after 1991 and the independence of Ukraine.

By 1994 Dubrovskii shifted to a Trotskyist position, after being able to read *The Revolution Betrayed* and other books previously unavailable in Russia.

The final sections of the booklet describe another wave of strikes against the failure of the employers to pay wages. In the course of this struggle, new movements to democratise the unions and other workers' organisations began to develop. Dubrovskii concludes with a discussion of the possibilities of a new working class party emerging from such movements, and from the wider circulation of Trotskyist ideas amongst the workers. He sees educating workers in the history of the Russian Revolution as a key part in this process, making clear what were its ideas, and showing how they were perverted by the Stalinists.

Simon Pirani is a man who takes his internationalism seriously, and conducts it with practical determination. He has previously contributed substantially to our knowledge of the revolutionary movement in Vietnam (through his own publications and his preparation of Ngo Van's book). His reports from Russia and the FSU, especially from the mining districts, have provided important source material, and this booklet adds more.

JJ Plant

Hal Draper, *The Adventures of the Communist Manifesto*, Center for Socialist History, Berkeley, 1994, pp344

THIS BOOK is a rare commodity; it is not only highly useful and authoritative, but lively and entertaining as well. It provides a new translation, publishing history (1848-1895), and textual analysis of Marx and Engels' *Communist Manifesto*, although as Draper makes very clear, 'the probability is great that the actual text of the *Manifesto* was solely from Marx's pen, however much weight we give to Engels' contributions preliminary to the final draft'. In this he does not seem to be going quite as far as David McLennan in his well-known biography of Marx, which states categorically that 'the actual writing of the *Communist Manifesto* was done exclusively by Marx'.

Prior to Draper's book there was only one work which explored the detailed history of the *Manifesto* as a publication — Bert Andreas' *Le Manifest*

Communiste de Marx et Engels. Histoire et Bibliographie 1848-1918 (Milan, 1963). It is bibliographical, and not in narrative form, but Draper pays it considerable tribute, clearly stating where he differs in his conclusions. 'The *Adventures*', he states, 'has been mined and quarried from its pages.'

In later years, despite many requests, Marx refused to rewrite the original *Manifesto*, as he termed it 'an historic document' that he did not feel he had the right to change. This was not because he held that it was true for all time, but that it related to a particular set of historical circumstances, and that in crucial ways his thought had progressed, although he continued to endorse its principles. This was clearly shown in the first of seven prefaces that Marx and Engels produced (although only two were signed by Marx) for Liebknecht's 'fake' German edition of 1872: 'No matter how much conditions have changed in the last 25 years, the general principles set forth in this *Manifesto* still on the whole retain their complete correctness today... The practical application of these principles — so the *Manifesto* itself states — will depend everywhere and every time on the historically existing state of affairs.' Incidentally, the edition was 'fake' because, although Marx and Engels used its papers to send to other countries for translations, it was never distributed in Germany itself. The story of how this happened is just one of the many 'adventures' of the *Manifesto* well chronicled by Draper in a very useful first section.

That Marx's approach is essentially undogmatic comes through clearly. It was not published as the *Manifesto of the Communist League*, the organisation that commissioned it, but with its original title of *Manifesto of the Communist Party*, although no Communist Party existed at the time. As Draper states: 'The decision to issue a manifesto not of the League itself but of the Communist point of view in general, reflected an attitude looking away from sectarianism... The title of the *Manifesto* was an advance notice of the de-emphasis of the sect... So when the manifesto was to be written, it was not a manifesto of the Communist League, but a manifesto presented on behalf of a broader aspect of politics than was contained in the organisational walls of any league.' This was completely in line with Marx's view that 'the Communists do not form a separate party opposed to other working class parties', a point that is always worth repeating. (It was the German edition mentioned above which first used *Communist Manifesto* as the official title, as ideas were erroneously perceived as less likely to be banned at the time than a document purporting to come from a political party.)

Most of Draper's book is taken up by parallel texts of three English translations of the *Manifesto* — the original translation by Helen Macfarlane of 1850 (starting with the infamous 'a frightful hobgoblin stalks throughout Europe'), the Authorised English Translation of 1888, and a New English Version, as well as the 1848 original in German. There are copious annotations bringing out significant differences which are often extremely illuminating. Like the original German version, the 1888 translation by Moore stands by right as an 'historic document', as it was the only one in which Engels had complete involvement, and its particular phrases have longed seeped into Socialist consciousness in the English-speaking world. In no way does the new translation given in Draper's book seek to claim superiority — its aim is to be supplementary, often setting down 'another alternative — not necessarily because it is better, let alone more "correct" — but simply to show the differences'.

It is instructive to see some of the assumptions behind the 1888 translation. Draper states that Engels' expectation that the ideas of the *Manifesto* could penetrate Anglo-Saxon skulls only 'with difficulty' was going to have an important effect on the formulations in the English translation. Marx and Engels both believed that German workers were more amenable to revolutionary theory than those in America or England, and for them 'plainer fare' was needed. Thus 'forms of consciousness' is usually rendered as 'general ideas' for the simpler English mind, while 'relations of production' is regularly translated as 'conditions of production', which is not the same at all. At best, it becomes 'social forms springing from...', etc.

Draper notes that a line-by-line comparison with the original German text produces an interesting characteristic. The Authorised English Translation is 'either extremely literal or else boldly revisionary'. There are few sentences that are in the grey area between the two. He deduces from this that Moore provided the literal bits, and that the revisions were made by Engels, who ultimately controlled the translation. He rightly concludes that Moore would not have made such revisions on his own initiative. A most valuable part of the book is the complete list and explanation of the changes. Draper does not attempt an interpretation of Marx's ideas — this is not the purpose of the book. His explanations, however, inevitably do throw light on Marx's ideas, and are of more value than many an explicit interpretation of the *Manifesto*.

There have been other English translations. In 1928 Eden and Cedar Paul produced one for Martin Lawrence (later Lawrence and Wishart), which Draper ironically comments had higher literacy qualities than the Authorised English Translation of 1888. However, translating it on the same basis as a novel makes the whole work an extremely risky base from which to draw conclusions about Marx's ideas.

Lawrence and Wishart followed this up with another edition around 1935 which purported to be the Authorised English Translation, but with key unacknowledged changes (Draper notes at least 56). This was perhaps the largest ever mass production of the work; there were hundreds and thousands of copies. Some changes are stylistic, others, such as the change of the Authorised English Translation's 'win the battle of democracy' to 'establish democracy' were clearly done to support the Communist Party's Popular Front politics of the time, although Draper does draw back from making this obvious point. Indeed, this is the joy of the book; there is so much raw material from which readers can draw their own conclusions. There is later a very interesting discussion of how best to translate the 'winning of democracy' from the German original, concluding that Marx was in many ways hedging his bets with the expression, and that the Authorised English Translation version had at least the merit of being as 'virtually as cryptic' as the original German. The ambiguity towards the concept of representative institutions of parliamentary democracy within the Marxist movement has continued ever since.

At a time when capitalism is finally reaching world-wide domination with the consequent widening gap between rich and poor predicted by Marx evident even in the most advanced industrial societies, the Marxist analysis of capitalism becomes increasingly relevant. In such a context it is important to go back to the classic texts of Marx and Engels unencumbered by later, and often spurious, interpretations. Thus, a book like Draper's is to be very much welcomed. It is very much a labour of love, but one that is not, as so often, clouded by a preconceived ideological position.

One small quibble: Draper points out that it was impossible to use a grammar or spell checker on the Macfarlane translation, in order to preserve the original misprints and slips. However, it would perhaps have been a good idea to use one on other parts of the text where no such constraints apply. For example, on page 43 we finds two strangers called 'EngelsLafargue' and 'Bakounine', and on page 44 an odd sort of social institution called a 'Commmune' appears.

Chris Matthews

Jesús Hernández, *How the NKVD Framed the POUM*, Pitt Productions, London, 1995, pp27, £2.00

THIS PAMPHLET, which consists of excerpts translated from the memoirs of Jesús Hernández, is an insiders' view of the repression of the POUM by the Stalinist secret services during the Spanish Civil War, and, as such, will be welcomed by all those concerned with the fate of the Spanish Revolution. The autobiography of Hernández has frequently been impugned; he was a founding member of the Spanish Communist Party in 1921, joining the Politbureau in the early 1930s, before serving as a loyal apparachik during the Civil War. Having proven his Stalinist credentials, in the immediate postwar years in exile, Hernández found his desire to become party leader thwarted by the old guard, and, as a frustrated *arribista*, embraced Titoism. Although Hernández wrote with the characteristic fury of a scorned bureaucrat, his account of the repression of the POUM, and in particular his version of the brutal interrogation, torture and eventual murder of former party leader and ex-Trotskyist Andreu Nin at the hands of the NKVD, has since been confirmed both by the memoirs of other Spanish Republican leaders, and by the most recent research conducted in the Moscow archives. This pamphlet, therefore, is a corrective to the hypocrisy of those apologists who, as Bob Pitt indicates in his valuable introduction, continue to obscure the nature of Stalinist terror by talking of Nin's 'disappearance', which is little more than a euphemism for the scurrilous and groundless accusation that Nin fled Spain for exile in Fascist territory. Moreover, despite the leitmotifs of Comintern policy in Spain — the public celebration of unity and petit-bourgeois Republican legality — the memoirs of Hernández highlight the willingness of the Stalinists to spread disunity amongst the anti-Francoist forces, and to perpetrate bloody terror against their rivals on the left.

But it must also be recognised that Hernández's testimony cannot be accepted uncritically. Firstly, it is extremely likely that Hernández exaggerated his opposition to the repression of the POUM. If he initially resisted the NKVD to the extent he claims, it is difficult to explain his recklessness in leaving for the USSR at the end of the Civil War, let alone how he survived his spell there. Secondly, his tendency to blame counter-revolutionary terror in Spain almost exclusively on the malign personality of Stalin — a view which received new currency in the 1970s following Santiago Carrillo's conversion to Eurocommunism — ignores the manifest guilt of both the Spanish and Catalan Communist Parties in the repression of the POUM. Indeed, at times, the testimony of Hernández attenuates the fierce invective directed at Poumistas by local Stalinists to such a degree that the reader is left with the impression that fraternal relations existed between the official and dissident Communist Parties; in fact it was the unrelenting and virulent political campaign against the POUM in the Spanish and Catalan Stalinist press which was instrumental in creating the climate in which the physical and political elimination of Spanish anti-Stalinists could take place. Nevertheless, this does not detract from the unquestionable value of a pamphlet that reveals how the international isolation of the Republic and its dependency upon Soviet supplies facilitated the exportation of NKVD police terror to Spain and the murder of Nin.

The scale of Stalinist power in Spain during the Civil War is emphasised if we look at an earlier attempt to frame Nin. I am referring here to a little known episode in 1933, when Nin, then a leader of the Trotskyist Izquierda Comunista de España, was detained by the Republican police in Barcelona and charged with possession of explosives. At the time, Nin was highly respected in Catalan cultural circles for his translations of Russian classics, including the major works of Dostoevsky and Tolstoy. His arrest was, therefore, greeted with widespread consternation and indignation, and prompted a spirited defence campaign, which led to his release in a matter of days. What is noticeable here was the support lent to Nin by leading Catalan intellectuals and academics, not to mention some petit-bourgeois Republican politicians who, though as anti-Communist as the unreconstructed monarchist police, knew that Nin was a professional revolutionary in the Bolshevik mould, and not a backstreet Anarchist bomber of the sort that abounded in Barcelona at the time, and which provided the main inspiration for police stereotypes of revolutionaries.

The arrest of Nin in 1937 provides a sharp contrast. The charges — that a lifelong revolutionary was a Fascist agent in the pay of German big business — and the 'evidence' — that Nin, despite his long experience of clandestine organisation, had personally signed a secret message to Franco with his own name — were far more preposterous than those in 1933. Despite all this, not a single Catalan academic or intellectual publicly denounced the arrest of Nin, nor were there serious protests from Republican politicians. Later on, when it was too late, and with Nin almost certainly dead, some Republican and Anarchist leaders did ask some 'awkward' questions, but these were always muted by the need to appease Soviet 'advisors' at any price, a price which included the repression of the POUM by the forces of Stalinism in defence of the bourgeois republic.

Chris Ealham

Alastair MacLachlan, *The Rise and Fall of Revolutionary England*, Macmillan, Basingstoke, 1996, pp431

DOES ENGLAND have a revolutionary tradition? MacLachlan thinks not. He argues that the radical left of the 1930s and 1940s merely tried to reinvent a tradition of an English revolution in their analyses of seventeenth century history, and especially the period of Cromwell and Charles I.

This book is centred on an assessment of the influence of the Communist Party's Historians' Group. MacLachlan contrasts the early Marxist interpretations of Christopher Hill and others with their later works. It is a periodised review which assesses the 'battle of ideas' for a revolutionary past in the Communist Party between Marxist theory and peoples' history. He traces the shifting ground on which the Marxist historians have rethought their positions in a post-Stalinist era. MacLachlan dovetails the historical analyses of the period with the contemporary political developments in the Communist Party and the New Left.

MacLachlan begins with an overview of the earlier historical studies which 'rediscovered' the Radical, Leveller and Ranter movements. Historians such as Guizot wrote convincingly of the similarities between the English and French Revolutions. The traditionalist Whig view of England's 'Great Rebellion', as a defence of ancient rights against the alien innovations of the Stuarts, came under increasing attack. The Marxist model of structural contradiction, class conflict and revolution became more influential. The Civil War became a bourgeois class struggle involving a transition from a feudal mode of production to a capitalist one. The Victorian period saw Cromwell resurrected in Carlyle's *Letters and Speeches*. Even the definitive works of Whig narrative written by Gardiner recognised a 'Puritan revolution' in the events of the seventeenth century. The stage was set for the Marxists to 'reclaim the revolution' for history.

MacLachlan's chapter 'Reclaiming the Revolution' explores the high profile given to the Leveller and Digger movements and the figure of Winstanley in the works of the 1930s and 1940s. The Putney Debates of Cromwell's Army were compared with the Eighth Army 'parliament' of 1941. The development of a 'Peoples History of England' is traced, in which Hill's work explained the Civil War as a class conflict involving a bourgeois attack on the hierarchical order. The chapter is also of interest for giving examples of the bitter doctrinal disputes for which the Communist Party was justly infamous, as Robin Page Arnott, Rajani Palme Dutt and others strove to impose a party line on the work of the Historians' Group. The chapter on Marxist history in a Cold War era reveals how Stalin's Cominform led to greater central control over the meetings of the Historians' Group. Despite the Cold War polemics, the Group's work was not deformed beyond recovery. Historians like Hill and Eric Hobsbawm were felt to be able to take an 'intellectual disengagement from Stalinism'. MacLachlan believes the Marxist model was beginning to come apart just as their political decay accelerated.

The Twentieth Congress of the CPSU and the failure of the leadership of the Communist Party to admit the faults of the Stalinist era created a party crisis in 1956-57. This had a devastating effect on the Historians' Group. Over half of its membership, including Hill, resigned from the Communist Party.

The analysis of the period of the 1950s to the 1970s is viewed as one in which Hill, Lawrence Stone and others tried to 'save appearances' in a retreat from the earlier position of class struggle and bourgeois revolution to one of a more ideological revolution. The change of approach was consistent with the contemporary movement away from an authoritative Soviet model of change to one in which Britain would reach Socialism by its own road. The revolutionary struggle of the 1640s was progressively broadened out by Hill into a longer process, as evidenced in the title of his book *A Century of Revolution*.

Hill's book *The World Turned Upside Down* showed his increasing interest in the history of the 'common people'. The revolution was redefined through its radical legacy — a process MacLachlan labels as 'levelling out the revolution'. Hill's book became a radical text — a map of past experiences which broadened the scope of the English Revolution.

Hill's work increasingly focused on 'what went wrong' with the English Revolution. Hill wrote in his book *God's Englishmen* of the contradiction of Cromwell's quest for a settlement after 1649, but he continued to defend the revolutionary consolidation achieved by the Protectorate.

MacLachlan explores the debate between EP Thompson and Perry Anderson on the place of the seventeenth century revolution within England's past, and the more overtly revisionist studies popularised in the 1970s and 1980s. He traces the developments in the New Left and its treatment of history in a period of its own political disarray. During the 1980s history departments all over the country witnessed the retreat of the revolutionary version of England's history. MacLachlan argues that the Marxists' inability to come to terms with the normative features of most societies critically weakened their credibility. Yet the new revisionism didn't resolve issues, and by 1993 Hill wrote of a return to a more social interpretation of the period. In the chapter entitled 'Revolution as Text and Discourse', MacLachlan shows how Hill's works on the life of Milton reasserted that the key to his life was to be found in his revolutionary politics and radical religious ideas. Hill's work on Milton helped to 'hold the line' against the general move to the right.

The concluding chapter, 'The End of the Line', provides an historical retrospect on the Marxist historians' views in modern Britain. MacLachlan claims to balance a critical analysis with a sympathetic reappraisal of their rhetorical worth. He briefly refers to the Socialist Workers Party's analyses in *International Socialism*, and particularly their criticism of Hill, Hobsbawm, et al for failing to identify a revolutionary bourgeoisie and for defending the rôle of Cromwell, the 'revolutionary Stalin'. The final chapter is anecdotal, with references to the implosion of the Soviet Union, and to Hobsbawm's latter-day description of the October Revolution as a 'vast detour in world history'.

MacLachlan concludes that Isaac Deutscher's perception of an academic 'red decade' of the 1960s declined rapidly into revisionism in a period of political conservatism. He argues that the enlightened and grand narrative approach of Marxism in seeking to explain events in seventeenth century England has failed. Yet he argues that the New Right has not succeeded in imposing itself on social and historical thinking. Against this background, MacLachlan believes that Hill's work in particular will remain of interest, despite his failure to fashion an indigenous revolutionary past.

Those on the left will find some uncomfortable reminders of their own decline in contemporary influence mirrored in the modern 'non-revolutionary' interpretations of seventeenth century English history. Yet the failure of the New Right's approach provides the left with an opportunity for recovery. MacLachlan's book reminds us that for long periods of history the progressive rôle played by Cromwell, the Protectorate and the various radical and revolutionary groups of the period was hidden from view. In more auspicious times, the importance of their contribution becomes more accepted. With this in mind, the work of Hill and others of the Historians' Group should retain their central place on the bookshelves of those interested in understanding English history, and particularly the Civil War period.

Peter Swingler

Dario Renzi, *La lunga marcia del trotskismo: 1. Dalle sconfitte delle rivoluzioni al dopoguerra,* Prospettiva Edizioni, Rome, 1992, pp148, Lit12 000
Piero Neri, *Nahuel Moreno,* Prospettiva Edizioni, Rome, 1994, pp178, Lit20 000

THESE TWO books, published by Socialismo Rivoluzionario, the Italian Trotskyist organisation, are by their leader, Dario Renzi, and by one of their founder members, Piero Neri, respectively. Established in 1990, SR was born of the Lega Socialista Rivoluzionaria, itself dating back to 1976. The LSR and its offspring organisation have had long-standing relations with Moreno and, later, with the LIT, hence the dedication of Renzi's book to the memory of Moreno, and the inclusion of the Argentine Trotskyist in the SR's series of monographs entitled *Ritratti di Famiglia (Family Portraits).*

Both books try to analyse the history and development of Trotskyism internationally, roughly beginning with Trotsky's exile from the USSR, and, within this context, also situate the contribution of SR in Italy as part of the Fourth International. All quotations are my translation, and where possibly, the authorised English translations have been given. This review will concentrate for two reasons on a number of key theoretical issues largely common to both books, firstly, because it is only in this light that the relevance and contradictions of these works can come to the fore, and, secondly, because a more interesting picture of the theoretical debate will emerge, pointing to the marked differences between the frameworks adopted by two exponents of the same organisation.

The declared aim of Renzi's book is, as he repeatedly states, that of emphasising the continuity of the struggle and activities of Trotskyism internationally towards the goal of a future revolution, albeit through moments of crisis and setback. This 'march of Trotskyism' was, and is, however, based on a core of shared principles and purposes, with successive generations of Trotskyists worldwide who have taken the struggle on from their founder since 1938, and continued along the same path. Renzi's book goes up to the years following the Second World War. Despite some good initial intentions and a certain degree of objectivity on Renzi's part, who, in the chapter devoted to the Left Opposition in the USSR, could still concede that Trotsky might have been mistaken in his excessive hopes in the self-reforming capabilities of the party apparatus, and in hesitating in taking the reins of the Opposition. But by the final chapter, on the Trotskyist movement, Trotsky has become 'the creative disciple of Marx and Lenin' (p105). In the intervening chapters, Renzi stresses the absolute convergence of Lenin's and Trotsky's Marxism, with good old Rosa Luxemburg thrown in for good measure to complete the 'triad'. Trotsky himself, while still vulnerable to error in the first half of the book, from 1938 onwards becomes almost infallible and, above all, a misunderstood figure by the 'less flexible' and 'more dogmatic' sections of the Fourth International.

These, however, are not merely Renzi's methodological problems. They are the necessary consequences of the comforting but increasingly contradictory story he tries to tell, and they should be understood in this light. The theoretical shortcomings of Renzi are indicative of the main issues being debated by Trotskyism for decades. The factual content of this book is well established, and offers little new data. Renzi himself recognises the problem, and calls for its rectification. In the introduction we read that, especially in the light of the disclosure of new sources of information after the 'epochal turning point of the August 1989 revolution in the USSR' (p10), and 'proportionally to the development of democratic revolutions in the East' (p12), there still is an almost complete silence on the 'historical and critical assessment by the various currents within Trotskyism as to their history. This, too, is a sign of the political retardation which afflicts the movement itself.' (p13) In this light, therefore, SR's willingness to discuss the history of Trotskyism is to be applauded, but unfortunately its failure lies precisely in its incapacity to open a debate on the strongest-held convictions of Trotskyism before and after the war.

Some of Renzi's shortcomings will be pointed out by Piero Neri in his book on Moreno, so we will leave them until later. The wide subject of inquiry of Renzi's work makes it impossible to stress all the potential difficulties in this short review, but three issues will serve to illustrate the point: the debate on the nature of the Soviet Union, the actions and line to follow on the eve of the Second World War, and the understanding of the nature and rôle of the Communist International. The more difficult and contradictory nature of some of Trotsky's proposals in these respects, formulated towards the end of his life and in exile, and Renzi's unwillingness to cast doubt on their validity and theoretical value, are also worthy of note, and it is a shame that Renzi's entire and otherwise worthy enterprise is founded upon manifestations of Trotsky's theoretical involution.

These three issues are, of course, closely interlinked. The story begins on familiar ground. The Bolsheviks allowed 'free and dialectical confrontation on all major issues of the proletarian dictatorship in Russia and the revolution worldwide' (p20). However, Lenin and Trotsky increasingly understood that 'the revolution could serve as no substitute for the necessary preparation of the revolutionary forces' (p22), and founded the Communist International in 1919. This new International included the best exponents of international Marxism, but 'coming from different experiences and backgrounds, with consequent fragility' (p25). Meanwhile, in Russia the New Economic Policy was an 'audacious and indispensable' measure to save the soviets (p31), and by the mid-1920s the internal debate in the Central Committee of the Soviet Communist Party had greatly diminished, partly due to Lenin's 'error in ratifying politically a practically necessary measure, that is, the temporary ban on internal factions' (p34). Increasingly, a bureaucratic caste was on the rise, which would ultimately expropriate the workers and take power in the USSR (p41). The reasons for this process are, according to Renzi, the weakening of proletarian forces and their state and party political representatives; the rise of counter-revolutionary forces in Russian society, infiltrating the party and soviets; the rise of the 'NEP men'; the proletariat's exhaustion; the accommodation of some Bolshevik leaders to the new situation (as in the case of Bukharin); and, obviously, the failed revolution on the international plane. For Renzi, 'there is a very close cause-effect relationship between the defeats suffered by the revolution and the collapse of the revolutionary leadership, its beating heart' (p42). To counter this, in 1926 the Joint Opposition stressed the need to revert to a 'truly international policy, to restore party democracy, to put an end to the concessions granted to rich peasants at the expense of the working class, and to pursue a serious planning of the economy' (p51). Undoubtedly, these facts are objectively true, but no attempt is made to link these consequences to any underlying causative reason. We are therefore left largely in the dark as to how the situation in Russia should so swiftly deteriorate. As for Trotsky, 'despite from the point of view of theory, politics and — above all — practice, the ruling bureaucratic faction moved closer and closer to imperialism, it had nevertheless not totally crossed the class divide' (p71). Trotsky, motivated by 'various and complex reasons' (p74), continued to maintain a policy of 'reform'. In 1933 the first conference of the International Left Opposition 'reconfirmed its character of faction, not party' in the official Communist movement (p78), and in the August of that same year the Plenum of the Opposition stated that it would defend the USSR in the event of war. Renzi admits that 'with the exception of the Left Opposition in the American Communist Party... the real building work for Opposition groups in other countries did not begin until the 1930s (p81). These attempts, followed in 1933 by the 'Declaration of the Four', failed because of the 'limitations of the other signatories... deep sectarianism and the poor tactical flexibility of Trotsky's colleagues' (p87). This 'lack of flexibility', which resurfaced towards Trotsky's entrist policies, which were 'not understood, or rejected, or badly applied' (p88), is sharply condemned, despite Renzi's admission that the Communist leadership had become the strongest obstacle to workers' emancipation and to future revolutions, and that this strength derived precisely from the revolutionary tradition. Nevertheless, Trotsky, convinced that 'his reasons were the reasons of Marx, Lenin, Rosa Luxemburg and above all the international proletariat' (p80), fought against strong opposition within the Fourth International and the American Socialist Workers Party, and argued for support for the USSR. If the reader should begin to see a problem here, Renzi comes to the rescue: 'To attribute this situation to any errors or intrinsic limitations in our project would mean totally to fail to comprehend the great laws governing revolutionary policy, and hence also its organisation. Obviously many errors were made and many limitations existed, but they must be considered within the worldwide context of the prevailing tendencies of the time.' (p90)

On the eve of the war the 'fundamental problem for the Fourth International, and which — in different terms — we still find today, is the enormous disparity between the socio-economic and the political conditions for the Socialist revolution' (p93). In this respect, Trotsky's 'vision of war' and of the tasks of revolutionaries was an attempt to understand the specific character of the new world conflict. Crucial to these proposals were, once again, the nature of the Soviet state, and some of Trotsky's practical strategies, such as the entry of revolutionaries into the imperialist armies. Renzi sharply accuses the Fourth International for 'relative inertia', which did not allow it to exploit the 'colossal opportunities' offered by the imperialist slaughter. In this section of Renzi's book the quotations from Trotsky become several pages long. For our purposes, it is significant that the 'colossal opportunities' offered by the doubtful prospects of having governments pay to train militarily workers and the granting of workers' officers, trained at their places of work, not to speak of the possibility of military training for workers under their control (see Trotsky, 'On The Question of Workers' Self-Defence'), amounted to a 'navy fraction' of the American SWP, approximately 150-strong, whose activity was 'necessarily only one of propaganda' (p110).

As for the defence of the USSR, here Renzi is at his most creative, and following his arguments will prove instructive. Incredibly, it seems that we won, and we do not even know it. The author informs us:

'The events and consequences of the war were to show without the shadow of a doubt that the Old Revolutionary got it essentially right. It could seem as if he underestimated the resourcefulness and capacities for recuperation of Stalinism, which came triumphant out of the War, as the world bulwark against Fascism. However, if we analyse events with a minimum of depth, we can immediately understand that this success, achieved despite the systematic betrayal of the interests of world revolution, fundamentally depended on the extraordinary response of the Soviet proletariat faced with the Nazi invasion. With immense sacrifices and overcoming all obstacles, including Stalin's war crimes, the cost of which in human lives cannot even be quantified, the Russian people repelled Hitler, and gave Stalin the chance to become victor. So, precisely that "defence of the Socialist fatherland" supported by Trotsky had won.' (pp108-9)

Oh well, that's alright, then.

Taking the discussion further, to Pablo, Mandel and the situation in the 1950s, the question of the nature of the USSR returns when tackling the processes involving the countries of Eastern Europe, most notably Yugoslavia. Here, Renzi accuses the Fourth International of formalism, of relying on 'established revolutionary Marxist *norms*, rather than on the new *events*' of the current situation (p117, original emphasis). Trotsky, by the way, had somehow predicted this too, when facing opposition on the workers' state analysis of the USSR. However, what Renzi does is to oppose to this supposed formalism yet more formalism by Trotsky. In the longest quotation of this book, he reproduces verbatim Trotsky's analogy between a workers' state and a liver poisoned by malaria (see Trotsky, 'Not a Workers' and Not a Bourgeois State?'), which amounts to nothing else than an equation between state ownership of the means of production and the Socialist nature of the state. If we follow Trotsky, who also proposed that trade unions with policies directly opposed to the interests of the proletariat (in his specific example, the AFL) are nevertheless trade unions, we would be left with formalism indeed, as if the name determined the substance of an organisation, and as if having the word 'Socialist' or 'Labour' in a name were a guarantee of revolutionary intent (just ask any Liverpool docker).

Renzi's 'march' comes to an end leaving more questions unanswered than solved. What is most disappointing about his work is not so much the content, which is no better or worse than in many other 'official' histories of Trotskyism, but that events, choices, directions are simply stated as given or supposedly determined by outside events, without any attempt to clarify the possible causative relations between them. We are none the wiser as to the nature and structure that the International should take, or the internal development of the Bolshevik party, and we are ultimately left with a sense of defensiveness and powerlessness against each new enemy, be it Stalinism, Nazism, Pabloism or the enemies of the future, only doomed to repeat past errors and take the best remedial action.

Piero Neri's biography of Nahuel Moreno is an altogether better book, in more ways than one. Neri knew Moreno personally, having been the delegate of the Italian LSR at the founding meeting of the LIT in Bogota (on which occasion the LSR broke from Moreno's current, re-establishing relations only in 1986), and during Moreno's stay in Italy in 1986, shortly before his death. This personal involvement on the author's part, whose warm friendship and respect for Moreno are plain to see, does not prevent him from presenting a highly critical picture of the Argentine Trotskyist, in which no merit is denied, but no blame is spared. Moreover, the value of this book lies in the fact that such criticisms are not confined to Moreno's activities, but are put in a direct relation with the general theoretical difficul-

ties of the movement — as well as Moreno's own shortcomings — and therefore acquire relevance for anyone wishing to avoid the repetition of the past.
Neri defines Moreno as 'the best leader produced by the Trotskyist movement from the aftermath of the war until now' (p11). In his view, we can
legitimately speak of 'Moreno's Marxism', thanks to a 'constructive revisionism' (p14) which combined firmness of principles with theoretical original-
ity, and was characterised by an attempt to maintain the independence of
the programme and policies of revolutionary Marxism, while building its
concrete expressions, that is, revolutionary organisations and the Fourth
International (pp12-13). Moreno attempted to overcome the deep separation
between theory and practice seen in Trotskyism after the war (p21). The
entire activity of Moreno towards this goal consisted in 'analysing and char-
acterising the situation, elaborating a line and a political orientation, and
then synthesising this in passwords' (p43), so as to break with that 'minority
mentality and intellectualistic "philosophy" embraced by the great majority
of the Trotskyist movement after the war' (p43), 'culminating in the 1950s
in an "entrist" policy in reformist organisations, which continued for decades' (p44). Moreno tried to 'analyse revolutionary processes, in an attempt
to derive lessons and generalisations from them' (p74). This attempt brought
him into conflict with the 'international left bureaucracy'. He also maintained a polemic against large sections of the revolutionary left which, by
calling for the support of the Cuban or Chinese revolutions, identified
themselves as Maoist or Castroist. Moreno criticised the attempt to describe
guerrillaism and Sandinism as 'new surrogates for Marxism' (p90).

   This work by Moreno took on various forms, and he waged various battles with the Fourth International over the years. Moreno's entire enterprise, however, was undermined by his erroneous understanding of revolutionary activity aiming to establish Socialism internationally, and this incorrect understanding, in turn, was to result in Moreno's mistaken view of the
rôle of the party and the International. Neri locates a few of the roots of
Moreno's mistakes in some general errors of the Trotskyist movement. Central to these issues is the analysis of bureaucratic states as 'workers' states',
since, according to Neri, their planned economy was given a Socialist, if limited, content. This, says Neri, mainly amounted to an arbitrary generalisa-
tion of some, in fact few, of Trotsky's positions on the USSR in the 1930s,
for example, the need to defend the Soviet workers' state in the event of an
imperialist attack, or to the contradiction posed between the existence of a
political superstructure to fight — the totalitarian state — and an economic
base to defend — Soviet planning (p13).

   More specifically in the case of Moreno, Neri points to a serious limita-
tion, again shared by the whole movement: that of the exclusion of Rosa
Luxemburg's current. Significantly, Moreno stated in his *Actualización del
programa de transición*: 'The existence of Lenin and Trotsky and the Bolshevik Party guaranteed the victory of the October Revolution, while in Germany the absence of a Lenin and a Trotsky ensured the failure of a Socialist
revolution.' (Cited on p22) In Moreno, this initial error of interpretation
became a profound theoretical shortcoming. The reduction of historical revo-

lutionary Marxism to Bolshevism distorted the relation between it as a current and theory, and also facilitated superficial simplifications and the rise of intolerance (p23). Moreno 'considered Lenin's and Trotsky's Marxism far more homogeneous than they actually were. Trotsky's decisive contributions after Lenin did not constitute an "evolution" of Leninism in Trotskyism.' (p24) Trotsky, therefore, is not seen by Neri as the highest expression of historical Marxism, and he also points to a further consequence of this understanding, that is, the use of historical analogy by Moreno. In fact, he came to see the 1917 revolution and the Socialism of the first stage of Soviet power as the model for all future revolutionary developments. The adoption of this model, furthermore, conditioned the dynamic of Moreno's understanding of the 'relationship between political, social and economic change' (p28). This is despite the Bolsheviks' appeal to their comrades to do better than they could do in 1917.

Moreno's concept of revolution evolved further, and led to a division of the revolutionary process into stages, which therefore does not constitute a truly dialectical model. In the first stage, the rising and ascent to power are envisaged, whereas the Socialist revolution in its proper sense only begins later. In this framework:

'... socialisation... is removed or postponed to a distant future, and so becomes separated from revolution, and is subordinated to the consolidation of state power. The state is conceived as a guarantor of socialisation, and this leads — not coincidentally — to a confusion between socialisation and nationalisation. [Moreno]... sees the birth of Socialism as characterised by the consolidation of the workers' state — with an important guarantee being given by the revolutionary party — and by the nationalisation of the means of production. But this dynamic is different from integral socialisation, and certainly does not necessarily initiate it.' (pp30-1)

Moreno gives absolute priority to the state as opposed to society in the struggle for Socialism, often identifying it with 'the struggle to establish the dictatorship of the proletariat and a revolutionary workers' state... Therefore, he calls for a strengthening of state institutions for an entire, long phase, until the international resolution of the fight with imperialism.' (p31) Neri is quick to note that this amounts to the inescapable logic of all forms of nationalisations, and that this future state would be far too similar to an overthrown bourgeois state (p31). In Moreno's Socialism, therefore, the dictatorship of the proletariat basically signifies party dictatorship (again, based on his model of the Bolshevik party). Perhaps the most serious consequence of this interpretation, as Neri rightly stresses, is that the Socialist consciousness of revolution is reduced to the revolutionary party, with a process in which just one of the methods of Marxist activity becomes absolutised. Moreno's conception of Marxist activity and elaboration is thus an exclusively political one (pp44-5), with an increasing importance being given to agitation work as the crucial revolutionary activity. Thus, as Moreno puts it in his *El partido y la revolución*, Leninist-Trotskyist parties should:

'... mobilise the masses, not the vanguard... With the transitional programme... the party must give those passwords that mobilise the masses against their exploiters, starting from their immediate needs and consciousness, and must continue to elevate the level of these passwords proportionally to the growth of the masses' consciousness and the creation of new needs brought about by this very same mobilisation, up to the final password and struggle for power.' (Cited on p51)

This accommodation to the level of the masses' consciousness sees theory becoming little more than a tool for tactics and politics, and also goes firmly against the grain of Trotsky's theory as presented, for example, in his *Transitional Programme*.

Historical analogies emerge again in Moreno's understanding of revolution. We have already pointed to his understanding of revolution 'by stages'. One of Moreno's strongest-held conviction was in fact that revolutions are endlessly dissimilar in their development and dynamics, and that the task of Marxists was to strive to understand them in all their manifestations. Ironically, however, his correct fight within the Fourth International at the time of the Nicaraguan revolution (as the Bolshevik Tendency and, later, as the Bolshevik Faction) found no parallels when theorising revolution itself. The Russian revolutions of 1917 became once again Moreno's terms of reference. This time, 'February' and 'October' were turned into universal categories which could, by themselves, be the sole analytical tools sufficient to explain any new revolutionary process. In his *Actualización* Moreno explained: 'The February revolution is an unconsciously Socialist revolution, while the October revolution is consciously Socialist. Paraphrasing Hegel and Marx, we could say that the former is a revolution *in itself*, while the latter is a revolution *for itself*.' (Cited on p79, original emphasis) So, for example, the 1974 Portuguese revolution was 'a great February revolution which did not develop into an October' (p93). It would follow that the world has seen various types of 'Februaries' but, presumably, no 'Octobers' since 1917, on Moreno's own definition (p80).

When faced with the issue of the tasks of the International, these instances of formalisation and contradiction remain firmly in place. In particular, between 1974 and 1979 Moreno's current (the BT, later to become the BF) initiated a lively polemic, among others, with the American SWP. This led to a break with the United Secretariat, which had never recognised 'Moreno's Argentine current as an official organisation', and which had 'isolated it as a result of various differences' (p97). The BF then began a disastrous but mercifully brief experiment with the Organisation Communiste Internationaliste headed by Pierre Lambert, and two years later, in 1982, established the LIT. The Italian LSR, until then part of Moreno's international current, did not join, and broke with the LIT until 1986. Among the points of disagreement was precisely Moreno's concept of the International.

In previous years, Moreno's current had come to propose an equation between the International and the need for international centralisation. This centralisation, which we have already witnessed in the importance given by

Moreno to the party at the national level, is here generalised in a concept of a 'world party'. This need, moreover, was felt to be an a priori condition, so that this 'world party' should be firmly in place before the dynamic of class struggle and revolutionary developments could come into being. Moreno thus argued that a political current should become a faction. Possibly by generalising the actual situation of his own current, he then went on to theorise an 'International Faction' (p98), and by the time of the establishment of the LIT the International fundamentally envisaged a preliminary stage, a victory in Argentina after the fall of the dictatorship, which due to the perceived importance of that country and the southern region of Latin America, was to become the axis around which the entire International would orbit. Neri rightly stresses the 'self-affirming and defensive character' of this formulation (pp100-1), and also casts doubt on Moreno's arguments as to the frictionless continuity among the four Internationals, which the LIT used to postulate its 'iron law' of the absolute priority of the International and its leadership. As is often the case, after the death of its leader this organisation exacerbated the elements of formalism present in his thought, and came to think of the existence of the International and its leadership as the automatic guarantee of revolution. Neri, however, reminds us that, in the history of all the Internationals, if anything it was disagreements, not conformism, which had allowed the more meaningful revolutionary developments to occur. Ultimately, Moreno's understanding of the International as a 'chief of staff' to coordinate and allocate resources and activities according to the specific situations in various countries, amounts to the transfer to the international plane of his previous subordination of the tasks of the International to mere agitation in the national sphere, again at the expense of theory. Internally, this International would be governed by 'democratic centralism', elevated by Moreno to 'a principle denoting the revolutionary programme itself, at the national and international levels' (p111).

While all these developments should not be seen in isolation or as examples of individual deviance, but as part of a general problem within the entire Fourth International, Neri admits that some limitations are nevertheless unquestionably attributable to Moreno.

Once again, therefore, these two books serve, on the one hand, as a strong reminder of the absolute necessity for complete openness and honesty when faced with the past, and, on the other, of the disastrous consequences of a separation between theory and practice for revolutionary Marxism, and of the non-existence and futility of 'short cuts' or dogmatism in the task of building the necessary theoretical basis for a Socialist revolution.
Barbara Rossi

Nadezhda A Joffe, *Back in Time: My Life, My Fate, My Epoch*, Labor Publications, Detroit, 1995, pp245

THE WRITING of memoirs has a special place in the culture of Russia, and the growth of literacy that was achieved under the Bolshevik regime encouraged the practice. The Central Museum of the Revolution, in Moscow's

Tverskaya, houses a large collection of manuscript memoirs assembled from many sources. (The work of mining this irreplaceable resource will take many decades, and historians concerned with the task of understanding and interpreting the October Revolution ought to be as concerned with the regular threats to the budget of this museum from the Yeltsin regime as they are to the problems of the more prestigious venues such as the Institute of Marxism-Leninism and the Lenin Library.) Often during the Stalin terror, revolutionaries were granted a stay of execution in order to be able to write their memoirs, even when there was no hope of them emerging from the capacious files of the Lubyanka. The destruction of memoirs by the forces of the state has always been regarded as an especially vile crime. (Larina's memoirs were seized and burned several times, and the fate of the manuscripts seized from Serge and Rakovsky remains a subject of active speculation.)

These memoirs serve many purposes, personal, political and literary. For the survivors of the Stalin terror, it has been particularly important to set the record straight, to rescue and preserve the memories and knowledge which Stalin and his regime set out to expunge, and to name the criminals and collaborators who thought the Stalinist regime would last forever.

In his foreword to Nadezhda Joffe's memoirs, David North points out that the 'survivor of Stalinism memoirs' have become a literary genre. Here he echoes Stephen Cohen's introduction to Larina's memoirs. And the same point has been validly made elsewhere, in relation to volumes by Nadezhda Mandelstam, Irina Ratushinskaya and all too many others (curiously, North's list of examples excludes the memoirs of Maria Joffe, *One Long Night*).

The regime created by Stalin to defeat the October Revolution marked one of the most extreme points of savagery and repression that humanity has ever perpetrated and suffered. It ranks with the Nazi holocaust, the slave trade and the century-long war between the 'mongol hordes' and China.

The memoirs of survivors of the Stalin terror are central in shedding personal light on the process of the long civil war which Stalin waged against the revolution. They illuminate and add force to the historical research of writers such as Conquest and Rogovin. But they do more than this. They can, at their best, demonstrate the survival of some tiny kernel of humanity in the face of the most immeasurable oppression. In this sense, Joffe's memoirs, and others of their kind, go beyond the range with which a revolutionary historical journal is directly concerned, to some of the questions that call up the revolutionary spirit.

It is proper to consider the book in the first instance as historical material. It has to be said that the notes are sadly inadequate, pointing only to well-known public sources. They cannot be the author's own notes, since the memoirs are dated 1971-72, but the notes refer to later material such as Trepper (1979) and Carr (1981), or to material to which Joffe is unlikely to have had access in Moscow (Trotsky, Deutscher). Of course, there would have been good reason for reticence in the early 1970s, but not in notes prepared for an English edition in 1994. There is also a curious reference (p39) to one of Broué's books on Trotsky. Was this material really available in Moscow in 1972? In another indication that the text was revised later than the 1971-72 sign-off date, she refers to the publication of the Riutin platform. I have not traced any publication of the platform before 1990 in Russia (it is clear from the context that Joffe is not referring to any of the fragmentary publications of 1932).

Joffe's own words and recollections provide some useful information. The early chapters deal with her early life, and give an account of her father's life and career. Adolf Joffe was a figure of exceptional importance in the revolution, and in the development of the Opposition. As the Soviet Ambassador to Berlin, he met important personalities, including Mehring. Nadezhda also met Rakovsky, Bukharin and Dzerzhinsky, and recalls these giants as daily visitors during her childhood. She also recollects Trotsky as a warm, friendly individual who had a good rapport with children (contradicting Larina's description of him as a cold, frightening figure).

She also provides us with an all-too-brief glimpse of the dazzling intellectual life of revolutionary Moscow — meeting Lunacharsky, Yesenin and Mayakovsky. She witnessed the famous Lunacharsky-Vvedensky debate, and tells a tale of Lunacharsky delivering a brilliant lecture on Campanella without notes or preparation. These bright days were to come to an early end. Joffe happened to be present for Krupskaya's announcement of Lenin's death.

We do not get an analysis from Joffe of the rise of the Opposition — she was very young in the early 1920s. Almost the first we hear from her is her voting against a resolution in 1926 condemning Trotsky. She begins her political material from the death of her father, denied access to overseas medical treatment by the vindictive party bureaucracy. The translation of Trotsky's funeral oration for Joffe differs from that in the Pathfinder collection *Portraits Political and Personal*, but does not seem to change any of Trotsky's meaning.

She also presents the full text of Joffe's final letter to Trotsky, and adds a few details to the account of Joffe's funeral — the booing and shouting down of Riutin (the Central Committee representative).

She reminds us of Sedova's work in preserving antiquities and monuments after the revolution, especially the old quarter between Red Square and the old city wall. Most of this was later cleared by Stalin, and eventually became the site for the huge, hideous and cockroach-infested Hotel Moskva. But little of this is first hand. She was, after all, a teenage girl at the time. She sets down a few memorised fragments of poems dedicated to Trotsky, which were probably excluded from the history of Soviet literature entirely by the mid-1920s.

The beginning of her oppositional activity is briefly described, from the autumn of 1927 in her third year at the Plekhanov Institute (apparently a year after her 1926 vote ended her 'party career'). She even quotes from a leaflet she wrote for distribution by the Moscow Komsomol Centre — how was this preserved? She shows that when Radek, Preobrazhensky and Smilga began the first wave of capitulations in May 1929, this was not simply an individual political realignment. It triggered a vast new wave of repressions against the Opposition. (They would have known that this would be the consequence of their action, since the same thing had happened a year earlier when Zinoviev and Kamenev 'repented'.) For Joffe, this resulted in her first arrest in the spring of 1929, leading to exile in Krasnoyarsk in the summer. There she met some notable oppositionists, including Dumbadze (Serge campaigned in his defence after being expelled from the USSR. He cannot have been at Krasnoyarsk long, as a letter published in *Cahiers Léon Trotsky* refers to him at the Cheliabinsk isolator in the autumn of 1929) and AS Yenukidze, but we don't get any details on their politics or their activities.

She describes meeting Rakovsky in Moscow after his readmission to the party. He convinced her that there existed a layer in the party that could, gradually and carefully, be influenced. She added her signature to his political statement. She tells us nothing more about activity in the Opposition, or how this legal 'influencing' in the party was carried out.

She may have maintained some level of activity which even in the 1970s could not safely be written about, because when she was arrested for the second time, in 1936, her flat contained 'seditious literature', including Trotsky's *Collected Works*. She was charged only in relation to her earlier oppositional work up to 1927.

At this point, the Opposition as such disappears from her account, although we get information about some individual oppositionists that she meets. We are now on grimly familiar territory, the dismal details of interrogations, the bleak architecture of the Butyrka and other prisons, and the dehumanised and dehumanising administration of the gulags.

Along this desolate road, in Magadan, Joffe met Trotsky's first wife Aleksandrovna Lvovna Bronstein (née Sokolovskaya), and carried her parting message of defiance across the decades: 'If you ever read somewhere or hear that I have confessed to being guilty, don't believe it. This will never happen, no matter what they do to me.' This is probably the last sighting of Sokolovskaya. Joffe was later returned to Magadan, but learned that Sokolovskaya had been moved to central Siberia. A small enough historical detail perhaps, but as an example of indomitable courage and determination, this last message from Sokolovskaya to the future is of incomparable value.

The case of Olga Ivanovna Grebner, whom Joffe met in Kolyma, sheds another grim sidelight on the Stalin regime's morbid fear of Trotsky's ideas. Grebner received a five year sentence. Her 'crime' was that her husband's niece had been the first wife of Sergei Sedov, Trotsky's younger son. Grebner herself had hardly even met Sedov, but even this remote link was enough to strike fear into the regime.

As late as 1938 there are occasional signs of oppositional activity. Joffe met a young Leningrad student who had learned from 'seditious literature' how all of Lenin's closest collaborators had been purged as 'enemies of the people', and had been imprisoned for this knowledge. But even before this, most of the Opposition had been stamped out. The mass arrests of 1937, according to Joffe, brought to the camps not Trotskyists but loyal Stalinists with records of action against the Trotskyists, who were sentenced more harshly than previous waves of accused (in fact as early as May 1936 Serge had warned Trotsky that the mass arrests were not of new oppositional elements).

Much of the rest of Joffe's account is concerned with her eventual release (she long struggled to be reunited with her daughters), her peremptory rehabilitation, and her restoration of her father's grave at the historic Novodevichy Convent site. (It is only in relation to the grave of AA Joffe that she mentions his second wife, Maria — author of another excellent gulag memoir, *One Long Night*). There is no indication that Joffe took any part in any of the oppositional movements of the 1960s or 1970s, focusing on samizdat publications and occasional illegal demonstrations, and she expresses no opinion on them. (In an undated introduction, presumably prepared for the English edition, she does remark that she expected her memoirs only ever to be read in samizdat form.) This would have been difficult in the early 1970s, of course, but it would have been possible for the publishers in 1994 to ask her for a supplementary comment, which would have added substantially to the value of the book.

To summarise, as a work of history, Joffe's memoirs add some valuable details to our knowledge of the Opposition, but change nothing of substance. As a personal memoir, they present an inspiring example of courage and determination to hold onto whatever can be retained of humanity and decency through one of the most appalling periods of history. And perhaps, too, there is the suggestion that we should not judge those we too casually refer to as 'capitulators' too harshly.

JJ Plant

Mikhail Baitalsky, *Notebooks for the Grandchildren: Recollections of a Trotskyist Who Survived the Stalin Terror*, Humanities Press, New Jersey, 1996, pp427

'LIFE HAS become better, comrades, life has become more joyful', announced slogans on the walls of the labour camp barracks at Vorkuta for badly-fed, badly-housed prisoners to read each day as they went to and from forced labour in the mines. These phrases were taken from a speech by Stalin.

Baitalsky, a member of the Komsomol in the 1920s, who as a boy had fought against Denikin, the leader of the counter-revolution in Southern Russia during the Civil War, was later to be arrested three times as a supporter of the Trotskyist opposition (even after the Trotskyists in Russia had all been murdered). He served two terms in Vorkuta labour camp with others dubbed 'enemies of the people', referred to as Trotskyists, which had become a general term of abuse. It was not difficult to become an 'enemy of the people', for anyone making an irreverent joke about the Stalinist bureaucracy, organising a school on Marxism or Leninism without permission, being related to an 'enemy of the people', falling foul of the local bureaucracy — all these could result in a sentence of from five to 25 years in the camps. This was in addition to those accused of sabotage, largely engineers, because they had failed to complete a five year plan in the stated time. And, as we know, those Russian servicemen captured by the Germans during the Second World War returned not as heroes, but also to be incarcerated. With regard to prisoners of war, Baitalsky states that the Nazis knew that the Geneva Convention need not apply to captured Russians, because Stalin's government would make no complaint at their treatment. In the camps also were members of foreign Communist parties disbanded by Moscow. Baitalsky claims that at any one time the camps held at least 15 million prisoners. There were also common criminals in the camps, but these (as in the Nazi concentration camps) were given trusted positions over the other prisoners, and generally had shorter sentences.

The members of the bureaucracy and petty bureaucracy, in competition with each other in the finding of 'enemies of the people', were as likely as anyone else to end up as prisoners in the camps. Baitalsky tells of the executions at Vorkuta, prisoners hurried across melting rivers to be shot down by machine-guns, 50 men at a time. Later, the bureaucrat in charge of these executions was himself arrested and was heard screaming from a window of the Kotlas prison where he awaited execution: 'Tell the people that I am Kashketin! I am the one who shot all the enemies of the people at Vorkuta!' Baitalsky remarks: 'And when these Moors had done their duty, they were charged with exceeding their authority and shot.' In this way Stalin wiped his hands clean of the terror.

Baitalsky remained a Leninist, having read Lenin's *Testament* 30 years before it became generally available. With regard to Trotskyism, he was unaware at that time as to whether any remained anywhere in the world. However, he raises some important questions for us with regard to the nationalisation of property. Nationalisation of the means of production has always been regarded by us as more efficient than production in private hands, in that planning should result in a higher standing of living for the population. However, as Baitalsky points out, the nationalised economy of the Soviet Union became distorted because it was harnessed firstly to the needs of the state — the large bureaucracy (which required private clinics, private shops, private schools, etc), the security services, the military, 'show' or status projects, such as space exploration, and so on. Therefore, the standard of living continually lagged behind that of the Western world. To allay discontent, shortages were blamed upon 'enemies of the people' or 'Trotskyists' who were sabotaging Socialist development.

Apart from this distortion of the economy, it is a fact that technological invention requires intellectual freedom, which did not exist in the Soviet Union. Baitalsky spent some of his imprisonment in the First Circle (also written about by Solzhenitsyn). In this prison were gathered engineers and others with technological knowledge, instructed to 'invent' within a specified time an object of technology already in use in the West. Trade magazines from the West were treated as blueprints, and were locked away in a safe.

Baitalsky speaks also of the changing face of the working class in a peasant country. Following the forced collectivisation, starving peasants poured into the towns, and sat begging homeless in the streets. Stalin met this problem by reintroducing the Tsarist pass laws, which resulted in these dispossessed peasants being forced 'home' to starve. An added advantage to Stalin of these pass laws was that peasants, without any working class experience, could be introduced into the workforce in an organised manner.

Baitalsky also writes of anti-Semitism in the Soviet Union, and claims that after the Second World War when the Nazi concentration camps were revealed to the world, the population of the Soviet Union were not told that Jews were the main victims. Every nationality was stated to have been found in the camps, but not Jews, but by this time 'cosmopolitanism' had also become a dirty word in Russia. This meant that Jews had relatives and other contacts outside Russia, and were therefore suspect.

In the light of the present war by Russia against the Chechens, it is of interest to know that there is a history relating to this, for the Chechens were one of five peoples deported from their homelands as 'unreliable' when the Soviet Union entered the Second World War. History might not always repeat itself, but it certainly colours events. For instance, Baitalsky states that one of Stalin's great heroes was Ivan the Terrible!

Baitalsky writes also of his private life, his first wife and the mother of his two children, whom he met in the Komsomol, but who became a committed Stalinist, and his friends from Komsomol days who disappeared into the camps, or who lived in poverty. This is a book that's well worth reading, it's thought-provoking, and poses many questions on the nature of bureaucracy and the state.

Sheila Lahr

Letters

Hull and the Blue Union

Dear Editor

Tom Cowan's review of my *How the Blue Union Came to Hull Docks* (*Revolutionary History*, Volume 6, nos 2/3, pp280-2) manages to combine praise for the pamphlet for being 'interesting and factual' with an attempt to disprove those 'facts' that do not fit into Cowan's theory that the move to the Blue Union on the Hull Docks in August 1954 was 'initiated by Gerry Healy's Club'. The two disputed areas in the review are the date of the Hull decision to move to the Blue Union, and the rôle of JW Murphy.

I wrote that the Hull dockers voted on Wednesday, 18 August 1954 to join the NASD or 'Blue Union' prior to the arrival of Gerry Healy, Bob Pennington, Bill Johnson and Danny Brandon on the morning of Sunday, 22 August 1954. Tom Cowan writes that 'the proceedings of the Wednesday meeting do not appear to have been known to any of the participants at the time'. This statement can easily be disproved, thus showing that the decision was indeed taken on Wednesday, 18 August 1954, and that JW Murphy was a key player in the events. Some of these sources were unknown to me when I wrote the pamphlet.

Former Birkenhead docker Danny Brandon was one of those who travelled to Hull with Gerry Healy. In an interview with Dave Baines in June 1982, he explained:

'It was in July [it was actually August — KS] 1954, I read three lines in one of the national newspapers that Hull had sent two men to see the London Executive of the NASD with an application to join the Blue Union, and so I set off hot-foot for Hull. One Saturday night in the company of Bill Johnson and people from the *Socialist Outlook* group, we took a train to Leeds and stayed overnight. We got the van there and carried on to Hull, arriving on the Sunday. We had contacted the people there and told them we were coming. Jim Murphy was the principal contact and principal leader, yet he didn't work on the docks then. He had, but he was then running a small kennels and pig farm. It was a peculiar place, Hull. That sort of thing would not be tolerated on Merseyside. Once off the dock, you're not a docker, and that's it, no matter how wrong it was for them to put you off.'

How could Danny Brandon have known about the decision to move to the Blue Union if the decision was not taken until after his arrival in Hull on the Sunday morning?

Cowan questions the importance of the *Hull Daily Mail* report showing that the decision to move to the Blue Union was taken on the Wednesday, several days before the visit of Gerry Healy et al.

If no decision had been taken to move to the Blue, then what is the explanation of the headline in the *Hull Daily Mail* on Saturday, 21 August saying 'New Union Forms Rushed to Hull', with the sub-heading 'Definitely going ahead with our breakaway — Albert Hart'? In the same edition, we read that the strike leader Albert Hart told the Friday evening mass meeting that 'a representative of the NASD — which the Hull men want to join instead of the Transport and General Workers Union — will be present' at Sunday's meeting.

Additionally, if the decision to move to the Blue was taken on the Sunday morning, is it not just a little surprising that the following day's *Mail* article reporting that meeting does not mention the 'momentous decision' to leave the TGWU, that Tom Cowan believes was taken on that day? The *Hull Daily Mail* on the Monday has a detailed report of the Sunday meeting without any suggestion that the initial decision to move to the Blue was taken there. It's not even as if they had a stunning alternative headline — 'Hull Dock Strike Goes On'.

Tom Cowan's attempt to use Bob Pennington's article in *International Socialism* (no 2, Autumn 1960) to support his position is completely unjustified. This is what Pennington wrote:

'On 16 August 1954 4000 Hull dockers struck work against the dangerous method of unloading grain referred to as "hand-scuttling". Automatically the local TGWU officials, led by Parnell the area officer, opposed the strike. Just as automatically the men formed their own rank-and-file committee. This committee, consisting of four men (Hart, Oakes, Eastwood and Brady), next day raised before the mass meeting on Corporation Field the attitude of the TGWU officials. Hart, acting as the committee's spokesman, made the call for going over to the NASD, and a telegram was sent to Barrett, the Blue Union General Secretary, applying for membership.'

Regarding JW Murphy, Pennington stated in an interview with Dave Baines in 1982:

'Hull had never been a port notorious then for its advanced leadership, either at a trade union or a political level. It was considered a bit of a backwater. When these workers came into struggle and strike, having no established leadership, they looked elsewhere for leadership — to Murphy. We went to see Murphy, who introduced us firstly to the strike leader, a young bloke called Albert Hart, and another bloke called Eastwood.'

In his thesis *The Unofficial Movement on the Docks and the Rivalry Between the Blue and the White* (Warwick University, 1982) Baines writes:

'Unlike London or Liverpool, Hull dockers didn't have a permanent Port Workers Committee or an acknowledged unofficial leadership. There was no organised political group active amongst the dockers, or even a group of dockers with any experience of industrial militancy. A strike committee was elected from the floor of the mass meeting, consisting of raw industrial workers with no experience of organising strikes, and consequently they turned to the only person they knew who had experience of organising a dispute, a certain James Wilcox Murphy. During the 1945 strike, Murphy was the acknowledged leader of the Hull dockers, and though he had resigned from the docks in 1946, he kept in regular contact with the docks, as well as with some of the unofficial leaders in London and Liverpool.

'Immediately after consulting with the strike committee, Murphy sent a telegram to Dick Barrett, General Secretary of the NASD, asking him to accept the Hull dockers into the Blue. On 20 August the Hull strike committee announced that the NASD had decided to consider their request.'

The Birkenhead dockers' leader, Bill Johnson, was interviewed by Fred Lindop in the early 1980s. Speaking of his visit to Hull, Johnson states:

'I went across to Hull during that dispute when the talk was in the air — how fed up they were with the T&G! Their mind had already been made up, they were going to seek membership, arrangements had been made for Albert Hart and somebody else to go to London.'

This is in addition to the letter, quoted in my pamphlet, to Murphy from Jimmy Ginley, the Hull NASD official, stating that it was 'largely due to your endeavour that the NAS&D was formed in Hull'. Baines also writes that 'Murphy's position was frequently commented on in scathing reports from TGWU Docks officers. He had regular contact with a number of Blue militants from 1945 onwards, especially Bert Aylward, and was in regular contact with the Birkenhead Committee from 1950.' Letters from Murphy to Harry Constable have also survived. Its also interesting to note that John McIlroy refers to Murphy, in passing, in his article on the 1945 dock strike in the same issue of *Revolutionary History*.

Hart, Pennington, Johnson, Brandon and Baines all therefore emphasise the importance of Murphy's rôle, and support the view expressed in my pamphlet that the decision to move to the NASD was made by the Hull dockers on Wednesday, 18 August 1954.
Fraternally
Keith Sinclair

Apparachiks and Stewards' Committees

Dear Editor
In his article published in *Revolutionary History* (Volume 6, nos 2/3, pp160-76), Alan Christianson appears to be regarding the old Revolutionary Communist Party as a mass party. How can there be 'Apparatus Men' in a party of a few hundred people? Apart from that, it was necessary for the leadership of the RCP to tackle all the nitty gritty work of the office — typ-

ing, duplicating, stuffing envelopes, cleaning up, etc — hardly the work of apparachiks!

The import of Christianson's article is that there is no need for a revolutionary party because the shop stewards' committees had taken over all functions 'political, trade union and economic'. Such a theory might have appeared relevant in 1955 when this article was written, but it has not stood the test of time. Therefore, Christianson did not discover a great revolutionary truth, but only a flash in the pan! Obviously, rank and file movements, shop stewards' committees, etc, are at their height during periods of full employment. Perhaps Christianson imagined that welfare capitalism was here to say. If so, I've got news for him!

Christianson claims that the leadership of the RCP lost interest in the trade union movement, and turned away from mass struggle. I disagree here entirely, for all of us, right up to the end, were expected to attend our trade union branches, be elected to Trades Councils, and so on. Regular meetings were held at the centre for members of each union represented, to coordinate work. And it has to be remembered that the membership of the RCP was largely working class.

No doubt Christianson has fond memories of stewards' Central Committee meetings in the pub, but this nostalgia is not enough on which to build a revolutionary theory.

Fraternally
Sheila Lahr

Harry McShane

Dear Editor

In his review of Les Forster's *Rocking the Boat* (*Revolutionary History*, Volume 6, nos 2/3), Ray Challinor states that 'Harry McShane died cursing Tony Cliff and the SWP'. I have no doubt that Challinor is being scrupulously truthful in this claim, but political honesty requires that it be placed against the background of historical record.

Harry McShane became a member of the editorial board of *Labour Worker* (forerunner of *Socialist Worker*) when the paper moved to Glasgow in May 1963, and remained one, contributing to the paper, until it returned to London in September 1964. He continued to collaborate with the International Socialists and the Socialist Workers Party until his death in 1988. Contrary to Challinor's claim that he was not allowed to make a 'political contribution', he made many such contributions. Thus he wrote a page-long article, 'Realm of Freedom', in the first issue of *Socialist Review* in April 1978, spoke — alongside Eddie and Ruth Frow — on the early years of the Communist Party of Great Britain at the SWP's Skegness rally in 1980, and addressed a meeting at the conclusion of the IS-inspired Right to Work March in 1976 — the first time he had ever spoken at the Albert Hall.

In 1978 McShane published his autobiography, *No Mean Fighter*, written in collaboration with a (then) SWP member, Joan Smith. In this he commends the IS/SWP for their 'Neither Washington nor Moscow' line in

CND, and for the way they built the Right to Work Campaign. He continued to attend Glasgow SWP meetings until shortly before his death. In *Socialist Worker* (8 March 1986) Paul Foot records that McShane, aged 93, had attended a meeting at which Foot spoke; he also scrupulously notes that McShane criticised him, saying 'there wasn't enough about the Russian betrayal, Paul'.

McShane was not in total political agreement with the IS/SWP. As he made clear in his autobiography, he aligned himself politically with Raya Dunayevskaya, and was involved with a small group of 'Marxist humanists' in Britain, as well as writing many letters to the American *News and Letters* in the 1960s and 1970s.

Dunayevskaya's ideas were not those of the IS/SWP, but there is no evidence that McShane expected the IS/SWP to provide him with a platform to propagate 'Marxist humanism'. Rather, in all the published examples I have consulted, he stressed what united him with the SWP. I know of no public utterance of McShane's in which he criticised the IS/SWP, or in which he repudiated the positive things he said about it in his autobiography and elsewhere. Presumably neither does Challinor — or he would cite them, instead of relying on deathbed curses.

McShane showed considerable courage in breaking from the CPGB at an age when others would have been thinking only of retirement; it is unlikely he would have been intimidated from making a political break from the SWP if he had wished to do so.

Challinor's review shows some of the dangers inherent in the current fashion for 'oral history'. Oral testimony can provide a valuable source for historians, but should always be balanced against other evidence. The facts I have quoted are all available to any researcher in published material; they cannot be negated by hearsay and gossip.

Fraternally
Ian Birchall

A Clarification

Dear Editor
In the last issue of *Revolutionary History*, I contributed a biographical note on the life of Alan Christianson, and in that note I wrote that while in France, a member of the Union Communiste introduced us to a meeting of the printers' union, and I made the following comment: 'On 26 January 1946 the printers' union initiated large-scale strikes against the de Gaulle-Stalinist government.' In the piece as published, this was altered to: 'On 26 January 1946 the printers' union was to strike against the de Gaulle-Stalinist government.' Not quite the same thing. Why anyone should have altered my remark, I do not know. It was not empty speculation on my part, but was based on the report of the Renault strike of 1947 which appeared in *Revolutionary History*, Volume 2, no 1, Spring 1989. The report was taken from *Jeune Révolutionnaire*, April 1971. It refers to the printers' strike of 27 June, and a strike of the postal workers from 29 July to 4 August 1946, and

goes on to say 'from this strike a national strike committee sprang up... which convened a conference of strike committees... Two revolutionary organisations were represented among these people... all of them trade unionists of the CGT.'

One was the Union Communiste, which survives today in the paper *Lutte Ouvrière*, and the other was the PCI (French Section of the Fourth International), today the Organisation Communiste Internationaliste (for the Reconstruction of the Fourth International). These two groupings put down roots among the workers of the Renault Billancourt plant. This led to a strike of 20 000 on 23 April 1947, which ended on 12 May. During this strike, the print workers printed and distributed at their own expense the appeal of the Central Strike Committee. On page 18 of this issue of *Revolutionary History*, it is pointed out that Renault opened the lock-gates, and a wave of strikes swept through France.

The bland phrase 'the printers' union was to strike against the... government' does not adequately reveal the rôle the printers' union played in the struggles of that period.

Fraternally
Ernie Rogers

The OCI to which Ernie refers has changed its name twice since the publication of the original article, first to the Parti Communiste Internationaliste, and lately to the Courant Communiste du Parti des Travailleurs — Editor.

Readers' Notes

Soviet Union and Stalinism

Guardian, 4 May 1996. 'Moscow, 21 March 1922', and 'The Caucasus, 25 March 1933', Arthur Ransome on the New Economic Policy, and Malcolm Muggeridge on collectivisation; WT Goode, 'An Interview With Lenin'; 'Reinforcements Against Denikin'; 'The Bid for Petrograd', from 21 October 1919 issue.

Observer, 5 May 1996. Zhang Xianliang, 'Madness, Mao and Mass Starvation', extract from his *My Bodhi Tree* on the Great Leap Forward.

International Workers Bulletin, 6 May 1996. Vadim Rogovin, 'The Origins and Consequences of Stalin's Great Terror'.

Workers Press, 11 May 1996. Peter Fryer, 'Trotsky and Artistic Freedom'.

Socialist Worker, 25 May 1996. Paul McGarr, 'Trotsky 1906: On Trial for Leading the People'.

Marxist Review, May 1996. Ray Athow, 'In Defence of Trotsky: A Reply to Dmitri Volkogonov'.

Workers Liberty, May 1996. John O'Mahoney, 'Trotsky and the Jews'.

Workers Press, 15 June 1996. Peter Fryer, 'That "Secret Speech"', memories of 1956.

Workers Vanguard, 7 June 1996. 'Richard Pipes: Exorcising the Russian Revolution'. See also Paul Siegel, 'The Pipes School of Falsification', in 30 August issue.

Socialist Review, June 1996. Judith Orr, 'The Struggle for Power', Lenin's *State and Revolution*.

Independent, 2 July 1996. Stephen Vines, 'Here They Met, Back in 1929 [sic]', and 'Comrades Who Waste No Time on Ideals'. Seventy-fifth anniversary of the founding of the Chinese Communist Party.

International Worker, 13 July 1996. Dick North and Richard Pipes, 'Leon Trotsky and the Moscow Trials', an exchange of letters.

The Times, 16 July 1996. 'Music and Art in Russia', Lunacharsky and the stage, from 16 July 1926 issue.

Guardian, 17 July 1996. Morgan Philips Price, 'Kronstadt After the Revolution', from 17 July 1917 issue.

Workers Liberty, July 1996. Max Shachtman, 'Remembering Leon Trotsky', and '1939: Trotsky and his Critics'; Sean Matgamna, 'Trotsky and "Trotskyism"'.

Socialist Review, July-August 1996. Sean Vernell, 'From Left to Centre', a look at Lenin's *Left Wing Communism*.

The Times, 5 August 1996. 'The Famine in Russia', from 5 August 1921 issue.

The Times, 21 August 1996. 'Russians March into Czechoslovakia', from 21 August 1968 issue.

The Times, 24 August 1996. 'Moscow Trial Verdict', from 24 August 1936 issue.

Observer, 8 September 1996. Andrew Higgins, 'Westerners Keep Going to Mao's March to Revolution', the Maoist tourist trail.

Guardian, 10 September 1996. 'Mao Poems Mark Anniversary', volumes 3 to 5 of his *Collected Works* published on the twentieth anniversary of his death.

The Times, 30 September 1996. Owen Matthews, 'The Death of a Party Man', investigation into the death of Boris Bikitov, a Ukrainian party secretary purged in 1937.

Workers Liberty, September 1996. Frank Higgins, 'When Stalin Murdered the Revolutionary Generation', the Moscow Trials; Max Shachtman, 'Trotsky's Contribution to Marxism'.

Independent, 20 October 1996. Teresa Poole, 'Long March, But It Was Worth It', interview with a veteran of the Chinese Long March.

Marxist Review, October 1996. Dave Wiltshire, 'Leon Trotsky and How the Revolution Armed', part one; parts two and three in November and December issues.

Socialist Standard, October 1996. Eddie Grant, 'Calling the Kettle Black', Ho Chi Minh's massacre of the Vietnamese Trotskyists.

Observer, 10 November 1996. Paul Webster, 'Hero of the French Left "Sent Comrades to the

Hangman'", Koral Bartosek reveals Artur London as a Stalinist agent. See also Jean-Jacques Marie, 'Lise London répond', *Informations Ouvrières*, 13 November; Jean-Jacques Marie, 'Les Truquers à l'oeuvre', *Informations Ouvrières*, 27 November; Jean-Michel Krivine, 'Les Archives de l'aveu', *Rouge*, 26 December; Jean-Michel Krivine, 'Bartosek, London et le travail d'historian'; 'Les Supplices de la mèmoire', *Rouge*, 13 February 1997.

Sunday Times, 17 November 1996. Carey Scott, 'Fear Revisits Stalin's House of Fear', the GPU's headquarters.

Workers Vanguard, 22 November 1996. 'Peasant "Anarchism", Pogroms and the Russian Revolution', Makhno and Soviet power.

Socialist Action (USA), November 1996. 'Moscow Conference Called to Commemorate Leon Trotsky's *The Revolution Betrayed*'. See also Marilyn Vogt-Downey, 'Moscow Conference Marks Sixtieth Anniversary of Trotsky's Classic *Revolution Betrayed*', in January 1997 issue; Simon Pirani, '*Revolution Betrayed* Discussed in Moscow', *Workers International Press*, February.

Workers Liberty, November 1996. 'Natalia Trotsky's 1956 Broadcast to Russia'; Max Shachtman, 'Trotsky and Marxism'.

Against the Current, November-December 1996. Paul LeBlanc, 'On the Trotskyist Opposition'; John Marot, 'A Rejoinder'.

International Worker, 11 January 1997. Vadim Rogovin, 'Social Inequality, Bureaucracy and the Betrayal of Socialism'.

The Times, 17 January 1997. Richard Beeston, 'Skeletons Revive Horrors of Stalin's Purges', bones in the Tbilisi Security Ministry.

International Workers Bulletin, 27 January 1997. Vadim Rogovin, 'The Program of the Opposition Embodied a Genuine Socialist Alternative'.

Weekly Worker, 13 February 1997. 'In Russia', from *The Call*, 8 February 1917.

Socialist, 28 February 1997. Christine Thomas and Helen Redwood, 'The Russian Revolution: Eightieth Anniversary: Opening Shots'.

Marxist Review, February 1997. Jim Graham, 'Trotsky and the British Socialist Revolution', part one; part two in March issue.

International Worker, 8 March 1997. 'Because I Have Remained a Socialist, I am a Declared Opponent of Stalinism', interview with Nathan Steinberger.

Guardian, 18 March 1997. 'Moshe Pijade, Red Buffoon', from 18 March 1957 issue.

Independent, 27 March 1997. 'Stalin Finds Favour in Former Soviet Republic', nostalgia in Belarus; Keith Flett, 'Baffled by 1917? Just Ask Trotsky'.

Sunday Times, 30 March 1997. John Harlow, '"Brilliant" Historian is Accused of Plagiarism', fur flies as Richard Pipes accuses Orlando Figes of nicking lumps of his books. See also Orlando Figes, 'Historian Puts the Record Straight on Russia, *Sunday Times*, 4 May.

Socialist Outlook, March 1997. Alexandra Kollontai, 'International Women's Day', from 1920.

Workers Liberty, March 1997. Clive Bradley, 'Eisenstein and Revolution'.

Sunday Times, 6 April 1997. Sir Reginald Hibbert and Tony Northrop, 'Old Albanian Feuds', Enver Hoxha in the Second World War.

Marxist Review, April 1997. Mike Driver, 'Towards a New Revolutionary Art', Trotsky on art and the class struggle.

Workers Liberty, April 1997. Martin Thomas, 'State Capitalism in the USSR'; Jim Noble, 'A Bureaucratic Revolution?'.

What Next?, no 3. Jonathan Joseph, 'Lenin's Concept of Hegemony'; Max Shachtman, 'Lenin and Rosa Luxemburg'; Bob Pitt, 'Lenin, Levi and Ultra-Leftism'.

Black Flag, no 207. Albert Meltzer, 'Why Ex-Kings are Dangerous', an inaccurate attack on Trotsky.

Europe-Asia Studies, Volume 48, no 3. Ian Thatcher, 'Trotsky Studies After the Crash: A Brief Note'.

The Hungarian Revolution, 1956

Independent, 25 June 1996. Adrian Bridge, 'Hungary Divided Over Martyr's Case', the debate over Imre Nagy.

Independent, 20 October 1996. Neal Ascherson, 'A Land Once Fit for Heroes'.

Independent, 21 October 1996. Paul Neuburg, 'My Class Struggle'; Adrian Bridge, 'The Day a Nation Turned on Its Masters'; Imre Karacs, 'Communist Rule Meant Singing Silly Songs'.

Guardian, 23 October 1996. Julian Borger, 'How China Killed a Revolution', Chinese pressure on Khrushchev to crush the Hungarian Revolution.

Independent, 24 October 1996. Adrian Bridge, 'Hungarians Honour Heroes of 1956 Revolt'.
Workers Press, 26 October 1996. Balázs Nagy, 'Hungary 1956'.
Socialism Today, October 1996. Phil Hearse, 'Hungary 1956'.
Militant, 1 November 1997. Dennis Rudd, 'Hungary: Tanks Replaced by Banks'.
The Times, 6 November 1997. 'Iron Curtain on Hungary', from 6 November 1956 issue.
Socialist Outlook, 9 November 1997. John Lister, 'Hungary 1956: Turning Point for Stalinism'.
Workers Press, 9 November 1997. Balázs Nagy, 'The Message of the 1956 Hungarian Revolution'; Peter Fryer, 'The Day They Bombed Budapest'.
News and Letters, November 1996. Raya Dunayevskaya, 'Hungary 1956: The Light of Freedom'; Laszlo Gati, 'Hungary 1956 Recalled'.
Workers Liberty, November 1996. Kate Buckell, 'Workers Against Stalinist Tanks'.
International Worker, 8 February 1997. Sybille Fuchs, 'Hungary 1956: A Revolt Against Stalinism', part one; part two in 22 February issue.
Workers International News, March 1997. Peter Fryer, 'The Hungarian Revolution Remembered'.

Labour Movement

Workers Vanguard, 12 April 1996. Joseph Seymour, 'Marxism vs Anarchism: From 1848 to the Bolshevik Revolution; part four: Anarchism and Syndicalism in Pre-World War I Era'; part five, 'The Syndicalists', in 24 May issue.
Workers Press, 20 April 1996. James D Young, 'Hitler's Fascism and German Socialist Resistance, 1933-44'.
The Times, 2 May 1996. Sarah Baxter, 'Labour's Patriotic Prophet', Eric Hobsbawm's ideas. See also Andrew Roberts, 'Eric, A Chip Off the Old Soviet Bloc', *Sunday Times*, 5 May.
Militant, 3 May 1996. Bill Mullins, '1926 General Strike: When Workers Took Control'.
Guardian, 8 May 1996. Alan Travis, 'From Peterloo to the Poll Tax', a history of protest.
Socialist Worker, 18 May 1996. Paul McGarr, 'Robert Owen: Boss Who Turned Against the System'.
Rouge, 16 May 1996. Jan Malewski, 'Ignace Reiss, vie et mort d'un révolutionnaire', a Swiss film on Reiss; Rodolphe Prager, 'Les Nôtres', the murder of Pietro Tresso by the Stalinists.
Workers Press, 20 May 1996. Peter Fryer, 'Hobsbawm Wonders Why', a Stalinist history conference.
Workers Press, 25 May 1996. John Plant, 'Murders of Trotskyists in World War'; Brian Pearce, 'Paris Commune'; Cliff Slaughter, 'More on 1926 — and 1936', the General Strike.
Socialism Today, May 1996. Lynn Walsh, 'Betrayal of a Generation', the General Strike.
Workers Liberty, May 1996. DR O'Connor Lysaght, 'Lenin Got It Right', the Irish national question; Edward Conze, 'The Unity of Opposites'.
Against the Current, May-June 1996. Charlie Post, 'The Flint "Sit-Down" for Beginners'; Sol Dollinger, 'Flint and the Rewriting of History'; Nelson Lichtenstein, 'A Comment on Historiography', the Flint strike and Stalinist interpretations.
Organizer, May-June 1996. Frank Wainwright, 'Leon Trotsky on the Formation of a Black Political Party'.
Workers News, May-June 1996. Al Richardson, 'Scargill's SLP in Perspective'; 'Towards the New Workers Party', from *Fight*, 12 December 1936, a symposium on the Independent Labour Party.
Workers Liberty, June 1996. Stan Crooke, 'Stalinism and the British General Strike'; Roger Clarke, 'The Nations and the Marxists'; Tony Dale, 'The Essence of Shachtman'; Edward Conze, 'The Unity of Opposites'.
Socialist Worker, 8 June 1996. Hassan Mahamdallie, 'Bronterre O'Brien: The "Schoolmaster" of Chartism'.
Weekly Worker, 6 June 1996. 'Why the Strike Failed: Communist Party Statement', from *Workers Weekly*, 4 June 1926; SL Kenning, 'Understand History: Don't Repeat It', Communist affiliation to the Labour Party.
The Times, 14 June 1996. 'Child Communist's Trip to Russia', Young Communist League trip, from 14 June 1927 issue.
Socialist Worker, 29 June 1996. Mike Simons, 'France 1936: Struggle Returns, But Who Will Lead?'.
Trotskyist International, June-September 1996. Dave Stockton, 'The Fight for the Fourth International'.
New Interventions, Spring 1996. Ted Crawford, 'Technology and Naval Mutiny'; Paul Flewers, 'A Few Words on James Klugmann's *From Trotsky to Tito*'; Chris Gray, 'Trotsky's Theory of Permanent Revolution'; Dave Hollis, 'Will the Real Rosa Luxemburg Please Stand Up!'.

Organise, Spring 1996. 'Anarchist Communism in Britain', a history.

Revolutionary Perspectives, Spring 1996. 'The General Strike, 1926'

Socialist Worker, 6 July 1996. Hazel Croft, 'Tom Mann: Incitement to Class Struggle'.

Independent, 13 July 1996. Nancy Sorel, 'When J Edgar Hoover Met Emma Goldman'.

Workers Press, 20 July 1996. Brian Pearce, 'Engels and Genocide'; Charlie Pottins, 'Land and Liberty', Stalinist attempts to hijack André Breton.

Rouge, 25 July 1996. Gabriel Peyrot, 'Vrai semblable exécution'; Rodolphe Prager and Gabriel Peyrot, 'Un interview d'Albert Demazière', the Stalinist murders of French Trotskyists in the Second World War.

New Yorker, 29 July 1996. Paul Berman, 'The Romantic Revolutionary', CLR James.

Workers Liberty, July 1996. Jane Ryan, 'Starry-Eyed About James', CLR James; Edward Conze, 'Contradiction and the Cause of Change'.

Against the Current, July-August 1996. Charlie Post, 'Rethinking CPUSA History' and 'The Comintern, the CPUSA and the Activities of Rank and File CPers'; Paul LeBlanc, Letter on CLR James.

Socialism Today, July-August 1996. Sam Baskett, 'Jack London's Call of Socialism'.

Workers Power, July-August 1996. 'Building the International in War-Shattered Europe', part five of the history of the Fourth International; part six, '1948: A Turning Point for Trotskyism', and part seven, 'The Collapse of the FI into Centrism', in September and October issues.

Guardian, 3 August 1996. Margaret Busby, 'Storming the Pavilions of Prejudice', CLR James.

Guardian, 13 August 1996. James Meikle, 'Campaigners Seek Pardon for Welsh "Martyr"', Dic Penderyn, a participant in the Merthyr Uprising.

Socialist Outlook, August 1996. Salah Jaber, 'Seminar Discusses Ernest Mandel's Open Marxism'.

Guardian, 3 September 1996. Paul Webster, 'Old Comrades Trade Insults over Che'.

Informations Ouvrières, 18 September 1996. Jean Boyer, 'André Breton et les procès de Moscou'.

Workers Press, 21 September 1996. Charlie Pottins, 'Artist's Rôle', Trotsky, André Breton and Diego Rivera.

Weekly Worker, 26 September 1996. William Gallacher, Wal Hannington, Albert Inkpin, Harry Pollitt, William Rust, 'Five Communists' Message', jailed Communists protest, from *Workers Weekly*, 24 September 1926.

Workers Press, 5 October 1996. Phil Edwards, 'The Battle of Cable Street'. See also Charlie Pottins, 'East Enders Stopped Mosley by Reversing CP Policy', in 12 October issue; Ruth Carlyle, 'Cable Street and the Defeat of British Fascism', *Workers Liberty*, October; Charlie Bain, 'People Power that Beat the Fascists', *Independent*, 7 October.

Socialist Review, October 1996. Clare Fermont, 'Workers' Springtime', Rosa Luxemburg and *The Mass Strike*; Frank Henderson, 'Why I Became a Socialist'.

Workers Power, October 1996. Clare Heath, 'Women and the Struggle for Socialism', Klara Zetkin.

Independent, 7 November 1996. Christopher Bellamy, 'The Reading Room Rebels', the defunct tradition of political exile in Britain.

Workers Press, 9 November 1996. Peter Fryer, 'In Defence of John Maclean'.

Guardian, 16 November 1996. Richard Boston, 'Anarchy Amongst the Anarchists', a history of Anarchism.

Workers Liberty, November 1996. Sean Matgamna, 'The Life and Death of Peter Graham, 1945-71'.

Rouge, 12 December 1996. Jean-Michel Krivine, 'Quand Staline "conseillait" Maurice Thorez', conversations between Stalin and Thorez on how to betray the struggles of 1945.

Bulletin, Autumn 1996. 'The Tragic Split in the Socialist International'.

International Socialism, Autumn 1996. Ian Birchall, 'The Babeuf Centenary: Conspiracy or Revolutionary Party?'

New Interventions, Autumn 1996. Paul Flewers, 'The Dog That Didn't Bark', *Tribune* and Soviet foreign policy; Theodor Bergmann, 'After the Deluge: Rebuilding a Marxist Organisation in Germany After 1945'.

Revolutionary Marxism Today, Winter 1996. Ernest Mandel, 'Vanguard Parties', a speech from 1983; Jim Miles, 'Joseph Hansen and the Marxist Theory of the State'.

Workers Liberty, March 1997. Brian Pearce, 'How the Labour Party Began'.

Daily News (Sri Lanka), 6 January 1997. T Perera, 'Appreciations: Edmund Samarakkody'. See also T Perera, 'Edmund Samarakkody: A Pioneer of the Left Remembered', *Sunday Observer* (Sri Lanka), 5 January.

News and Letters, January-February 1997. Kevin Anderson, 'Uncovering Marx's Yet Unpublished Writings'.
Guardian, 16 April 1997. 'Chez Marx', a Prussian police spy looks at Marx's house; 'Cheers to Marx's Fine Tradition', Marx and Engels on drink.
Socialist Worker, 19 April 1997. Sam Ashman, 'Rosa Luxemburg: The Flame of Revolution'.
Workers Liberty, April 1997. John O'Mahoney, 'The Apostle of Labour Solidarity', Jim Larkin.
Rouge, 1 May 1997. Eric Lafon, 'Une Interview de Raymond Vacheron', details of the murder of Pietro Tresso.
Lobster, no 31. Charlie Pottins, 'How Britain's Stalinists Spied on the Left'.
Revolutionary Perspectives, no 1. 'The Indispensable Engels'
What Next?, no 2. Jean Van Heijenoort, 'The German Revolution in the Leninist Period', from *Fourth International*, March 1943.
What Next?, no 3. James D Young, 'John Maclean: Clydeside Socialist'; Edmund Samarakkody, 'The National Question in Sri Lanka'.

Spanish Civil War Anniversary

Ham and High, 24 May 1996. Roger Blitz, 'Director Evokes a Glorious Revolution', inaccurate report of showing of *Land and Freedom* at Marx House.
Independent, 18 July 1996. Tunku Varadarajan, 'Civil War Taboo Keeps Spanish Historians Cowed'.
The Times, 20 July 1996. Hugh Thomas, 'The Spanish Civil War: A Memoir'.
Independent, 21 July 1996. Brian Cathcart, 'They Kept the Red Flag Flying', Stalinism and the Spanish Civil War.
Independent, 22 July 1996. Paul Vallely, 'Romancing the Past', a Stalinist view of the Spanish Civil War.
Militant, 26 July 1996. Mike Morris, 'The War for Land and Freedom'.
Informations Ouvrières, 31 July 1996. EN, 'À propos l'emission d'arte sur l'assassinat d'Andrès Nin', a film about Nin's assassination.
Socialist Review, July-August 1996. Andy Durgan, 'The Spanish Revolution: Fighting on Two Fronts', a reply to Paul Preston that the *New Statesman* refused to publish.
Informations Ouvrières, 7 August 1996. AT, 'Lettre de Barcelone', the murder of Andreu Nin.
Observer, 1 September 1996. Rita Grosvenor and Arnold Kemp, 'Spain's Falling Soldier Really Did Die that Day', Capa's famous Spanish Civil War picture.
Workers Press, 24 August 1996. Charlie Pottins, 'Copic's Fate', the purging of the commander of the Fifteenth International Brigade.
Morning Star, 28 August 1996. George Hallam, 'Casting Light on Spanish Illusions', Stalinists still try to smear the POUM. See replies by Gerry Downing, 'A Putsch or Stalinist Counter-Revolution?', in 6 September issue; and Bob Pitt, 'Rôle of German Agents in the Puzzling "Putsch"', in 9 September issue.
International Worker, 21 September 1996. Vicky Short, 'Lessons of the Spanish Revolution'.
The Times, 2 November 1996. Tunku Varadarajan, 'Carried Away to War', the International Brigades.
Observer, 3 November 1996. Neil McKenna, 'Heroes at Last, 60 Years After'.
Guardian, 4 November 1996. 'Spain Honours Anti-Fascists'.
Guardian, 9 November 1996. Adela Gooch, 'Spain Honours Its Debt to the Foreign Brigades'.
The Times, 6 March 1997. 'The Ordeal of Madrid: Thirty Months Besieged', from 6 March 1939 issue.
Guardian, 18 April 1997. Robert Dawson Scott, 'Sixty Years On, Fighting a Threadbare Cause'.

George Orwell and the Spooks

Guardian, 11 July 1996. Richard Norton-Taylor and Seumas Milne, 'Orwell Offered Writers' Blacklist to Anti-Soviet Propaganda Unit', including a letter from Orwell to Celia Kirwan.
The Times, 11 July 1996. Ian Murray, 'Orwell Was Recruited to Fight Soviet Propaganda'.
The Times, 12 July 1996. Derwent May, 'George Orwell's Cold War'.
Sunday Times, 14 July 1996. Andrew Roberts, '*Animal Farm*'s Rich Crop of Humbug'.
Independent, 14 July 1996. Ros Wynne-Jones, 'Orwell's Little List Leaves the Left Gasping for More'; Bernard Crick, 'Why Are Radicals So Eager to Give Up One of Their Own?'.

Guardian, 13 July 1996. John Lawrence, Stephen Lutman and David Ross, 'Some Propagandists Are More Equal Than Others', correspondence.
Guardian, 13 August 1996. Mervyn Jones, 'Fears that Made Orwell Sneak on his Friends'.
New Interventions, Autumn 1996. Paul Flewers, 'Orwell and the Spooks'.

William Morris Centenary

Guardian, 27 April 1996. Fiona MacCarthy, 'Walls of Fame'.
Guardian, 3 May 1996. Deyan Sudjic, 'Papering Over the Cracks'.
Independent, 4 May 1996. Jonathan Glancey, 'The Sentimental Socialist'.
Independent, 5 May 1996. Tim Hilton, 'Paper Tiger'.
Guardian, 6 May 1996. Oliver Bennett, 'Underneath the Paper, William Morris' Writing on the Wall'.
Guardian, 8 May 1996. Paul Hardwick, SCM McFarlane, HE Roberts, David Page and Roger Simon, replying to Sudjic.
Independent, 9 May 1996. David Grove, 'William Morris' Socialist Dream'.
New Statesman, 10 May 1996. Jonathan Glancey, 'A Peculiarly English Socialist'.
The Times, 10 May 1996. Richard Cork, 'The Man Who Traded in the Best of Taste'; John Russell Taylor, 'Did the Patient Seducer Have His Way?'; Alison Beckett, 'Morris Round-Up'.
Guardian, 11 May 1996. Martin Kettle, 'Defence of an Icon Who Still Inspires'.
The Times, 11 May 1996. Karen Kay, 'Vintage Year for the William Morris Miners'.
Independent, 12 May 1996. Clive Wilmer and Keith Flett, 'How Ruskin Saw Morris'.
Observer, 12 May 1996. Roger Tedre, 'Future is Far From Rosy for Morris' Red House'; William Feaver, 'William the Plunderer'.
The Times, 18 May 1996. Simon Jenkins, 'The Man Who Never Stopped'.
Socialist Worker, 22 June 1996. 'William Morris: Seeds of Revolution'
Socialist Review, June 1996. Solomon Hughes, 'A Bit of Agitation'; John Plant, 'London's Morris Legacy'.
Socialist Standard, June 1996. Steve Coleman, 'Socialists, Saints and Muffin the Mule'.
Workers Liberty, May 1996. William Morris, 'Ireland: Is Home Rule Enough?', from *Commonweal*, October 1895.
Workers Liberty, June 1996. Nicholas Salmon, 'Reclaiming William Morris'.
Independent, 17 July 1996. Andrew Marr, 'Art Lessons for New Labour'.
The Times, 23 July 1996. John and Kate Cooper, 'Exemplary Life of William Morris'.
Independent, 28 July 1996. Dorothy Biltcliffe, 'William Morris Sadly Neglected'.
Independent, 31 August 1996. David James, 'William Morris, Rest in Peace'.
International Socialism, Summer 1996. Hassan Mahamdallie, 'William Morris and Revolutionary Marxism'.
Independent, 7 September 1996. Dorothy Biltcliffe, 'William Morris' Neglected Grave'.
Independent, 10 September 1996. Michael Murphy, 'Grave Concern'.
Socialism Today, September 1996. Margaret Jones, 'William Morris: Revolutionary Socialist Pioneer'.
The Times, 5 October 1996. 'Death of Mr William Morris', from 5 October 1896 issue.
Socialist Campaign Group News, October 1996. Pete Willsman, 'William Morris'.
The Times, 23 November 1996. Andrew Yates, 'Where William Designed his Wallpaper'.
International Socialism, Autumn 1996. Paul O'Flynn, 'From the Kingdom of Necessity to the Kingdom of Freedom: Morris' *News From Nowhere*'.
Journal of the William Morris Society, Autumn 1996. Ian Birchall, 'Morris, Bax and Babeuf'.

Obituaries

Alec Acheson, Trotskyist and supporter of this magazine. Charlie Van Gelderen, 'Alec Acheson: A Convinced Marxist Revolutionary', *Socialist Outlook*, 25 May 1996; CVG and BH 'Alec Acheson: A Convinced Marxist Revolutionary', *International Viewpoint*, September.
Carl Cowl, veteran US Oehlerite. 'Carl Cowl: A Century of Revolution', *Socialist Worker*, 19 April 1997.
Deng Xiaoping. Derek Davies, 'Deng Xiaoping', *Independent*, 20 February 1997; 'Deng Xiaoping', *The Times*, 19 February; Richard Evans, 'The Man Who Mocked Mao'; John Gittings, 'Deng Xiaoping: Marching Through the Storm', *Guardian*, 20 February; 'Deng Xiaoping and the Fate of the Chinese Revolution', *International Worker*, 8 March.

Michael Economides, International Brigade veteran. Lala Isla, 'Michael Economides: Strong Voice Against Fascism', *Guardian*, 28 December 1996.

Patience Edney, long-term member of the Communist Party of Great Britain. Martin Green, 'Patience Edney', *Independent*, 2 December 1996; Claire Tomalin, 'Patience Edney', *Independent*, 3 December.

William Forrest, International Brigade veteran. 'William Forrest', *The Times*, 31 October 1996.

Vivienne Goonewardene (1916-1996), wife of Leslie Goonewardene. Florence Wickremasinghe; 'Vivienne: Woman of the Revolution', *Sunday Observer* (Sri Lanka), 6 October 1996.

Vernon Gunasekera, first General Secretary of the Lanka Sama Samaja Party. ZM Razik, 'Kandy Bar Pays Tribute to Vernon Gunasekera', *Daily News* (Sri Lanka), 14 November 1996.

Yutaka Hanya, Japanese novelist, opponent of Stalin in the Japanese Communist Party. James Kirkup, 'Yutaka Hanya: The Never-Ending Story', *Guardian*, 29 March 1997.

Ellis Hillman, member of *Revolutionary History* Editorial Board. Jonathan Margolis, 'Flat Mates', *Evening Standard*, 26 April 1996; 'If There's a Heaven, Then It's Probably Flat Too', *Camden New Journal*, 9 May; José Villa, 'Ellis Hillman: Dedicated Revolutionary', *Internationalist Bulletin*, August; Albert Meltzer, 'Ellis in Wonderland', *Black Flag*, no 207.

Douglas Hyde, former *Daily Worker* writer, author of *I Believed*. Steve Parsons and Solly Kaye, 'Crisis of Belief', *Guardian*, 21 September 1996; Kevin Morgan and Bruce Kent, 'Douglas Hyde', *Independent*, 26 September; 'Douglas Hyde', *The Times*, 3 October.

Karel Kynel, journalist during the Prague Spring. Philip Spender, 'Freedom's Late Spring', *Guardian*, 4 April 1997; Neal Ascherson, 'Karel Kynel', *Independent*, 3 April.

Frida Knight, minor Stalinist. 'Frida Knight', *The Times*, 1 November 1996.

Daniel Mayer, SFIO leader and Secretary of its wartime underground apparatus. Dave Bell, 'Drive on the Left', *Guardian*, 15 January 1997.

Albert Meltzer, Anarchist. Stuart Christie, 'Anarchy's Torchbearer', *Guardian*, 8 May 1996; Nicholas Walter, 'Albert Meltzer', *Independent*, 9 May; 'Albert Meltzer', *The Times*, 15 May; Gary Younge, 'And When I Die, Don't Send Me Flowers', *Guardian*, 25 May; Ros Wynne-Jones, 'After the Anarchy, the Comedy', *Independent*, 26 May; Charlie Pottins, 'Rascal', *Workers Press*, 1 June; Charlie Pottins, 'Under a Black Flag', *Workers Press*, 15 June; Sandra Barwick, 'Anarchy Reigns as a Comrade is Remembered', *Daily Telegraph*, 2 December.

Zdenek Mlynar, leading figure in the Prague Spring. Kate Connolly, 'Frost and Thaw in Prague', *Guardian*, 21 April 1997; 'Zdenek Mlynar', *The Times*, 22 April; Gabriel Partos, 'Zdenek Mlynar', *Independent*, 21 April.

Nick Origlass, Australian Trotskyist and supporter of Pablo. John Percy, 'Nick Origlass: A Life of Struggle and Principle', *Green Left Weekly* (Australia), 5 June 1996; John Minns, 'Nick Origlass, Revolutionary Opponent of Stalinism', *Socialist Alternative* (Australia), July; Paul True, 'Battler's Politico Unafraid of Risks', *Australian*, 4 June; Nick Beams, 'Nick Origlass (1908-1996): A Trotskyist Fighter Destroyed by Pabloism', *International Worker*, 5 October.

Bob Pennington, Trotskyist. Bill Hunter, 'Bob Pennington Remembered', *Workers Press*, 12 October 1996; Peter Fryer, 'Remembering Bob Pennington', *Workers Press*, 26 October; Jane Kelly, 'Bob Pennington: Revolutionary Militant', *Socialist Outlook*, 9 November; Bob Wood, 'A Bookie's Runner — But One Hell of a Recruiter', *Socialist Outlook*, March 1997; Patrick Avaakum, 'The Life and Times of Bob Pennington', part one, *Workers Liberty*, March, part two, 'Bob Pennington and the Trotskyist Archipelago', in April issue.

Raphael Samuel, historian. Bill Schwarz, 'Raphael Samuel: Keeper of Our Shared Memory', *Guardian*, 10 December 1996; Gareth Steadman Jones, 'Raphael Samuel', *Independent*, 11 December; 'Raphael Samuel', *The Times*, 11 December; David Selbourne, 'The Last Comrade', *Observer*, 15 December; Keith Flett, 'Raphael Samuel', *Independent*, 21 December.

Carl Sagan, astrophysicist who smuggled copies of Trotsky's *Revolution Betrayed* into the Soviet Union. Joseph Bradshaw, 'Carl Sagan (1934-1996)', *International Workers Bulletin*, 13 January 1997.

Pavel Sudoplatov, mastermind behind Trotsky's assassination. 'Pavel Sudoplatov', *Daily Telegraph*, 8 October 1996; Jeanne Vronskaya, 'Pavel Sudoplatov', *Independent*, 30 September; Isobel Montgomery, 'Doing the Dirty Work of the Revolution', *Guardian*, 1 October .

Ken Tarbuck, member of *Revolutionary History* Editorial Board. Jim Dye, 'Ken Tarbuck (1930-1995)', *Workers News*, May-June 1996.

Meyer Schapiro, US art historian and Trotskyist. Alan Wallach, 'Meyer Schapiro, 1904-1996', *Against the Current*, May-June 1996.

Ono Tozabuo, Japanese Anarchist poet. James Kirkup, 'Ono Tozabuo', *Independent*, 17 October 1996.

Marie-Claude Vaillant-Couturier, personal assistant to Jacque Duclos. Douglas Johnson, 'Marie-Claude Vaillant-Couturier', *Independent*, 14 December 1996.

Jorge Villaran, Peruvian Trotskyist leader. José Carlos, 'Jorge Villaran', *Informations Ouvrières*, 25 September 1996.

Ivan Vrachev, veteran of the Left Opposition. Victor G, 'In Memory of Ivan Vrachev', *Workers Vanguard*, 7 June 1996.

Wang Li, Chinese Stalinist. John Gittings, 'Wang Li: A Revolutionary Out of His Depth', *Guardian*, 24 October 1996; 'Wang Li', *Economist*, 2 November; 'Wang Li', *The Times*, 4 November.

Ryan Worrall, pioneer Trotskyist in Britain and scientist. Walter Kendall, 'Ryan Worrall', *Guardian*, 25 May 1996.

Reviews

John Archer, *The Struggle for an Independent Trade Union by the Dockers in Merseyside and Hull During 1954-55*. Richard Price, 'Healy and the Blue Union', *Workers News*, May-June 1996.

Chris Arthur, *Engels Today: A Centenary Appreciation*. Mike Driver, 'A Tribute to Engels', *Marxist Review*, November 1996.

Mikhail Baitalsky, *Notebooks for the Grandchildren*. Abraham Bromberg, 'A Better Lenin?', *Times Literary Supplement*, 23 August; Paul Siegel, 'Recollections of a Trotskyist Who Survived the Stalinist Terror', *Socialist Action* (USA), November.

Benigno (Colonel David Alarcon Ramirez), *Vie et mort de la révolution Cubaine*. Hugh O'Shaughnessy, 'How Castro "Betrayed" the Cuban Revolution', *Independent*, 26 May 1996.

Greg Benton, *China's Urban Revolutionaries*. Neil Murray, 'China's Urban Revolutionaries', *Socialist Outlook*, August 1996; Pierre Rousset, 'G Benton sur le trotskysme en Chine', *Rouge*, 1 August; Ray Athow, 'Trotskyism in China', *Marxist Review*, July; Peter Main, 'Hidden History of the Chinese Revolution', *Trotskyist International*, January-June 1997.

Jasper Berker, *Hungry Ghosts* (on Mao's Great Leap Forward). Jonathan Mirsky, 'Spirits Allowed to Speak', *The Times*, 20 June 1996; 'From the Messiah to Mao', *Sunday Times*, 26 May.

Robin Blackburn, *The Making of New World Slavery*. Darcus Howe, 'What We Owe to Slavery', *Guardian*, 20 March 1997; Anthony Julius, 'Chain Reactions', *Observer*, 23 March.

Pierre Broué and Raymond Vacheron, *Meutres au Maquis*, the Stalinists' murder of Pietro Tresso. Jacques Faucher, 'Meutres au Maquis', *La Commune*, March 1997.

Vladimir Boukovski, *Jugement à Moscou*. Norman Stone, 'A Dissident Roaming the Kremlin Archives', *Times Literary Supplement*, 31 January 1997.

Pierre Broué, *Rakovsky*. 'Portrait d'un révolutionnaire', *Rouge*, 25 July 1996.

Paul Buhle, *A Dreamer's Paradise Lost: C Fraina/Lewis Corey and the Decline of Radicalism in the US*. Kevin Anderson, 'New Look at Louis Fraina (Lewis Corey) and American Marxism', *News and Letters*, November 1996.

Tony Cliff, *Trotsky 1927-1940: The Darker the Night, the Brighter the Star*. John Marot, 'The Trotskyist Opposition, 1927-1940', *Against the Current*, September-October 1996.

Daniel Coquema, *De Trotsky à Laguillier: Contribution à l'histoire de la IVè Internationale*. Jean-Guillaume Lanuque, 'De Trotsky à Laguillier, ou le contre-example d'une histoire du trotskysme'; Michel Lequenne, 'Notes sur notre histoire', *Critique Communiste*, Winter-Spring 1997.

Hal Draper, *War and Revolution*. Tom Rigby, 'Lenin, Trotsky and World War Three', *Workers Liberty*, September 1996; BC, 'A Petit-Bourgeois Attack on Revolutionary Defeatism', *Marxist Review*, January 1997; Paul Flewers, *New Interventions*, Spring 1997.

Theodore Draper, *A Struggle for Power: The American Revolution*. Megan Trudell, 'Who Made the American Revolution?', *International Socialism*, Winter 1996; *The Times*, 5 April 1997.

Alison Drew, *South Africa's Radical Tradition*. Charlie Van Gelderen, *Socialist Action* (USA), February 1997.

Andrew Durgan, *BOC 1930-1936: El Bloque Obrero y Campesino*. John Sullivan, *New Interventions*, Spring 1997.

John Ehrenberg, *Proudhon and His Age*. William Westwell, 'Proudhon and Marx', *Marxist Review*, February 1997.

Orlando Figes, *A People's Tragedy: The Russian Revolution, 1891-1924*. Mike Haynes, 'Unreliable

Witness', *Socialist Review*, October 1996; Norman Stone, 'Beyond the Revolution', *Sunday Times*, 18 August; David Pryce-Jones, 'Eager for the Smell of Blood', *The Times*, 29 August; Robert Service, 'Before Hindsight', *New Statesman*, 30 August; Andrew Solomon, 'The Peasants are Revolting...', *Observer*, 6 October; Ken Smith, 'Russia's Revolution: True and False', *Militant*, 10 January 1997; Erica Wagner, 'History of Russia Wins Book Prize', *The Times*, 26 March; Andrew Marr, 'Makers of Their Own Tragedy', *Independent*, 27 March.

Edmund and Ruth Frow, *The Liquidation of the Communist Party of Great Britain*. Harry Ratner, *New Interventions*, Spring 1997.

George Fyson, *Lenin's Final Fight*. Adrian Budd, 'A New Life for Lenin', *International Socialism*, Spring 1996.

Donny Gluckstein, *The Tragedy of Bukharin*. Paul Flewers, *New Interventions*, Spring 1997.

Ernest Haberkern and Arthur Lipow, *Neither Capitalism nor Socialism: Theories of Bureaucratic Collectivism*. Paul Flewers, *New Interventions*, Autumn 1996; Alex Callinicos, 'State in Debate', *International Socialism*, Winter 1996.

JL and B Hammond, *The Labourer*. Mark O'Brien 'The Bloody Birth of Capitalism', *International Socialism*, Spring 1996.

Neil Harding, *Leninism*. Bill Jenkins, 'Harding's Lenin: Revised for the New World Order', *Trotskyist International*, January-June 1997.

Christopher Hill, *Liberty Against the Law*. Keith Thomas, 'Stolen From the Poor', *Guardian*, 24 May 1996; Jonathan Clark, 'High Hill', *The Times*, 30 May; John Rees, 'Land and Freedom', *Socialist Review*, June; Bill Jenkins, 'Christopher Hill: Culture of Resistance', *Workers Power*, July-August; Charles Townshend, 'Diggers in the System', *Independent*, 25 August; Brian Manning, 'A Voice for the Poor', *International Socialism*, Autumn.

Baruch Hirson, *Revolutions in My Life*. Vusi Makabane, *Workers News*, October-November 1996; Richard Owens, 'Revolutions in a Life', *International Viewpoint*, May.

Bill Hunter, *They Knew Why They Fought*. Richard Tyler, 'A Deliberate Falsification of Working Class History', *International Worker*, 7 September 1996.

Klehr, Haynes and Firsov, *The Secret World of American Communism*. BC, 'New Documents From Soviet Archives', *Marxist Review*, February 1997.

Paul LeBlanc, *Lenin and the Revolutionary Party*. Adrian Budd, 'A New Life for Lenin', *International Socialism*, Spring 1996.

Lars Lih, Oleg Naumov, Oleg Khlevniuk, *Stalin's Letters to Molotov, 1925-1936*. Martin Malia, 'Misanthrope, Cynic and Fanatic', *Times Literary Supplement*, 31 January 1997.

George Lipset, *Rainbow at Midnight: Labor and Culture in the 1940s*. John Newsinger, 'From Class War to Cold War', *International Socialism*, Winter 1996.

Ken Loach, *Land and Freedom*. 'Popular Front Strangled the Spanish Revolution', *Workers Hammer*, April-May 1996; Michael Schreiber, '*Land and Freedom*: A Good Short Course on the Stalinist Betrayal of the Spanish Revolution', *Socialist Action* (USA), June; Valentine Cunningham, 'Comrades!', *Independent*, 20 July, the Stalinist backlash continues; Jack Jones, Derek Pattison and Brian Bamford, 'Across the Generations', *Freedom*, 3 August; 'Lessons of the Spanish Civil War', *Revolutionary Perspectives*, no 1; '*Land and Freedom*, A Film Made to Show that the Idea of Socialism is not Dead', *Socialist Action* (USA), October; 'Land and Freedom', *Black Flag*, no 207.

Nestor Makhno, *The Struggle Against the State and Other Essays*. Lew, 'A Third Force', *Socialist Standard*, July 1996.

Shirley Manganis, *Memories of Resistance*. Francesca Patai, 'Women Chronicle Spanish Civil War', *News and Letters*, March 1997.

Brian Manning, *Aristocrats, Plebeians and Revolution in England, 1640-1660*. 'The Left Wing in the English Revolution', *Marxist Review*, July 1996; Mark O'Brien, 'The Class Conflicts that Shaped British History', *International Socialism*, Winter 1996.

Henri Miczeles, *Histoire générale du Bund*. Abraham Brumberg, 'Unbreakable Bund', *Times Literary Supplement*, 10 May 1996.

Wesley Muthiah and Sydney Wanasinghe, *The Secret Files: World War 2 and the Sama Samajists*. Richard Owens, *International Viewpoint*, May 1996; Richard Price, *Workers News*, May-June; Ray Athow, 'The LSSP: From Revolution to Counter-Revolution', *Marxist Review*, August.

Mary Nash, *Defying Male Civilisation*. Francesca Patai, 'Women Chronicle Spanish Civil War', *News and Letters*, March 1997.

John Newsinger, *The Fenians in Mid-Victorian Britain*. Mark O'Brien, 'The Class Conflicts that Shaped British History', *International Socialism*, Winter 1996.

David North, *Socialism, Historical Truth and the Crisis of Political Thought in the USA*. David Walsh, *International Worker*, 19 October 1996.

Richard Pipes, *The Unknown Lenin*. George Urban, 'Hang Them High', *The Times*, 14 November 1996; Simon Sebag Montefiore, 'The Documents in the Case', *Sunday Times*, 17 November; Ken Smith, 'Russia's Revolution: True and False', *Militant*, 10 January 1997; Martin Malia, 'Misanthrope, Cynic and Fanatic', *Times Literary Supplement*, 31 January (see also correspondence between Malia and Pipes in 14 February and 7 March issues).

Mark Polizzott, *Revolution of the Mind* (biography of André Breton). Lachlan MacKinnon, 'A Total Revelation', *Times Literary Supplement*, 3 May 1996.

Elena Poniatowska, *Tinissima* (biography of Tina Modotti). Liz Jabey, 'Snaps of Modotti', *Guardian*, 27 February 1997.

Edvard Radzinsky, *Stalin*. Robert Service, 'The Great Terrorist', *Guardian*, 12 April 1996; Robert Conquest, 'Small Terror, Few Dead', *Times Literary Supplement*, 3 May; JH, *Sunday Times*, 16 March 1997.

Al Richardson (ed), *In Defence of the Russian Revolution*. Alistair Mitchell, *New Interventions*, Spring 1996.

John Saville, *The Consolidation of the Capitalist State*. Mark O'Brien, 'The Class Conflicts that Shaped British History', *International Socialism*, Winter 1996.

Cyril Smith, *Marx at the Millennium*. Chris Gray, *New Interventions*, Autumn 1996; Alex Callinicos, *Socialist Review*, June; John Robinson, 'A Sophisticated Attack on Trotskyism', *International*, July 1996; Mike Waddington, 'Marx at the Millenium', *Socialism Today*, May.

EP Thompson, *Witness Against the Beast*. Paul Foot, 'Crossing the River of Fire', *International Socialism*, Summer 1996.

Robert Thurston, *Life and Terror in Stalin's Russia, 1934-41*. Robert Service, 'The Great Terrorist', *Guardian*, 12 April; Robert Conquest, 'Small Terror, Few Dead', *Times Literary Supplement*, 3 May; 'Terror Apology', *Socialism Today*, June 1996.

Hillel Ticktin and Michael Cox, *The Ideas of Leon Trotsky*. Bill Hunter, 'A Polemic Against Trotsky', *International*, July 1996.

Enzo Traverso, *The Marxists and the Jewish Question*. Peter Drucker, 'A Problematic Theory and Practice', *Against the Current*, November-December 1996.

Jürg Ulrich, *Leo Trotski als junger Revolutionaer*. Jürgen Quick-Tomasevic, 'Young Trotsky', *International*, July 1996.

Dmitri Volkogonov, *Lenin: Life and Legacy*. Paul Siegel, 'Volkogonov's Assassination of Lenin', *Socialist Action* (USA), April 1996; Paul Flewers, *New Interventions*, Autumn 1996; Samuel Farber, 'The Uses of Volkogonov', *Against the Current*, July-August.

Dmitri Volkogonov, *Trotsky: The Eternal Revolutionary*. Robert Service, 'The Great Terrorist', *Guardian*, 12 April 1996; Abraham Bromberg, 'A Better Lenin?', *Times Literary Supplement*, 23 August; Corin Redgrave, *Marxist Monthly*, October-November; Penny Cole, 'Restoring Trotsky's Place in History', *Socialist Future*, Summer; Susan Weissman, 'Trotsky Assassinated Again', *Against the Current*, July-August.

Robert Whymat, *Stalin's Spy* (biography of Richard Sorge). Kevin Tool, 'When Not Cuckolding Husbands, Sorge was Carousing in Brothels or Covertly Photographing Top-Secret Code Books', *Observer*, 24 November 1996; Donald Cameron Watt, 'Out in the Cold', *The Times*, 14 November; Oleg Gordievsky, 'Sorge's Sad Story', *Times Literary Supplement*, 17 January 1997.

Kent Worcester, *CLR James: A Political Biography*. James D Young, 'The Artist as Revolutionary', *Workers Liberty*, June 1996.

Valdislav Zubok and Constantine Peshakov, *Inside the Kremlin's Cold War: From Stalin to Khrushchev*. Taylor Downing, *Observer*, 20 October 1996.

Zheng Yi, *The Scarlet Memorial* (on the horrors of the Cultural Revolution). Jonathan Mirsky, 'A Political Hunger Sated', *The Times*, 10 April 1997.

Revolutionary History, Volume 5, no 4. *Prométhée*, First Quarter 1997.

Revolutionary History, Volume 6, no 1. John Pole, 'Trotskyism in Poland', *Socialist Standard*, July 1996.

Revolutionary History, Volume 6, nos 2/3. Daniel Joseph, 'Writing Marxist History', *Workers Liberty*, October 1996; John McKee, 'Revolutionary History', *Workers Power*, October; *Prométhée*, First Quarter 1997.

Back issues

Volume 1

All sold out

Volume 2

No 1: Revolutionaries and major class struggles, £3.00

No 2: Trotskyism in Argentina and Scandinavia; glasnost and Trotsky, £3.00

Nos 3 and 4: Sold out

Volume 3

No 1: Stalinism and Communism in Eastern Europe, £3.00

No 2: Trotskyism in Vietnam, £3.00

No 3: Trotskyism in Greece, £3.45

No 4: Trotskyism and the Second World War, £3.45

Volume 4

Nos 1/2: Special double issue on the Spanish Civil War, 400 pages, £10.95 'A fascinating and indispensable statement of the case for "the primacy of revolution".' — Professor Paul Preston, University of London

No 3: The Bolivian Revolution of 1952 and the Trotskyist movement, 160 pages, £3.45

No 4: South African Trotskyism, 224 pages, £4.00

Volume 5

No 1: The German labour movement and the rise of Hitler, 1929-33, 160 pages, £3.45

No 2: Germany 1918-23: From the November Revolution to the failed October, 192 pages, £3.75

No 3: Victor Serge special, 288 pages, £6.95

No 4: Left Communism and Trotskyism in Italy, 256 pages, £4.75

Volume 6

No 1: Trotskyism in Poland, repression of the left in 'People's Poland', Solidarnosc, the church and the state, 224 pages, £4.75 'The scope of these documents has a considerable historical and political value.' — *Dalej*, no 22, Winter 1996-97

Nos 2/3: Double issue on revolutionary Marxism in Britain and Ireland, 320 pages, £6.95

Prices shown for UK, including postage. Overseas orders: Europe: add 50p, elsewhere add £1.50. Overseas orders in Pounds Sterling by International Money Order. Cheques or IMOs payable to Socialist Platform Ltd. Send orders to: **Socialist Platform Ltd, BCM 7646, London WC1N 3XX.**